Super Bitches and
Action Babes

Super Bitches and Action Babes

The Female Hero in Popular Cinema, 1970–2006

RIKKE SCHUBART

McFarland & Company, Inc., Publishers
Jefferson, North Carolina, and London

LIBRARY OF CONGRESS CATALOGUING-IN-PUBLICATION DATA

Schubart, Rikke.
    Super bitches and action babes : the female hero in popular
cinema, 1970–2006 / Rikke Schubart.
        p.   cm.
    Filmography: p.
    Includes bibliographical references and index.

    ISBN-13: 978-0-7864-2924-0
    (softcover : 50# alkaline paper) ∞

    1. Women heroes in motion pictures.   I. Title.
PN1995.9.W6S363   2007
791.43'652—dc22   2007005283

British Library cataloguing data are available

Cover photograph: Pamela Anderson as Barbara Kopetski in *Barb Wire*,
1996 (PolyGram)

Manufactured in the United States of America

McFarland & Company, Inc., Publishers
  Box 611, Jefferson, North Carolina 28640
    www.mcfarlandpub.com

Acknowledgments

I want to first thank the Danish Research Council for the Humanities for their one-and-a-half-year grant, which made it possible for me to write this book. Thanks also to the University of Southern Denmark for funding the illustrations.

I was fortunate to meet my friend and Norwegian colleague Anne Gjelsvik, who commented on every part of the book in its first, second, and third drafts. My work has benefited immensely from her keen eye for detail, her patience, and generous friendship. Another friend is Nicolas Barbano, who has been my guide in the area of extraordinary (some would say trashy) films. I must credit my film taste to his influence. Colleagues at the University of Southern Denmark have read, commented on, and helped me throughout the writing process, among them Heidi Philipsen, Bo Kampmann Walther, Pia Harritz, and Lotte Nyboe. Another group of people, whom I cannot name individually since they are so many, are my wonderful students. They are unaware that I learn as much from them as they from me. Discussing my female heroes with them has kept me in touch with a changing reality. Also thanks to René Kimose, Lars Jakobsen, Gunnar Albjerg, and Martin Gotfredsen, whose technical help made it possible for me to watch films and access information on my laptop.

Finally, my family has shared the pleasures of meeting super bitches and action babes and the frustrations of late night writings. Ditte and Rasmus, I cherish every moment we spent together at the cinema! And to Martin—I know it takes a man like you to love a woman like me. My debt is growing.

Table of Contents

Preface

As I write this preface, I realize with a sting of regret that my journey has come to an end. Over the last six years I have explored the vast and, to me, unknown territory of the female hero in popular cinema. As I scaled mountains to discover hidden highlands, dragged my feet through swamps and fell down unexpected chasms, my hardships were rewarded with the company of black super bitches and brave Amazons, Chinese wonder women with thunderbolt kicks, expert Japanese female samurais, evil dominatrixes, hysterical virgins, bad mammas, sweet angels, and killer brides. The female hero is all of this and more. I call her "female hero" and not "heroine" because the figure I set out to find is a woman who enters a man's world and plays the hero in "male" genres: action films, adventure films, martial arts films, war films, science fiction films, all genres with male heroes, male audiences, and male producers. Well, not anymore. As gender changes, everything in the plot changes, and I identify five female archetypes in this book: the dominatrix, the Amazon, the daughter, the mother, and the rape-avenger. Archetyping the hero both absorbs and adjusts to social change, allowing her agency as well as limiting her action.

The seed for my journey was planted in 1996 when I discovered American actresses Pam Grier and Cynthia Rothrock during research for my Ph.D. dissertation on American action cinema. As Pam castrated bad guys and bottled their private parts, and Cynthia performed her martial arts in more than thirty films despite Hollywood's rejection of her, I wondered why I had not heard of these women. Where were their sisters? Why didn't women know their films (as I discovered many *men* did)? Why had their history not been written? Apart from the rare article and Yvonne Tasker's groundbreaking *Spectacular Bodies: Gender, Genre and the Action Cinema* (1993), the subject of strong women was almost uncharted. As I received a one-and-a-half-year grant from the Danish Research Council for the Humanities in 2000, I set out to write an in-depth study of the female hero's evolution across different national cinemas and genres, exploring her composite nature as both sexualized spectacle and active hero, and her ambivalent appeal to a female audience.

When I visited the Margaret Herrick Library in Los Angeles, the Hong Kong Film Archive in Hong Kong and the National Film Center in Kyobashi, Tokyo, looking for films, reviews, press material and earlier research, it became clear that the female hero was ignored in her low-budget appearances. One reason might be the element of sexual exploitation: When Grier, dressed in torn clothes revealing a breast, points her shotgun, and when a busty Dyanne Thorne as Ilsa tortures naked men and women, this is pure Mulveyan use of woman as sexualized spectacle and object of a male sadistic gaze. So, of course, is the "nudge-nudge, wink-wink" costuming of today's protagonists as erotic dancers and dominatrixes in mainstream films like *Charlie's Angels: Full Throttle* (2003) and *Mr. and Mrs. Smith* (2005).

This clash of abuse and female agency is the central dilemma of the female hero, who is what I call *in-between*.[1] In-betweenness is the space between two usually joined poles—male-female, active-passive. The term captures the dual nature of the female hero composed from stereotypical feminine traits (beauty, a sexy appearance, empathy) and masculine traits (aggression, stamina, violence). Rather than unite two genders she is in-between, a position that may only last as long as the plot but which creates fascination and unease, ambivalent responses and conflicted interpretations. From a feminist perspective, she is a victim of patriarchy. From a postfeminist perspective, she represents female agency. "Is this advertising photo yet another misogynistic image of Woman, or is it a postmodern construction of a newly powerful female subjectivity?" a researcher asked in 1985 about a dominatrix photo.[2] In postmodern culture we construct identity as a flexible and adjustable notion according to our needs, abilities, and beliefs. In this work I use *representations* as well as *interpretations*. True, men construct the female heroes in popular film. But it is up to us how we read and use them. Sarah Projansky calls this "equality and choice postfeminism" and, ironically, her glowing feminist critique of postfeminism and popular culture made me convert from feminist to postfeminist.[3] As much as I share feminism's cause, I accept living in a world of ambivalence and contradiction where I compose my self with bits and pieces from the culture I consume. I identify with Grier shooting a cheating boyfriend in the crotch in *Coffy* (1973), and with Geena Davis and Demi Moore, respectively, yelling, "Suck my dick!" in *The Long Kiss Goodnight* (1996) and *G.I. Jane* (1997) when they have had enough. To ignore such pleasure is to negate "politically incorrect" desires and "wrong" objects of pleasure. Where feminism is utopian, postfeminism is pragmatic: if we want to influence society's gender roles, we must get in the ring and join the fight. It might turn out men are not the enemy, but merely an opponent.

As I prepared for my journey, the territory started to expand. The television series *Xena: Warrior Princess* (1995–2001) was followed by shows like *La Femme Nikita*, *Buffy the Vampire Slayer*, *Witchblade* and *Alias*. What had been the occasional mainstream film with a female hero, like *Alien* (1986) and *Terminator 2: Judgment Day* (1992), in the late nineties became a box office trend culminating with the *Charlie's Angels* and *Lara Croft* franchises and Quentin Tarantino's *Kill Bill Vol. 1* and *Kill Bill Vol. 2* in 2003 and 2004. Suddenly, female heroes were everywhere. I cannot claim discovery of any new land, as others have been here before and several overtook me on the way. Yvonne Tasker's *Working Girls: Gender and Sexuality in Popular Cinema* (1998) explores mainstream Hollywood while Bev Zalcock's *Renegade Sisters: Girl Gangs on Film* (1998) deals with exploitation cinema. Jacinda Read's *The New Avengers: Feminism, Femininity and the Rape-Revenge Cycle* (2000) introduced me to postfeminism, and the anthologies *Athena's Daughters: Television's New Women Warriors* (2003), *Action and Adventure Cinema* (2004) and my own *Femme Fatalities: Representations of Strong Women in the Media* (2004) edited with Anne Gjelsvik directed me to more female heroes.[4] I am indebted to all of these works and many more, but especially to the works of Tasker and Projansky.

Strong women now exist in a range of media from comics, computer games and television shows to films, role playing games and action dolls. The time required to research all these areas made me limit my study to popular film. Hopefully, my work will contribute a new view of the female hero in a global film history, tracing her archetypes across exploitation and mainstream cinema. I believe such a panoramic view—with Pam Grier's WIP films at one far corner and French auteur cinema at the other far corner—will reveal new contexts and changes. My intention has not been to produce a complete history or to provide a feminist critique—which I leave to better-suited film historians and critics—but to discover new female heroes, add to a developing postfeminist theory, provide critical analysis, and engage in pleasure and empowerment whenever possible. "Gender can be rendered ambiguous without disturbing or reorienting normative sexuality at all," Judith Butler points out in her new introduction to *Gender Trouble*. "Sometimes gender ambiguity can operate precisely to contain and deflect nonnormative sexual practice and thereby work to keep normative sexuality intact."[5] I will not claim the female hero is a feminist or that her inbetweenness subverts our present gender roles. But I *do* claim that she offers the *possibility* for change and empowerment. Sometimes, identifying with a super bitch or action babe is exactly what a woman needs. As Catwoman puts it in *Catwoman* (2004), "Freedom *is* power! To live a life untamed and unafraid is the gift that I've been given and so my journey begins."

Remember: you need not be Catwoman to begin that journey.

Introduction:
Female Heroes in an
Age of Ambivalence

> To see women strain against the world may be inspirational,
> but also at some psychic level unbelievable.
>
> —Richard Dyer[1]

It's not fair. Heroes can have broken teeth and squint like Clint East-wood, suffer from a speech defect like Sylvester Stallone, have foreign accents like Arnold Schwarzenegger and Jean-Claude Van Damme, be old like Charles Bronson, bald like Kojak, wear constant I-am-very-very-pissed-off expressions like Steven Seagal, or be just plain ugly like Chuck Norris. In short, men don't have to *look* good to be heroes. It's different with women. The first step to qualify as female hero in a man's world is to be young and beautiful. If not young, then she must be Botoxed to look young. If not beautiful, then she must have silicone breasts, be aided by plastic surgery, wigs, makeup and never ever a wrinkle on her pretty face.

In the seventies women entered film genres that until then had been thought of as "male": action films, science fiction films, westerns, war movies, martial arts films, revenge films. The world of action and violence was no longer a man's world. Kicking ass and shooting guns; acting as judge, jury and executioner; exploring; conquering; and going to war had been things *men* did. Men saved the victims, the day, and the planet. Men found the ticking bombs, the madmen, and the evil terminators. Men had the mus-cles and the dirty white underwear. Well, not anymore. Starting with black actress Pam Grier, the tables turned. She advanced in the late sixties from playing a prisoner or, alternatively, a prison guard in WIP (women-in-prison) movies to become action cinema's first female hero in *Coffy* (1973) and *Foxy Brown* (1974). Instantly famous as "Queen of Blaxploitation," Grier led the

5

way by moving from playing rape victim to playing rape-avenger, from trophy to hunter, from love interest to female hero. Following her example, women conquered cult and exploitation cinema during the seventies when they appeared as samurais (*Lady Snowblood*, 1973), prison commanders (*Ilsa–She-Wolf of the SS*, 1974), and rape-avengers (*I Spit on Your Grave*, 1978), and, moving into the mainstream in the eighties, martial arts fighters (*Above the Law*, 1986) and sword fighters (*Red Sonja*, 1985), until they hit Hollywood's blockbuster cinema playing astronauts (*Aliens*, 1986), secret agents (*Point of No Return*, 1993), gun fighters (*The Quick and the Dead*, 1995), action heroines (*The Long Kiss Goodnight*, 1996), elite soldiers (*G.I. Jane*, 1997), and computer game heroines (*Lara Croft: Tomb Raider*, 2001). Today, the actresses of *Charlie's Angels: Full Throttle* (2003) and *Kill Bill: Vol. 1* and *Vol. 2* (2003, 2004) are top billed and top paid. Female heroes have also taken over prime time television with series like *Xena: Warrior Princess*, *Nikita* and *Alias*. It seems, after all, feminism was wrong and there is no place a woman can't go.

Today's active, aggressive, and independent female hero is clearly a child of feminism. But to read her as an answer to or even as the end of feminism would be a mistake. The female hero is an ambiguous creature and whenever she appears, ambivalent reactions follow. On the one hand, a woman performing actions which society has so long associated with men has the instant taste of a revolt against traditional gender roles. On the other hand, a closer look at the actress playing the female hero reveals a figure deliberately composed as ambiguous. Take CIA agent Charly in *The Long Kiss Goodnight*; she is not only prettier and smarter than any of her colleagues, but she is also the *only female agent* in the film and thus exceptional in more than one sense: she is an anomaly. Despite the "realistic" narrative and a daughter, a boyfriend, and a job as a schoolteacher, Charly is not a "realistic" character, neither viewed from the audience's perspective nor from within the film. Charly is a fantasy about a woman *outside her natural place*. As she breaks society's gender expectations she also confirms them.

The female hero divides critics. Postfeminists welcome her as progressive and a sign of equality. From their point of view, her use of masculine violence and discourse signals the end of an outdated psychoanalytic taxonomy of male versus female (active versus passive, and so forth). She demonstrates that any gender representation is about "gendered discourses" rather than gendered bodies, as Yvonne Tasker has recently put it.[2] Feminist critics, on the other hand, perceive her as the opposite. In their view, she represents a backlash against feminism, and her plastic surgery is a sign of oppression. From this perspective Lara Croft is not a strong woman but, as Germaine Greer has called her, a "sergeant-major with balloons stuffed up his shirt."[3] Lara Croft is thus a relative of the fierce female warriors we meet in adventure and fantasy—a female writer of fantasy comics commented that they "acted like men, they talked like men, they were like men. But physically they were portrayed like centerfolds, with two watermelons stuck to their chests, in harem girl costumes."[4]

This debate of feminism versus postfeminism mirrors an ambivalence at heart of the female hero. The two—the female hero and the theoretical debate—reflect that we live in *an age of ambivalence*. It is not my mission to close the gap between silicone implants or between feminist and postfeminist views. I will not "judge" whether Ilsa in *Ilsa, She-Wolf of the SS* is "the first feminist," as actress Dyanne Thorne described her own role, or whether the film is "sickening exploitation," as reviewers found.[5] Such judgment misses the point: audiences read the film both ways. I want to acknowledge this ambivalence and my position in it: I, too, am caught between admiring Amazons like Pam Grier and Dyanne Thorne, yet being aware that they are invented and marketed as products by film production companies.

Rather than choose a "correct" position we must open ourselves up to another position: in-between. Just like the female heroine is placed between male and female gender roles, we, the audience, find ourselves caught between pleasure and guilt, between acceptance and denial. Talking about the gender ambiguity of masculine women—transvestites, tommies, drag kings, butches, lesbians—Judith Halberstam in *Female Masculinity* (2002) identifies in-betweenness as a site for subversion. The less identifiable a body is as a *gendered* body, the more troubling: "It is in-betweenness here and elsewhere in the history of butches in film that inspires rage and terror...."[6] The female hero is recognizable as feminine, yet her cross-dressing and cross-behavior represent degrees of in-betweenness. Reading in-betweenness as "difference," Sharon Willis (1997) acknowledges a similar unease: "[A]s films read our social field, they may both mobilize and contain the conflict, uneasiness, and overwrought affect that so often accompany the confrontation of differences in everyday practices."[7]

Female heroes "exhibit ambivalent mixes of desire and violence that respond to collective anxieties about shifting borders ... [Such] ambivalent representations often expose our most highly contested social and cultural sites."[8] In this study I focus on the pleasure as well as the unease that the female hero in a man's world generates. Although my book has become a chronological study, my intention was not to simply "map" the female hero historically but to recognize her as a contested site, a paradoxical and ambivalent creature open to feminist as well as postfeminist interpretations, a figure of oppression as well as liberation. Her aggressiveness is the result of feminism, yet, as chapter 12 will discuss, delivered by a body more artificial and "constructed" than ever before.

A classic in the "girl gang" genre of the exploitation film, Russ Meyer's *Faster Pussycat ... Kill! Kill!* (Eve Productions, Inc., 1965) had Varla (Tura Satana) break a man's back. Oscillating between pastiche and inflicting serious pain, such wild women are ancestors of the female hero.

Male Film Genres

What do I mean by male film genres? The term acknowledges two things: first, that films with female heroes are written by men, produced by men, directed by men, and intended for a male audience; second, that the "heroic" nature of the protagonist in male film genres is mythologically, psychologically, and culturally designed to function as *a role model of masculinity*. By this definition westerns, war movies, action movies, martial arts movies, spy movies, gangster movies, and road movies are male film genres. Romance, romantic comedy, and melodrama, on the other hand, are *female* genres with a female protagonist and a female audience.[9]

In her analysis of the woman's film in *A Woman's View: How Hollywood Spoke to Women 1930–1960* (1993) Jeanine Basinger divides films into male and female. "Action does not represent the woman's life in films the way it represents the man's. The ritual events of male films—taking an objective in combat, racing the bootleggers across the Canadian border, withstanding the Indian raid—are defined by the man's individual courage. The ritual events of female films—weddings, proms, births, and even the Happy Interlude—are defined by nature or society, and the woman is bound by the rules."[10]

The woman's film cuts across film genres. It is defined by a) having a woman as the center of the universe, b) presenting love as her true job, and c) allowing her a "temporary visual liberation of some sort"[11] between the beginning and end. The point of the woman's film is to articulate female "concerns, angers, and desires" and demonstrate proper female social behavior: "Accept that you're a woman in relation to love, marriage, men, and motherhood, or suffer or become paralyzed or die...."[12] According to Basinger male and female films serve different purposes; the first socialize men into heroes, the second socialize women into wives and mothers. "The woman's genre does not have a character at its center who is meant to triumph over exaggerated events and be elevated to the status of hero, as in films about men. Instead, it presents an exaggerated character, played by an extravagant beauty, who is to be brought low by love for a man and returned to a state of normal, ordinary womanhood."[13]

This description of male and female films brings to mind the definition by Thomas Schatz of film genres into two types, which he calls "rites of order" and "rites of integration."[14] The first type—rites of order—are the western, the detective film, and the gangster movie. The hero is a "redeemer figure" and conflicts are externalized as actions in open space and are resolved by the hero's use of violence. The hero is a loner, a marginalized figure mediating between civilization and wilderness, order and chaos, citizens and criminals. Will Wright described the same protagonist when he defined the classical plot of the western as "the story of a hero who is somehow estranged from his society but on whose ability rests the fate of that society. The villains threaten the society until the hero acts to protect and save it."[15] The second type—rites of order—are romantic comedies and melodramas. The protagonist is a couple, the narrative takes place at home, and the drama is about success or failure in romance, marriage, and motherhood.

Male and female genres serve opposite purposes: male genres depict an active, aggressive, and utopian masculinity with spectacular destructions of villains and father figures, featuring a vulnerable yet invincible hero and an absence of social obligations such as marriage, family and work. Really, this is the fantasy of a teen hero who has the appearance of an adult, but is without what anthropologist David Gilmore calls "the deep structure of masculinity": serving as protector, provider and procreator in society.[16] Male heroes are without social bonds and obligations. Female genres work opposite, teaching women social responsibility as wives and mothers.

What happens, then, when a woman enters a man's world? Is the female structure mapped onto the male genre? Does the figure of the hero change when "he" becomes a "she"? In a chapter called "The Woman in the Man's World" Basinger describes how male genres are feminized when they are invaded by women. This happens in two ways. One, "a woman is seen doing what is traditionally thought to be a job for men only ... illustrating the issue of what a woman's capabilities are."[17] An example is *Westward the Women* (1951) where a group of women travel in wagons from the east to the west coast through the wilderness. After killing Indians, suffering sickness, death, and hunger, they are married as soon as the journey ends. Two, "the woman's genre is grafted onto, or fused onto, a genre that would be called 'masculine' ... and there is a clear and brutal demonstration of how society and nature restrict women."[18] An example is *Anne of the Indies* (1951) whose hero, a woman pirate, chooses to die in battle because the man she loves exploits and rejects her. Either way, when a woman enters a man's world she is brought low if she does not accept that her true career—her *only* career—is love.

Basinger concludes, "When a male genre is feminized, it allows women a chance for freedom and heroism but also maintains a status quo in which the women themselves cannot, for example, win the war, only wait for the men to win it for them."[19] And, of course, the American woman of the west is a sex symbol. "She is brave and independent, and she has a job to do. Of course, she is also a platinum blond, wearing a snood on her hair, plaid ruffles on her dress, and a bunch of ribbons and flowers on her bonnet. She is a sex symbol who looks good while she slaps her boss and tells him off."[20]

Assassin Charly (Geena Davis) in *The Long Kiss Goodnight* (New Line Cinema and Forge, 1996) is an example of the female hero in an age of ambivalence: she is a mother *and* a spy, a nurturer *and* a killer. Here, she is shooting at the villains.

Basinger's subject was the woman's film from 1930 to 1960. What, then, about the female hero today? Is she brought low if she doesn't recognize that her only career is love? Made to suffer and put to death? Yes. And no. Somehow, things become muddy and work both ways. Charly in *The Long Kiss Goodnight* turns down a job offer from the president and quits the CIA (as any decent hero would have done in a male film genre). She returns to her daughter, her boyfriend, and her old job as a school teacher (as any decent heroine would in a woman's film)—but she also brings with her a suitcase full of money picked up during the plot. Is Charly brought low? Bathed in sunshine with her boyfriend smiling from behind and her daughter playing with a golden retriever, Charly smiles happily—then suddenly throws the knife she is using to cut an apple into a stump of a tree. Love and family, yes, but also financial and psychological independence.

Today's female hero is domesticated, but not tame. Catwoman in *Batman Returns* (1992) is electrocuted and dies, yet her shadow is cast on Gotham City's skyscrapers in the end. She is killed, but not dead. When we turn to the actresses playing the female hero, things are no less complicated. Pam

Grier became an icon of freedom, change, and independence because she had lines like, "You wanna spit on me and make me crawl? I'm gonna piss on your grave tomorrow!" Yet her protagonists also suffered beatings, torture, and rape, and the actor was frozen out of Hollywood when she abandoned her super bitch persona.

We can't say today's female hero is *not* degraded or traumatized or tortured or killed. We can't say she is *not* a platinum blonde with a snood on her hair. And we can't say she is *not* a sex symbol. In fact, she is all of these as *Kill Bill* so beautifully demonstrates. Beatrix Kiddo (Uma Thurman) is beaten, killed, raped, then killed again. Her child is cut out of her belly. But beware, because the female hero in a man's world rises from the dead and claims her right to vengeance, independence, and womanhood with or without men. She tortures and kills those who have harmed her. She is beautiful and lethal. Sensitive and vulnerable. Brought low by love then high by vengeance. Still a clotheshorse, but now also a self-sufficient single mother.

Feminism Versus Postfeminism: Is the Female Hero a Person or an Object?

Film theory took a long time to respond to this new female hero. Neither her entrance in exploitation cinema during the seventies nor her appearance in mainstream movies such as the Dirty Harry entry *Sudden Impact* (1983) or the adventure movie *Red Sonja* made any impact. The action and martial arts movie *China O'Brien* (1988), with American actress and martial arts fighter Cynthia Rothrock, was completely ignored by audiences as well as academics. Instead, a lot of energy went into debating Laura Mulvey's seminal essay "Visual Pleasure and Narrative Cinema," which at the time of its publication in 1975 presented a one-sided and highly subjective argument. Mulvey described woman as the passive object of the male gaze. Man was bearer of the gaze, he was the active subject, "the more perfect, more complete, more powerful ideal ego" who "can make things happen and control events."[21] He was the hero, and woman was the object of his quest.

Mulvey set the agenda of feminist film theory for the next decades. She was not wrong to point out that women are objects of male desire. But she was wrong to insist on a binary view of the actress as a passive pinup opposed to the actor in control of events. Men have undressed in cinema since Johnny Weismüller wore a fig leaf in *Glorifying the American Girl* (1929), and an eroticization of the male as well as the female body is part of our western culture as evidenced by Margaret Walters' study *The Nude Male: A New Perspective* (1979) and Richard Dyer's *White* (1997). Action icons Bruce Lee, Jean-Claude

Van Damme, Sylvester Stallone, and Arnold Schwarzenegger all earned their claim to fame by exposing flesh.

It is simplistic to see men as always powerful, in control, and sadistic. In the eighties studies of the representation of masculinity in films such as *Le Samourai* (1967), *Butch Cassidy and the Sundance Kid* (1969), *Saturday Night Fever* (1977), and *Raging Bull* (1980) demonstrated how male protagonists could be both aggressive *as well as* objects of the gaze, not in control of the plot, and punished heavily.[22] Looking at male film genres, it is clear that even the most stereotypical hero, like James Bond, exhibits homoeroticism, masochistic sufferings, exhibitionism, and other perverse desires which fall outside the Mulvian binary: Clint Eastwood's spaghetti westerns made the magazine *Citizen News* give him the decade's "open wound award" for their beating scenarios, Sylvester Stallone's sufferings in the *Rocky* and *Rambo* film series made critics call him a "Plastic Jesus," and Van Damme's popularity with a homosexual audience resulted in increasingly open homoerotic subtexts in his films.[23] Van Damme stripped in *Cyborg* (1989), *Universal Soldier* (1992), and *Inferno* (1999), and was beaten and chained in *Replicant* (2001). "It doesn't bother me to have gay fans. Maybe they like me because gay people love beauty in general. They have a high level of taste," Van Damme commented.[24]

Masculinity is not a homogenous concept. "Maleness" is biology (and even then ambiguous, as Halberstam points out in *Female Masculinity*, where masculine women have trouble entering the public men's and women's rooms), but "masculinity" is a socially constructed concept. Masculinity is not monolithic, even if it tries to pass itself off as that. Today, masculinity is acknowledged as heterogeneous and its representations raise multiple connotations. A straight guy's hero may well be a gay guy's pinup (as poster-art for Dolph Lundgreen demonstrates).[25]

The same goes for femininity. "Femaleness" is biology; however, "femininity" is a socially constructed concept open to multiple interpretations. A woman in a man's world may signify many things. To reduce her to one statement—feminist, nonfeminist, or postfeminist—restricts her potential. As Sharon Willis suggests, "We will do better to think of viewer identifications as scenarios rather than as fixations. Hardly confined to identifications with characters, then, these scenarios may equally well fasten on situations, objects, and places, or the cinematic apparatus itself."[26] Thus it is possible to take pleasure from Linda Hamilton's muscles in *Terminator 2: Judgment Day* (1991), while at the same time objecting to her portrayal as near-psychotic mother.

In the nineties feminist film theory finally noticed the female hero. The deconstruction of her began with two studies in horror: Carol Clover's

Men, Women and Chainsaws: Gender in the Modern Horror Movie (1992) and Barbara Creed's *The Monstrous-Feminine: Film, Feminism, Psychoanalysis* (1993), both focusing on women in slasher and horror films in the seventies and eighties. Clover argued that the function of the "Final Girl" (the last victim who kills the monster) was not to portray a strong *woman*. Instead, she served as a gender-neutral platform where the male viewer could experience a masochistic position. That is, the Final Girl was the sensitive body through which a male viewer identified with pain, fear, and vulnerability. "To applaud the Final Girl as a feminist development, as some reviews of *Aliens* have done with Ripley, is, in light of her figurative meaning, a particularly grotesque expression of wishful thinking. She is simply an agreed-upon fiction and the male viewer's use of her as a vehicle for his own sadomasochistic fantasies an act of perhaps timeless dis-honesty."[27] Clover argued that the Final Girl was not a woman, but a stand-in for male desires. She was neither an object nor a subject.

Barbara Creed chose another approach. The angry, phallic, and castrating women in *Carrie* (1976), *The Brood* (1979), *I Spit on Your Grave* and *Sisters* (1973) spoke not of men's fantasies about being subjected to feminine sensations, but of men's fear of castrating women and men's ambivalent fantasies about being subjected to monstrous and castrating women: "woman as archaic mother, monstrous womb, vampire, possessed monster, *femme castratrice*, witch, castrating mother."[28] Where Clover discussed men's relation to (their own) femininity, Creed's focus was on men's relation to *women* as well as to femininity in general. In Creed's opinion, the protagonists of *I Spit on Your Grave* and *Ms. 45* were not identity positions for male audiences, but reflections of men's fear of the *femme castratrice* and, at the same time, their fear of that hated feminist figure, the single career women. To Clover, the Final Girl was not a girl but an "agreed-upon fiction." To Creed, she was very much a woman—not in the sense that she represented a "real" woman, but that she represented men's real fears about women. "I am not arguing that simply because the monstrous-feminine is constructed as an active rather than passive figure that this image is 'feminist' or 'liberated.' The presence of the monstrous-feminine in the popular horror film speaks to us more about male fears than about female desire or feminine subjectivity."[29]

In Clover's view, the Final Girl was merely a stand-in for male identification, a *subject* for men to identify with. To Creed, the Final Girl is a result of male desire, an *object* to fear and desire. Both agree, however, that a female audience should not embrace the female hero in horror film. Clover and Creed represent the suspicious feminist approach, struck by the ambiguity of this new protagonist, who is both subject and object, both stand-in and pinup, both a reflection of men's femininity and a representative of

The three angels—Sabrina (Kate Jackson), Jill (Farah Fawcett), and Kelly (Jaclyn Smith)—in the television series *Charlie's Angels* (1976–81), present a sweeter and more conventional image of femininity than the lethal female heroes in cinema.

men's fear of women. Feminist film theory is attracted to the female hero, yet ultimately rejects her.

In the mid-nineties, postfeminism reached film theory. This contested term, coined in the late eighties by the American media, expresses a plurality of attitudes towards feminism and gender: first, we find a distance to the feminist movement which is declared "dead, victorious, and ultimately failed"[30]; second, a sense of living in a postmodern culture defined by hybridity, globalization, capitalism, ambivalence, and contradiction; third, a playful attitude towards products (clothes, movies, objects) that are perceived as signs expressing emotions rather than having an essence (in the sense that women are "free" to wear a push-up bra and makeup one day and be casual the next day according to who she "feels like" and not who she "is"); and, fourth, a sense of living with multiple and conflicting identities. Conflicting identities may not be a new phenomenon, but has nonetheless become a widespread reaction to an experience of maneuvering in more than one sphere (home, work, social network, national and global identities). Germaine Greer in *The Whole Woman* (1999) fears that "the career woman does not know if she is to do her job like a man or like herself."[31] Conflicting identities are also found in the (unintentionally) contradictory responses women give when asked by sociologists whether they have experienced gender discrimination in their lives. As one woman said, "Other than the constraints that I felt being a woman, I really don't think that I've ... missed out on opportunities ... because I'm a woman, luckily."[32]

Where feminism has a specific political and social aim (equality), postfeminism is more an attitude towards culture and gender. In her book *Watching Rape: Film and Television in Postfeminist Culture* (2001), Sarah Projansky divides postfeminism into five interrelated categories of "postfeminist discourses."[33] First, a *linear postfeminism* constructs feminism as "outdated" and dead or no longer needed; postfeminism is thus the logical development of feminism. Second, *backlash postfeminism* rejects feminism as a "victim" feminism responsible for making women frigid and neurotic, and turning women into lonely man-haters and murderous career women as Alex (Glenn Close) in *Fatal Attraction* (1987). In this discourse, feminism is regarded a threat to the family because it has misguided women. Third, in *equality and choice postfeminism* everything becomes a choice by a free individual. In this (political) discourse women cannot change the system, and therefore accept being part of it. Like men, they are free to choose which role they want to play—mothers, career women, both, neither, a stripper, et cetera. This is the postfeminism alluded to by journalist Elizabeth Wurtzel in *Bitch: In Praise of Difficult Women* (1999): "People like Camille Paglia who go on about the power and glory of strippers are so stupid. This is desperate work. I don't notice *her* doing it."[34] Equality and choice postfeminism is the famous "no, but" and "both ... and" position: women deny being feminists, yet share feminist values. In postmodern terms this is *identification bricolage*. From a feminist and modernist point of view it is alienation and schizophrenia. From a postfeminist and postmodern point of view it is the ultimate freedom to "chose who you want to be." Fourth, *(hetero)sex-positive postfeminism* rejects feminists as frustrated bra-burners who alienate men with their rejection of "feminine" behavior. Such feminists become lesbians out of desperation. Postfeminist women "have the freedom to 'choose' to engage in femininity ... [as] a style, easily acquired and unproblematically worn."[35] Projansky also calls this "masquerade postfeminism." Fifth, the postfeminist attitude holds that *men can be feminists too* and, in fact, "not surprisingly men turn out to be *better* feminists than are women."[36]

The central difference between feminism and postfeminism is the attitude towards *choice, identification* and *goal*. For feminism the goal is to be liberated from a "heteropatriarchal" culture as Halberstam calls it. For postfeminism the goal is, more pragmatically, to achieve equality between men and women, and identity is constructed playfully by "trying on" attitudes through identification with gendered discourses rather than fixed positions. Thus Yvonne Tasker suggests gender "can be best understood as a set of discourses that are contested, accepted and resisted within networks, rather than binaries. Instead of proposing an analysis of movies in which female characters tell us about femininity and male characters about masculinity, an analysis of gendered discourse opens up these qualities operating across characters, scenarios and narratives as well as interacting with other discourses."[37]

Tasker's book about the action cinema, *Spectacular Bodies: Gender, Genre and the Action Cinema* (1993), is contemporary with Clover and Creed, but represents a new approach to the female hero. Tasker reads the female action hero as a positive response to feminism and coins the now widespread term "musculinity" about the bodybuilt female action hero. Cynthia Rothrock's body in *China O'Brian* and Linda Hamilton's muscles in *Terminator 2* transgressed images of women as soft and petite. Tasker noted, however, how this was compensated for "by emphasizing her sexuality, her availability within traditional feminine terms," thus narratively relocating the female hero into the usual female stereotypes.[38]

A clear postfeminist attitude was formulated by Jeffrey Brown in "Gender and the Action Heroine: Hardbodies and the *Point of No Return*" (1996).[39] Finding "an awareness of the arbitrariness of gender traits" in the femme action movies of the nineties, Brown discusses how "recent action films challenge both cinematic and cultural assumptions about what constitutes natural or proper female behavior," and asserts that "the modern action heroine confounds essentialism through her *performance* of traditionally masculine roles" (italics mine).[40] About the dilemma of identification and gender, Brown suggested male and female viewers identify with the protagonist in the same way: "the same viewers can identify with both a Ripley and a Rambo, a Maggie and a Martin Riggs *in the same way*..." (italics mine).[41]

After killing a rapist on their weekend trip, Thelma and Louise (Susan Sarandon, left, and Geena Davis) refuse to take any more male abuse in *Thelma and Louise* (Metro-Goldwyn Mayer, 1991), the road movie which opened a decade of strong women in male film genres.

Before Brown, film theory debated the female hero in terms of *cross-dressing* and *masquerade*. The *cross-dressing* critique claimed that the female hero in a man's role was not a woman, but a man dressed as a woman. Nothing had changed, except putting a woman in a man's place and offering her as a sexual spectacle for a male audience. Thus reviews of *Conan the Barbarian* rejected the sword fighter Valeria (Sandahl Bergman): "*Conan* shows a world where there are two kinds of men—one of which has long hair and gorgeous tits."[42] Cross-dressing was also an issue in the reception of *Thelma and Louise* (1991), which divided critics between on the one hand reading the film as feminist, or, on the other hand, rejecting it because it "merely substitutes female 'buddies' for male ones in an otherwise conventional and regressive road movie."[43] The *masquerade* critique argued that the male behavior of the female hero is merely an act. In psychoanalyst Joan Riviere's classic essay "Womanliness as a Masquerade" (1929), a woman behaving as a man (by making herself noticed for her intelligence) uses feminine behavior to compensate for her transgression into male territory and avert a feared reprisal. "Womanliness therefore could be assumed and worn as a mask, both to hide the possession of masculinity and to avert the reprisals expected if she was found to possess it."[44] Film theory has translated such a psychological defense mechanism into a loosely understood notion of masquerade as "an act." The female hero is "taught" appropriate gender behavior so she can "choose" gendered actions like women choose clothes. An example is Luc Besson's French action movie *Nikita* (1990) about a secret agent who is taught to act like a stereotypical man and woman (disguising herself as waitress, prostitute, male diplomat). To feminists, such masquerade signals oppression of women. To postfeminists, it is not a masquerade but a sign of the freedom to navigate society's gendered signs and discourses.

Today, feminist and postfeminist attitudes intersect with and overlap each other. Bev Zalcock's *Renegade Sisters: Girl Gangs on Film* (1998) is an example of a feminist approach positive towards male genres with female heroes because they make transgressive female behavior visible. "[T]here is always a subversive element at play, even if it is only the foregrounding of the mismatch between the male universe and the female subject. The spin offs include some degree of empowerment for the female audience and the inadvertent indication of a 'wild zone'—the no-man's-land of female experience."[45] Another positive feminist response is the anthology *Reel Knockouts: Violent Women in the Movies* (2001), by Martha McCaughey and Neal King, whose introduction suggests that images of strong women may prevent men from using violence against women: "We like the threat that women's movie violence presents to the all-important divide between women and men. We wonder what effect such images could have on men who assault women partly because they're so confident that they'll win the fights."[46] A combined feminist and postfeminist approach to the female hero is Jacinda Read's *The New Avengers: Feminism, Femininity and the Rape-Revenge Cycle* (2000). Discussing the transformation of the rape-revenge figure, Read reads Catwoman in *Batman Returns* as an ambivalent figure composed of backlash postfeminism and heterosex-positive postfeminism: Selina Kyle is transformed from mousy secretary (the hated career woman) into sexy and aggressive female superhero Catwoman purring, "I don't know about you, Kitty, but I feel so much yummier." Read suggests we regard the dialogue between feminism and postfeminism as a terrain where we negotiate "everyday meanings of feminism and femininity ... based not so much on fixed identities but on flexible *identifications*" (italics mine).[47]

The flexibility of identification is central, if problematic, in postfeminism. Film theorists, critics, and audiences differ in their engagement with the female hero. Some view her as an instrument to please a male audience. Even if this is the case—and looking at Drew Barrymore, Lucy Liu, and

Cameron Diaz in the film *Charlie's Angels* there is little to deny—this does not prevent an audience from reading the female hero in different ways. Willis thus quotes a female journalist from the magazine *New York* writing about *Thelma and Louise* and *Terminator 2*: "To appeal to women repulsed or bored by male action movies, they have created these warrior women....

The new female hero is an icon of fashion, beauty, and extreme body control, as well as independence. Who could be more "fit" for the role as Catwoman than former beauty queen and model Halle Berry? *Catwoman* (Warner Bros., 2004).

What is important is that these women, created from male fantasies, have been released. Where can they go?"[48] Yes, where can they go, where will they take us? The journalist's point is that it is possible to take an object, put it in a different context, and by doing so turn it into something different. Thus feminists condemned I Spit on Your Grave when it came out, but two decades later it is standard in university curriculums for feminist film classes. Such changes tell us that representation is one thing, interpretation another. My experience from using I Spit on Your Grave in classes demonstrates the problem of interpretation. Male students read the film as feminist, because rape was avenged by a female hero. However, female students left the film during the rape, and thus couldn't appreciate the vengeance. They simply found the film too stressful to watch and (therefore) antifeminist. One viewer's feminist movie may very well be another viewer's antifeminist movie.

Opinions on postfeminism are divided. Next to the positive approaches to the female hero in a man's world are critical voices. Projansky's trajectory through rape cinema relentlessly points out how the discourse of postfeminism obscures a feminist view because "other options are closed down, other experiences are unaccessed, other possibilities are denaturalized, and other forms of activism are discouraged."[49] Also, a widespread critique of postfeminism and issues of class and gender are evaded. "Specifically, I argue that postfeminism's version of feminism assumes that antirape activism is no longer necessary, ultimately holds women responsible for responding to rape, often recenters white men in the name of feminist antirape activism, and perpetuates a long-standing tradition of excluding women of color, particularly Black women, from rape scenarios in ways that negate rape's complexity and frequency in their lives."[50]

Greer rejects postfeminism as neither positive nor empowering: "A 'new feminism' that celebrates the right (i.e. duty) to be pretty in an array of floaty dresses and little suits put together for starvation wages by adolescent girls in Asian sweat-shops is no feminism at all."[51] Greer criticizes women's representation in male spaces such as the police and the army. Men, says Greer, basically hate women and hate them even more when they enter male hierarchies because they reveal masculinity as a system. "The ultimate effect of the myth of masculinity is to generate anxiety in the vast majority of men who cannot live up to it."[52] Women in male systems have two choices: they can remain feminine and be rejected, or they can adopt men's behavior and perhaps be tolerated. "Women who are inducted into masculinist hierarchies are exported tissue, in constant danger of provoking an inflammatory response and summary rejection."[53] Recent harassment and rape trials in the police and the military in the U.S. and in Europe point to the first reaction—rejection.[54] But documentation of female soldiers participating in the torture of Iraqi prisoners by American soldiers in the spring of 2004 testifies to the second reaction—that women are tolerated in male hierarchies when they behave like men.[55] A postfeminist objection, however, would be that torture and sadism are not intrinsically "male" since the majority of men don't exhibit this behavior. That women turn sadistic in the company of soldiers is not due to being exposed to "male" behavior, but to war facilitating aggression and violence. Similarly, although violence has not increased among Danish youth, statistics show that girls are responsible for a growing percentage of youth violence. Sociologists and criminologists speculate that this is the result of increasing equality; violence is no longer an expression of male malcontent, but simply an expression of malcontent. The reason for violent behavior, statistics indicate, is not gender, but social factors.

To Greer and Projansky postfeminism is oppressive because it obscures questions of class and ethnicity; by obliterating differences between the masculine and the feminine, postfeminism accepts masculinity as the standard, just like the white middle class becomes standard. So here we are, in a battlefield where the number of sexual harassment trials in the military increases with the number of female soldiers. Where action for reducing gender inequality is opposed by invoking equality and arguing against, for instance, quotas for employment of women in public institutions as discrimination against men. Where the number of reported rapes have steadily increased in western society since 1970, but male rape remains a taboo yet to be broken by the media and society.[56] The new female hero is caught in a crossfire; she is both rejected and welcomed, she is both an icon of fashion, beauty, and extreme body control, as well as an idol of independence and strength.

There is not one answer, but many, to the ambiguous world of the female hero in male film genres. Two recent anthologies signal the deepseated ambivalence at the core of the female hero and the responses she generates in her audience. In their introduction to *Athena's Daughters: Television's New Women Warriors* (2003) Frances Early and Kathleen Kennedy conclude she "presents viewers with a polysemic image that enables both reactionary and progressive readings" and "the contributors to this anthology are both intrigued by the possibilities that the new woman warrior offers for alternative storytelling and acutely aware of her limitations as a model for feminism."[57] Similarly, in her introduction to *Action Chicks: New Images of Tough Women in Popular Culture* (2004), Sherrie A. Inness sums up that some tough women "do follow in the same footsteps as the Angels and a host of other beautiful women who battle the bad guys but whose fundamental purpose seems to be to function as eye candy," but, on the other hand, the same women "challenge the patriarchal social structure by defending women and acting against the men who threaten them."[58] This is the conflicted, provocative, fascinating, and empowering world of the female hero. My own position is pragmatic and postfeminist: To engage in close encounter and read the female hero as an expression of gender in contemporary culture, yet also to be sensitive to what opportunities she offers for change in the future.

Five Female Archetypes

It is easy being a hero. He is always some sort of Christ saving the world like Neo in *The Matrix*. Or he is an antihero, in which case he is still Christ sacrificing himself like The Man With No Name in *A Fistful of Dollars* (1964). Or he can be "a man of the wrong stuff" like McClane in the *Die Hard* movies who proves to be an archetypal action hero after all.

It's different with women. Heroism is not expected from a woman. She is not expected to rise to any occasion, and if she does, the occasion is usually minimal. Take Jordan in *G.I. Jane*, who proves that she is as tough as the male soldiers. Or Slim in *Enough* who beats her abusive husband to death. If the hero had been a man, this would not be impressive. In fact, most of the acts female heroes perform are about proving they are as good as men, better than men, or have had enough of men. The female hero is rarely mythological. She does not enter society and absorb social unrest and violence, and she is not cheered on by a crowd. We are up close and personal, rather than mythological and memorable. The female hero is a generic anomaly, and the narrative takes a lot of trouble to explain *why* she is in a man's world, *what* she is doing there, and carefully *exports* her out of the plot—perhaps not as abruptly as in *Westward the Women*, but it is hinted that her "mission" is over. Coffy puts down her shotgun, Megan is carried away by her detective lover in *Blue Steel*, Slim has a new boyfriend, and Beatrix Kiddo has found her daughter.

It is an exception that the female hero is cast as a traditional hero archetype (like Xena). Instead, surveying the field of popular cinema, we find that she is constructed as a female *type* of which five are so widespread and recurring that I call them *archetypes*: the dominatrix, the rape-avenger, the mother, the daughter, and the Amazon. My "archetype" is not universal in the Jungian sense of the term, where archetypes are believed to be universal and primordial symbols, mental images stored in a collective unconscious (Hero, God, The Tree of Life). In my use an archetype is a figure which becomes paradigmatic and gains iconic status through repetitive retellings in contemporary culture. Like a prototype is the first example of a new type, which may or may not be put into serial production (the prototype of a car), my archetype is a female hero who enters culture's serial production and becomes an archetype through mass repetition. Greek *arche* means first, superior, most, and is related to *arche* (origin, beginning) and *arkhos* (chief, leader). We have no way of knowing if a new female hero will become an archetype; only her recirculation in culture's narratives can prove this. The female hero may start as a feminized version of a male figure (the female rape-avenger) and develop into an archetype. And she can, as Sigourney Weaver's Ripley in *Aliens* was at first, be rejected as an unimaginative stereotype (a female Rambo or "Rambolina") but later recognized as an archetype (the mother). Sometimes it is possible to locate an archetype's *prototype*, that is, the figure that signals the birth of a new archetype or sums up all parts of an archetype, such as Luc Besson's *Nikita* and the daughter. On other occasions it is impossible to pinpoint one film character as the first of an archetype, like the Amazon, who originates from Greek mythology and has innumerable representatives in popular cinema.

Casting the female hero as archetype is a way of containing her polysemy (by reducing her conflicting elements to a recognizable pattern) and responding to cultural and social changes (by inserting changes in contemporary women's roles into new cultural archetypes, such as the daughter and the mother). Archetyping the female hero is not a solution to ambivalence, but a continuation of it. Whether an archetype is conservative or progressive depends on its use and representation, and on our reading of it.

The Dominatrix

Fundamental to the construction of the female hero in modern popular cinema is the archetype of *the dominatrix*. In male masochistic fantasy she is the woman punishing the masochist and fulfilling his perverse pleasures. She is not really cruel, since she serves her victim, and he is not really a victim, since he is a customer buying a service. Whereas the *femme castratrice* is an archaic figure in mythology, the dominatrix is a product of capitalism. She is related to pornography, to buying and selling, to the splitting of pleasure in "normal" and "perverse," where the first is located in marriage, the second in prostitution. The dominatrix is related to masochism, capitalism, and prostitution. It is rare to find her in a pure form. She is too close to pornography and thus an embarrassment to mainstream movies. But she is a strong component in most femme fatale cinema and prominent especially in low-budget films tailored exclusively to a male audience.

Being subjected to a beautiful, sadistic woman who has her way with the male victim is a scenario of male masochism. Such scenes are at the heart of the *Ilsa* movies where Ilsa, head of a prison camp, castrates her lovers. "I promised you, that you would never see the camp again," Ilsa laughs triumphantly as she cuts off the genitalia of a prisoner. Castration scenes are widespread in seventies exploitation cinema. The protagonists in *Coffy* and

Foxy Brown shoot a lover in the crotch and castrate a villain, and Jennifer in *I Spit on Your Grave* cuts off a rapist's private parts.

Moving from exploitation to mainstream cinema the dominatrix becomes a caricature, a role for the female hero to step in and out of, an act, and a self-conscious masquerade. During the eighties she more or less fades from sight but returns in the nineties where her bondage costume is fashionable. It starts with the black, shiny raincoat that Selina Kyle transforms into the skin of a newborn Catwoman, purring and stretching her paws complete with needles from Selina's sewing machine. Later, a long, black bullwhip appears out of nowhere—as my daughter commented when we watched *Batman Returns*, "Where did she get the whip from?" The whip (which Catwoman steals from a shopping mall) is part of the costume, and in her movies Ilsa uses bullwhips, horsewhips and a camelwhip (a version of a cat-o'-nine-tails).

Two movies provide examples of the centrality of the bond-

Former *Baywatch* star Pamela Anderson is Barbara Kopetski, a dominatrix archetype hero in corset, high-heeled boots, latex, and tons of makeup in *Barb Wire* (PolyGram, 1996).

age costume in the nineties. One is David Hogan's action movie *Barb Wire* (1996), a shameless and witty remake of *Casablanca* set in the future. Female hero Barbara Kopetski, or just Barb, played by former *Baywatch* star Pamela Anderson, is the politically neutral owner of a bar located on the border between freedom and Nazi-like tyranny. She makes her living as a bounty hunter, a job that has her frequently going undercover as stripper, erotic dancer, and prostitute. Barb is constantly dressed in black leather or latex, corsets, ultra-high-heeled boots, wearing tons of makeup, chains and dog collars, and handling phallic, shining guns (the film cover has her practically licking one). Pamela Anderson does not "wear" these costumes as much as she disappears into them and becomes as unrecognizable as Boris Karloff in his makeup as Frankenstein's monster. In one scene Barb poses as a dominatrix to a customer. They are both dressed in full-size latex suits, and the masochist also wears a diving mask. He hands her a rubber board and eagerly turns to get his smacking: "I have been a baaad boy." Barb then smacks him in the back and renders him unconscious.

The other movie with bondage reference is the French art film *Irma Vep* (1996) with Hong Kong actress Maggie Cheung in the leading role of the meta-movie about the remake of the French serial drama *Les Vampires* from 1915. The director has seen Cheung in Johnny To's stylish action movie *The Heroic Trio* and wants to add a modern touch to his production. The Chinese actress is equipped in a sex shop, where the latex catsuit is refitted to her size—"it has to be *tight*, it's bondage costume"—and the costumier chooses from masks with or without holes for her mouth and eyes. "Is this really what Henri [the director] wants?" Cheung asks. "Oh yes," the costumier responds, showing her a magazine clipping with a picture of Michelle Pfeiffer in her costume as Catwoman. "I say it's like hooker, but if he wants hooker, I say that's okay. Now we're in a shop for hookers." Cheung gets her costume, complete with a spray to make the latex shiny.

What separates the dominatrix from the femme castratice are connotations of capitalist economy—the purchase of a service—and the sense of being "dressed" in a costume that has nothing to do with the female hero's personality. The dominatrix is an erotic act rather than a person, and her actions are services rather than punishments. She is not perceived as a "person," but as a male fantasy. Is she a feminist figure? Well, Jacinda Read interprets Catwoman as a postfeminist critique of capitalism—perhaps because she uses her black bullwhip on the female mannequins in the magazine store belonging to Max Schreck, the boss who pushed her out the window and killed her and whom she eventually electrocutes. And Thaïs E. Morgan in "A Whip of One's Own: Dominatrix Pornography and the Construction of a Post-Modern (Female) Subjectivity" suggests we welcome pornography's dominatrix as a woman with potentials for female strength. Whether we like her or not, the dominatrix and her outfit have become archetypes in femme fatale cinema from Nazi officer Ilsa with her torture instruments to efficiency inspector Lucy Liu with her whip in *Charlie's Angels*. And as the face of the clothes brand Vila, Lucy Liu has proved the durability and attraction of a "dominatrix" star persona.

The Rape-Avenger

"Don't let her looks fool you. She's the fucking Energizer Bunny. Just do her and dump her. Don't try and get cute and play doctor first," the villain Timothy (Craig Bierko) warns co-villain Jack (Joseph McKenna), who is about to kill the unconscious Charly in *The Long Kiss Goodnight*. "I made that mistake. It nearly killed me." Jack ignores the warning and decides to play doctor. A wrong choice. Charly wakes up when he touches her and stabs him in the eye with the syringe he was about to use on her. Grabbing at his bleeding eye, Jack shoots Charly, who falls forty feet into the ocean from which she will be washed ashore with amnesia and be three months pregnant. CIA agent Charly now believes she is the schoolteacher Samantha, which was her cover identity on her last mission. The pregnancy tells us that Timothy was successful in "playing doctor" and that Charly's daughter Caitlin is the result of a rape. Timothy will pay later, just as Buck (who "likes to fuck") has it coming in *Kill Bill*, and every rapist in femme fatale cinema can be dead sure to get his money's worth. With a vengeance.

In Charly we see traces of the archetype of the rape-avenger. This is the woman who kills the man, or men, who raped her. She can even, as in *Ms. 45* (1981), kill men who haven't touched her yet, merely because they belong to the "predatory" sex. Rape has been a widespread motive in cinema since *The Birth of a Nation* (1915), where it served to "discipline independent women into vulnerability," as Sarah Projansky succinctly puts it.[59] When a woman was raped she became a victim, and men avenged victimization. "Raped and left in a hole to die. Who speaks for her?" Dirty Harry asked rhetorically in 1971, at a time when raped girls were not supposed to raise their voices. Read concludes that rapes before 1970 "are ultimately not about *trans*forming but about *con*forming; they are about positioning and fixing the female characters within established and accepted feminine roles."[60]

In the seventies the rape-avenger is born. A woman who takes vengeance into her own hands, who turns the tables on those who attacked her, who picks the time and the place for payback and who decides not to conform, but transform. With *Hannie Caulder* (1971), *Rape Squad* (1976), *Lipstick* (1976) and *I Spit on Your Grave* (1978) a new genre is born: The rape-revenge drama. Here, rape does not discipline a woman, but the opposite: it jerks her out of ordinary femininity and into the extreme role of lethal femme fatale.

Before she was raped the rape-avenger was "soft," sweet, fragile, often unsexy and single, like the young, mute, and mousy Thana in Ms. 45 who hides in her claustrophobic apartment. Then rape puts her in a new position, an in-between state of shock, where she recovers from the attack. After the rape the female hero transforms into a monster, a woman who can employ "feminine" signs such as cocktail dresses and makeup, and who can use "male" violence and weapons to get even. Thana starts out with a female "weapon," her iron, and then advances to guns. Read points out that this is the same linking of erotic anticipation with violence as in film noir. "Men are violently punished in these films ... in a context that is overtly erotic and punishment is frequently preceded by the promise of sexual pleasure."[61] Thus Thana dresses up as a nun for a Halloween party, with sexy underwear and heavy makeup as an invitation to the men—especially her boss. She steps into erotic role-play to attract men and becomes a femme castratrice in her dual role as femme fatale and castrating bitch. Castration can be symbolic—hanging or shooting the victim—or literal. Rape is, by the way, the only crime in popular culture which can justify literal castration.

The rape-avenger is characterized by three elements: As a victim of rape she is the victim of a certain kind of masculinity. As an avenger of rape she acts out a certain kind of male fantasy. And as a female avenger of male violence she has feminist potentials. Sue Lees, an English professor in women's studies, regards men who commit rape as participating in "the dominant hegemonic heterosexuality" of society. Rape in real life is not so much about women and sex as it is about power and masculinity. "The sexual act is not concerned with sexual gratification, but with the deployment of the penis as a concrete symbol of masculine social power and dominance."[62] Rape is a symbolic act defending masculinity against women, against homosexuality and against "feminized" versions of masculinity. About gang rapes, Lees notes that "[t]he men vent their interest in one another through the body of a woman, but this can also be on the body of a man who is not a 'real' man. The fact that the victim is often unconscious highlights her status as a surrogate victim in a drama where the main agents are the males interacting with each other."[63]

Clover points to the same drama of masculinity in I Spit on Your Grave, where five men rape Jennifer, one of them pressured by the leader. The uneasiness of masculinity is relieved through demonstration of power—here men's power over a woman's body. In Deliverance it is poor men's power over rich men's bodies. Rape is thus, in real life as well as in rape-revenge movies, about gender and social power rather than sex and pleasure.

In The Long Kiss Goodnight male rape is a theme with Charly's sidekick, private detective Hennessey (Samuel L. Jackson), who has been in prison four years and will do *anything* not to go back. In one of his scams he threatens a man: "I will see to it you spend the next ten years in prison getting ass fucked. And if the case is thrown out because my arrest was too violent I will personally hire men to ass fuck you in the next ten years. So, if you're an ass fucking fan you go ahead and mouth off." Hennessey could well have been "ass fucked" during his time in jail and attacks on him are symbolically visualized as rapes: beaten up, he is left naked in a cellar, glistening with blood and sweat. In another scene Timothy throws a knife which lands inches from Hennessey's crotch. Charly is the rape victim killing her rapist, but Hennessey is a male rape victim being remasculinized with the help of a woman.

Vengeance is a strange thing in rape-revenge narratives, where it feminizes an unsexy woman into seductive femme fatale and turns her into an active and aggressive killer. The rape-avenger's violence is aimed at the "performance" of her victims, thus the "dick jokes" surrounding her in mainstream movies ("Oh honey, only four inches?"). Rape and performance are, of course, themes in the action movie. "I'm not the one who got butt fucked on national television," McClane tells his superior in *Die Hard*. With male heroes, however, rape remains in the realm of the symbolic. With female heroes it is carried out.

Critics disagree about many things in femme fatale cinema and most of all about the significance of the rape-avenger. Clover sees her as a standin for male desires and men's identification with "female" sensations. Creed sees her as a modern day representation of the archaic figure of the *femme castratrice* playing up to male masochism: "[T]he *femme castratrice* becomes an ambiguous figure. She arouses a fear of castration and death while simultaneously playing on a masochistic desire for death, pleasure and oblivion."[64] Read finally sees the rape-avenger as an ambivalent figure, "not as relatively progressive or reactionary but as an attempt to make sense of feminism, not as reflecting or deflecting authentic feminist politics but as constructing popular versions of feminism."[65]

The Mother

"You're just gonna be written off as some crazy mummy who kidnapped her own kid and died with her in a blizzard," Timothy tells Charly as he locks her and Caitlin in a freezer room to die. "She's a complete psycho, a total loser," John characterizes his mother who is doing push-ups in a cell in the secured wing of the mental hospital in *Terminator 2*. And in *Aliens* Ripley looks at a photograph of her long-dead daughter and whispers, "I promised her I'd be home for her birthday. Her eleventh birthday." Ripley has accidentally slept for fifty-seven years in her ship lost in space.

The psychology of the mother as an archetype is simple: The good mother is nurturing and reproductive, and constitutes the mental space of the family. She is not with her family. She *is* the family. She is the womb where the family grows. She is the cultural symbol of "mother nature" and "mother earth." In contrast to the good mother, the bad mother has expunged her womb. She has cut the umbilical cord and left her family. She is no longer the home, the family. We find images of bad mothering in Ripley, who was late for a birthday. In Sarah, who was pregnant in *Terminator* and abandoned her son in *Terminator 2* because she was obsessed with saving the world. And no sooner does Charly recover from her amnesia than she turns her back on Caitlin: "Samantha had the kid. Not I!" Even "normal" abandonment—a working mother—can lead to disaster. Thus in *Eye for an Eye* (1996) a helpless Karen can hear her daughter be raped and killed over the cellular phone—while stuck in traffic on her way home from work in the city.

The mother is not bad in the sense that she maltreats her children (as the evil mother in the horror movie), is a bad cook or cheats on her husband. No. She is a bad mother because she wants to be in a man's place. To have a job. A career. To do what men do: work. This proves incompatible with being a mother, at least with being a traditionally good mother. The mother must choose between motherhood and career. Her mission is to right wrongs, to turn back time, and undo her earlier failures—to make up for wrong behavior.

The bad mother in male film genres is a different figure from the archaic mother in horror films, which Creed describes as "the mother as primordial abyss, the point of origin and end" and the "primeval 'black hole.'"[66] The archaic mother represents the truly horrifying image of a femininity threatening to "swallow" men. The mother in male film genres, on the contrary, is a maternal figure *within* patriarchy—a mother with a child—and like the other female archetypes she functions as an object of desire. She is played by beautiful actresses like Geena Davis, Sigourney Weaver, Linda Hamilton (who played Beauty in the television series *Beauty and the Beast*), Jennifer Lopez, and Uma Thurman.

It is striking how women in male film genres never learn from other women. They depend on men for education, help, fatherly advice, weapons instruction, and sensibility training. Sarah receives sensibility training from her son, who teaches his cyborg to cry and his mother to care. Ripley is taught to "handle herself" by corporal Hicks. Charly learns responsibility and loyalty from Hennessey, who picks up a photograph of her daughter Caitlin that she tore up and threw out: "It's two days to Christmas, you should phone your daughter." It takes a man to help the bad mother change her ways.

The mother is a postfeminist role model. Her transformation is not simply from good to bad and back to good. It is a move forward to a third position, where the masculine discourse she has been using is integrated into her nature. Two scenes in *The Long Kiss Goodnight* show the changed status of male discourse. The first scene is when Charly (the forgotten spy) returns

A tough mother and an example of the mother archetype. The physical shape of actress Linda Hamilton playing Sarah Connor in *Terminator 2: Judgment Day* (Carolco Pictures, 1992) made critic Yvonne Tasker coin the term "musculinity" about female action heroes with muscles.

for the first time in Samantha, who is teaching her daughter to skate. Caitlin falls and hurts her wrist. Sweet Samantha becomes harsh Charly, saying, "Life is pain. Get used to it. See, you will skate all the way to the shore, princess. And you will not fall again. Am I understood?" These are words Samantha probably heard from her father when she was a child. This is what boys are told, not girls. Later, Charly drags Caitlin out of a truck loaded with explosives. Charly is wounded and orders her to run: "Go! I'm right behind you, baby. Go! Don't look back." Caitlin runs. "Good girl." Charly falls to the ground, her eyes open and lifeless. When Caitlin discovers that Charly is not behind her, she returns to her mother. "Mummy, no. It's okay. I'm sorry I left you. Please get up." But forgiveness does not bring back the dead. Caitlin beats Charly with the cast on her wrist (yes, the one broken while skating) and echoes Charly's words on the ice: "Life is pain. You just get used to it! So stand up right this minute, Mummy." Motherly love doesn't bring back the dead—but fatherly discipline does. Charly blinks her eyelids, stands up, and saves the day.

Like the rape-avenger the mother is about *trans*forming. The rape-avenger combines elements from the femme fatale with the femme castratrice. The mother also unites several features: she unites the nurturing qualities of the good mother with the "bad" ambitions of the bad mother (that is, the desire to enter a man's world and have a career) by integrating qualities our culture traditionally associates with men—responding with violence when threatened, being brave, strong, resilient, committed, ambitious, intelligent.

The mother has three phases: good mother, bad mother, new mother. The latter integrates feminine and masculine qualities in her capacity as a mother. This is Ripley with a flame torch saying, "Get away from her, you *bitch*," to the alien queen attacking little girl Newt. This is Charly screaming, "Suck my dick!" to the men trying to kill her. This is officer Karen Walden responding, "I gave birth to a nine-pound baby, asshole, I think I can handle it," to the pain of being shot.

The Daughter

When a woman becomes a hero in a male film genre the question is always why? How did she get to be this (unnatural) way?

As the daughter became an archetype in the nineties an answer surfaced. Daddy told her to. Or rather, Daddy *taught* her to "be this way." He raised his little girl, educated her, trained her, gave her weapons, and handed her a job. The heroine is *his* little girl. His creation. Besson's *Nikita* (1990) is the prototype that sums up the daughter. In this stylish action movie a young drug addict kills a police officer and gets a life sentence. A state agency fakes her suicide complete with a funeral and an empty grave and hands her an ultimatum: be a secret agent and killer working for the state or be terminated.

We find three themes: education by a father, masquerade, and prostitution. The female hero, as mentioned before, has no mother. Quite remarkable, since there are mothers in other genres; the evil mother in horror, the fuzzy mother in comedy, the dominating mother in drama. But not in male film genres. Instead, the female hero has a father.[67] It can be a biological father, as Charly in *The Long Kiss Goodnight* who was raised by her father, a Royal Irish Ranger, and after his death was adopted by a friend of her father's, who happens to be chief of the CIA. Or he can be a symbolic father figure like the old men who teach the female heroes to fight in *Hannie Caulder*, *Red Sonja* (1985), *Lady Dragon* (1992) and *Kill Bill: Vol. 2*. He can even be a spirit as the dead father guiding Lara in her dreams in *Lara Croft: Tomb Raider*. Whatever his status, his mission is to transform an ordinary young woman into an extraordinary hero. Nikita must "learn to read, walk, talk, smile and even fight. Learn to do everything." Pygmalion carved his ideal woman from cold marble and the father carves his ideal daughter from a human frame.

Part of the education is to fight like a man. Another, more prominent part is to learn to look and act like a woman—an *attractive* woman. Nikita has to sit in front of the mirror and apply makeup, put on a wig, and force some sort of smile onto her angry face. "Smile when you don't know something. You won't be any smarter, but it's more agreeable to those who look at you," a female agent tells her. The agent is The Beautiful Woman whose job it is to teach new female agents to *appear* as "man's perfect companion, a woman," with black cocktail dress, civilized behavior, and feminine manners. Impressed with the transformed Nikita, agent Bob exclaims, "You've really outdone yourself this time!" He is not talking to Nikita, but to The Beautiful Woman, who replies, "Yes, about this one I am pleased." The daughter is not a person. She is—as they say in *RoboCop* (1987)—a "product."

This is a masquerade with the daughter putting on a costume in a drag-like overacted performance of femininity. Think of Charlie's angels, his sweet little girls willingly masquerading as masseuses, strippers, hot and horny little devils almost giving a chauffeur a heart attack on the race tracks and keeping male crowds breathless with their dances, outfits, and silly rodeo bull rides. It brings to mind Joan Riviere's previously mentioned essay, "Womanliness as a Masquerade" (1929). Femininity is a protective shield, the "I'm-just-a-little-girl" act. When we compare this use of masquerade with the daughter, something has changed. Now men teach the daughter to use the mask of femininity. Riviere astutely observed in her essay that there is really no difference between our notion of femininity and the mask of femininity; they are one and the same. The daughter, however, demonstrates that there *is* a difference; in her private and "real" self, she turns out to be sweet and loving and social, the opposite of her "badass" persona.

Speaking of cross-dressing, Yvonne Tasker points out the "delight in sequences of transformation" which are traditionally "represented through montage sequences with an upbeat soundtrack ... offered as cinematic spectacle that takes place, like the numbers in Hollywood musicals, in a space to one side of the narrative."[68] But this is not to one side of the narrative. This *is* the narrative of the daughter. Her masquerade is the whole point. Tasker notes that such scenes aim to discover some kind of truth about "who the cross-dresser *really* is." Also with the daughter. But things are rather complicated, because truth is not found in the cross-dressing scenes, but in the daughter's female nature. Truth lies not in masquerading, but in essentialism.

Just as fashion scenes were central in classic Hollywood films, masquerade scenes are ubiquitous in male film genres with female heroes: it can be the female hero cross-dressing to have a male or masculine appearance—Joan cutting her hair in *The Messenger: The Story of Joan of Arc* (1999), Jane shaving her head in *G.I. Jane*, the angels posing as men. It can be up-dressing to turn a "wrong" femininity into the "right" femininity—as the female heroes up-dress in *Nikita* and *Point of No Return*. Or it can be cross-class-dressing to change one's social position—usually the female hero dresses "down" when she poses as prostitute, but it is also Nikita dressing "up" when she transforms from rag-clad drug addict to single career girl. From a postfeminist perspective, this is freedom. Speaking of *Point of No Return*, Jeffrey A. Brown argues, "We witness the easy fluidity with which Maggie performs both masculinity and femininity. In this regard, a biological female is free to enact either or both of the most stereotypical of masculine or feminine and female behaviors."[69] Brown is referring to Maggie's ability to switch between male and female behavior when she is cornered by a bodyguard; she pretends to surrender, and because she looks like a stereotypical woman—petite, fragile, beautiful—he falls for the scam and she immediately shoots and kills him.

Is this freedom? Nikita and Maggie don't think so. "I know you and your sadistic game. You're sick, Bob," Nikita tells her boss. She is wearing an enormous hat and a short dress with large red polka dots to underline the cliché that femininity is created from fashion. "I'm happy to see you. I miss the time when I had you to myself every day," he responds as he hands her another assignment. Like a pimp, he is cashing in on his daughter who is forced to dress up to do his "dirty" jobs.

The Amazon

The last archetype is the Amazon. My daughter knows Amazons from the animated television series *Justice League* where Wonder Woman (the former Amazon princess) is among the team of superheroes. The Amazon is related to women and war. Thus in the television movie *A Soldier's Sweetheart* (1998), the young Marianne gives up her innocent "college girl" image and joins the green berets on their raids into the Vietnamese jungle. Her boyfriend blames the other soldiers for filling her with "all that crap about Amazons!" Xena from the television series *Xena: Warrior Princess* is a warrior, not an Amazon, but her costume and her mentality are Amazonian: militant, independent, erotic.

In Greek mythology the Amazons are a race of women warriors descended from Ares, the god of war, and the nymph Harmonia. Amazons loved war and to fight without impediment they cut off their right breasts— "Amazon" meaning "those who have no breasts." They hated men and refused to marry, bred once a year and only raised girl children. In *Amazons: A Study in Athenian Mythmaking* (1984) Blake Tyrrell sums up the nature of the Amazon: "Unique to her is the combination female, militant, fighting against men, sexual attraction, dominance in marriage."[70] The Amazon myth, says Tyrrell, was constructed as men's fantasy of a frightening, yet fascinating, antithesis to the Athenian society. In the Greek patriarchal society women stayed home, men ruled, and men went to war. In Amazon society men were excluded, women ruled, and women went to war. "What the myth says of Amazon customs and homelands derives neither from inquiry nor from independent creation. It is a product of the Greek view of the human condition as civilized, mortal, Greek, and, most of all, male. When men cease to be men, the world ceases to be ordered; and the topsy-turvy world of the Amazon results."[71]

Most topsy-turvy about Amazons is the way they disrupt sexual order. They are aggressive and erotic creatures who kill, castrate, and even rape men to fulfill their own desires. "When I want a man I just take him. Grab him," says Zula with a dark smile in *Conan the Destroyer* (1984). Zula is played by actress Grace Jones, a black model and singer who with her short hair, flat chest and slim body represented an androgynous and raw, animal-like sexuality during the eighties. Tyrrell points out that Amazons are androgynes rather than women. He calls the Amazon a "daughter in limbo" because she is neither man, nor woman, nor nubile girl. Like the dominatrix, this archetype is not a "real" person, but a fantasy, a role rather than a real figure.

The Amazon is a monster to be feared, desired, and conquered. To become a great warrior the Athenian was supposed to slay an Amazon. Either that or marry her, whereby she ceased to be an Amazon and was reduced to a "normal" wife.

In male film genres the Amazon mirrors masculinity and patriarchy. It isn't that these institutions are disrupted or shattered or anything like that; rather, their structure is *made visible* and can be experimented with in the playful form of fiction, spectacle, and modern myth telling. In Greek mythology Amazons were "evil" because they were outside men's control. They became "good" when killed or domesticated in marriage. In contemporary popular film we find two versions of the Amazon: the good Amazon and the bad Amazon. The good Amazon is young, beautiful, heterosexual, and in favor of patriarchy. She doesn't live in a tribe of Amazons, but is a single warrior. She can be almost a wild animal, like the warrior Zula who joins Conan's company. Or she can be a wandering woman warrior in a male world, sometimes serving the system, sometimes just serving herself. Thus the thief Valeria in *Conan the Barbarian* is part Amazon in her love for sword fights and independence. Secret agent Cleopatra (Tamara Dobson) in *Cleopatra Jones* is not an Amazon, but is still clearly Amazonian in appearance and attitude (strikingly tall, with a fiery and proud expression, short hair, militant behavior). It is the Amazon's nature to love war and fighting.

The evil Amazon comes in several versions, where the common feature is that she does *not* favor patriarchy. She is always on her own side. "Why be an angel, when I can be God?" says ex-angel Madison in *Charlie's Angels: Full Throttle*. Like Madison, the evil Amazon is often lesbian and a generation older than the heroine—that unspecified age between young and old. She can even have her very own harem of female prostitutes, as the lesbian villains Mommy and Dragon Lady in *Cleopatra Jones* and *Cleopatra Jones and the Casino of Gold*. She is greedy, asocial and amoral, like Madison who shoots her partner in cold blood. Some evil Amazons are godmothers with their own criminal organization and, like godfathers, the power to kill people. Other evil Amazons are just small fish, hired villains, or companions to the female hero's adversary (in which case they are bisexual).

Today's visual rendering of the Amazon is seldom androgynous, but focuses on the female body. Thus cover art for *Barbarian Queen* (1985) has five women in string bikinis and makes the statement, "No man can possess her. No man can defeat her." Guinevere in *King Arthur* (2004) is an example of a modern Amazon with her painted body and bondage-inspired costume of leather straps. Guinevere, like the Greek Amazon, is domesticated through marriage.

Today, a dominatrix outfit is a natural part of any female hero's wardrobe. Shown here is wife and secret killer Mrs. Smith (Angelina Jolie) in *Mr. and Mrs. Smith* (New Regency Pictures, 2005).

Observations

The female hero in a man's world has many faces. Some are provocative and subversive, some are entertaining and exploitative. Some are sexy super bitches, bad mamas, and castrating femme fatales. Others are vindictive, hurt, angry. However, whatever their archetypal nature, they are always beautiful and sexy. Such are the female hero's possibilities—and limitations.

So, is she a role model? Let me be clear: there is no simple "yes" or "no" answer to this question. I do not believe in directly linking political critique with pleasure and popular entertainment. In my view, a film is not "better" because it is politically correct, nor is it "worse" because it is politically incorrect. The pleasure of a film lies in the emotions we invest in the fiction. Thus, the huge lesbian fan audience for Xena cannot be wrong, as a fan wrote.[72] There *had* to be a liberating (in this case, lesbian) aspect to Xena. Interpretations differ. And even if they are unanimous, they may change over time. What once was sickening and inappropriate can become university curriculum. I was an example of this, when I recently gave a presentation on *Ilsa, She-Wolf of the SS* at the Danish Film Museum as part of a film series entitled "Lust and Sexuality in Film." What once was "pure" exploitation may later inspire changes, like my daughter starting karate after watching the high-kicking heroines in *Charlie's Angels*.

I will not claim that the female hero is a progressive role model, or a feminist, or that she subverts patriarchy. It is for an audience to decide how to read her. But neither will I deny her the potential for feminist critique and postfeminist action. She represents a cultural field where today's male and female generations negotiate gender, feminism, patriarchy, and women's roles in society. Hopefully, this book can be part of this dialogue.

PART ONE

The Rise Against Men

1

"Godmother" of Them All: The Rise and Fall of Pam Grier

You want me to crawl, white motherfucker? You wanna spit on me and make me crawl? I'm gonna piss on your grave tomorrow!
　　　　　　　　　　　　　　　　　　　—*Coffy* (1973)

I'm going to make movies the way I see fit. No threatless, mindless women. No dumb situations. I know I have to go slow. But I'm going to sneak up on them little by little and then I'm going to create a monster. This girl isn't just another body for their cameras.

　　　　　　　　　　　　　　　　　　　—Pam Grier[1]

The biggest, baddest, and most beautiful of all female heroes in popular cinema is Pam Grier, who transformed low budget exploitation into cult cinema in the seventies. She made her debut in WIP films (women-in-prison films), worked her way through horror films and swords-and-sandals films and finally became famous as "Queen of Blaxploitation" through her action roles in *Coffy* (1973) and *Foxy Brown* (1974). Today, she remains the undisputed Queen of femme fatale cinema.

She was marketed by American International Pictures as a sexy, aggressive, and cool super bitch, a bad mama who dished out violence in its most extreme forms: shooting, killing and castrating men; stabbing them with broken bottles, hair pins and metal hangers; hiding razor blades and guns in her high afro and serving lines like, "Have I bruised your masculinity?" Her film persona was based on aggression towards men and an unabashed exploitation of her body. Mixed with the action were always rapes, beatings, torture, kinky femme fights, sex, *anything* to expose that incredible flesh. On film Grier *never* let men get her down. In real life, however, her career was terminated when she rebelled against her "super bitch" image and called the films she had made for AIP "jerk jobs."

The films of Pam Grier dared me to begin my own journey into the territory of female heroism. I was caught between pleasure and pessimism. On the one hand, her films were a mind-blowing experience to watch for a viewer—in this case me—used to "nice" female Hollywood stars. There is nothing "nice" about Grier. Not at all. She is—as the poster for *Coffy* promises—"the baddest One-Chick Hit-Squad that ever hit town." Yet her fate underlines the central dilemma of femme fatale cinema: Mixed with the misogyny and exploitation produced to please a male audience, there is created a space for feminist identification with a sexy super bitch. It is there all right, as all the female friends and students I have introduced to Grier's world have experienced. The star Pam Grier was born in this space. But this space is dangerous to occupy. Thus, the *actress* Pam Grier was not allowed to tap into the power of her star persona. Instead, she fell victim to it.

Birth of "Big Bad Mama"

Much has been made of the fact that Pam was raised in Europe on American military bases and that her father didn't say "yes" and "no," but "affirmative" and "negative" to his children and called the kitchen "the mess."[2] Pamela Suzette Grier was born on May 26, 1949, in North Carolina, and when she was five, her father, a maintenance mechanic for the United States Air Force, was transferred to a base in England. Perhaps this is where the aggression and sense of isolation in her characters come from? She played with toy missiles as a child and when she returned to the States at fourteen, Pam felt as alien as her British accent. She was never popular at school and wanted to be a doctor. After her parents were separated, her mother told her to get an education so she could be financially independent.

Pam never dreamt about becoming an actress; one could say that her body made the decision. When she was nineteen she entered two beauty contests to earn money for college. She was the only black contestant. Part Caucasian and part African American from her father's side, part American Indian and part Asian from her mother's side, she was five feet eight, a tall, strikingly beautiful woman. She had skin the color of creamed coffee, a proud aquiline nose, almond-shaped eyes and her measurements of 36-23-36 should make Barbie envious. Once she became a star, journalists, male as well as female, inevitably commented on her appearance. "Her skin is light caramel. It looks five inches deep, and you want to roll in it.... And her nose, easily her best feature, juts away from her face defiantly—a warning or a dare."[3] Or "Pam Grier is the most winning example of a miscegenated person I have ever seen.... Her skin is the exact color of the pancakes in the Little Black Sambo book. Her nose is the kind that was meant to flare when someone disgusts her. She has the kind of lips that look comfortable smiling, pouting, or pursing."[4] Pam didn't win any beauty contests, but got a prize for her singing and dancing (yes, that is her singing the title song "Long Time Woman" in *The Big Doll House* which Tarantino later used in *Jackie Brown*). And she was spotted by Hollywood agent David Baumgarten whose offer she turned down. Her mother, however, had dreamt about becoming a movie star and convinced her daughter to give it a try. Pam moved to Hollywood to work as a receptionist and switchboard operator for three years, first with Baumgarten's agency, then with AIP.

In 1969 she managed to land a bit part in Russ Meyer's *Beyond the Valley of the Dolls* (1970). However, her part as "the fourth woman" was left on the cutting table. Then she auditioned for Roger Corman, who was looking for a white, aggressive, and sexy girl. "Corman had me try out for the part of a white girl. He said he wanted someone who was aggressive and bouncy and I thought if I could show him how aggressive and bouncy I was nobody would care about my color. When the director told another actress to shove me, I shoved her back. Roger thought it was great. For me it was a natural reaction. Nobody bullies this kid, not even in fun. Not where I come from."[5] The attitude proved right. The film was *The Big Doll House* (1971), the first of a string of WIP films produced cheaply in the Philippines for Corman's new company, New World Pictures.[6] This is where the unique Amazon persona of Grier is born. After playing an angry lesbian prisoner in *The Big Doll House*, directed by Jack Hill, Grier was cast as a sadistic lesbian warden in *Women in Cages* (1971), directed by Gerardo de Leon, then as a revolutionary-turning-prisoner in *The Big Bird Cage* (1972), also directed by Jack Hill. She was an imprisoned prostitute in Eddie Romero's *Black Mama, White Mama* (1973), and finally an enslaved Nubian princess in Steve Carver's gladiator-and-WIP film *The Arena* (1974).

Later, as Grier reached action film level, she was hailed as a feminist trend in Hollywood. But not while she did WIP films. With one exception—an American film colleague—I have not met any woman (besides myself) who watches WIP films, and thus no woman who has claimed that these films should be feminist. Not one. I have, on the other hand, met numerous men who enjoyed WIP films and read them (or, at least, said they read them) as fables of female rebellion offering women new role models.

They are, partly, correct. WIP films present strong, independent, and erotic women burning with desire, energy, and willpower. However, WIP films are also produced by men, aimed at a male audience, and designed to satisfy male, not female, desires. They promise two kinds of erotic violence: Women maltreated by men and women maltreating men (actually, there are also women maltreating women, today made notorious by the *Ilsa* series, but usually not announced in trailers or publicity material). "Soft young girls behind hard

prison bars.... They'd do anything for a man—or to him! They caged their bodies, but not their desires!" the poster for *The Big Doll House* announces with
a drawing of five female prisoners in a golden bamboo cage suspended in the
air like a birdcage. The poster for *Black Mama, White Mama* had the two female
leads, Pam Grier and Margaret Markov, dressed (or, depending on one's point
of view, *undressed*) in rags, strangling a male guard with their chains under
the slogan "Chicks in chains—where they come from this is ... FUN!" *The
Arena* showed female gladiators with the slogan "See wild women fight to
the death." In its new design the cover of the DVD advertises, "Four sexy
savages beat the Romans into submission." The female heroes of the seventies WIP movie were presented as Amazons who love to fight and kill, hate
men, burn with sexual desire and delight in violence and destruction.

Pam Grier (left) on the run as the prostitute Lee chained to the revolutionary Karen (Margaret Markov) in the classic women-in-prison film
Black Mama, White Mama (American International Pictures, 1972). Less
sadism and more character development established Grier's "bad mama"
action persona and gave her a break into mainstream cinema. (Courtesy
of the British Film Institute.)

Originally, WIP films were modeled after the male prison movie. Thus, *The Big House* (1930) was followed by *Ladies of the Big House* (1931). In prison the freedom of the outside world is substituted by rules, restricted space, and control over time, bodies, and behavior. In the end prisoners escape or riot against the system. In its female version, prison films were social realist melodramas whose prison was meant to reform women, so they could be returned to their proper social duties in the outside world.[7] Mostly, of course, prison did the opposite and turned women into hardened criminals, masculinized women, or victims, destroying their families, children, bodies and minds in the process. The point was educational and contradictory: See what happens to anyone who strays—and yet the heroic protagonist was a criminal who rebelled against the system. During the sixties the American WIP movie died out. Corman revived and altered the genre formula partly by taking inspiration from Italian director Jess Franco's sadistic take on the genre and partly by incorporating the new social changes from the sixties— women's liberation, the black civil rights movement, and the counterculture movement. There were now two new characteristics of the WIP film: Softcore sexual violence and a thin narrative of political revolution.

The classical narrative opens with the "new fish" arriving at The Women's Rehabilitation Center, as the prison camp for example is called in *Black Mama, White Mama*. The camp is located on an unspecified Asian island where life is cheap, the temperature high, and the women hardly dressed. Apart from a dozen American actors, the rest of the film crew consists of dubbed locals who seem ignorant of what is going on. The plot is straightforward: The female hero may be innocent, as Jeff (Jennifer Gan) in *Women in Cages*, who has been framed by her lover, but she is usually guilty, as the prostitute and thief Lee (Grier) in *Black Mama, White Mama*. Mostly there is a link to some revolutionary movement. Thus Bodine (Pat Woodell) in *The Big Doll House*, Blossom (Grier) in *The Big Bird Cage*, Karen (Markov) in *Black Mama, White Mama* and Bodicia (Markov) in *The Arena* are revolutionaries. However, though leftwing politics are represented, they are not condoned; handcuffed to each other the revolutionary Karen and the prostitute Lee escape. Karen wishes to join the revolution which Lee refuses:

KAREN: We're trying to set this island free. Christ, you're black, don't you understand?

LEE: I've spent the last few years living with a prick I hate so I could beat him of enough cash to get what I've been after all my life. Now, there's a boat waiting to get me and my money out of here for good. And some jive-ass revolution don't mean shit to me!

KAREN: I've had money all my life.

LEE: Oh, my heart bleeds for you! Is this two-bit hick island important to you? If it is, maybe your good life at home got old ... and this is the little rich kid's new toy! How about it, little sister?

(Yes, Jonathan Demme's story for *Black Mama, White Mama* was a switch-around from *The Defiant Ones*, 1958) with escaped convicts Tony Curtis and Sidney Poitier chained together). Solidarity, though, does not come easy in prison, where new and old inmates fight over power and rank. Who gets to be Queen Bee? Harsh conditions, however, force the women to unite and escape or riot. In the final confrontation with the guards, all lesbians, revolutionaries, and evil men are killed. Most of the prisoners die as well, allowing one or two to make it. "The basic formula to this is that you show these women in depraved, oppressive conditions, exploit the hell out of them sexually with the camera, and at the end it's always about the women rising up and revolting against their oppressors. And they succeed. Women-in-prison films are parables of liberation, while satiating the perverse, decadent tendencies of people like myself," says Darius James, author of *That's Blaxploitation*.[8]

Of what nature are these "perverse, decadent tendencies"? first, there is little "normal" sex in Grier's WIP movies or, in fact, in *any* of her movies. Sex falls into three categories: voyeurism, sadism, and fetishism, happily joined together and spiced up with lesbianism. Standard voyeuristic scenes are the *initial examination* new prisoners undergo. In *The Big Doll House*, the women are stripped naked and laid on a table, where they are examined by a fat, ugly, grunting, Asian female guard, who wipes her fingers off on her jacket. Nice little detail, just in case we missed what the camera didn't show. There is also the *shower scene* with long showers, tits and ass, and playful splashing water on each other and displaying oneself to a peering audience (in *The Big Doll House* the fruit vendor Fred has a peep, in *Black Mama, White Mama* a lesbian guard masturbates as she secretly spies on the women in the shower). "Strip 'em and get 'em wet," a guard commands in *The Big Doll House*. Voyeuristic are also *torture scenes* where women—in these films it's almost never men—torture other women. "Is this how you get your kicks?" the female hero Jeff exclaims, strapped to the wheel in the "Play Pen" room and tortured by lesbian chief warden Alabama (Grier) in *Women in Cages* (1971). Lesbian wardens are evil and perverse, most spectacularly so in *The Big Doll House*, where the torture chamber has a royal chair for a mysteriously hooded figure in fetishistic outfit (whip, boots, gloves) who watches when chief guard Lucian (Kathryn Loder) works her wonders on the victim on the rack. A memorable moment is a hissing cobra lowered onto the naked Collier (Judy Brown). As James Robert Parish comments in *Prison Pictures from Hollywood* (1991), "The multi-leveled sexual implications of this segment are enormous!"[9] Mixing sadism and voyeurism are also the *femme fights* taking place in the canteen—throwing food at each other—and in the work field where scores are settled and positions lost and won, as when Alcott (Roberta Collins) dethrones Grear (Grier) by beating her up in a fight that ends as a mud wrestle. *Rape scenes*, more rare than one would expect, come in several variations: men raping women, lesbians raping women, and women raping men. "Get it up or I'll cut it off," says Alcott to Fred (Jerry Franks) and forces him to have sex with her. In *The Big Bird Cage* a group of women force a male guard to perform at knife point. "It'll last or he'll lose it."

WIP movies do not contain the traditional meat shots and money shots of the porn movie, and although the content is pornographic, the cinematography stays carefully within soft-core boundaries. The camera prefers tits and ass, drawing away from the genital area and rarely displaying frontal nudity (and *never* male frontal nudity). The tall Amazonian Karen (Karen McKevic) running naked through the fields to beat up another girl is an exceptional sight. "Stop her!" a girl yells. "I can't, she's all slippery. She's covered in chicken fat," another girl yells back. Hard-core violence is kept offscreen as well, displaying the woman either waist up or legs down. Thus the rape of Bodicia in *The Arena* shows her waist up when lecherous, repulsive old Romans with hairy backs leer over her.

The pleasure of female pain falls within psychoanalysis' conception of male sexuality as aggressive and sadistic. However, after the torture of the women the viewer is treated to the spectacle of male humiliation, a repeated feature in Grier's WIP films. Whereas everyone writing about these films notes sadism and female heroism, this specific feature is overlooked.[10] But exactly male humiliation will become central in Grier's star persona. In *The Big Doll House*, fruit vendors Fred and Harry (Sid Haig), who constantly fantasize about the girls, end up strolling in the woods in identical white underwear because the escaped women have substituted their prison dresses with the men's clothes. Thus demasculinized Fred and Harry furthermore have to be content with raping the lesbian and schizophrenic warden instead of the foxy inmates, who had promised sex if the two men helped the women escape. *The Big Bird Cage* takes male ridicule one step further by making two unsympathetic male guards homosexual. They are the viewer's point of comic relief. The revolutionary Django (Haig) poses as homosexual in order to get into the camp and free his lover, Blossom (Grier). In the men's room one of the guards stares at Django's penis. "Big show. Fourteen and a half," Django laughs in a falsetto. The girls also laugh when they rape the same guard: "You're finally gonna use that thing for what it's made for." There are similar scenes in *Black Mama, White Mama* where the gangster Ben (Haig) forces two men to show their privates. "Which of them has got the biggest pecker?" he asks a prostitute, who has slept with both of them. "The cop—eight. He [a ministerial adviser] has four, maybe four and a half." Ben then checks, "No, three, maybe three and a half." And in *The Arena*, the homosexual roman—who three times insists that *he* will certainly not touch the female slaves—is killed.

Male humiliation occurs in a much lighter tone than the torture of women (but will be pushed to sadistic extremes in the *Ilsa* films). In his analysis of penis-size jokes in mainstream Hollywood cinema, film critic Peter Lehman points to three possible viewer positions:

> The men who create and enjoy such jokes may be denying their vulnerability by positioning themselves as superior to the objects of the joke. Or, in heterosexual, masochistic desire, they may be identifying with the male judged inadequate by the desired woman and thus enjoying that vulnerability. Or, in a disavowal of homosexual desire, they may be using the woman to deny their own homoerotic desires to look at and evaluate other men's penises. In accordance with my earlier argument about multiple and contradictory male subject positioning, all three perspectives may be simultaneously occupied and all or any combination of them is amenable to Freudian analysis.[11]

Indeed, all perspectives are at play: sadistic, masochistic, and homoerotic. The male viewer can choose between identifying with either supermale Ben or the humiliated men, or they can choose to desire Ben, or, in *Women in Cages*, to desire Django and identify with the guard. The multiple identification positions are repeated in Grier's action films, whose focus on vulnerable male privates didn't pass unnoticed (a journalist exaggerated somewhat, reporting that Grier shot off four pairs of genitals instead of one in *Coffy*).[12] Anxiety about performance, size and masculinity is played as a joke.[13] The point, however, is to open up to *both* a masochistic masculinity *and*, as a male student pointed out to me, at the same time ridicule men who do not live up to traditional masculinity, thus establishing traditional, aggressive, and heterosexual masculinity as the social standard.

Tracing female desire through Grier's WIP characters there are contradictory perspectives. On the one hand, they are beaten (*The Big Bird Cage*), gang raped (*Women in Cages*), and sexually exploited (*The Big Doll House*). Women are portrayed as constantly aroused—"Do you know they are so horny you can hear them honk in the night?" Harry tells Fred, "I ain't gonna rape one of them. One of them is gonna rape me"—and although women are free to feel desire, they are rarely granted freedom. The heroine escapes in *The Big Doll House* but is picked up by a car that will take her back to camp; only two female gladiators remain alive in *The Arena*; and only "black mama" escapes in *Black Mama, White Mama*. However, in her WIP films

Grier comes across as strong, attractive, independent, and always defiant. A modern Amazon. "I like being on top," her lesbian character says mockingly in *The Big Doll House*, standing up for her sexual preferences. Grier's character has the critical dialogue about men: "You are rotten, Harry! You know why? Because you're a man. All men are filthy; all they ever want is to get at you. For a long time I made them get at me, that's why I'm in this dump, but no more. You hear me! I'm not gonna let a man's filthy hands touch me again." In her second role as the sadistic and lesbian warden Alabama, Grier's character was developed further. "A man raped me, a woman might as well kill me," Alabama says towards the end, and to Jeff's question, "What kind of Hell did you crawl out of?" replies, "It's called Harlem, baby, and I learned to survive. Never have pity. This game is called Survival. Let's see how well you can play it. I was strung out and high on smack at ten. And worked at the streets when I was twelve." Her third character, revolutionary Blossom, was on top of all situations, whether this was dealing with an unfaithful lover ("I told you I was gonna cut it off if you pulled that shit on me") or being a new fish in prison ("Which one of you dikes run this place? My name is Blossom, but that don't mean shit. From now on, I'm gonna run this place!"). As the prostitute Lee, her fourth WIP role, Grier suffered neither torture nor rape and managed to escape with forty thousand dollars. And in *The Arena* she played Mamawi, the strongest and proudest of the female gladiators, who corrects a gladiator who tries to rape her. After slapping him in the face she decides to have sex with him anyway—like Amazons who have sex if they want to.

Pam Grier's WIP movies today strike the viewer as innocent. There is sex and sadism, but the hard-core stuff is offscreen and the tone is light, often comical. From the posters one could expect—I did—more sadism, whereas the films in fact are less shocking than Grier's action movies.

Black Mama, White Mama was the movie that convinced audiences of Grier's star potential. Critics hated the movie and John L. Wasserman predicted in *San Francisco Chronicle* that "as soon as *Black Mama, White Mama* is seen by members of the motion picture industry ... [not only would] director Romero and writer Christian be out of work ... [but] that situation will be permanent."[14] Audiences and grosses certainly proved him wrong.

"Godmother"

There is a direct connection from Grier's WIP films to her action films and from her WIP persona to her action persona: Jack Hill, the director of *The Big Doll House* and *The Big Bird Cage*, wrote and directed *Coffy* (1973) and *Foxy Brown* (1974), the two films that made her queen of blaxploitation.

Director of AIP Sam Arkoff approached Jack Hill with the idea of a woman blasting a man's head off as the opening scene for a film about female vengeance.[15] There was no plot or further development, just a scene and a strong, violent female protagonist. AIP felt cheated out of *Cleopatra Jones* whose director had left in the middle of negotiations and taken his film elsewhere. Now AIP wanted their own black female hero. And Hill wrote the manuscript with Pam Grier in mind. The title came from a woman, who years ago had described the color of her skin to him over the phone as "coffee-colored." That wording hadn't left Hill's mind.

The poster for *Coffy* displayed a voluptuous Grier in a bikini top and low-cut white pants, a shotgun resting casually at her hip and the phrase, "She's the 'GODMOTHER' of them all.... The baddest One-Chick Hit-Squad that ever hit town!" The poster for *Foxy Brown* had Grier in a long, white dress with a gun hidden in high heeled shoes, small images of women fighting at her feet and the text, "Don't mess aroun' with FOXY BROWN. She's the meanest chick in town! She's brown sugar and spice but if you don't treat her nice, she'll put you on ice!"

Her action persona was a paradoxical creature. Whereas her WIP characters had been pure Amazons, her action characters were decent, all–American happy-go-lucky girls at heart, forced to take vengeance because the world is corrupt, the law is impotent and criminals destroy the innocent. These young women had brothers, fathers, boyfriends, and friends, all there to be mutilated, killed, destroyed, and avenged. And when it came to vengeance, her sweet and caring babes turned into explosive killer Amazons.

Coffy opens with a bang: A black pusher king is called out of a nightclub by one of his dealers. "I brought you a piece of tail." "A piece of what? What are you talking about? Look over there, I've got more tail than I can handle, I've even got *white* tail," the pusher exclaims and gestures towards his women. However, no mortal man can resist Coffy, who is waiting in his car in a skimpy dress, pretending that she will do anything for a fix. In his bedroom she pulls out a shotgun with the words, "This is the end of your *rotten* life, your motherfucking dope pusher," and blows his head off—a threat even Dirty Harry didn't go through with. The camera shows the exploding head (quite hard stuff for an audience who had to wait a few years for David Cronenberg's famous exploding head scene in *Scanners*). Coffy then moves in on the dealer, "It was easy for him because he didn't believe it was comin.' It's not gonna be easy for you because you better believe it's comin'!" At gunpoint she forces him to take an overdose and relates her motive, "My name is Coffy. Loubel Coffy is my little sister. She's only eleven and you made her shoot dope. Her whole life is gone and she can never get it back and you're living real good. That ain't right."

No, that ain't right, and Coffy is a woman with a strong sense of justice. After killing the two men she turns up at a hospital, where she works as a nurse. She is now a black "sister" dressed in white, symbol of her innocence and goodness. Coffy is both a saving angel and an avenging vigilante, a mender of bodies and a cleaner of corruption. When a nurse is sick during operation the doctor calls for the dependable Coffy.

At this point in her vigilante career, Coffy is not sure about the justification of her acts, and after a visit to her comatose little sister in a clinic she discusses crime and punishment with her cop friend Carter (William Elliott). "Carter, wouldn't you want to kill somebody who'd done a thing like that to your little sister?" But Carter does not believe in vengeance. "What? To shoot some pusher who's only selling dope so he can buy for himself? What good would it do, Coffy, when he is only part of a chain that reaches back to some poor farmer in Turkey or Vietnam? What would you do? Kill all of them?" Indeed, she would. Coffy knows why the law can't arrest them. "The law is in for a piece of the action." When Carter refuses to be on the take like his new partner, he is beaten into brain damage in his own living room, and Coffy is back on her vigilante track. She gets the name of the biggest pusher in town from a prostitute, whose face she sewed up at the hospital.

Apart from the effective shotgun, her best weapon in the war against drugs is—not surprisingly—her body. Disguised as a Jamaican prostitute with the name Ms Deek, Coffy tricks her way into King George's (Robert DoQui) stable of escort girls. "Now, I don't do no leather work, man," she tells him at their first meeting. "No whips, ropes, chains or any of those fetish freaks. Just plain sex. But for that I don't mind saying that I am the very best in my business." Coffy may be good at plain sex, but there is nothing plain about her character, who tells the same male sadomasochist drama as her WIP persona: first the men torture the women, then the women kill the men.

Exploiting herself in the name of vengeance Coffy makes King George forget sense, security, and his leading lady Meg (Linda Hayes), who is furious. "Ms Dick, what kinda name is that?" she asks, suspecting the newcomer with the improper name. At a party Coffy starts a femme fight with the other escort girls to get the attention of the mafia man behind the city's drug trafficking and political corruption, Mr. Vitroni (Allan Arbus). Vitroni, she has learned, is turned on by wild, exotic women, and Coffy kicks, punches, and pulls hair, tricking Meg into cutting herself on razor blades hidden in Coffy's afro. Vitroni *is* turned on. "She's like a wild animal. I've got to have that girl. Tonight!" During the fight the girls' dresses are accidentally torn open to expose their breasts to the male guests and the film audience—a striking feature carried over from Grier's WIP films.

Before visiting Vitroni, Coffy prepares by hiding her shotgun in a teddy bear which she tucks into her bag, a scene accompanied by Roy Ayers' song "Coffy Baby" performed by Denise Bridgewater. In his hotel room Vitroni makes Coffy crawl at his feet in her high-heeled boots and opened dress, spitting in her face and calling her "dirty nigger bitch" and "black trash." "Oh, please, I know I'm not good enough for you but let me have your precious white body just once," Coffy begs. Then, in a scene parallel to the opening blast, she gets out her gun. "You want me to crawl, white motherfucker? You wanna spit on me and make me crawl? I'm gonna piss on your grave tomorrow!" The image of a suppressed woman is replaced by kinky female anger, both images imported from the WIP genre, and both essential to the Grier persona. However, vengeance must wait till the end and for now Coffy is knocked out by Vitroni's henchman, Omar (Haig).

In the action cinema, the law is always impotent. If there is a good cop he is sure to do his heroics outside the law or without the law's blessings. In vigilante cinema the good cop—if there is one—is killed like Michael in *Foxy Brown* or brain damaged like Carter in *Coffy*. The vigilante is on her own. And it comes as no surprise that Coffy's suave and rich boyfriend Howard, a black politician running for Congress, is tied in with the rest of the dope dealers. Vitroni kills King George and summons Howard to ask if he had anything to do with Coffy's attack. In his public speeches Howard (Booker Bradshaw) talked of the "vicious attempt of the white power structure to exploit our black men and women" by creating "narcotic addicts." He laughs, "You've been listening to my political speeches. I thought you'd be more intelligent than to listen to crap like that. Now, for God's sake. Black, brown or yellow. I am in it for the green. The green buck." He barely looks at Coffy on the floor, surrounded by men. "She's just some broad I fuck.... I'll tell you how much she means to me: Take her out and kill her."

Vitroni orders three men to execute Coffy and dump her body. But he underestimates the power of an Amazon. Vengeance time has finally come and once again the Grier physique solves the problem. They give her what they believe is an overdose of King George's heroine (which Coffy had earlier substituted with sugar). Coffy promises Omar one last sexual service (like all men, he thinks women "like it" that way) and during sex, she stabs him in the throat with a hairpin. Then she kills the two corrupt policemen pursuing her, steals their shotgun, and steals a car from a guy thinking he had picked up the woman of his dreams. Coffy is, like most of Grier's characters, an unstoppable force of nature running amok and never short on ideas and resources. She crashes through Vitroni's house and kills everyone present.

Howard is dealt with last. When Coffy turns up exhausted, beat-up,

All it takes is the right costume. Female avenger Coffy (Pam Grier) tricks her way into King George's (Robert DoQui) stable of escorts by posing as a Jamaican prostitute with the dubious name Ms. Deek in *Coffy* (American International Pictures, 1973).

betrayed at his house on the beach, he almost sweet-talks the avenging angel back into his arms. "Now, don't be naive, baby" (despite their violent ways, Grier's characters are naive when it comes to love), "you think if I wasn't mixed up with the racket, there wouldn't be any racket?... Sometimes you have to do a few little wrong things in order to do one big right thing." Coffy wants to believe him and when he ends with, "All you have to know, baby, is that I'm your man and I'm gonna take care of you and I'm gonna steer you straight." She is about to put down the shotgun when a naked, white girl appears from Howard's bedroom. "Coffy, baby, you've got to understand, I thought you were dead," Howard desperately explains. Right! Dead, killed, and resurrected, as they always are, avengers. Coffy's war, we understand, is not against crime and corruption, but against *male* crime and *male* corruption. She shoots Howard in the crotch and puts an end to future conquests. Dawn breaks as she walks out on the beach, and Wayne Garfield performs Roy Ayers' "Shining Symbol" to comfort the new action queen baptized in blood.

"I don't know how I did it. It seems like I'm in a dream," Coffy says towards the end of a vengeance spree leaving nine men dead. Apparently reviewers liked Sam Arkoff and Jack Hill's dream. "A statuesque actress with a body she doesn't hesitate to show, is strongly cast and conceivably could appear in a folo-up focusing on her talents," *Variety* wrote and called the movie "a smashing, no-holds-barred tale of retaliation."[16] *Boxoffice* predicted superstar status: "Judging by the talents she displays in this action drama, Pam Grier may yet emerge as the first black female superstar in today's market. Miss Grier is a capable and good-looking performer who averages two or three nude scenes per film. She won't let her fans down here."[17] *L.A. Times* was positive towards the film—"'Coffy' ... is a very well-made, very filthy and obscenely violent release"—but negative towards Grier, "who reads her lines rather stiffly and childishly and who shouldn't be able to fool anyone ... with that phony Jamaican accent." *L.A. Times* found Coffy "a great looking but totally unsympathetic black chick," a view partly supported by *Variety* who called Coffy a "black tart" (*tart?*). Clearly, her persona had struck a chord as being provocative and *not* nice.

Coffy put down her shotgun, but Grier had just started. The following year she reprised her action character in *Foxy Brown*. The first half of the film is an incoherent attempt at motivating vengeance: Foxy Brown (Grier) has a brother dealing coke and an FBI boyfriend recovering from an assassination attempt. Both are killed by evil drug queen Katherine Wall (Kathryn Loder) and her evil lover and second in command, Steve (Peter Brown), who protect their business by providing free escort service to corrupt judges and politicians. To get even Foxy poses as an escort and this is when the action begins.

The sexual pattern is the same as in *Coffy*: Maltreatment of men mixed with maltreatment of Grier's character and, as dessert to this rich dish, savage female vengeance. This time male humiliation comes in two versions: Mild ridicule and harsh castration. Ridiculed is an elderly judge, whom Foxy and escort girl Claudia (Juanita Brown) are sent out to service. The girls arrive in a hotel suite full of judges with half-naked escorts on their laps, laughing, drinking, and watching hard-core porno movies. The girls take

Opposite: In the case of actress Pam Grier, the poster art does not exaggerate. *Foxy Brown* (American International Pictures, 1974) delivered all the kinky sex and action any man could ask for—including castrations, rapes, and femme fights with evil lesbians. Foxy *was* the meanest chick in town.

judge Fenton (Harry Holcombe) into a single bedroom, push him down on the bed and pull his pants off. Then they look at his privates and laugh.

FOXY: Will you look at that? Baby, is this what you are gonna use on me?

JUDGE: What?

FOXY: I mean, I've heard of a meat shortage, but that's ridiculous.

JUDGE: Well, you've gotta, well.... The other girls liked it.

FOXY: I'm sure I'll like it. But I just can't find it. Claudia, help me find it. I think I see it somewhere (the women laugh and examine him).

FOXY: The charge, Your Honor, is assault with a very undeadly weapon.

CLAUDIA: I mean, talk about a blunt instrument.

The judge, however, takes no offense, but is quite pleased with the development of the game. "I can play along with the gag as well as the next fellow. What happens next?" Next, Foxy undresses and opens her arms, almost letting him have a taste of that incredible flesh, then pushes him out the door on his back and yells, "You pink ass corrupt honky judge. Take your little wet noodle out of here and if you see a man anywhere, send him in, because I *do* need a man." Left in the hotel hall in a shirt and without underwear the judge is beaten with umbrellas by a group of bourgeois-stereotyped women his own age. This scene, leaving the judge at the mercy of political correctness, obviously plays male masochism for laughs.

The "fun" gets more dramatic as Foxy allies herself with a group of Black Panther-esque revolutionary brothers who cut off Steve's private parts on her orders. Leaving the screaming Steve the camera cuts to Foxy handing Katherine a pickle jar. "I brought it for you, Mrs. Pimp, it's from your faggot boyfriend." The drug queen can't make out what the jar contains and inspects it at close range—dropping it with a scream as the nature of the contents becomes clear. At this point Foxy extracts a gun from her afro, kills two henchmen, and maims Katherine. "Why don't you kill me too, I don't wanna live," Katherine screams. "I know," Foxy calmly responds, "that's the idea. The rest of your boyfriend is still around and I hope you two live a long time and get to feel what I feel. Death is too easy for you, *bitch*. I want you to *suffer!*"

The Amazon has become a *femme castratrice*. To justify such extreme measures a rape motive was provided to turn Foxy into both a vigilante and a rape-avenger. As Foxy helped Claudia escape to the airport where Claudia's husband and little son were waiting, she was caught by Katherine's men. Unfortunately for Foxy who is beaten up, tortured and sent to "the ranch" down south, but fortunate for the audience, who are in for a special treat, namely the most painful moment in Grier's career.

A tender moment with politician boyfriend Howard (Booker Bradshaw) in *Coffy* (American International Pictures, 1973). When Coffy (Pam Grier) later finds him cheating, she shoots him in the crotch. Who said "super bitch"?

KATHERINE: Give her a shot of heroine and send her down to the ranch.

STEVE: You know what the boys at the ranch will do to her?

KATHERINE : She'll probably love it, and when she's got a good habit we'll send her down to the islands. She should bring a good price. Maybe she'll pay us back for some of the trouble she has caused us.

STEVE : If there is enough of her left when the boys are through with her.

At "the ranch" two fat, old, dirty, white rednecks (called "degenerates" in the film's press sheet) take turns beating, doping, and raping Foxy. The scene has a disturbing tone similar to *The Texas Chain Saw Massacre*, leaving a viewer uneasy. This is heavy stuff even by contemporary WIP standard and stands out from the film's otherwise tongue-in-cheek approach and cartoonishly drawn characters. Foxy escapes by picking up a razor blade from the bed table with her tongue (an inventive and far more kinky scene than the rape), bends two steel hangers into a weapon to attack her captors (like Laurie in the later *Halloween*) and sets the house on fire with gasoline.

Even if it clearly had an exploitative nature, *Coffy* had a coherent plot, a believable female protagonist—believable, that is, from a narrative point of view—and an undeniably realistic tone. *Foxy Brown* made no attempt at either realism or coherence. Director Jack Hill knew what audiences expected and delivered an action package on the verge of tripping back into exploitation. Thus, when Foxy picks up Claudia in a bar it is—quite inexplicably—populated with angry lesbians (!). Obviously, the point is to include the big femme fight from the WIP film. Also, in contrast to *Coffy*, the dialogue in *Foxy Brown* is aware of Grier's bad ass image and provides cool lines like "It's as American as apple pie" about vigilante justice and, when the brothers later ask Foxy if the justice she asks for isn't revenge, she responds, "You just take care of the justice and I'll handle the revenge myself."

Narrative gaps are bigger than the Grand Canyon—how exactly does she make contact with Katherine's escort service?—and where Coffy displayed doubt, desperation, and misery, Foxy possesses none of such weak spots and never begs for mercy. "That ain't gonna do it, you'll have to kill me or I'll kill you," she tells Katherine. However, realism had nothing to do with Grier's box office success, and *Foxy Brown* delivered Grier the way audiences liked her: A contemporary black sister with an Amazon personality, proud, angry, ready to maim, kill, have sex, and castrate to win her cause. "That's my sister and she's a whole lot of woman," says Link (Antonio Fargas) proudly after Foxy smashes his home because he deals drugs and has tipped Katherine about Foxy's FBI boyfriend.

The chemistry between Hill and Grier was perfect. "Bosomy black starlet Pam Grier and writer-director Jack Hill, who hitched a ride on the b.o. gravy train with last year's 'Coffy' are at it again," wrote *Variety* in a review that wasn't positive towards "his current stew of lumpy sex and indigestible violence" but had to respect a winning formula. "Viewers either have a stomach for this kind of fare or they don't, and no amount of media moralizing is going to eliminate such arguably grotesque samples of 'entertainment.'"[18] Again, the screen presence of Grier made an impression. "Grier is developing an audience following, and it's not hard to see why. She's reasonably competent and self-assured, has an expressive face and is certainly mamarily blessed. It would be interesting to see her in another kind of role under a director whose abilities extend beyond the grisly."

This critique was right. It could be interesting to see Grier in a role "beyond the grisly." The only problem was that such a role did not fit with the Grier persona. It did not meet audience expectations. And it did certainly not meet economic expectations. Detective drama *Sheba, Baby* (1975) was the last movie produced under her contract with AIP. Grier plays private detective Sheba Shayne, who is called back to her hometown Louisville when a white mafia boss, Shark (Dick Merrifield), attempts to take over her father's loan company. Director William Girdler, who had written the story with David Sheldon, played down Grier's Amazon persona and created a lighter and contemporaneous "independent woman" character. Sheba is an affectionate daughter and ambitious career woman, who has quit her boyfriend and job as police detective in Louisville to move to Chicago and be independent—financially as well as sexually. When former boyfriend Brick (Austin Stoker) wants to know if she sleeps alone, Sheba replies, "If you are asking, 'Do I sleep alone every night?' I'd have to say no. But then, if you asked if I was going steady with someone, I'd say no. So what are you asking?" And when her father tells her to stay out of his problems, Sheba says, "Dad, I know you think I'm doing a man's job, but I'm not going to sit on the sidelines just because I'm a woman." Sheba is denied the police protec-

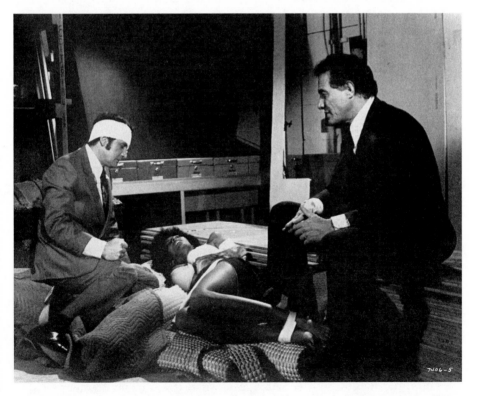

Foxy (Pam Grier) is caught, beaten, and about to be sent down to "the ranch" for further abuse and rape in Jack Hill's blaxploitation film *Foxy Brown* (American International Pictures, 1974). The film was the high point of Grier's career, but would also be her last hit until Quentin Tarantino wrote *Jackie Brown* for her in 1997.

tion she requests for her father, and when Shark's henchmen kill him, she goes vigilante. Again, Grier poses as an escort (for the third time), there is a big femme fight (without exposed breasts), and Sheba teases the villain with the self-conscious, "Have I bruised your masculinity?" However, no kinky sex, no kinky violence, no story, and a tame Grier did not do the trick this time. "[B]land escapist fare which could use a dash of passion or even a pinch of vulgarity to make it more palatable," *Los Angeles Times* wrote and noted "an embarrassing lack of electricity between Miss Grier and Stoker."[19] Also, songs by Cleveland and Rancifere were unimpressive, performed routinely by Barbara Mason who could not convince audiences that Sheba was dangerous and could take care of herself.

Her last leading role in the seventies was in *Friday Foster* (1975) by director Arthur Marks, a comic action thriller with Eartha Kitt as a fashion designer, Carl Weathers as a hit man (one year before he hit the jackpot in *Rocky*), and Grier, trying to be a comedienne instead of an action hero, as fashion photographer Friday Foster living with her little brother. She didn't beat up or kill anyone, but had sex with every rich black man in the plot. first a senator, then the richest black man in the US, billionaire Blake Tarr (Thalmus Rasulala). "Who is Friday?" Blake wants to know. "Well, first I'm a woman. Second, I'm a photographer and a big sister.... And I like cats and dogs and horses and men, but not necessarily in that order. I make my own decisions—and I'm a Gemini," Friday responds. The plot about an assassination attempt on Blake and some secret plan called "Black Widow" fell apart as dull standard blaxploitation. The dialogue tried to make Grier "a woman" with Friday saying silly things like, "You treat a person like a person and a woman like a woman" to billionaire Blake, and "I don't hustle for no one" to a pimp trying to get her in his stable of ladies. "That gal has got more balls than brains," a policeman says when Friday takes off in a hearse to pursue a suspect during a funeral. "She's just all woman," her friend Colt comments. This "all woman" character was dumb, unsexy, and uninteresting, even when played by Pam Grier. Her time as a Hollywood star was over for the next two decades.

Whose Pleasure Is It Anyway?

Pam Grier never regretted or excused her violent and sexy characters. "Yes. I did nudity. So what? And guess what? It was by my insistence and not the producers'. How can you play a rape victim or a hooker and not show nudity?"[20] She took the roles Hollywood had to offer, and together with names like Barbra Streisand and Liza Minelli she became one of the few leading *and* bankable actresses in the seventies, a name that could carry a film without being backed by a male lead, and the first female action hero. She was proud of her success. "I took the parts no other Hollywood starlet would touch because they didn't want to be demeaned or mess up their nails. It was a risk but I didn't know any better and somehow I came out on top. I don't know why, I just played myself and audiences liked me. I am where I am because I took those tough roles. If I had held out for those sweet, pretty, demure parts I'd still be waiting."[21]

To begin with, men welcomed Grier's tough action persona as sexy and dangerous, while women found it new and intriguing. Mark Jacobson in an article in *New York* entitled "Sex Goddess of the Seventies" (1975) told readers, "I saw one woman in a 42nd Street theater smack her boyfriend's arm ... [after watching Pam Grier in *The Arena* and say] 'See, fool, I'm going to get myself together like her, so next time you think you're superman, watch out,'"[22] a bit that was quoted in later articles about Grier. And a big interview in feminist journal *Ms.* was infatuated with Pam Grier. "She can so effortlessly dominate a scene that everything and everyone else in it become incidental," Jamaica Kincaid noted and compared Grier to her childhood memory of a film with actress Eve Arden who "had ability, presence, brains, and what seemed to me the courage to control and impose order on a world outside the house. I have wished many times that I could propel myself through life with the same spirit as that celluloid image. It is, I believe, that same kind of triumphant spirit and character that holds 'Coffy,' 'Foxy Brown' and 'Sheba, Baby' together."[23]

Audiences were also served black Amazons Tamara Dobson and Gloria Hendry in *Cleopatra Jones* (1973) and *Black Belt Jones* (1974). However, they did not do nudity and kinky scenes like Pam Grier, and neither of them possessed her screen presence. Dobson, a former model, was tall and certainly statuesque at six feet two, but also high class and socially out of reach. Hendry, a former Playboy Bunny, was pretty and slim, but unsexy and unconvincing. In the action business, Grier was the only one to hit the winning formula.

"I created a new kind of screen woman. Physically strong and active, she was able to look after herself and others," Grier described her contribution to film history. "You'll see she was the prototype for the more recent and very popular white Bionic and Wonder Women." Actually, Grier is wrong to compare her characters to these white female superheroes, who were meek and constructed to please prime time television audiences.[24] Grier's female heroes were far more complicated: angry Amazons and sweet sisters, castrating bitches and resourceful black women, archetypal male masochist fantasies and liberated career women, all of them fiercely independent yet submissive once in a lover's bed. This Amazon, raised in a modern U.S. and ready to break a bottle and swing it at someone's face, was far from Wonder Woman. The triumph of beating men in a man's world is quite different, when that world is your own. "[T]hey are the only films to come out of Hollywood in a long time to show us a woman who is independent, resourceful, self-confident, strong, and courageous," concluded Ms.[25]

Grier's characters, however, were fictitious creatures created by AIP, the film production company that produced and distributed Grier's films and gave her star treatment. When Pam Grier tried to break with AIP and leave her tough mama persona, that star persona was exposed as a construction. Grier's attitude towards it was ambivalent: on the one hand she rebelled against it, on the other hand she tried to tap into its strength. She became critical of AIP. "AIP's policy is to give the niggers shit. They don't like me but they want to work with me because I make them money. They don't like it that I talk about the cheesy way they work or that I say the movies that I did for them were jerk jobs. They think I am being ungrateful because they discovered me and made me a star.... They have lived in Beverly Hills for too long, and they don't know from nothing because they are not exposed to anything."[26]

Grier decided to kill off her action persona. She turned down a ten thousand dollar offer from *Playboy* for a December centerfold, and set up her own film company, Brown Sun Productions. No more waiting around for men to write her roles and offer her work, she wanted to expand her acting talent and create a new cinema for black women. "The bigger I became, the bigger the fuss. My nerves were shot a lot of the time. I never felt I was *that* Pam Grier."[27] She wanted to be bigger, be *real*, and be a factor to be reckoned with in the future. "They want me to be a noble slave or a doormat," Grier ironically said. "I read the trades, I know I'm big. I can get investors. And I'm going to make movies the way I see fit. No threatless, mindless women. No dumb situations.... I'm going to sneak up on them little by little and then I'm going to create a monster. This girl isn't just another body for their cameras."[28]

But the times were against the proud and outspoken Grier. In 1975 blaxploitation died suddenly at the box office, the films no longer appealed to a black or a white audience due to their repetitiveness, television wouldn't transmit the violent movies, and Europe didn't care for their black themes. A few black actors moved into "white" movies, but, except for Grier, none of the black actresses survived. The press that had promoted Grier to super star proportions now seemed to gloat over her downfall. "There is nothing visibly tough about Pam Grier ... she was a product that was carefully packaged for a particular market," wrote Alan Ebert in *Essence* in 1979. "Underneath the image of tits-and-ass and sex-and-violence is a very nice, rather conventional young woman ... [who] creates the impression of a little girl who dresses up in her mama's clothes to pretend she is all grown up."[29]

After *Friday Foster* in 1975 Pam Grier's next leading role came with Quentin Tarantino's crime drama *Jackie Brown* in 1997. He wrote the role of Jackie Brown especially for Grier, who had auditioned for a role in *Pulp Fiction*. In the twenty-two years in between, however, Grier was reduced to minor roles. Hollywood does not easily forget an actress who dares tell the press, "Should I sit around and wait for these cigar-smoking-conservative-high-water-Bostonian-wing-tipped-shoes-businessmen-lolling-in-their-studios to give me a job? I don't wait for anything."[30] But time and lack of jobs broke the Amazon. "I've paid my dues," she said in an interview in 1979. "I no longer want to be political. I want to work. To be political means to hurt me and the people trying to help me."[31] Four years without a leading role had erased the pride.

It is beyond the scope of this book to examine the many interesting roles of Pam Grier after *Friday Foster*.[32] She was excellent as a sex slave in Steve Carver's *Drum* (1976), and convincing as homicidal prostitute in Daniel Petrie's *Fort Apache: The Bronx* (1981). She was also entertaining as The Most Beautiful Woman In The World in Jack Clayton's *Something Wicked This Way Comes* (1983) and—in my opinion—back in excellent "tough mama" shape as the high-school-teacher-and-modified-killer-cyborg Ms Connors in Mark L. Lester's impressive (and highly exploitative) *Class of 1999* (1990). Here she mixes teaching with killing, appearing as a mix of a strict, sexy teacher and a Sherman tank. Grier regained her cool with *Jackie Brown*, but had had two minor hits before that in John Carpenter's *Escape from L.A.* (1996), where she was a criminal leader and drag queen, and Larry Cohen's homage to blaxploitation, *Original Gangstas* (1996), where she was a self-defense instructor. Recently she appeared as regular character Kit Porter in the television series *The L Word* (2004–) about lesbians in Los Angeles.

Pam Grier kicked the door open to future female action. She was no switch-around of a traditional male hero in a male film genre, no sexy adventure figure like Emma Peel in *The Avengers*. Neither was she a violent teen-drop-out in a Russ Meyer movie. She was a new item: A combination of a dominatrix, a rape-avenger, and a contemporary Amazon, fighting for a just society, killing men with hairpins, broken bottles, shotguns, and steel hangers. Had she bruised AIP's masculinity? Absolutely. When she took her critique of men from the fantasy world of Hollywood into the real world of film production, she crossed over from a pleasurable male fantasy to male anxiety. Pam Grier—the dark, feminine continent—was quickly conquered and domesticated. The rise against men, however, had just begun in Hollywood cinema.

Pam Grier Action Filmography (Selective)

The Big Doll House (1971) Dir. Jack Hill, filmed in the U.S. and the Philippines. Lesbian prisoner Grear, WIP

Women in Cages (1971) Dir. Gerardo de Leon, filmed in the U.S. and the Philippines. Lesbian chief warden Alabama, WIP

The Big Bird Cage (1972) Dir. Jack Hill, filmed in the U.S. and the Philippines. Revolutionary and prisoner Blossom, WIP

Black Mama, White Mama (1972) Dir. Eddie Romero, filmed in the U.S. and the Philippines. Prisoner, prostitute, and thief Lee, WIP

Coffy (1973) Dir. Jack Hill. Avenger Coffy, action

The Arena (1974) Dir. Steve Carver, filmed in the U.S. and Italy. African princess, prisoner, and gladiator Mamawi, WIP

Foxy Brown (1974) Dir. Jack Hill. Avenger Foxy Brown, action

Sheba Baby (1975) Dir. William Girdler. Private detective Sheba Shayne, action

Friday Foster (1975) Dir. Arthur Marks. Photographer Friday Foster, drama

Bucktown (1975) Dir. Arthur Marks. Girlfriend, vengeance drama

Fort Apache: The Bronx (1981) Dir. Daniel Petrie. Drug addict and prostitute Charlotte, action

Above the Law (1988) Dir. Andrew Davis. Police officer Delores, action

Class of 1999 (1990) Dir. Mark L. Lester. Cyborg teacher Ms Connors, action

Escape from L.A. (1996) Dir. John Carpenter. Criminal Leader and Drag Queen Hershe Las Palmas, action

Original Gangstas (1996) Dir. Larry Cohen. Self-defense instructor Laurie, gangster

Jackie Brown (1997) Dir. Quentin Tarantino. Stewardess and thief Jackie Brown, crime

No Tomorrow (1998) Dir. Master P. Diane, action

Wilder (2000) Dir. Rodney Gibbons. Detective Della Wilder, action

Bones (2001) Dir. Ernest R. Dickerson. Girlfriend Pearl, horror

The L Word (2004–) Showtime, television series. Lesbian Kit Porter, drama

A Pure Dominatrix:
Ilsa, She-Wolf of the SS

To have never seen an *Ilsa* film is to have truly been deprived the
joys of one of the last great exploitation sagas.
—Review of *Ilsa, She-Wolf of the SS* (1974)

Blond, beautiful, bosomy, and dedicated to pain and perverse pleasure, Ilsa from the WIP film *Ilsa, She-Wolf of the SS* from 1974 has entered
film history as a pure example of *the dominatrix*. Her mission is to please the
male masochist by acting out his most taboo fantasies. She is not a female
hero in any ordinary sense, yet she is a strong, active, and aggressive protagonist, who has become mythical in Western culture.

Her cruel acts left little to the imagination—one of the first scenes was
the castration of a screaming male prisoner—and the film provoked three
reactions: First, audiences for exploitation movies embraced Ilsa with such
an enthusiasm that a movie filmed in nine days on a budget of 150,000 dollars became a cult phenomenon worldwide. Actress Dyanne Thorne was
buried in fan mail and today still receives hundreds of fan letters each
month.[1] The success of director Don Edmonds' *Ilsa, She-Wolf of the SS*
spawned three sequels: *Ilsa, Harem-Keeper of the Oil Sheiks* (1976), also by
Edmonds; *Ilsa, The Tigress of Siberia* (1977) by Jean LaFleur; and *Ilsa, The
Wicked Warden* (1977), an unofficial sequel by Spanish director Jess Franco
with Dyanne Thorne. Ilsa's popularity remains undiminished; recently the
four films were reissued on DVD, beautifully restored in uncut versions
including commentary tracks with Dyanne Thorne, Don Edmonds, and
producer David Friedman. In 2000 the fan publication *The Ilsa Chronicles*
was published and out of print a year later.[2]

The second reaction came from mainstream audiences and reviewers
who absolutely hated the movie. The ardor of their condemnation fully
equaled the enthusiasm of the former group. "The movie is so nauseating

that it is impossible even to hint at its specific scenes without making my typewriter stink," a Danish reviewer wrote and deemed the film "perverse, sadistic pornography of the most sickening and exploitative kind."[3] In an interview a cinema owner described how he had to operate the movie projector himself, because his film operator refused to watch the film. The director eventually removed the movie from the program, commenting, "Ilsa was so disgusting and her methods of torture so repulsive that the audience was sick."[4] Dyanne Thorne lost close friends and though her husband was coproducer, her mother-in-law left the pre-screening in disgust. Even today, reviews of the DVDs mix cult praise with uneasiness. "To have never seen an *Ilsa* film is to have truly been deprived the joys of one of the last great exploitation film sagas,"[5] one review opens, while another begins with the confession, "I actually watched this one a couple of months ago and have been wrestling with how to write a review about it ever since."[6] Incidentally, all comments are by men. I have not come across any review, commentary, or article on the *Ilsa* films by a female author.

The third reaction provoked by *She-Wolf* came from film research. It was—silence. An utter silence, which to my knowledge is broken now.[7] The *Ilsa* films do not figure in mainstream movie guides such as Leonard Maltin's *Movie & Video Guide*. They are not listed in James Robert Parish's *Prison Pictures From Hollywood: Plots, Critiques, Casts and Credits for 293 Theatrical and Made-for-Television Releases* (1991). They aren't even included in the chapter on WIP movies in Bev Zalcock's *Renegade Sisters: Girl Gangs on Film* (1998). And the few academic articles on WIP pictures—incidentally, all written by women—do not mention the *Ilsa* movies at all.[8]

This third reaction—silence—is significant. It indicates that something is "wrong," even by the standards of exploitation.[9] Of what nature, then, are the "sickening," "perverse," "nauseating," "disgusting," and "repulsive" pleasures that make *Ilsa, She-Wolf of the SS* the ultimate see-if-you-dare movie celebrated by fans, condemned by critics, and muted by researchers? A word running through reviews, comments, and articles is "sadistic."[10] A word I have *not* found is "masochistic." Yet, this is where I want to locate the taboo pleasures of the *Ilsa* films.

A Parade of Atrocities

First a summary: *Ilsa, She-Wolf of the SS* laid down the archetypal structure of the series, and I shall use this film as my main point of departure, making references to the other three in the series (hereafter called *She-Wolf*, *Harem-Keeper*, *Tigress*, and *Wicked Warden*). The film opens with a warning:

The film you are about to see is based upon documented fact. The atrocities shown were conducted as "medical experiments" in special concentration camps throughout Hitler's Third Reich. Although these crimes against humanity are historically accurate, the characters depicted are composites of notorious Nazi personalities; and the events portrayed have been condensed into one locality for dramatic purposes. Because of its shocking subject matter, this film is restricted to adult audiences only. We dedicate this film with the hope that these heinous crimes will never occur again.

The text, presented as a legitimization of the story that will unfold, is accompanied by a speech by Hitler ending with repeated *Sieg Heils*. The camera then cuts to a bedroom and pans slowly across the bourgeois interiors: White silk ballet shoes hang on a hat stand, flowers, rococo bed table, two mirrors wherein we see a couple make love, a radio playing classical music, and finally a close-up of the woman saying, "Not yet, no, please." The man, we understand, ejaculates. "You should have waited," she mumbles. She has an orgasm in the shower and then wakes up her lover: "Time to go." The camera zooms back from her hand with dark-red nail polish to the woman in black SS-uniform. "But you promised I didn't have to go back to camp!" Two female officers take the man away. Strapped to an operating table he is castrated by the three women, the final cut made by a smiling Ilsa: "My little man, I kept my promise—you will never leave the camp again!"

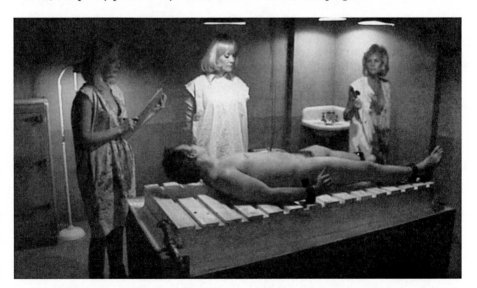

The perverse pleasure of *Ilsa, She-Wolf of the SS* (Aeteas Filmproduktions, 1974): Male masochism at the hands of three blond and busty women. Notice that Ilsa's two female helpers are naked underneath their blood-stained white coats.

The means for castration are demonstrated in *Ilsa*. Here is the scalpel, framed between a swastika and a bloodstained breast.

After these eight minutes, titles roll across the screen as female prisoners arrive to Medical Camp 9, where SS officer Ilsa and a doctor are in charge. The prisoners are presented naked to Ilsa, who divides them into two groups: One to be sent to German camps as prostitutes, the other "to serve the Third Reich." During the inspection one woman, Anna (Maria Marx), stands out as proud and defiant. She becomes Ilsa's favorite torture victim. Afterwards, a female nurse shaves the women's genitals. Next new male prisoners arrive at the camp. They, too, are inspected by Ilsa, first in the court, then naked in the men's barracks. "You call yourselves men? I see no manhood between your legs!" Again, one prisoner stands out. "Size is not everything," the blond Wolfe (Gregory Knoph) replies. He is an American and will become Ilsa's lover.

Life in camp is short and unpleasant, consisting of sex, torture, and death. In the women's barrack the prisoners are in various stages of terminal illness, infected with diseases by Ilsa. Their leader, Kala (Nicolle Riddell),[11] is horribly disfigured by syphilis, and Anna immediately talks about escape. During Ilsa's daily inspection of her experiments we see a woman killed in a decompression chamber, another woman has an open wound in her thigh alive with maggots infected with typhus, a third woman is boiled alive in a bathtub. Even worse off are the selected few who are used in Ilsa's private experiment to prove that women can withstand more pain than men.

In Ilsa's torture chamber a woman has her toenails plucked out with pliers. When Ilsa discovers Anna's plan to escape, Anne is subjected to days of torture in Ilsa's special room. The women not used for experiments are punished for minor sins by being gang raped by the male guards or flogged to death by Ilsa's female duo, the two female soldiers who serve directly under Ilsa.

Although the men are not used for medical experiments, their fate is no less enviable. While digging a grave, Wolfe and Mario (Tony Mumolo) discuss the strange nature of Ilsa, who castrates her lovers. "Castrate? Why?" Wolfe exclaims. "Perhaps it is her way of punishing a man who makes her feel like a woman, yet fails to satisfy her cravings for more. Who knows? Only one thing is certain: Once they have served her, it's the end of him as a man," says Mario. "My God, did you kill her?" Mario later exclaims, when Wolfe has survived a night with Ilsa. Wolfe explains his secret: He can hold back ejaculation for as long as he wants, thus satisfying a woman again and again. "You wanna know something: That never-control just about drove her up the wall," Wolfe boasts.

Breaking the routine is the visit of a general coming to inspect Ilsa's results. She throws a lavish dinner party in his honor with a table laid with food and, in the center, a naked female prisoner, who balances on a block of ice with a noose around her neck. During dinner Ilsa is awarded the Heinrich Himmler Cross and when they toast, the block of ice has melted and the woman is strangled. Later Ilsa offers herself to the general, who begs her to urinate on him. She does so, clearly disgusted, and next morning sends for Wolfe. "I need a real man." As part of their sex games he ties her to the bed, steals her gun, and starts the planned revolt. In what is the film's only action sequence—involving guns, explosions, and slow motion (in a film aesthetic otherwise transparent and primitive)— the prisoners take over the camp and execute their guards. Wolfe and Rosetta escape, while the rest stay and exact revenge. Amidst the uprising German tanks arrive and destroy the camp. A blond officer, who had also attended the dinner party, executes Ilsa in her bed and calls headquarters. "General, your orders have been carried out. Camp 9 has ceased to exist. You may tell the Reichführer that the allies will find nothing. They will never know." The last picture freezes Wolfe and Rosetta outside the wire looking at the burning camp. On the soundtrack is a boy's choir singing a cheerful song in German.

The setting and period change in the sequels; in *Harem-Keeper* we are in the Arabian desert in the seventies, *Tigress* places Ilsa in Stalin's Gulag during the fifties and in Canada in the seventies, and *Wicked Warden* has her in the seventies in South America. The recurring traits are her role as dominatrix, torturess and leader of an "institution"; her two female servants; and her destruction at the end of each film.

Perversion: A Revolt Against the Order of Things

WIP movies tell two stories: The first is a plot of suppression, rebellion, and liberation where female prisoners rise against oppressors to gain freedom. The second story is a string of perverse situations such as lesbian sex, shower scenes, torture scenes and rape scenes. The two stories—the dramatic plot and the erotic fantasies—are intertwined, the one justifying and motivating the other.

In She-Wolf the first story almost disappears, leaving the second story—the string of perverse situations—to dominate the narrative. More than a drama, the film reads as an inventory of taboo fantasies, which explains the frequently reported unease from watching the film. We find the stereotypical WIP narrative in the arrival of new prisoners to the camp, their maltreatment, and their final uprising. However, the plot is so thin and the "heroic" characters of Wolfe and Anna so poorly developed that they fail to engage us. Instead, we are left with the perverse fantasies.

According to Freud all sexual activities that do not lead directly to heterosexual genital intercourse are "perverse" in their diversion of sexuality from its primary aim, procreation. In her book *Male Subjectivity at the Margins* (1992) American film scholar Kaja Silverman discusses perversion as not only a diversion from genital intercourse, but furthermore as a subversion of the hierarchical structure on which social order is built. "Perversion ... subverts many of the binary oppositions upon which the social order rests: it crosses the boundary separating food from excrement (coprophilia); human from animal (bestiality); life from death (necrophilia); adult from child (pederasty); and pleasure from pain (masochism)." Perversion is a revolt against the order of things—but paradoxically simultaneously a confirmation of this very order. In the denial of order is confirmed its existence. "It is crucial, then, that we grasp the double nature of perversion, that we understand it as simultaneously a capitulation and a revolt."[12] Even though perversions appear radical, they are not sites of political subversion.

She-Wolf could be interpreted as one long fantasy enjoyed by the man, who in the opening scene falls asleep and wakes up to his lover dressed as an SS officer. This ties in with the ending where every trace of the camp—and thus of the fantasy itself—is erased. Burning down the camp and killing guards and prisoners removes all evidence of the atrocious acts and serves as a repression of the historical or "collective" memory. "They will find nothing." It also conveniently serves as the audience's repression of perverse pleasures, thus relieving them from feelings of guilt. This explains why prisoners must die with the guards; in the world of perversion, everyone is equally guilty. No matter their role or function, they are all part of the perverse structure.

In *She-Wolf* such a subversion of binary oppositions is everywhere. The opening scene establishes the radical nature of the subversion where every element is turned into its diametrical opposite: First in the filmic *genre*, where a pseudo-documentary opening is subverted into sexploitation. Then in the *iconography*, where the bedroom becomes the torture chamber below Ilsa's private quarters, the soft bed turns into a hard operating table, bourgeois wallpaper becomes bare grey walls. Then with the *characters*, where the formerly willing mistress becomes a harsh tormentor and the lover a male victim. Also the *sexual aim*, phallic victory—ejaculation—ends in phallic defeat—castration—and potency is transformed into impotence. Finally, a *high culture aesthetic*, marked by classical music and the ballet shoes, is transformed into the extreme opposite: the primitive, un-adorned and pre-cultural world of torture. The confrontation between *bourgeois culture* and *primitive violence* is repeated in the dinner banquet scene, when the camera crosscuts from the naked woman, silent and immobile on the ice block, to the elegantly dressed dinner guests toasting with their crystal glasses.

The producer, David Friedman, had his name removed from the film when he saw the final cut, and only admitted to the film twenty years later. Friedman had earlier produced gore films such as Herschell Gordon Lewis' trilogy *Blood Feast* (1963), *Two Thousand Maniacs!* (1964), and *Color Me Blood Red* (1965), but "those were made for fun, no one took them seriously," he says on the commentary track. Friedman immediately stresses, however, that the *Ilsa* films were also intended as not serious, they were "fun" to make and the team had a "great" time during the nine days of filming. He is right: As most exploitation movies, *She-Wolf* employs several tongue-in-cheek elements to serve as comic relief amid the tension. Wolfe's remark that "size is not everything," and the cheerful music accompanying him as he self-satisfied struts from Ilsa's bedroom after having survived a night without being castrated, are "funny" elements within the nightmare world. However, the real world took *Ilsa* seriously when it premiered, and the mixing of the historical Nazi period with the perverse fantasies was perceived as an unheard-of provocation. Which it was. Earlier movies that had linked Nazism and perverse eroticism were Lee Frost's much lighter *Love Camp 7* (1969) and Luchino Visconti's serious drama *The Damned* (1969). *Ilsa* pushed WIP films from the dark eroticism of Pam Grier's Philippine pictures to a new violent level and inspired the "Nazi sex & death" subgenre.[13]

Male Masochism

Some perversions are more subversive than others. Sadism, Freud notes in his writings, is a biological part of the libido and therefore poses no threat to the sexual and social order. It serves "the need for overcoming the resistance of the sexual object by means other than the process of wooing."[14] Otherwise with masochism, which Freud describes as "mysterious" and "incomprehensible" in "The Economic Problem of Masochism" (1924) and views as a dangerous perversion, because it subverts the pleasure principle itself by having pain as its primary aim. "If pain and unpleasure can be not simply warnings but actually aims, the pleasure principle is paralysed—it is as though the watchman over our mental life were put out of action by a drug. Thus masochism appears to us in the light of a great danger, which is in no way true of its counterpart, sadism."[15]

Freud describes the *manifest content* of the masochistic fantasies as "being gagged, bound, painfully beaten, whipped, in some way maltreated, forced into unconditional obedience, dirtied and debased."[16] He comments that these fantasies leave a less "serious impression" than "the cruelties of sadism" (I wonder if this is because they are "softer" than sadistic fantasies, or because their pain is aimed at the subject himself and not at an external object.) We might find a motive for Freud's comment in his explanation of the *latent content* of the masochistic fantasies. "[T]hey place the subject in a characteristically female situation; they signify, that is, being castrated, or copulated with, or giving birth to a baby."[17] The binary opposition between libido and death instinct, masculine and feminine, sadistic and masochistic, active and passive, men and women, strong and weak, recur in Freudian psychoanalysis. This is how Freud perceives the natural order of the sexes— and this is exactly the order masochism subverts. Thus, it is easy to understand why Freud rejects masochism as "mysterious." Mysterious indeed, because it places men in the role sadism usually reserves for women: the passive, painful role of the victim.

I shall not deny that sadism is part of the pleasures of the *Ilsa* movies. But I do not believe it is the central pleasure. Instead, the parallel between Freud's description of masochism and the scenarios in *She-Wolf* is striking: A male victim is whipped to death by a topless woman (one of Ilsa's servants) and when dead he is hung in an exhibitionist manner outside Ilsa's quarters; another is urinated on, lying on the floor; a man is castrated by three beautiful, smiling women; naked men have their genitals inspected by a cold, beautiful woman dressed in uniform; and so forth. These scenes continue in the American sequels; in *Harem-Keeper* a man is beaten publicly by two naked women who, with the approval of Ilsa, tear off his genitals. In

Tigress a man is eaten alive by a tiger, another has his arm chopped off by a chainsaw, a third is speared through the mouth. All these scenes belong within male masochism.

Here, I am not concerned with the psychological reasons why men become masochists—Freud presents this as the boy's repression of a homosexual attitude towards his father, the wish "to be loved by the father" repressed into the fantasy "to be beaten by the father," which again is further repressed into the conscious fantasy "to be beaten by the mother."[18] It is this last fantasy we see played out in the "beating scenarios" where a woman equipped with "masculine attributes and characteristics" punishes her male victim. Whether male masochists repress homosexual desires or not will not be discussed here. Rather, I am interested in the "silence" male masochism is met with, when it is quite flagrantly portrayed as in *She-Wolf*.

Is Freud correct to assume masochism to be a "feminine" perversion due to its self-inflicted pain and passivity? I think not. The German psychoanalyst Theodor Reik and the French film theorist and philosopher Gilles Deleuze both disagree in their respective studies of masochism. In *Masochism in Modern Man* (1941) Reik concludes from his patients that men are more masochistic than women, and that male fantasies are more "orgiastic" than the "anemic" female fantasies. "The woman's masochistic phantasy very seldom reaches the pitch of savage lust, of ecstasy, as does that of the man ... One does not feel anything of the cyclonelike character that is so often associated with masculine masochism, that blind unrestricted lust of self-destruction."[19] In Reik's view, the intensity, lust, and aggressive savagery are "masculine" traits, turning pain into an active rather than passive component.

Attacking Eyes and Genitals: Images of Castration

Of the "female situations" Freud mentions in masochism—castration, copulation, birth—only the last strikes me as specifically female. The first, castration, is on the contrary a conspicuously *male* situation. About castration Freud writes, "Being castrated—or being blinded, which stands for it—often leaves a negative trace of itself in phantasies, in the condition that no injury is to occur precisely to the genitals or the eyes."[20] But when it comes to male masochist fantasy, Freud is mistaken. The genitals and the eyes are *exactly* the objects which are attacked.

To take the eyes first: Throughout the *Ilsa* series, damage is inflicted on eyes. In *She-Wolf* the leader Kala has half of her face disfigured by syphilis, including the eye, and Anna's left eye is destroyed. In *Harem-Keeper* the right eye of a female victim is pulled from its socket and eaten by a man. And in *Wicked Warden* one girl has the hollow of one eye covered by grey scar tissue. The mutilation itself is not shown, but the wounds and scars are displayed in close-ups and graphic makeup. Eye injuries are only inflicted on women, where they serve as warnings to a male audience, displacing castration anxiety onto a female body.

An act *not* displaced onto female bodies is castration. Let us look at one of the masochistic fantasies Reik reports from a male patient:

> To an ancient barbaric idol, somewhat like the Phoenician Moloch, a number of vigorous young men are to be sacrificed at certain not too frequent intervals. They are undressed and laid on the altar one by one ... They must satisfy certain requirements as to physical beauty and athletic appearance. The high priest takes the genital of each prospective victim in his hand and carefully tests its weight and form. If he does not approve of the genital, the young man will be rejected as obnoxious to the god and unworthy of being sacrificed. The high priest gives the order for the execution and the ceremony continues. With a sharp cut the young men's genitals and the surrounding parts are cut away.[21]

Reik points to a number of characteristic features in masochism: The *demand* for punishment; the ritualized and theatrical nature of the *elaborate fantasies* where the punishment occurs; the *suspense factor* of delay and anticipation; and the *exhibitionistic* character of the display of suffering.

Let us now return to the castration scene in *She-Wolf*: In the torture chamber the lover awakens and finds himself strapped to an operating table and surrounded by Ilsa and her female guards. They are wearing white, blood-spattered coats and the two guards are naked underneath to underline the erotization of the violence. "When a prisoner has slept with me, he will never sleep with a woman again. If he lives, he remembers only the pain of the night," Ilsa tells the victim. She instructs the women to castrate him and then orders them to leave. "I will finish it!" Holding the instrument in full view of the camera she slowly walks around the victim, the camera tracking her. "There is a doctor Baum in Berlin. He believes that inferior races prove their inferiority through part of their body. And can you guess what part that is? The part that makes man. The doctor has a collection which proves his theory and yours will be sent to him." She cuts off the penis, shown in a semi-total shot where we see the screaming man from the side, his body shaking violently, and Ilsa with her back to the camera, cutting. She turns around and the camera zooms in on her sadistic smile. "My little man, I kept my promise, you will never leave the camp again," she laughs.

The similarities between Reik's masochistic fantasy and the castration scene are striking: a) *Inspection and measuring*: Like the young men inspected by the priests, Ilsa chooses her lovers during inspections. And just as the genitals of the men are weighted and approved or disapproved, Ilsa measures and judges the genitals of her male victims (at a point Wolfe asks Mario, "Mario, did she cut off your..." "No! Would have spoiled the doctor Baum's theory.") b) *Delay and anticipation:* In the fantasy, the mutilation is delayed by the ceremony to raise the anxiety level. Likewise, the castration is delayed by Ilsa circling her victim and giving her speech, which anticipates the act. c) *Detail and ritualization:* The fantasy is imagined in great detail adding music, a number of participants, colors. Ilsa's castration is also displayed in detail—as opposed to the castration scene in *Foxy Brown*—complete with blood on the white coats (the blood must come from former "operations" since the castration has not been performed yet), close-up on all participants and music. The camera is "neutral" in contrast to a later scene where German soldiers gang rape a female prisoner, shown in slanting and fragmented takes.

All these elements—inspection, anticipation, ritualization—serve the exhibitionist character of the masochist fantasy.

Final Boys and the Masochistic Gaze

To determine whether such castration scenes are sadistic or masochistic, we need to examine the point of identification being offered. About the masochistic fantasy Reik notes, "whether the phantasy is primarily masochistic or more sadistic in character must rest on information as to the person with whom the patient identifies." Reik's patient fantasizes about being a spectator, identifying "usually not [with] the one who is just being castrated but with the next, who is compelled to look on at the execution of his companion. The patient shares every intensive affect of this victim, feels his terror and anxiety with all the physical sensations since he imagines that he himself will experience the same fate in a few moments."[22]

The viewer, likewise, is "compelled to look on" at the castration, and in *She-Wolf* we expect Wolfe, the male character with whom the male audience identifies, to be "next." Reactions to the film indicate a similar identification with the victim position: On the commentary track there is uneasy silence, then humorist Martin Lewis (who is interviewing the director, the producer, and the star) comments, "With this picture you are not laughing, this is a shocker." As Ilsa, however, laughs and holds her instrument high, the interviewer asks star Dyanne Thorne, "Ilsa, why are you laughing here?" The uneasiness is a break in tone from the otherwise humorous conversation that treats the movie as a "funny" cult phenomenon. The movie itself foregrounds this masochistic point of view. In *She-Wolf* with close-ups of the screaming man begging for mercy, in *Harem-Keeper* with a reaction shot where a man next to Ilsa turns away from the castration with nausea.

What, then, is the reaction of the male audience?[23] An anonymous reviewer on the Internet comments on the difference between torture in standard WIP films and torture in the *Ilsa* movies:

> In these settings [a Nazi slave labor camp or Japanese wartime prison] we seem to cross the line from the taboo/power narrative into the arena of full-blown degradation. Is there really a large market for that? Maybe it is just me, but I think there is a qualitative difference between standard women-in-prison movies and movies like *Ilsa*. WiPs usually play on the common male fantasy of having power over a large number of beautiful women in which torture (often whipping with the woman's cries being played at the line between excitement and pain) is part of establishing the D/s [sic] relationship. In *Ilsa* torture is lovingly presented in great detail as an end in itself. Although Puritans of both the left and right might not see the difference, it seems pretty clear to me.[24]

In WIP films torture has a purpose—to have power over women—whereas in the *Ilsa* movies it seems purposeless—torture as "an end in itself." This is exactly the difference between the role of pain in sadism and masochism: In masochism the pain is turned against the subject, which in this case is the viewer. He chooses to understand the movie as "a dare, or a challenge, or a gross-out contest." Other reviewers agree, commenting that this is "gory, sleazy wallowing in nauseating excess," that "the basic appeal of *Ilsa* is a parade of tortures"[25] and that "this one is certainly not to be watched by the weak of stomach."[26] The "nauseating" element is perceived as a "quality" of the movie, and it requires "guts" to watch it.

In the Mulveyan tradition of feminist film theory, spectatorship is perceived as male, sadistic, and voyeuristic. Silverman, however, points out that in masochism the viewing position is "a vantage point from which to see and identify with the whipping boys."[27] To be a spectator to pain means to be gripped in the anxious anticipation of being "next." "This is a very disturbing movie," is a repeated comment in reviews. Disturbing not only due to its sadism, but also—and especially—due to its masochistic pain and viewer position.

In *Men, Women and Chain Saws: Gender in the Modern Horror Film* (1992) Clover introduced the concept of the Final Girl. The Final Girl is the victim who survives being stalked in slasher films like *Halloween* (1978) and *Friday the 13th* (1980). It is through her terrified eyes a male audience experiences fear and anxiety, a process which Clover calls "cross-gender identification." Based on the common reaction to horror movies—fear—Clover assumes that a male audience's identification is with the victim, the Final Girl. Clover argues that "crying, cowering, screaming, fainting, trembling, begging for mercy belong to the female" and is "gendered 'feminine'."[28] To keep traditional masculinity intact, "feminine" emotions are experienced vicariously through a woman, so it is possible to share her feminine fears, yet distance oneself from her female body. "I am scared like her, but this happens to her because she is a woman. It will not happen to me." The Final Girl is a stand-in for male identification, and the violence of horror is a symbolic castration. Thus, the Final Girl in the slasher movie is threatened with castration by a knife-wielding psychopath.

The positions of male monster and female victim are reversed in the *Ilsa* movies. Here, a man is placed in the role of Final Boy, and a beautiful woman threatens the victim with castration (and executes the threat).[29] But as in the horror movie, a masochistic viewing position is still foregrounded by the film.

Ilsa: *Femme Castratrice*

The time has come to meet Ilsa, the *femme castratrice* of the film series. As embodied by actress Dyanne Thorne she could not fulfill the wet dream of male masochism more perfectly.

Several reviews note the convincing performance and arresting face of Thorne. "Dyanne Thorne is a frightening Amazon of a woman. She plays a Nazi commandant like she was one and she even looks the part. Although she is amazingly endowed, her hard facial features literally draw your attention away from most everything else."[30] Indeed, the harsh features of her face are more striking than her body, and her tight lips, penetrating gaze, over-acting, and campy German accent, which would be phony in any other context, all serve to underline the essential nature of the fantasy: The masquerade of masochism.

Ilsa travels through time and place, from Nazi Germany to Stalin's Gulag in Russia, from the Arabian desert to the South American jungle. The characters around her change, but she remains the same. Dressed in a uniform—a standard prop in masochism—and high heels. The fetishism is developed further after the success of *She-Wolf*, where her costume is fairly simple (although one wonders why she wears riding pants since the camp has no horses). In *Harem-Keeper* she wears a desert costume with mini-shorts and long boot-stockings, and she attends the Sheik's feast wearing a tight black outfit held together by red string and holding a chained greyhound in each hand. Her two black servants, Satin and Velvet, have helped her into the outfit and tightened all the strings, thus emphasizing the "costuming" of Ilsa. Gaylyn Studlar, writing about the costuming of the German actress Marlene Dietrich, notices the use of "striptease" and masquerade as "erotic metamorphoses" in masochism. The costumes are used to "fetishistically idealize the woman as they are used to play out the masochistic rituals of punishment and disguise."[31] Thorne is equipped with guns, sables, dildos, spurs, and various whips—a short black horsewhip, a white rod, and a long brown animal whip. All phallic attributes of the dominatrix.

Ilsa is characterized by a mixture of cruelty and coldness, the same mixture which Austrian author Leopold von Sacher-Masoch admired in his women, and that Gilles Deleuze took as the title of his famous study of masochism, *Coldness and Cruelty*. She is indifferent to the pain she inflicts on women and smiles sadistically during castrations. Pain, it seems, is not so much the point, as the object. "They are his to do as he wishes, she is lucky it was not worse," she coldly comments, as a doctor laments the sheik's maltreatment of his mistresses in *Harem-Keeper*. Ilsa's coldness is contrasted by the "hot" sadism of the sheik, who smiles and laughs excitedly when Ilsa demonstrates her "vaginal bomb" on an unconscious girl, whose abdomen is blown to pieces. The gimmick is a bomb placed deep within the vagina, exploding at the height of intercourse. The sheik can thus send a beautiful female "bomb" as a gift to his enemies. Later Ilsa ties the sheik to the same operating table and has a girl, equipped with the bomb, make love to him. As our hero, Adam Scott (Michael Thayer) enters the torture room, Ilsa is surprised that he looks away in disgust from the remains of the sheik.

The uniform, the beautiful and harsh appearance, the fierce pride, and the cold cruelty are all features of the dominatrix, who is here, quite literally, a "castrating bitch." She is a hypersexual creature, fully devoted to her job, and always in search of satisfaction. It takes a special man to satisfy this woman, and the Final Boy is special when it comes to potency and performance. In contrast to the sadistic character called "The Greek" in Sacher-Masoch's novel *Venus in Furs*, the heroes in the *Ilsa* movies are never sadistic or cold. They represent an ideal American masculinity—active, strong, optimistic, politically devoted to democracy—and are equipped with "unusual powers." "I discovered that I can hold back for as long as I want to," Wolfe explains to Mario. "I still can. All night if necessary. I guess you can call me a freak of nature. Sort of human machine. A machine that can set its control to fast, slow or never." The Final Boy is the ultimate performer, and thus the perfect companion to the sexual insatiable Dominatrix. When he is done with her, he terminates the masochistic "contract" and quits the game.

Originally the part was to be played by Phyllis Davis, who had been the lead in the WIP movies *Sweet Sugar* (1972) and *Terminal Island* (1973), but she left the production in protest to the "golden shower" scene where Ilsa urinates on the general. Instead forty-two-year old Dyanne Thorne (fifteen

Top: The symmetrical fetishism of the masochistic spectacle in *Ilsa, Harem-Keeper of the Oil Sheiks* (Mount Everest Enterprises, 1976). Here, Ilsa (Dyanne Thorne) with her two helpers Velvet (Marilyn Joi) and Satin (Tanya Boyd). *Bottom:* Satin and Velvet punish a man by beating him and ripping off his private parts.

years older than Davis) got the role. She had been a dancer in Las Vegas and acted in low budget exploitation movies such as *Blood Sabbath* (1972) and *Wham Bam Thank You Spaceman* (1972). Her age, her over-acting and her campy star persona successfully united in the role that would make her immortal.

The Utopian Reading: Ilsa as Feminist

How shall we read Ilsa? Is she a strong woman who subverts patriarchy by being a female aggressor inflicting pain on men? Does she turn the stereotypical gender roles upside down?

On the DVD's commentary track Dyanne Thorne, without hesitation, characterizes Ilsa as a feminist: "This is the first [film], where they had a female villain and also this is the first one where she was, like, the leader of the feminists if you will, which many of the magazines had said, this was the first feminist. See, even with this particular scene [the male castration scene in *She-Wolf*] the victim was the male, and the three females standing there were in total control."

As mentioned earlier, I have not found any academic articles on Ilsa. However, in the academic articles written by women on WIP films, the idea of female strength and independence is seen as an indication of feminism or feminist potential. Pam Cook is the first (writing in 1976) to suggest a subversive content in this genre, focusing on *Terminal Island* which is the only WIP film directed by a woman, Stephanie Rothman. In *Terminal Island* the women reform the men, who have initially abused them on the prison-island, where male and female prisoners have been abandoned. "They cannot in any sense be described as feminist films," Cook admits, but points to "contradictions, shifts in meaning which disturb the patriarchal myths of women on which the exploitation film itself rests."[32] A decade later, a German article by Birgit Hein in *Frauen & Film* locates a subversive content in the portrayal of lesbian sexuality and women's use of violence in the WIP films *Mädchen in Uniform* (1931), *Ausgestoßen* (1982), and *Chained Heat* (1983). "I was infatuated with the women from the very first film ... They fight excellently. They are familiar with the use of guns and knives. They are sly and without scruples. They also turn each other on sexually and, when necessary, stick together and are brave" (my translation from German).[33]

Hein argues that lesbian sex and female violent behavior subvert traditional gendering of female sexuality as passive, clean, and delicate. Finally, an article by Suzanna Danuta Walters (2001) discusses aggressive women as representing a repressed image of "woman-as-other" within patriarchal order. "Female criminality, female violence, female desire—so firmly negated by mainstream popular culture—here emerge in all their overblown glory. Not only do these bizarre films explore the unexplored with humor and a certain postmodern verve, but they often allow women to be victorious over the forces of male violence."[34]

Is Ilsa, then, a feminist? That depends, like in the perverse fantasies of Reik's patients, on which point of view we take. Certainly, within the context of the films and their reception by mainstream as well as exploitation audiences, she was not perceived as a feminist. She was first and foremost read as a commercial element, a break with all taboos so radical as to command attention, whether we like it or not. In the world of exploitation cinema, attention means money. Ilsa signified an innovation of the WIP film, both by the explicit construction of her figure as dominatrix, and by the fact that a villain became protagonist. Her figure foregrounded a male masochistic element that had been a subtext in the WIP film and in exploitation cinema.

Perverse fantasies work by subverting order and transgressing taboos, as in the use of power scenarios where unequal or inappropriate partners have sex: Master and slave, Nazi and Jew, doctor and patient, adult and child. Perversion is the motivation behind the subversion of order, which the above quoted female (and part feminist) readings of WIP films note. But is this subversion progressive? Silverman rejects a utopian reading of perversion and points out that, for instance, masochism's revolt against patriarchy is post–Oedipal and not, as Gilles Deleuze presents it in his somewhat optimistic study of masochism, pre–Oedipal. This means that masochism is quite aware of itself as a perversion, a deviation from the "normal" order of things, and the practitioners of the perverse pleasures are also quite aware of "playing" a game limited by certain rules, domains, and situations. Or, as director Don Edmonds puts it, "it's only fun." In his *Eroticism* Georges Bataille writes, "The transgression does not deny the taboo but transcends it and completes it.... Organized transgression together with the taboo make social life what it is."[35]

The function of the *Ilsa* series is the display of a perversion—male masochism—that is taboo and therefore fascinating. With Dyanne Thorne the series became a cult phenomenon and a must-see among young men, where it became part of modern-day male initiation rites. Or, in Bataille's words, "organized transgression." In these rites, the playful exploration of alternative sexual behavior (sadism, masochism, cannibalism) and the subversion of social order are acted out in the "safe" setting of watching an exploitation movie. This transgression does not subvert social order. On the contrary, my experience is that men who have enjoyed the "nauseating" and "sickening" pleasures of Ilsa have turned out to become quite normal social beings. Perversion is a step in the process of constructing masculinity. This, in turn, may say more about the nature of "normal" masculinity than about the "disgusting" nature of Ilsa.

Ilsa Filmography

Ilsa, She-Wolf of the SS (1974) Dir. Don Edmonds.

Ilsa, Harem-Keeper of the Oil Sheiks (1976) Dir. Don Edmonds.

Ilsa, The Tigress of Siberia (1977) Dir. Jean LaFleur.

Ilsa, The Wicked Warden (also called Greta—Haus ohne Männer; Greta the Torturer; Greta, the Mad Butcher; Greta, the Sadist; Ilsa: Absolute Power; Wanda, the Wicked Warden) (1977) Dir. Jess Franco, filmed in the U.S., Switzerland and Germany.

3

Enough! Birth
of the Rape-Avenger

Come on. The thing with you is a thing any man would have
done. You coax a man into doing it to you. Look, a man gets the
message fast, and whether he's married or not, a man, he's just a
man. Hey, first thing you come into the gas station and you expose
your damn sexy legs to me walking back and forth real slow making sure I see 'em good. And then Matthew delivers the food to
your door. Why, he sees half your tits peeking out at him! And
then you're lying in your canoe ... in your bikini ... just waiting
... like bait.

—*I Spit on Your Grave* (1978)

When she awakes, the Bride's first kills in *Kill Bill: Vol. 1* (2003) are
two men. One has just paid to have sex with a comatose woman. The
other is the male nurse selling the Bride's body for seventy-five dollars
per twenty minutes and returning to check if his customer is finished. The
customer is and so is Buck. The Bride has killed the customer and now
smashes Buck's head in with the door in the doorway. The men have nothing to do with her vendetta against Bill, and she is not raped again. Shot,
beaten, and buried, yes. But not raped. The scene is Quentin Tarantino's
homage to one of the little-known female heroes from the seventies: the
rape-avenger.

Men, Rape, and Revenge

The rape-avenger belongs in the rape-revenge film, which would be
some obscure subgenre within exploitation cinema had it not been for Carol
Clover's poignant study of it in *Men, Women, and Chain Saws* (1992), which
has become a key text in feminist film studies. The rape-revenge film evolved
in the seventies' exploitation cinema, seeped into the mainstream during
the eighties, reached blockbuster status in the nineties with *Eye for an Eye*

83

(1996), and is today found in Hollywood blockbusters (*Enough*, 2002) as well as in French avant-garde cinema (*Irreversible*, 2003).

The rape-avenger is a woman who is raped and kills the man, or men, who raped her. The subgenre is born from crossing rape as a motive with the vigilante movie, and its key scene is the protagonist's transformation from victim to avenger. As Jacinda Read puts it, "Rape-revenge can be seen as constituting a sequence of narrative events (rape, transformation, revenge) occurring in a particular order, combined with a specific set of character functions or spheres of action (victim, rapist, avenger)."[1] Really, the number of rape-revenge films is too small to claim it as a genre, but then again, the narrative structure and the rape-avenger are too striking to be ignored. Like film noir, the rape-revenge film falls between categories. Clover places it as a subgenre of the horror movie, but Read argues that rape-revenge is a narrative structure, because its plot is found across genres: there are rape-revenge westerns (*Hannie Caulder*, 1972), rape-revenge court room dramas (*The Accused*, 1988), rape-revenge horror movies (*I Spit on Your Grave*, 1978), rape-revenge thrillers (*Ms. 45*, 1981), rape-revenge dramas (*Lipstick*, 1976), and so forth. What unites these different films is that rape functions as plot, as a motive for vengeance, and as the element that transforms the film's protagonists from victim to avenger. Thus, I agree with Read that the rape-revenge film is not a subgenre of horror, but a narrative structure.

Before the seventies, rape had, in folkloric terms, been a "motif." It was an assault committed against women as an act of violence and desire, or it was punishment for inappropriate female behavior. An example is Sam Peckinpah's *Straw Dogs* (1971), where David's wife Amy (Susan George) is raped by two village men. The film, however, hardly portrays her as rape victim; first, she sexually teases the men and gives in to the first rapist; second, she functions as part of her husband's transformation from "feminine" mathematician to "masculine" defender of home and property. Amy is David's "property," which the men "take" to prove that they have the power to do so. David (Dustin Hoffmann) and Amy did not report the strangled cat in their bedroom closet, and Amy does not report the rape to the police or to David. Rape is a crime on a par with intrusion, theft, and vandalism. During the seventies rape "graduated to a tale-type"[2] with a handful of films: In Burt Kennedy's English western *Hannie Caulder* (1972) a woman learns to shoot so she can kill the men who murdered her husband, burnt her home, and raped her. In Bob Kelljan's drama *Rape-Squad* (1974) raped women formed a group that caught and castrated their rapists. Lamont Johnson's drama *Lipstick* had a model take her rapist to court, lose, then shoot him after he rapes her younger sister. Finally, Meir Zarchi made rape-revenge infamous with *I Spit on Your Grave* (1978) about a writer from New York who rents a house in the country for the summer, is raped by four men, and kills all four rapists.

The film credited as the "birth" of the rape-revenge film is John Boorman's drama *Deliverance* (1972), where men rape men, not women.[3] The film's masculinity-in-crisis plot was related to titles like *Point Blank* (1967), *Madigan* (1968), *Straw Dogs*, *Dirty Harry* (1971), and *Death Wish* (1974), which featured men whose masculinity was under pressure. Male crisis was a theme in Hollywood represented by actors such as Lee Marvin, Dustin Hoffmann, Clint Eastwood, Charles Bronson and Burt Reynolds. With its rape scene, however, *Deliverance* became *the* "traumatized-men-struggling-for-survival" movie to which later rape-revenge films would return.

The plot is simple: four city men go on a canoe trip down "the last wild, untamed, unpolluted, unfucked-up river in the south," as Lewis (Burt Reynolds) puts it. "We're gonna rape this whole goddamn landscape. We're gonna *rape* it!" he exclaims as they drive down to the river that is about to be dammed in and become an artificial lake, which will produce electricity for the city. When the city men meet the locals, they treat them with contempt. "Talk about genetic deficiency," Bobby (Ned Beatty) exclaims loudly. On the second day of the trip, the men in the first canoe are attacked by two mountain men who sodomize Bobby and are about to rape Ed (Jon Voigt) orally—"you're gonna get on your knees and do some prayin' for me, and you better pray good"—when the second canoe arrives and Lewis kills one of the attackers with bow and arrow. They decide not to report the incident to the police, bury the body, and continue downstream. On a violent rapid Drew (Ronny Cox) is shot by the second attacker,[4] both canoes capsize, and Lewis breaks a leg. It is now up to Ed, who the day before was unable to shoot a deer, to sink to the occasion: He must scale a gorge wall; kill the mountain man waiting at the top to kill them; hide the man's body and Drew's body; fabricate a story for the police; and get himself, Bobby, and Lewis safely back to civilization.

The masculinity-in-crisis theme was recognized widely. *New York Times* wrote, "[T]he film is a devastating critique of machismo ... the journey has no purpose; nothing is achieved, nothing gained. The last images express a sense of total desolation. There is no sentimentality in the film; it is a serious and meaningful challenge to the belief in rites of manhood."[5] A review in *The New Yorker*, however, was critical of the male mythology. "The story is simple to the point of obtuseness, and a ragbag of all the myths about maleness that an analyst's couch ever put up with ... in overcivilized, over-analyzed countries it works like a very smooth and exciting piece of toy machinery for men at Christmas."[6] But exactly what *kind* of game was this? In James Dickey's novel, on which *Deliverance* was based, Ed made contact

with his inner Iron John and proved himself to be a "real" man.[7] In Boorman's version the plot was twisted: The rite of manhood became a tale of a
civilized masculinity raped by "genetically deficient" mountain men and
raped by the river that the city men thought *they* were raping. Why canoe
down the river, the locals had asked? "Because it's there." Being *there* is an
invitation to rape and for a man to be a man means having to prove your
masculinity by committing rape.

What does masculinity-in-crisis, a male rape, and a failed descent down
a river have to do with a *female* rape-avenger? Pretty much, as we shall see
shortly. The female hero pushes the hero down from his pedestal and takes
his position. Viewed from a man's perspective, she challenges patriarchy and
disrupts masculinity, because masculinity is structured in binary opposition
to femininity (male versus female, strong versus weak), and strengthening
the female position means *weakening* the male position. Rape springs from
anxiety about masculinity. Barbara Creed comments on *I Spit on Your Grave*,
"The rape scenes at the beginning can really only be understood retrospectively as the actions of a group of men who are terrified of women."[8] To rape
is to defend and protect one's masculinity. Research in rape shows that "coer-
cive buggery of men indicates that, like the rape of women, sexual violence
is more about power and domination than eroticism ... It is the use of sexuality to dominate, humiliate and degrade."[9] According to Sue Lees in *Ruling Passions: Sexual Violence, Reputation and the Law* (1997) "a rape victim is
not merely a victim, whether male or female, but a victim of the gendered
power relations between men and women."[10] Men rape to establish what Lees
calls "the dominant hegemonic heterosexuality." Dominant because it does
not respect other kinds of masculinity (homosexuality and "soft" variations
of masculinity), hegemonic because it wants to conquer all territory, and
heterosexual because it is opposed to femininity. Thus, rape is not about
sex, but about the *power* to decide what *kind of masculinity* is dominant (who
gets to be rapist) and what kind is marginalized (who gets to be rape victim).
"It looks like me got a sow instead of a hog," the mountain man jokes before
raping Bobby's soft, fat, white, naked body. The raped body is the symbolic
battle field where "the deployment of the penis ... [is] a concrete symbol of
masculine social power and dominance."[11]

Gender identity is socially constructed. "Masculinity is not, as is often
believed, genetically programmed," says Lees, "but is socially constructed
and is only meaningful in relation to constructions of femininity. Achiev-
ing manhood involves a permanent process of struggle and confirmation."[12]
Men prove their manhood in a struggle against what is valorized "feminine,"
be it a woman, a man, or a river. The city men with their expensive leisure
time outfits (canoes, tents, life vests, rubber suits, modern archery) were not

out on a weekend trip for fun, but out on a rape date with nature. They had it coming. They *asked* for it with their smug remarks about the locals—"Isn't that a pitiful sight!"—whose home will soon be at the bottom of a lake. The locals are the "feminized" other against which the city men measure themselves. Like the locals, the river is a "she" to be conquered. Killing an Amazon proved a warrior's courage in ancient Greece and a ride down the river makes civilized man a "real" man. The city men expected to "find" themselves in nature. "There is something out here in nature that we lost in the city," says Lewis at one point.[13]

The point of *Deliverance* is that modern men cannot find themselves in nature because there is no "real" masculinity out there. The name of the game is Survival, as Lewis calls it, but it is a competitive game *within* the male group. Thus Lewis rejects Ed's colleague Bobby—"Can that boy handle himself?"—and throws him out of his canoe on the second day of the trip. "You take that chubby boy today," Lewis tells Ed. Clover comments on the male rivalry among the four rapists in *I Spit on Your Grave* which ends as "Johnny the winner, Andy a strong second, Stanley the loser, Matthew on the bench."[14] In *Deliverance* the four city men—and if we accept the river as "a lady" they are also rapists—regroup as Ed the new leader, Bobby a weak second, Lewis the dethroned leader, and Drew a quitter (Drew wanted to go to the police and dies on the river). Rape is about inscribing macho-masculinity. When women are not available, this is done on male bodies.[15]

In the previous chapters I linked Grier's Bad Mama star persona and Ilsa's dominatrix figure to male desire and masochist fantasies. In the rape-revenge film, representations of rape and revenge are more complex. They are both related to male desire *and* to men's anxiety about masculinity, to men's ambivalent fear of and desire for women *and* to a sensation that civilization "femininizes" and castrates men.

Why Men Rape Women

After *Deliverance* (whose metaphorical name could not be more fitting) the newborn rape-revenge plot finds a female body. What began as a masculinity-in-crisis plot becomes a female rape drama haunted by feminism and the instability of gender in postmodern age.

The mountain men rape the city men because they were provoked. The city men flaunted their civilized softness and leisure time game of Survival. They didn't know what it was like to be a mountain man and an endangered species. They *asked* for it. Women in rape-revenge also ask for it, at least as seen from men's perspective. When the mountain men disappear all men are an endangered species, and women get to play the part of the four city men. That is, women represent a civilization which is seen as "rap-ing" men, and women represent the soft city men who (symbolically) raped the local mountain men and became avengers. Thus, women in rape-revenge are at one and the same time *symbolic* and *social* rapists, as well as also being rape victims and rape-avengers. They are the uneven battle field where men return a symbolic rape with a real rape in the flesh.

Lipstick (1976) is symptomatic of this complexity. The model Chris (twenty-one-year-old model Margeaux Hemingway) is a single career woman whose job presents her as a "constructed" image of femininity. The film opens with a photo shoot. The male photographer is ecstatic. "Oh boy, look at her making it. So beautiful, so beautiful. Wauw!" Chris poses naked in bed, then in a silver dress, then with a black feather boa draped around her naked body. A female client constantly corrects the photographer, who hisses, "You want the camera? Do you want to take the picture?" "No." "Then let me get *one* picture I like, just *one* frame." It is difficult for men to concentrate on doing their jobs as shapers of femininity amidst such female disturbance. The campaign is for lipstick and Chris' red lips are on huge billboards in town. In the next scene she poses naked on the beach, which is where rapist Gordon Stuart (Chris Sarandon) sees her. Later, during the trial, large photos are presented to the jury. "Do you use sexy thoughts to make you hot," Gordon's defense attorney asks. Chris testifies that she uses thoughts of being overpowered to make her "hot." Steve, her boyfriend, calls her "the hottest model in the business." "But why like this?" Chris' female attorney asks. Chris responds "it's my work" and "because I'm supposed to look like every woman wants to look like." The photographs are society's ideal of femininity constructed by the male photographer and the female client in unison, they do not reflect a "natural" femininity. Chris acts out the role assigned to her by capitalist society. She sells dreams. "I agree there was a rape, but it is impossible to tell who the victim was," the defense con-cludes. The jury believes Gordon's lie—that he wanted to have sex with Chris and when she asked him to act out her sadomasochistic fantasies, he consented because he wished to please her.

Seen from his perspective, this is not far from the truth. Chris had invited her sister's music teacher to the beach to play his compositions for her. The shoot ran late and she instead invited him to her apartment next day. The scene prior to the rape is a "confrontation scene" parallel to the scene in *Deliverance* where the city men meet the locals. Chris is in the shower when Gordon arrives, and she opens the door with her hair wet and dressed in a bathrobe. Clearly uninterested in his music, she asks him to get himself a drink while she dresses. With a French beer Gordon waits in the tastefully furnished living room with photos from safaris and private photographs of Chris with Warren Beatty and Paul Newman. The stuttering teacher—"may-maybe this isn't the-the right time"—is clearly no match. Chris interrupts his jarring electronic music mixed with recorded bird screams to answer a phone call from Boston. "I know how you feel," she apologizes. "You don't know me. How do you know what I feel?" Gordon replies. Chris does not know how he feels, it isn't her music being cut off by a phone call, and she doesn't care. Why was he invited? Because Chris pleased an elevenish-year-old sister who begged her to listen to the teacher's compositions. "He is Cathy's *school teacher*," Chris later explains when her attorney asked why she invited him. As if this changes everything. Is a man "safe" because he is a teacher? Does the "teacher" part transform a stranger into someone you can invite into your livingroom to have a beer while you get dressed? Will a teacher not react to a woman's naked body reflected in the mirror as Chris' body is reflected to Gordon? Does she not bother to close the door because a teacher is "feminine" and a male teacher thus not a "real" man? Male school teachers are rare in films. Charly's cover identity in *The Long Kiss Goodnight* is indeed a school teacher, which is logical because she poses as an average woman. But when a man is a school teacher, *Lipstick* argues, it compromises his gender identity.

Gender and sexual attraction are at the core of rape-revenge. Victims

Model and rape-avenger Chris (Margeaux Hemingway) in makeup and fashion dress grabs the hunting rifle from her car and takes aim at acquitted rapist Gordon (Chris Sarandon) in the rape-revenge film *Lipstick* (De Laurentiis and Paramount Pictures, 1976).

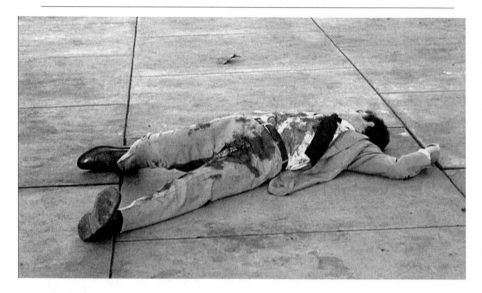

The dead rapist at the end of *Lipstick* (De Laurentiis and Paramount Pictures, 1976).

are always played by strikingly beautiful actors; Margeaux, granddaughter of Ernest Hemingway, French sex idol Raquel Welch (*Hannie Caulder*), ex-angel Farrah Fawcett (*Extremities*, 1986), singer and super star Jennifer Lopez (*Enough*, 2002). Rapists, on the other hand, are unattractive and played by unknown actors. No wonder women hardly consider them men. Before Gordon rapes Chris, he searches for the red lipstick and smears it on her lips: "Nice, huh? Because it makes you look good enough to fuck! Am I good enough to fuck?" No, he is not. He is not sexy, attractive, or strong, neither is he psychologically "fit," and he has no social status because he is not famous like Newman or Beatty. Gordon is not a real man. If we should miss this point he is nervous, manipulative, and psychologically unstable, all "feminine" characteristics. The movie furthermore hints that he is a pedophile; he is only confident with little girls, he jokes in a childish tone with Cathy, and when he rapes Cathy this assault seems to spring from repressed pedophile desire rather than the burning anger directed towards adult sister Chris. We also find insecure masculinity in Chris' boyfriend, who regrets taking the rape to trial when he learns that the chances of winning are small. He leaves Chris when she loses.

Chris had a boyfriend in *Lipstick*. Even if tenuous, there existed an intimate relationship between the sexes. This is lost in Meir Zarchi's low budget production *I Spit on Your Grave* (1978), where the representation of men and women is reduced to five roles: the four rapists and the rape-avenger. Beside these we catch brief glimpses of a priest, a grocer, Johnny's wife and two children. This is one reason why the film is almost unbearable to watch; we are in a world trimmed down to violent sex and sexualized retribution, the two balancing each other with the rape lasting thirty-two minutes and the revenge taking twenty-six minutes (this is in the film's original ninety-eight minutes, now available on DVD, which at the time of its theatrical release in the US were cut to eighty-one minutes).

The film opens with Jennifer's drive from New York. She has rented a house to finish a novel and pulls over for gas after a three hour drive. While Johnny (Eron Tabor) fills her car she stretches her legs with a walk in her high heels and tight summer dress. Two men, Andy and Stanley, play a silly game with a knife in the grass. This is the film's first confrontation scene. Johnny is dressed in a worn blue worksuit, and Andy and Stanley push each other around like little boys. Clearly, like Gordon Stewart, the men are no match for a beautiful career woman. Johnny comments she will like it so much she will stay the year, but Jennifer (Camille Keaton) calmly replies that it's only for the summer. The second confrontation scene is when the mildly retarded Matthew (Richard Pace) delivers groceries. "Here is a tip from an evil New Yorker," she jokes and hands Matthew a large tip. "Do you have a boyfriend?" "I have many boyfriends." "Can I be your friend?" Matthew asks. "Sure." Like Chris, Jennifer is kind and condescending, because the men are not real men, not "good enough to fuck." They are servants like Johnny, dumb imbeciles like Matthew, or unemployed imbeciles like Andy and Stanley. Even Johnny's wife yells and pushes them away, when she can't find her husband at the gas station, "Why do you hang out here, get the fuck out of here, fucking bums."

The men pass the time restlessly like stray dogs. On a nightly fishing trip they fantasize about women. "You know," Andy (Gunter Kleemann) says, "sometimes I look at these gorgeous looking chicks, I mean, ones with *real* knockouts, sexy, you know, and I wonder. I wonder if they gotta take a shit too." "All women are full of shit," Stanley (Anthony Nichols) responds. Women are attractive but unattainable and "full of shit." They are not persons with whom men can have meaningful relationships. Instead, men have relationships with men, sharing work time and leisure time and rape time. Women are objects to be used. Thus Johnny, Andy, and Stanley take Jennifer and offer her as a gift to Matthew, who is a virgin. When he is unable to perform they rape her. First Johnny in the woods. They let her go, then circle her in and Andy sodomizes her on a rock in a clearing. They release her again and wait for her in the house, where Matthew attempts intercourse and Stanley rapes her with a bottle and tries to make her fellate him. Jennifer is almost unconscious and passes out when he beats her and screams, "I want total submission in a woman!"

Next, Jennifer plans her revenge. Matthew is killed first, he is hanged during intercourse as he ejaculates. Next is Johnny, who at gun point explains, "Come on. The thing with you is a thing any man would have done. You coax a man into doing it to you. Look, a man gets the message fast, and whether he's married or not, a man, he's just a man. Hey, first thing you come into the gas station and you expose your damn sexy legs to me walking back and forth real slow making sure I see them good. And then Matthew delivers the food to your door. Why, he sees half your tits peeking out at him! And then you're lying in your canoe ... in your bikini ... just waiting ... like bait!" Unable to see that his behavior is in any way wrong, Johnny actually believes that Jennifer wants more when she lowers the gun and kisses him. "I knew you were gonna like it here." In the bathtub at her house, Jennifer cuts off Johnny's penis and leaves him to bleed to death in the locked bathroom while she listens to classical music downstairs.

With its gritty realism *I Spit on Your Grave* stirred a controversy. Film critics Gene Siskel and Roger Ebert warned that the film inspired violence against women. And it was no excuse that director Meir Zarchi in interviews explained that his inspiration for the film had come from finding a rape victim in a park in New York. One evening when he was driving in his car, he had seen a naked woman who had been raped and badly beaten. Still, the rape scenes in *I Spit on Your Grave* provoked critics. James Wolcott in *Village Voice*, "I'm suspicious of the crusading tone Siskel and Ebert take against these films ... but the clips themselves did have a sickening impact ... [And about the rape in the house where the men laugh and tear up Jennifer's manuscript] How could actors *play* this scene? How could any director bring himself to shoot it? Layer by layer, the people who make films like *I Spit on Your Grave* ... seem to be trying to peel off any sense of dignity or compassion or tenderness from what's left of our social skins."[16] A later review in *Variety* rejected the film as "generating laughter instead of audience involvement" and as "a padded, unconvincing exploitation film."[17]

If *I Spit on Your Grave* had no intentions beyond exploitation, Abel Ferrara's stylish low budget thriller *Ms. 45* (1981) used the rape-revenge plot to deliver a message: Relations between men and women are, as they say in Steven Spielberg's *Saving Private Ryan*, FUBAR. Fucked Up Beyond All Recognition. The film skips the confrontation scene and has its protagonist, the mute, beautiful, and extremely shy Thana (Zoë Tamerlis) who irons clothes in a designer's workroom, raped twice the same day by two strangers. First in a back alley by a man wearing a clown mask, and when she returns home a burglar rapes her in her living room. Thana knocks the burglar out with a paperweight at the time of his orgasm, then kills him with her iron, cuts up his body, and dumps the parts around New York. She uses the burglar's .45 gun first to defend herself (she shoots a man who runs after her to return a bag with a body part she had left in the street), then to punish men who come on to women (a sleazy fashion photographer), who attack women (like a black pimp beating a prostitute and four attackers in a park), who buy women (an oil sheik mistakes Thana for a prostitute), then, finally, Thana shoots *any* man because all men are potential rapists. Her killing spree leaves sixteen dead before Thana's colleague Laurie (Darlene Stuto) stabs her in the back with a knife. As Thana turns, her last word uttered in surprise is "sister."

"Its no longer a man's world" the publicity poster for *Ms. 45* announced with the image of a woman's hand with red fingernails holding a gun, and dropping a black plastic bag out of which falls a man's hand. The text above these two hands implies that it *was* a man's world until Thana came along. But the film presented a masculinity-in-crisis scenario, where men were victims from the outset. In the opening scene Thana's boss, Albert (Albert Sinkys), must suck up to an arrogant female customer who is choosing among his dress designs for her chain of clothes shops. Looking colder than Ilsa, she has brought an androgynous secretary. Clearly, the female customer is a castrating woman who makes Albert sweat. When his employees go to lunch, they walk in a city which is a bustling jungle of male aggression where men yell things like, "Hey, Baby," and "Do you wanna sit on my face," or "Hey, what's the matter, I got bad breath or somethin'? Or maybe I ain't good enough for you?" Lowlife and rejected men come on to women from every corner. In the bar where they have lunch, a man who was kissing his

Rape-avenger Thana (Zoë Tamerlis) dresses as a nun with a gun for the Halloween party, where she will shoot and kill seven men in Abel Ferrara's *Ms. 45* (Navaron Films, 1981).

fiancée hits on them when she has left. "Fuck off," Laurie yells, "you heard, get fucked! Get bent! Get the hell out of here!" Chris and Jennifer's conde-scending kindness has been replaced with verbal abuse as defense mecha-nism.

Symbolism is simple in *Ms. 45*: Thana's name comes from Greek *Thanathos* (death), and her muteness signifies the impossibility of commu-nication (except for the burglar, none of the men she kills notices that she is mute). Likewise, the mask that the first rapist wears points to masculin-ity as a ridiculous act, a masquerade. Indeed, at the film's final Halloween party gender is a masquerade with women pretending to be men, men in white wedding dresses pretending to be women, and Thana dressed as a nun with sexy underwear. Attraction and desire are reduced to ambivalent farce and endless nagging (at the party lovers argue and a group of men discuss the price of virgins in Mexico). Like the Halloween party the film, too, is a turbulent sea of scenes rubbing against each other, one more bleak and angry than the other. When leaving a murder, Thana walks straight into a group of men looking for a gang rape. From there she walks right into the arms of a fat oil sheik waving his money, and so forth. One scene stands out for its downplayed desperation. This is where Thana picks up a man in a bar intending to kill him. He is talking non-stop, first to a man at the bar, then to Thana on a bench by the water:

> I was fed up. I had to find out. I told her I was working late one night, real late. And I hid across the street in some garbage cans. She walked down the street a cou-ple of blocks and went into a building ... So, I tried the door and it was locked ... I tried the side door, the one they bring the garbage out in. So. I went in the back. There's a dark window. I looked in. There's a candle light. And I saw her with her arms around another woman [pauses]. And I got back to our place, went to the bathroom, brushed my teeth, washed my face, and I went in the bedroom, changed my shirt, then I went out in the kitchen and *I strangled her cat.*

When Thana pulls her gun, it clicks. The man takes it from her: "Is this some kind of joke?" He then looks at the gun, looks Thana in the eyes, puts the gun to his head and with a smile pulls the trigger. Suicide is a relief in a world where drowning men struggle for air. The traditional gender roles from the fifties—or rather, the *idea* of these roles as "traditional" and sta-ble—dissolve in the seventies. Vigilante Paul Kersey had a family to lose in the *Death Wish* saga, but the family is gone in the eighties. Women leave men to get a job, a career, a life without men. Instead, men are reduced to crawling in the garbage, a recurrent metaphor in the seventies. The rapist with the clown mask and the husband spying on his wife both hide with the garbage.

The gun is another symbol. "The .357 Magnum Harry carries is a surrogate penis, gigantic and under his complete control, a fantasy of the terrified and the impotent," says Joan Mellen of Dirty Harry's gun in *Big Bad Wolves: Masculinity in the American Film* (1977).[18] The gun represents the penis and the penis represents a virile masculinity which again stands for power and control. The penis, however, is *not* a sign of phallic power. Gilles Deleuze remarks about the penis and the phallus, "just as the absence of a penis need not indicate lack of the phallus, its presence likewise need not indicate possession of the phallus..."[19] Guns, like penises, have become signs of impotence instead of potency. In the rape-revenge film, the penis-gun metaphor is nervously untied from male and female bodies and instead related to abstract notions of masculinity and femininity. "Paradoxically enough—and the generalization extends beyond the rape-revenge film—it is the man who is deprived of the phallus who must live by the penis," says Clover.[20] Men do not attack women with their penises. They *defend* themselves against women in a sea of free-floating gender symbols.

How can the penis make an impression, if women don't want it? How can sex return to normal, when a wife cheats on her husband with a *woman*? In *Straw Dogs*, the strangled cat and the raped wife were attacks on David's home. In the rape-revenge film, the very same acts are defensive gestures against women's attacks on a man's symbolic "home"—his masculinity.

From Victim to Avenger

In primitive cultures it is a common belief that girls naturally "grow" into women. Boys, on the other hand, must be transformed into men. The painful initiation rites push the boy from child to adult.[21] Ed in *Deliverance* has a deer at close range but lowers his arrow because his hands are shaking. They still shake when he aims at the mountain man, yet this time he hits the target because circumstances force him to change his behavior. He must become an adult and find it in him to kill a man, hide the body, and lie to the police. Rape is the initiation rite that pushes women from being "soft" victims to becoming "hard" avengers. This is equal rights and equal opportunities. They, too, must find it in them to kill a man, hide his body, and lie to the police. Violence is no longer a man's domain and if a woman wants a man's position, she must learn to play the game of Survival. Rape transforms her into one of two rape-avengers: the *femme fatale rape-avenger* or the *rape-avenger-as-new-woman*.

The femme fatale rape-avenger is a relative of the femme fatale in forties film noir, a beautiful and lethal woman who is driven by desire. The film noir fatale is greedy, guilty, and is punished in the end. The femme fatale rape-avenger is neither greedy nor guilty, and is usually not punished in the end. But like her sister, she is sexy and lethal. "The initially rather plain rape victim," says Read, "is transformed into a deadly but irresistible femme fatale."[22] The rape victim does not have to be plain to begin with. Chris is "so beautiful!" and Jennifer is highly attractive in her high heels and makeup. However, at the moment of her rape, the victim is usually as clean as newfallen snow and soft as a "natural" woman. Chris is just out of the shower and without makeup, Jennifer is sun bathing in bikini with her hair loose, and shy Thana is looking down into the ground as always when she is in the public realm. Just as women are unaware of the privileged position they have gained in society at the expense of men (so men feel), they are unaware of the physical effect they have on men. Only after the rape do they learn that sex is a battle field, genitals are weapons, and to be in the public sphere unaccompanied by a man is an open declaration of war. "As soon as a woman enters a male preserve," says Germaine Greer, "be it the police, the military, the building site, the law, the clergy, she finds herself in an alien and repellent world which changes her fundamentally even as she is struggling to exert the smallest influence on it. As these masculine realms have been constructed to withstand outsiders and have grown stronger and more effective in doing so over many generations, they are virtually incapable of transformation."[23]

The single career woman enters a male preserve and is violently repelled. But she will not keep out. She arms herself with guns, butcher knives, saws, makeup, and a killer outfit. For the first time in the new femme fatale cinema makeup is thematized as a pose *constructing* rather than *hiding* an angry woman. On her last photo shoot, Chris wears makeup as a burden; since the rape she has lost her ability to get "hot" and before driving up in the mountains with Cathy she must finish a last job. Dressed in a sparkling red dress and her lips glistening with lipstick, she shoots Gordon Stewart with six shots at close range in the mall's parking area. A *public* demonstration of anger. Close-ups of her face and reflections of her body in the windows multiply the representations of the beautiful femme fatale rape-avenger. Jennifer, too, is empowered by anger and a new wardrobe: She appears in church in the clichéd black outfit signaling death and action. The audience does not really think that she packed a pair of long black trousers and a black shirt for a summer holiday. No, this is the rape-avenger's new costume, a simple forerunner for later action outfits which become increasingly elaborate, expensive and fetishized. "Time to accessorize," purrs Catwoman when actress Halle Berry (former model and Miss America) jumps on her stolen bike and hits the mall to catch the right jewelry for her costume in *Catwoman* (2004).

The costume is central to both the femme fatale rape-avenger and the female hero, and we shall return to the costume in chapters 8 and 12, "Daddy's Action Girl" and "High Trash Heroines," where action equals a striking pose. At this point in our investigation, rape-revenge cinema exposes femininity as a disguise, a masquerade, and a visual way to simultaneously hide and flaunt a desired object—the female body. Thana quickly learns to apply makeup, she wears increasingly sexy outfits (red blouse, latex trousers, skirts, high heels, black stockings), and she indulges in her new looks in front of the mirror. "What's with all that makeup, good heavens, I've never seen you look like that, your eyes and your lips are so heavily made up," her landlady exclaims on the stairs. Yes, these are the rape-avenger's killer looks. Quoting the scene in *Taxi Driver* where Travis draws his gun in front of the mirror and says "Are you talking to *me?*," Thana dressed in black stockings and wearing the head set of a nun costume also draws her .45 and aims at an imaginary target. Commenting on the scene where Albert lifts the skirt of Thana's nun costume and discovers the gun tucked in her stocking, Read concludes that "this highly erotic image surely plays on a whole range of male sexual fantasies."[24] Indeed. Death, masochism, and castration being some of them. Yet, as Deleuze points out, having the penis—in this case the gun—is not the same as having the phallus.

Mary Ann Doane describes the femme fatale as "a symptom of male fears about feminism" and "an articulation of fears surrounding the loss of stability and centrality of the self, the 'I,' the ego." Doane is referring to a *male* ego and to *men's* loss of a sense of stability. Men lose power; women gain it. The femme fatale in film noir was killed in the end. "Her power is of a peculiar sort insofar as it is usually not subject to her conscious will, hence appearing to blur the opposition between passivity and activity," says Doane. "In a sense, she has power *despite herself*."[25] The femme fatale in film noir is punished for her trespassing. The rape-avenger, however, is relieved of guilt. "This woman has just chopped, broken and burned four men beyond recognition ... But no jury in America would ever convict her!" the poster for *I Spit on Your Grave* promised. The femme fatale rape-avenger is invited to take what men claim as their God given right: revenge. Her retribution is staged in the bedroom or the bathroom, that is, in intimate situations. She is the phallic woman from Freudian psychoanalysis, the *belle dame sans merci* who, says Creed, is "playing on a masochistic desire for death, pleasure and oblivion."[26] She represents women's new permission to use femininity as a mask and turn it against men.

The femme fatale rape-avenger is an erotic display with a just cause, a combination of the angry male vigilante and the murderous femme fatale, a justified killer with the mission to educate men who have not adjusted to modern society. She doesn't know where she is going, hardly knows what she is doing, but she knows that she has had enough. The next step is the rape-avenger-as-new-woman who evolves from pinup to person. She appears in the nineties, when the rape-revenge plot is mapped over stories of raped and killed daughters, battered wives, and stalked women in spousal-revenge dramas and "women-take-back-their-lives" dramas. She is often a "maternal avenger" as Read calls the mother who avenges a daughter's rape in the television drama *In My Daughter's Name* (1992) and the film *Eye for an Eye* (1996).[27] In the latter, Karen (Sally Field) kills her teenage daughter's rapist after a trial is dismissed due to the prosecutor mishandling evidence. Here I want to focus on the drama *Enough* (2002) with Jennifer Lopez, which, admittedly, is only partly a rape-revenge film, since it has no rape. Instead, like in *Sleeping with the Enemy*, an abusive husband substitutes for the male assault on a woman.

Like the femme fatale rape-avenger the maternal rape-avenger is initially a "soft" woman in a man's world. Karen in *Eye for an Eye* may be a successful career woman, but she dresses in high heels and short skirts and is stuck in a traffic jam when the rapist kills her daughter. She is "caught" in a space where action is limited to screaming, falling, and dropping your cellular phone on the sidewalk. Slim (Jennifer Lopez) in *Enough* is also caught

Maternal failure in the rape-revenge drama *Eye for an Eye* (Paramount Pictures, 1996). Caught in traffic, career woman Karen (Sally Field) is helpless when she hears her daughter raped and killed over the phone.

in a claustrophobic space after financial problems forced her to quit college and become a waitress. When she is picked up by rich Mitch (Bill Campbell) in what we later learn is a scam by him and his police friend Robbie, she mistakes marriage for happiness. When she discovers that he is unfaithful and she refuses to tolerate it, he becomes abusive. With the help of friends she escapes with her daughter Gracie and gets involved with a former boyfriend from college. When Mitch finds her and tries to kill her, she decides to turn the tables: She learns Krav manga defense technique and meticulously plans a confrontation in Mitch's home where she will beat him to death in a fist fight.

The approach to vengeance has changed. The rape-avenger realizes that killing one man won't solve the problem. It is still his world. When he hits her, Mitch explains, "I make the money so I set the rules. We have to take the good with the bad. That's what marriage is ... Today is the price you pay for having such a great life." Slim's mother-in-law comments, "What did you say to him?" thinking that Slim provoked Mitch into beating her and thus condoning her son's behavior. Even Slim's colleague and friend Ginny (Juliette Lewis) blames Slim's attitude on masculinity: "The problem is you wanted a man-man. Meaning his veins run thick with testosterone which is good. But then he can turn around without any warning and hit you." Neither is the law of any help when Slim inquires at the police

Determined to avenge her daughter's rape and death, Karen (Sally Field) learns to shoot a gun in *Eye for an Eye* (Paramount Pictures, 1996).

station about wife battery, and later when she's on the run has her case rejected by an attorney, "You had two chances to go to the police, file a complaint, put his violence on record. You ignored them both ... It's too late. There isn't anybody who can help now."

The only way to survive is do like the city men in *Deliverance*: adjust. "Here goes," says Slim and throws away her wig, the masquerade, the running and hiding. It's time to strike back, and the film's transformation scene is not when the female hero disguises herself as another woman but when she learns Krav manga, an Israeli defense system developed "to give their women soldiers the ability to defend themselves in even the most excruciating hand-to-hand combat."[28]

TRAINER: So how do you win? How?

SLIM: I attack.

TRAINER: And what do you do after you attack?

SLIM: Nothing.

TRAINER: Why nothing?

SLIM: Because *I never stop attacking.*

The new woman finds strength and confidence. Slim learns Krav manga, Karen joins a gun club, and they then invade the rapists' territory. Karen leaves a trace in the rapist's apartment that will make him come to her house, where she is waiting with a gun. "Self-defense is not murder," Slim calmly informs Mitch. She breaks into his home, searches for knives and guns with a metal detector, and fakes evidence. Everything is set up for a confrontation on *her* terms. "What are you gonna do? You are gonna fight me? Man against man?" "Woman, Mitch." And yes, she *is* gonna fight him dressed in the new woman's version of the black killer outfit: fitness clothes and boxing bandages on her fists. Uplifting music accompanies the punches sending Mitch to his death.

Unlike the femme fatale rape-avenger who wears her killer outfit as a dazzling costume, the skills of the new woman rape-avenger are integrated into personality and behavior. This is no masquerade. The rape-avenger stalks her target, returns aggressive banter, and beats her opponent at *his* game on *his* turf. In contrast to male vigilantes she is not a loner, but part of a social network. Thus Jupiter (Fred Ward), "almighty, powerful king of the Gods," as Slim ironically calls her father, sets her up with a trainer, a body double, and more money. During the fist fight with Mitch, Slim finds support over her cellular phone in her friend Ginny, who is taking care of Slim's daughter Gracie while mum goes on a vengeance trip. Ginny assures Slim, "You have a divine, animal right to protect your life and the life of your offspring."

Placing the new woman in a political frame, she is strikingly postfeminist. Her attitude towards life resembles Projansky's definition of a fifth post-feminist discourse, the *equality and choice feminism*, which is a choice made by a free individual. You choose in life, and if your choice is wrong, it is up to you to make a different choice. The new woman rape-avenger refuses to cash in on her gender, and even when the rape-avenger is played by Hollywood icon Lopez, surprisingly little is shown of the star's body which was rumored to be insured for one billion dollars. The new woman uses male codes, not because they are male, but because they take her where she wants to go. Her refusal of eroticization makes her an ordinary person and a representative of reality, which was picked up by the media. "These are not movies of prefabricated Rambo-esque revenge, but rather ones that tap into the public's outrage about real social problems that our civic leaders have been unwilling or unable to solve," Lael Lowenstein wrote in *Los Angeles Times* and compared *Enough* to the real cases of paroled Cheryl Sellers ("a woman convicted of murdering her abusive husband") and murdered Nicole Brown Simpson ("failed in life and death by the legal system").[29] The conservatism of such belief in free agency, however, was commented on under the headline "Girls Just Wanna Have Guns" in *Time*, which refused to regard the new woman as progress. "[T]he new women-in-peril films betray a simultaneous naiveté (that the heroine will triumph) and cynicism (that moviegoers won't believe justice is done unless they see the bad guy blown away) ... it doesn't make for a truly adult cinema about complex men and women."[30]

But entertainment need not be about "complex men and women." Even if entertainment cinema is not "adult" (whatever this means), it can and does address issues of real concern in contemporary society. It just doesn't do it in a straight-forward manner. Thus, the female hero, on the one hand, is determined to get even without playing the dominatrix card. On the other hand, she is careful to distance herself from the image of a "crazy woman." "I am not this person," Slim cries when she becomes a battered wife and "I am not a crazy person, I swear," when she barges into the attorney's office. Karen tells her husband, "Don't treat me like I'm some neurotic," to which he replies, "Well, don't act like one." This is the "desidentification" Charlotte Brunsdon speaks of, "the othering structure ... so as to denounce that which formed it."[31] To hold out at arm's length that which *is* your historical past. Because this *is* exactly where the rape-avenger-as-new-woman comes from: male masochism and images of crazy, battered, and neurotic women.

There is a social subtext of *Enough*, however, which echoes Projansky's critique of postfeminism as capitalist, consumerist, racist, and middle class. Slim is the prototype of a middle class, WASP consumer.[32] She comments

on Ginny's smell of sweat, she refuses shelters because she doesn't want Gra-

Top: The postfeminist avenger Slim (Jennifer Lopez) in *Enough* (Columbia Pictures Corporation and Winkler Films, 2002) is fit to fight after taking lessons in Krav manga so she can beat her abusive husband to death. Bottom: "What are you gonna do? You are gonna fight me? Man against man?" the husband (Bill Campbell) asks in *Enough*. "Woman, Mitch." And yes, she *is* gonna fight him—to the death.

cie to become "tainted," and her "house rules" only allow ex-boyfriend Joe (Dan Futterman) to lie on her bed fully dressed ("How can I forget with Gracie here?"), as if having sex while a six-year-old is in the house would emotionally disturb the child. When Slim and Gracie are on the run they are sheltered by Indian friends of Phil (Slim's boss at the diner and a father substitute), and Gracie suspiciously comments on the food ("What is it?") to which Slim, equally suspicious, replies, "It's food," as if Indian food is below their "taste." Scenes with credit cards being refused are tragic, whereas a scene where Jupiter sends her a bunch of fifty dollar notes is accompanied by pop music. Independence may mean farewell to upper class luxury, but it does *not* mean sinking into the working class. Slim miraculously finds a lost father who turns out to be a helpful millionaire and a forgotten boyfriend who is sweet, single, and educated. He is, by the way, an example of Projansky's fifth type of postfeminism: the *men can be feminists too*. Why did Slim leave Joe? Because he didn't live up to her idea of masculinity; rich Mitch with his construction company, infidelity, and psychopathic behavior did. Well, she got smarter.

In conclusion, Read suggests, "with the maternal avenger, the rape-revenge cycle may have run its course."[33] Not quite. Slim and Beatrix Kiddo are both mothers killing their daughters' fathers, even if only Beatrix is literally raped. Rape remains a plot, a motive, and a symbol in popular cinema, which Slim and Beatrix are two different examples of: Slim is the new woman rape-avenger who exchanges a prefeminist and failed marriage with a postfeminist relationship with Joe. Supported by patriarchal structures, Slim is helped by several father figures and visualized in the desexualized archetype of the mother. After her detour into vengeance territory, she returns to an ending that could fit in the woman's film, where love is a woman's only obligation. Perhaps Slim finds love with Joe. Different with Beatrix, to whom we shall return in chapter 12. Beatrix is a postfeminist female hero who has it all: she remains single after her "divorce" from Bill, her character is eroticized and sexualized, and she leaves the plot cast in the ambivalent mise-en-scene of film noir, complete down to a black and white image.

Rape-revenge Filmography (Selective)

Strawdogs (1971) Dir. Sam Peckinpah. Avenger David and rape victim Amy

Deliverance (1972) Dir. John Boorman. Rape victim Bobby, avengers Ed, Lewis, Bobby, and Drew

Hannie Caulder (1972) Dir. Burt Kennedy, filmed in the UK. Rape-avenger Hannie Caulder

Last House on the Left (1972) Dir. Wes Craven

Rape Squad (also called Act of Vengeance; The Violator) (1974) Dir. Bob Kelljan
Lipstick (1976) Dir. Lamont Johnson. Rape-avenger Chris
I Spit on Your Grave (also called Day of the Woman) (1978) Dir. Meir Zarchi. Rape-avenger
    Jennifer
Ms. 45 (1981) Dir. Abel Ferrara. Rape-avenger Thana
Sudden Impact (1983) Dir. Clint Eastwood
Savage Streets (1984) Dir. Danny Steinmann
The Ladies' Club (1986) Dir. Janet Greek
Extremities (1986) Dir. Robert M. Young
Hunter's Blood (1986) Dir. Robert C. Hughes
Positive I.D. (1987) Dir. Andy Anderson
The Accused (1988) Dir. Jonathan Kaplan
Lady Avenger (1989) Dir. David DeCoteau
In My Daughter's Name (1992) Dir. Jud Taylor. Television movie
Dirty Weekend (1993) Dir. Michael Winner
Eye for an Eye (1996) Dir. John Schlesinger. Maternal rape-avenger Karen
A Time to Kill (1996) Dir. Joel Schumacher
Enough (2002) Dir. Michael Apted. Maternal rape-avenger Slim
Irréversible (2003) Dir. Gaspar Noé, filmed in France. Female rape victim Alex, male rape-
    avengers Pierre and Marcus
Kill Bill: Vol. 1 (2003) Dir. Quentin Tarantino. Maternal rape-avenger Beatrix

PART TWO

From the Margins

4

Meiko Kaji:
Woman with a Vengeance

I am a woman walking at the brink of life and death
Who has emptied my tears many moons ago
All tears of compassion and dreams
The snowy nights and tomorrow hold no meaning
I have immersed my body in the river of vengeance.
        —"Shura No Hana" (Flower of Carnage)

The Japanese WIP film *Female Prisoner Scorpion: Jailhouse 41* from 1972 opens with a monotonous, scratching sound. The camera tracks slowly backwards, tilts, moves into a prison, glides down corridors and into the bottom of a hole, where a woman is lying with her hands and feet tied. It rests in a close-up of her face lit by blue light. A face with a spoon between soft, full lips. She patiently grinds the spoon on the uneven floor, turning the harmless shape into a knife. This is Matsu, the female prisoner nicknamed Scorpion. And this is Meiko Kaji, a hauntingly beautiful, enigmatic, and seductive actress who became a star in Japanese femme fatale films during the seventies. Today, to most Western audiences Meiko Kaji is just a beautiful voice. She sings the song "Shura No Hana" towards the end of *Kill Bill Vol. 1* when Beatrix has just chopped off the top of O-Ren Ishii's Chinese-American head, and "Urami Bushi" during credits in *Kill Bill Vol. 2*. Connoisseurs familiar with Asian cult cinema and Japanese manga, however, will recognize the songs from the films featuring Kaji's famous characters, Scorpion and Lady Snowblood.

Meiko Kaji is to Japanese cinema what Pam Grier is to American cinema: A queen of cult cinema and erotic bloodshed. Two of her films, *Lady Snowblood: Blizzard From the Netherworld* (1973) and *Lady Snowblood 2: Love Song of Vengeance* (1974), were available on DVD with English subtitles years before Tarantino convinced Uma to wield her Hattori Hanzo sword. I picked them up in 2001 in a bookshop run by the Danish Film Museum, whose bookseller was well oriented in art cinema, as well as exploitation, cult, and Asian cinema. Meiko Kaji's film represented the best of those categories, he assured me. He was right.

Meiko Kaji

While going through stills from Kaji's films at the research library in the National Film Center in Kyobashi, Tokyo, it struck me how the studios had chosen to focus on her big eyes, her long, straight, black hair, and her body as an immobile and brooding figure. Often holding a weapon—a knife, a piece of glass, a rifle, a samurai sword—and always looking *away* from the action around her and the other characters, and directly into the camera and the eyes of the audience. She did not smile in any of the stills, not a single one, but remained a lonely existence immersed in darkness, either in intimate close-up or as a remote figure. She resembled a female version of Clint Eastwood's character The Man With No Name in Sergio Leone's spaghetti westerns. Not quite wrong, as she personally requested the directors of the *Scorpion* series and the two *Lady Snowblood* films to remove most of the dialogue from her characters, just like Eastwood convinced Leone to remove the name and most of the dialogue from his character, thus creating a mythical hero.

The Japanese film library had articles and interviews with Meiko Kaji (surprisingly few); however, they are in Japanese. There were stills and film posters from all her films in the library's stills department and she was clearly

Meiko Kaji as prisoner Matsu in Japanese WIP film *Female Prisoner Scorpion: Jailhouse 41* (Toei Studio, 1972), patiently grinding her spoon into a weapon. With its experimental visual aesthetics, this WIP film is more avant-garde than it is exploitation cinema.

a famous Japanese actress, as my failed attempt to buy stills with her in film shops showed. My knowledge about her is thus compiled from American and French Internet sites and from the information on the DVDs issued with English subtitles.[1] Meiko Kaji was born on March 24, 1947, as Masako Ota. Her film career started with minor roles in 1967 with the studio Nikkatsu under her real name. In 1970 she had her first starring role credited as Meiko Kaji in *Stray Cat Rock: Sex Hunter*, the third in a series of five films about a girl gang, The Alleycats, of which Meiko played the leader in two entries (1970, 1971). When Nikkatsu turned their production exclusively into "Roman Porno" (romantic soft-core porn films), Kaji switched to the film studio Toei, where she starred in the WIP series *Female Convict Scorpion* based on a manga from the sixties by Tooru Shinohara. The character Sasori (Scorpion) had an obscene language (characteristic of the erotic manga), and Kaji requested a change into the almost mute film character, which would become her trademark. Nudity, too, was removed from the character. In this WIP series the protagonist (in the four entries with Kaji) had only one scene in which her right breast is displayed; all other scenes involving nudity were transferred from Sasori to fellow female convicts, thus enhancing the exceptional and aloof nature of Meiko's film persona. The silence was continued in the two *Lady Snowblood* films produced by Toho Studios. *Lady Snowblood* was also based on a manga, *Shurayukihime*, by Kazuo Koike who had written the immensely popular manga *Kozure Ôkami*[2] (*Lone Wolf and Cub*, also known as *Baby Chart*), which Toho Studios was turning into a film series, producing four films alone in 1972. *Lone Wolf and Cub* dealt with a *ronin*, a masterless samurai, whose family had been killed and now traveled the countryside as an assassin with his infant son. The female version, *Lady Snowblood*, similarly had a young woman traveling the countryside as a professional assassin seeking revenge over the men who destroyed her mother.

Japanese *chanbara* cinema (swordplay cinema) had seen a female swordswoman in *The Crimson Bat* series of four films between 1969 and 1970 about a blind swordswoman, a feminization of the *Zatoichi* series about a blind swordsman.[3] However, actress Yoko Matsuyama was ordinary and sweet, lacking the dark sensualism that would make Kaji a future cult figure.

The actress Kaji appears as enigmatic as her characters. During the seventies she became a huge star appearing in television series and historical film dramas as well as chanbara films, experimental films, and exploitation films. In 1978, however, she vanished from the film arena and only returned occasionally in a handful of roles in films and television series over the next two decades (in 2003 she was in a television series). Sites on the Internet wonder why she withdrew—studios offered her roles, but Kaji turned them down and quit her role as Sasori in the *Scorpion* series, which continued in two films in 1976 and 1977 with actress Ryôko Ema. Also, the *Lady Snowblood* films could have become a series. Instead, Kaji joined in the silence of her characters and leaving the fame of the film star, she chose to become a singer.

Cool Alleycat

Two features of Kaji's star persona are present in the character Mako in *Stray Cat Rock: Sex Hunter* (1970): A cool, silent, and arrogant behavior best compared to Eastwood's Man With No Name, and a stubborn pride to even consider surrendering to superior forces. A third feature I found in the films with Kaji is a critique of Japanese values as represented by the patriarchal structures in power—like the critique a hero always represents when he or she "rights wrongs" in society.

The plot of the third film in the *Stray Cat Rock* series revolves around national identity and genetic purity. Two gangs operate in the city: The all-female gang The Alleycats led by Mako (Kaji) and the all-male gang The Eagles led by the Baron (Tatsuya Fuji). In the beginning the two gangs socialize with Mako being the Baron's girlfriend and the Baron's second in command, Susumu (Jiro Okazaki), being in love with Alleycat Mari. However, things change when Mari falls in love with halfbreed Ichiro, and Mako falls in love with halfbreed Kazuma (Rikiya Yasuoka), who is searching for a lost sister who was adopted when he was a child. A "halfbreed" is a person of mixed Japanese and foreign descent. The foreign descent in this film is thematized as being American, which is indicated by flashbacks to the invasion during the second world war, by the Baron's flashback to halfbreeds raping his sister, and by the film's use of jazz music and American culture (soft drinks, dance, songs, clothes, music). It is hinted that Kazuma's father may be American as well.

The status of "halfbreed" is ambiguous; it signals genetic impurity as well as possibility for change in contrast to the purity of Japanese blood and traditional Japanese culture, which is portrayed as impotent.[4] "Baron—why don't you ever fuck me?" Mako asks the Baron. "Aren't you up to it?" When he tries, it turns out he *is* impotent. He compensates by beating up halfbreeds. Halfbreed Ichiro leaves town, but Kazuma refuses to leave, and when the Alleycats help him, the Baron cons them into a rape party. The Baron has made a deal with the mafia and while he is in bed with Mako, her gang is "right now being gang banged at the party."

The style is cool, tragic, and romantic. The rape works on a symbolic rather than physical level: Symbolically speaking, The Alleycats are "fucked over" and "sold out" by The Eagles. Mako returns to the party with Molotov cocktails and frees her gang. Kazuma's sister Megumi was ashamed of being halfbreed and has kept her foreign descent a secret. When she finally accepts her heritage and returns to the place where The Eagles tortured Kazuma she is gang raped by The Eagles. The end is a showdown between The Eagles and Kazuma.

The film is as stylish as Mako's black and white costume, which elegantly mixes the dress code of an American gun fighter with that of a Spanish ranch owner. The genre template is the western—a stranger comes to a town, two gangs, the showdown at dawn—and visually the film opens with a close-up of Mako's black hat, zooms out to The Alleycats, and closes with a zoom in on Mako, who puts on her black, broad-brimmed hat in existential pragmatism: To love is to suffer and die.

Scorpion: Sting of Death

Like its American counterpart, the Japanese WIP film series about the female prisoner Scorpion combines plots of rebellion with scenes of sexual violence. But unlike any WIP film I have seen, it does so in a surrealist visual style and with a tragic heroine.

Matsu (Kaji) was betrayed by her police-lover, who manipulated her to infiltrate the mafia, then turned out to be corrupt like Howard in *Coffy*. He enters the room during the gangsters' rape of Matsu, laughs, and disappears as the back wall turns like a turning theater stage, abandoning Matsu to her sad fate. The rape is filmed from below a glass floor to enhance the theatrical setting. In the series' first film, *Female Prisoner # 701: Scorpion* (1972), Matsu escapes after three years of prison and returns to the city to kill her lover and his corrupt associates. In the start of the second film, *Female Convict Scorpion: Jailhouse 41* (1972), Matsu is removed from the hole where she has been isolated for a year. Her first act is an attempt to cut out the director's eye with her spoon-turned-knife (his first eye having been lost in the first film). He punishes Matsu by tying her in a Christ-like position to a huge branch and having his men gang rape her in public, masked and dancing around her in a circle.

The attempt to break Scorpion is in vain. She is unbreakable, a mute symbol of male betrayal and social injustice. Like the rape-avenger, her mission does not stop with the death of her lover. Her goal is not the man who caused her downfall, but the system which he represents. Scorpion is raped and beaten; however, it has no effect, and even tied in a cell she can make a female guard scald herself with hot soup, and she can cause an epileptic seizure in another female guard who laughs when Scorpion is punished.

Her powers are nearly mystic. She seduces a female guard who, disguised as a prisoner, tries to make her talk. The woman begs her superior to be returned to the cell to have another try, but the love marks on her breasts reveal her failure.

Scorpion's long black hair frames her face, lustrous and well kept in contrast to the other prisoners, whose hair is rumpled, unkempt, and lusterless. The hair hangs down each side of her face covering her face and eyes like curtains. Or like a lens, opening and closing to allow light into a camera. Such a comparison makes Matsu's face the equal of an "eye" looking back at the men and back at the male audience. In feminist film theory the gaze belongs to men—and that the series had a male audience is clear from the beginning of the first film, where the women parade naked in the jail yard as a punishment for Matsu's attempt to escape (she is in her cell, dressed). However, Matsu returns this male gaze with her black eyes wide open like an abyss where every insult, every abuse, every maltreatment, is absorbed. In the iconic close-up of the spaghetti western, the men's eyes are narrow lines which hardly allow light to enter. In the ultra close-up, Matsu's eyes are wide open, showing the white around the iris. A terrifying abyss.

In the cinema, the wide-open eyes belong to the victim of the horror film. Carol Clover draws attention to the fact that modern horror cinema has two gazes: *assaultive* and *reactive* gazing. The first—the assaultive gaze—is in line with the traditional Mulveyan gaze, the male gaze which can be either voyeuristic (sadistic, controlling, and punitive) or fetishistic (turning woman into an icon). This is the prison guards leering at the naked women, the prison director triumphantly looking down at Matsu lying tied in the

Matsu (Meiko Kaji) returns the gaze of the men raping her, refusing to be a victim and using her black, wide open eyes to promise castration and death in *Female Prisoner Scorpion: Jailhouse 41* (Toei Studio, 1972).

hole in isolation, the police-lover looking at Matsu being raped by the gangsters. The second gaze—the reactive gaze—is one of the "blind spots," says Clover, in Mulvey's theory. This is the frightened gaze, the eye wide open in terror. Clover quotes Georg Metz who also distinguishes between two gazes, a projective ("casting" itself over things) and an introjective (where things are illuminated by the gaze and "deposited" within the spectator, the things being "projected" onto his or hers retina, so to speak).[5] This last gaze, the introjective gaze, is where we look at things and retain them in our minds, where they may come back to haunt or please us. Clover compares her reactive gaze to the introjective gaze—the gaze of the victim looking at horrible things, a gaze mirrored by a frightened audience (who also keep the images in their minds). Some WIP films represent the reactive gaze in scenes where female prisoners are being tortured. Often, however, female prisoners refuse to be intimidated into the position of the victim and reactive gazing.

Like Matsu. "Why do you stare at us like that?" a new jail director asks in *Jailhouse 41*. He has come to succeed the former (one-eyed) director, and as Matsu suddenly strikes out with her knife at the old director, the new director collapses in shock and wets his pants. Not only does Matsu refuse to enter the position as victim and use the reactive gaze (being scared), she even exposes the male gaze as a fraud. This gaze pretends to be phallic and in control, when, in fact, it is not a gaze but just a look. Clover compares the relationship between the gaze and the look to that of the relationship between the phallus and the penis: The first (gaze and phallus) is the fantasy of mastery; the second (look and penis) is the biological "tool" and weapon of mastery. And this latter weapon *is* vulnerable and soft, as the castrations and mutilated eyes in rape-revenge cinema and WIP films tell us. Where fantasy can triumph, flesh might fall.

The scene where Matsu is raped in *Jailhouse 41* makes an interesting case: The guards cover their eyes with masks, thus hiding their eyes. As they rape Matsu, who is tied crucifixion style, she lifts her head and stares wildly at them in return as her only weapon of defense. The camera shows no nudity but focuses on her face. Her eyes are wide open, not in terror as in the reactive gaze, but trying to terrorize the men with her gaze and show them that she is *not* subdued, will *not* surrender to the humiliation and pain they inflict upon her. She uses her eyes as an assaultive gaze, a projective gaze "casting" itself on the attackers and seeking out and focusing on (like a lens pulling an object into focus) the jail director standing at the brink of the sand grave. Returning the male gaze turns Matsu into a monster, like Medusa. Or a witch who can "cast eyes." "I hate you for destroying my eye. Other things don't matter. I'll make you go mad," the director tells Matsu.

The dark and lonely figure of Matsu, the female prisoner in the fourth *Scorpion* film, *Female Prisoner Scorpion: # 701's Grudge Song* (Toei Studio, 1973), the WIP series which made Japanese actress Meiko Kaji a cult star. She starred in *Lady Snowblood* the same year (Toho).

However, Matsu is not a castrating "bitch" like the usual rape-avenger. Bitches dissimulate, manipulate, and seduce; they operate in a field of male lust and female strategy. Scorpion never smiles, never opens her body to men. She does not participate in the prisoners' later rape of the male guards. Her desire is not for flesh, and her look is not seductive. It is assaultive. Like a "castrating" witch.

The witch powers are manifest in the surreal visual style. An example is when a female prisoner attacks Matsu in the shower in *Female Prisoner # 701: Scorpion*: The traditional shower scene—giggle, naked breasts, rubbing and masturbating—is turned into a surrealist nightmare where the attacker's face is painted as a demon, thunder strikes and the shower transforms into a hellish maze of glass, water, and naked, screaming women. Matsu remains calm in contrast to the attacker who, by mistake, stabs the director in his right eye. An example from *Jailhouse 41* is when seven escaped prisoners find an old woman in an abandoned village. The woman is a ghost or a witch, who releases their inner demons. Behind flames they sit in a row wearing white kimonos, the old woman sits behind them bathed in purple light, and a male voice narrates their crimes: One killed her two children because her husband was unfaithful, drowning her two-year old son and stabbing the unborn fetus to death in her uterus. Another killed her lover, because he maltreated her son from a former marriage. A third killed her father, who tried to rape her. And so on. Before she dies, the witch curses the guards, and when she is dead, a sudden autumn turns the sky purple; the colors change from dark blue to bright red, purple, and yellow; and a strong wind lifts Matsu's hair and blesses the knife that the witch has given her.

The style may be inspired by the original manga, which I was unable to find. The imagery is strikingly beautiful and surprisingly effective, with tilted and upside-down images, radiant colors, and magical transformations, turning an exploitation film into a cry of existential anguish. The text on the back of the DVD describes *Jailhouse 41* as "as subversive as Donald Cammell and Nicolas Roeg's *Performance*, John Boorman's *Point Blank* and Jean-Luc Godard's *Weekend*." In fact, the film is far more subversive, because it unites strategies of art and exploitation cinema not in order to create "high art," but to create "high exploitation." A utopian mission Tarantino would pick up years later.

The first two films in the series are hailed as the best of WIP cinema. In a way, they are far too experimental, well crafted and lacking in sexual sadism to be representative of the WIP genre. There is sadism, as when the prisoners beat Scorpion because they believe she sold them out. But it isn't gruesome. And there is sexual violence, as when a group of men rape the female guard who helps Matsu in the third film, *Female Prisoner Scorpion: Beast*

Stable (1973). But it isn't graphic. Nudity and torture are scarce and no match to Grier's Philippine WIP films or the *Ilsa* films. And most of the violence is done to men, as male guards being beaten in the first film, a guard being castrated in the second film, the torture of the film operator in the third film, and a policeman having his arm cut off in the fourth film, *Female Prisoner Scorpion: # 701's Grudge Song* (1973). Also, the explicit politics are unusual for WIP cinema—a critique of *all* men and *all* masculinity being destructive by nature. This is represented by the three businessmen on vacation who, when they stumble upon one of the escaped prisoners, immediately rape and kill her for fun. No wonder the female prisoners hate men! Their crimes relate to betrayal and disappointment, to anger and jealousy, and to the impossibility of female dignity in a patriarchal society. In the last image of *Jailhouse 41* the escaped female prisoners run in the streets of Tokyo. A truly surrealist and subversive sight.

Here, Kaji develops her unique star persona in collaboration with Shunya Ito, the director of the first three *Female Prisoner Scorpion* films. They changed the female protagonist in the manga from being foul-mouthed and vengeful to become a mute image of female mystery, dark sensualism, and primordial abyss. A castrating femme fatale in the monstrous-feminine tradition of Barbara Creed's female monsters—not literally but symbolically castrating, as when Matsu stabs out the jail director's last eye at the end of *Jailhouse 41*. The series was a huge commercial success, but when budgets diminished and the new director Yasuharu Hasebe failed to keep the standard in the fourth entry, Meiko left for another project developed with her in mind by Toho Studios: *Lady Snowblood.*

Lady Snowblood

It is interesting that in a Western culture which considers itself democratic and with equal opportunities for women and men, female heroes are met with surprise—"it's a woman!"—or with strong negative or positive reactions ranging from incredulity (*I Spit on Your Grave*), mild surprise (*Long Kiss Goodnight*), and brutal rejection (*Alien 3*), to cult worshipping (*Coffy*) and trendy admiration (*Kill Bill*). Negative or positive, the issue of gender never seems absent in Western cinema. In Asian cinema characters within the films' diegesis express no surprise that the hero is a woman. This is especially intriguing since Asian culture until recently was more conservative in gender relations than Western culture. Yet it is in Asian cinema we find some of the most subversive examples of female heroes.

Take Lady Snowblood, child of the netherworlds, born out of her mother's desire to take vengeance on the four people who murdered her husband, took her son, and raped her for three days. When she is convicted for the murder of one of the culprits, she has intercourse with as many guards as possible to ensure an offspring who can exact vengeance on her behalf. "You have a destiny that needs to be realized. Forget joy, forget sorrow, forget love, and forget hate. Except for vengeance, these must be forgotten," Yuki's adoptive father and instructor Dôkai (Kô Nishimura) teaches her. "You are a beast, a devil, not even Buddha can save you now."

Yuki Kashima, or Shurayuki-hime (Kaji) as the child is called, is a tragic figure. "Shu re" means "netherworlds," "yuki" is "snow," and "hime" means "lady." This "tragedy," as the male narrator calls the story, is divided into four chapters entitled "Vengeance Binds Love and Hate," "Crying Bamboo Dolls of the Netherworlds," "Umbrella of Blood, Heart of Strewn Flowers" and, finally, "The House of Joy, the Final Hell." A young audience will recognize this narrative device of dividing the film into chapters with titles from Kill Bill. Lady Snowblood is, indeed, one of the "master texts" behind the American blockbuster. This is where the frozen images with information about characters comes from, like the assassins caught by the camera, their names written in blood: Tsukamoto Gishiro, Banzô Takemura, Tokuichi Masakage, Okono Kitahama. From my experience with Chinese and Japanese cinema, this use of chapter titles, frozen images, and manga (comics, parallel to Tarantino's use of anime, Japanese cartoons) is strikingly modern and has a Brechtian effect of Verfremdung, which draws attention to the height of the drama, the depth of the tragedy, the high-strung sentiments, the exceptional beauty of the woman, and the superhuman fatality of her destiny. With such extreme devices we are in a world of Shakespearian proportions. Tarantino has said that Kill Bill was the first film made entirely from within his "movie-world," meaning that everything originated from movies and not reality. The same must be said about Lady Snowblood.

The plot is narrated by jumping back and forth in time, opening with Yuki's birth in 1874 in prison, then going forward twenty years to when she as a young woman dressed in kimono slices five men to death with a samurai sword hidden in her umbrella. The last victim gasps, "Woman, wh... wh... who the hell are you?" "Lady Snowblood." This is the beginning of Yuki's revenge and as she proceeds with the three murderers still alive (her mother had killed the first), we get the background filled in through flashbacks from her mother's death in prison, from the terrible crime, and from Yuki's training as a child by adoptive father, priest and former liege vassal Dôkai. Yuki secures the help of a beggar king, Sir Matsuemon, whose army of beggars track down Yuki's targets. The first man, Banzô (Noboru Nakaya), has been reduced to a pathetic drunk and a gambler, living off his daughter who works as a prostitute. Yuki saves Banzô's life in a casino so that she can confront him with old debt. "You and I have some business to take care of" (echoed in the Bride's words to each of her targets, "You and I have unfinished business"). The man begs for his life; however, the answer is predictable, "An eye for an eye." Second in line is Okono Kitahama, the malicious woman restraining Yuki's mother while the men murder her husband. Okono owns a restaurant where Yuki fights her bandits (the inspiration for the sword battle in O-Ren Ishii's restaurant). Okono hangs herself, but to be sure she is dead, Yuki slices the body in half with a single sword blow. Blood spurts everywhere in red geysers blasting out of the molested body. At this point a curtain falls (a *real* fabric curtain). The final murderer and mastermind behind the crime is Tokuichi Masakage (Takeo Chii), a smuggler and political opportunist who hosts a party for the Japanese elite and the foreigners. In the ballroom Yuki jumps from one balcony to another, kills Tokuichi, and flees fatally wounded by gunshots. Outside in the falling snow Banzô's daughter stabs Yuki, who falls to the ground, her white kimono stained by blood. When the sun rises it caresses Yuki, who opens her eyes, the music rises optimistically and the screen goes red with blood spurting from the sides to frame Yuki's face.

The character Yuki is connected to a savage nature of uncontrollable forces surrounding a fragile civilization. She exercises with her sword in the woods, wanders on top of the black, tall rocks beaten by the blue ocean below, elegantly battles without stumbling in her traditional women's sandals of wood. The second film, *Lady Snowblood: Love Song of Vengeance* (1974), opens with Yuki visiting her mother's grave in the cemetery. When she leaves, a group of policemen attempt to arrest her. Moving slowly, never interrupting her feminine walk with short steps constrained by the tight kimono and the clicking sandals, and never batting an eyelash, Yuki handles her sword so swiftly that we hardly notice it. Like Matsu, she is invincible, and she can only be captured when she surrenders out of existential *Weltschmertz*. Wounds heal magically as Yuki survives being shot several times in both films, being cut and stabbed by swords, having her foot crushed in an animal trap, and being touched by the plague. Magical powers seem to protect Yuki.

Witches, writes Barbara Creed, are known by all cultures. "The witch sets out to unsettle boundaries between the rational and irrational, symbolic and imaginary. Her evil powers are seen as part of her 'feminine' nature; she is closer to nature than man and can control forces in nature such as tempests, hurricanes and storms."[6] Christianity links witches to the devil and female nature to evil. A medieval manual for inquisitors, *The Malleus Maleficarum* (1484), described women thus, "What else is woman but a foe to friendship, an inescapable punishment, a necessary evil, a natural temptation, a desirable calamity, a domestic danger, a delectable detriment, an evil of nature, painted with fair colors!"[7] Other cultures, however, associate witches with nature and magical powers of healing, positive aspects explored in contemporary popular culture with television series like *Sabrina the Teenage Witch* (1996–2003) and *Charmed* (1998-), films like *Practical Magic* (1998) and cartoons like *W.I.T.C.H.*[8] Yuki is not explicitly called a witch, but she is—like Matsu—magically embedded in a savage nature supporting her quest.

Yuki is a relative of the maternal rape-avenger, but unlike her Yuki is a daughter who avenges her mother's rape and death. In the manga, Yuki is repeatedly gang raped, abused, and beaten, and her naked body is a central visual point of attraction in the manga. But in the films Yuki is a pure virgin in a white kimono, unblemished except for the blood spurting from the people she kills. To compensate for the missing rape of Yuki, the films show the men raping her mother. The rape weighs heavier than the husband's death, which is just shown once. What drives vengeance is not maternal anger, but desire for revenge. Compared to Kaji's two former characters, Mako and Matsu, and to the American rape-avengers, Yuki has an exceptional status: She is attacked by men, but never raped. Her body remains intact, unopened, sacred, like a child's body. Instead, like in the *Ilsa* films, we have a Final Boy who functions as a witness to the crimes and as a torture victim. In the first film this is the character Ashio, a writer and journalist who is chronicling Yuki's life. "Suffer! Suffer a lot more! Suffer!" Okono screams, as her men beat Ashio and cut his face with a knife. In the second film the anarchist Ransui is tortured to bleeding pulp, scalded with boiling water and injected with the plague, after which he dies. Each film relates Yuki to a man—Ashio and Ransui—who admires and helps her, but is not allowed to have a romance with her.

The star persona of Meiko Kaji is located between the extraordinary powers of a castrating gaze and the existential malaise of a female killer. Kaji's characters are haunted, if not by the past, then by a sense of not belonging, of being out of place and out of time. In this, they resemble the mythic hero. They are exceptionally beautiful, yet out of reach emotionally. Their weapon skills are at the expense of inner balance. They move faster than any opponent but lose track of life. Why live, if not to kill, as the police chief points out? Watching the anarchist, Yuki senses his passion for his wife, for poetry, and for the poor. But like the anarchist's brother, a disillusioned doctor who dies from the plague, she is incapable of reaching into her soul. She has been taught to kill emotions. The daughter-father connection between Yuki and her adoptive father is presented as sadistic, incestuous, and pedophilic when Dokai with his sword cuts the clothes off the body of a little eight-year-old Yuki, who then fights him naked. In another scene he throws her down a hill in a barrel. Sensitivity is not an option.

The archetypes of daughter and rape-avenger blend into a proud creature, a cold and fiery female killer, who has compassion for lost souls (such as Banzô's sad daughter working as a prostitute), yet lacks the ability to experience, to *feel* compassion. Coldness points to the archetype of the dominatrix, yet the coldness is counterbalanced by the warm anger of the witch casting her gaze. The iconic figure used in promotional stills for the last two *Scorpion* films underlines the witch aspect: Kaji is clad in a long black coat, wears a large black hat and is accompanied by animals, black crows and a huge black dog. There is no victimization in Kaji's star persona, neither in her films nor in the extratextual reception of her. Like all stars in femme fatale cinema, her star persona was created by men (the authors of the manga, the owners of production companies, and the film directors). However, unlike Pam Grier, Kaji participated in the design of her persona. And, also in contrast to Grier, withdrawing as an actress was a choice made by Kaji, not by any film company.

Kaji and Beyond

A later adaptation of the *Lady Snowblood* manga, *The Princess Blade* (*Shura Yukihime*, 2001), updated the period to a futuristic Japan where the government is using a tribe of masterless ronin, the House of Takemikazuchi, as assassins who hunt down and kill rebels. The Takemikazuchi were once "guards to the rulers of a neighboring kingdom" but became unemployed when reformers ended the monarchy. The day before her twentieth birthday Yuki (Yumiko Shaku) learns that her mother was killed by the head of the Takemikazuchi, and that she is the princess of the House who must rule on her twentieth birthday. As her attempt to kill the leader fails, she flees and hides with a young, disillusioned rebel, Takashi (Hideaki Ito), whom she falls in love with. His love transforms Yuki from being cold and unemotional ("Are you never sad?" he asks. "I make it go away. Like pain.") to get in contact with her feelings. In the end she confronts and kills the leader, assumes leadership of the House and dissolves it. When she returns to Takashi to live happily ever after as in the fairy tales, he has been killed by a fellow rebel because he refused to plant more bombs. Before dying in her arms his last words are, "Live. Be happy. Live for me."

Love, youth, and happiness are central in *The Princess Blade*, as they also are in two recent Japanese femme samurai war epics, *Azumi* (2003) and *Azumi: Death or Love* (2005), that eroticize their heroines as young teenage girls and not as adult women. Even if actress and former underwear model Yumiko

Kazuo Koike and Kazuo Kamimura's manga *Lady Snowblood* (GaGa Communications and Oz Productions) was modernized in 2001 in the film *Shura yukihime* (*The Princess Blade*), which turned the nineteenth century female samurai into an expert assassin in a future Japan.

Shaku is twenty-three years old, she looks like a young teenager, an impression supported by the promotional material: In stills she is dressed in a white dress resembling a five-year-old girl with an innocent, sulky, and childish facial expression. In comparison, Meiko Kaji was almost the same age, twenty-five, when she played Scorpion, and twenty-six when she played Lady Snowblood. She appeared *older* than the twenty years her character is in *Lady Snowblood*.

The sexy child "nymph" is a contemporary trend in Japanese manga, anime and computer games. And, it seems, also in femme fatale cinema. With her dark sensuality, brooding mood, and mute despair, Meiko Kaji was no nymph. She was a woman "walking at the brink of life and death."

Meiko Kaji Filmography (Selective)

Stray Cat Rock: Sex Hunter (Nora-neko rokku: Sekkusu hanta) (1970) Dir. Yasuharu Hasebe. Mako, leader of girl gang

Stray Cat Rock: Wild Measures '71 (Nora-neko rokku: Bôsô shudan '71) (1971) Dir. Toshiya Fujita.

Female Prisoner # 701: Scorpion (Joshuu 701-gô: Sasori) (1972) Dir. Shunya Ito. Prisoner Matsu "Scorpion"

Female Convict Scorpion Jailhouse 41 (Joshuu sasori: Dai-41 zakkyo-bô) (1972) Dir. Shunya Ito

Female Prisoner Scorpion: Beast Stable (Joshuu sasori: Kemono-beya) (1973) Dir. Shunya Ito

Female Prisoner Scorpion: # 701's Grudge Song (Joshuu sasori: 701-gô urami-bushi) (1973) Dir. Yasuharu Hasebe

Lady Snowblood: Blizzard from the Netherworld (Shurayukihime) (1973) Dir. Toshiya Fujita. Female avenger Yuki Kashima, "Shurayuki-hime" (Lady Snowblood of the Netherworlds)

Lady Snowblood 2: Love Song of Vengeance (Shura-yuki-hime: Urami Renga) (1974) Dir. Toshiya Fujita.

Japanese Femme Fatale Filmography (Selective)

This filmography includes female swordfighters, gunfighters and martial arts fighters. The Sister Street Fighter films are contemporary martial arts, the Black Angel films are contemporary gangster, and the Crimson Bat and Azumi films are samurai films set in the Edo period.

Crimson Bat—Blind Swordswoman, The (Mekura No Oichi monogatari: Makkana nagaradori) (1969) Dir. Sadaji Matsuda

Trapped! The Crimson Bat (Mekurano Oichi jigokuhada) (1969) Dir. Sadaji Matsuda

Watch Out, Crimson Bat (Mekurano Oichi midaregasa) (1969) Dir. Hirokazu Ichimura

Crimson Bat: Wanted Dead or Alive (Mekurano Oichi inochi moraimasu) (1970) Dir. Hirokazu Ichimura

Sister Street Fighter (Onna hissatsu ken) (1974) Dir. Kazuhiko Yamaguchi

Sister Street Fighter 2 (Onna hissatsu kenikki ippatsu) (1974) Dir. Kazuhiko Yamaguchi

Sister Street Fighter 3 (Kaette kita onnan hissatsu ken) (1975) Dir. Kazuhiko Yamaguchi

The Black Angel (Kuro no tenshi vol. 1) (1997) Dir. Takashi Ishii

The Black Angel 2 (Kuro no tenshi vol. 2) (1999) Dir. Takashi Ishii

The Princess Blade (Shura yukihime) (2001) Dir. Shinsuke Sato

Azumi (2003) Dir. Ryuhei Kitamura

Azumi 2: Death or Love (2005) Dir. Shusuke Kaneko

"Beautiful Vase Made of Iron and Steel": Michelle Yeoh

One may speculate that without Hong Kong there would have been no Trinity suspended in bullet time in *The Matrix*, no high-kicking *Charlie's Angels*, and definitely no martial arts skilled Deadly Viper Assassination Squad.

Yet, despite the marks of wire works aesthetics and Hong Kong action choreography left on today's action and science fiction films, Chinese actors struggle to catch our attention. After Bruce Lee's death, only Jackie Chan, Jet Li, and Chow Yun Fat have become international male action stars. Odds are even higher when it comes to female heroes. Even if Hong Kong for the last four decades has produced hundreds of female action heroes, few are known in the West. Angela Mao earned a small reputation for her role as Lee's sister in *Enter the Dragon* (1973), which reached an international audience. And after the success of Johnny To's *The Heroic Trio* (1993) Maggie Cheung starred as herself in Olivier Assayas' French meta movie *Irma Vep* (1996), which, among other things, was homage to cinema, spectacle, and female sexuality.[1] But only a single actress has been able to export her action persona from Hong Kong to international territory and at the same time deepen her star persona. This person is Michelle Yeoh.

The Young Yeoh

Where the male martial arts stars *are* experts in martial arts—Bruce Lee, Chuck Norris, Jean-Claude Van Damme, Steven Seagal (who was the first non–Japanese to open a *dojo*, karate school, in Japan)—most female martial arts stars are *not*. They are beautiful, graceful, and skilled (in that order) and Michelle Yeoh is no exception to the rule—even if she would become famous for doing most of her stunts herself.

The five-feet-four-inches tall actress was born to Chinese parents in Malaysia in 1962 and danced ballet from the age of four. At fifteen she went to England to study ballet, but a serious back injury forced her to give up ballet and turn to jazz and contemporary dance. She holds a bachelor degree from London's Royal Academy of Dance and returned to Malaysia in 1983 where she won Miss Malaysia. Her mother had sent her pictures to the contest and convinced her to go. Yeoh (pronounced Yoh) considered opening a ballet school in Malaysia, but then quit dance studies when Jackie Chan invited her to Hong Kong to do a commercial with him in 1984. Here she joined D & B Films Co. and debuted in *Owl and Dumbo* (1984) billed as Michelle Khan.

Yeoh's star persona was from the beginning that of a "new woman": single, strong, independent, and intelligent, with intense energy and willpower. She was no sweet comedienne like Maggie Cheung and no sexy fatale like the late Anita Mui, her two co-stars in *The Heroic Trio* (1993). Her career can be divided into three phases: In the first phase, from 1984 to 1988, she made six films, among them the action movies *Yes, Madam* (1985) and *Royal Warriors* (1986) and the Indiana Jones-inspired adventure film *Magnificent Warriors* (1987). In 1988 she married D & B owner and producer Dickson Poon and, at the height of a career as the most popular action actress in Hong Kong, retired from acting. The second phase began when she returned to film after a divorce in 1992. Her star persona was still that of a strong and single woman, now often frustrated over (the lack of) a romantic relationship. In *Wing Chun* (1994) she plays a spinster, in *The Heroic Trio* her lover dies, and in *Butterfly and Sword* (1993) her love is unrequited. Several of her films in the second phase are *wuxia* films, a chivalric martial arts tradition parallel to the Japanese *chanbara* (swordplay) films, dealing with issues of heroism, honor, and fighting skills. With the dramas *The Stunt Woman* (1996) and *The Soong Sisters* (1997) a third phase began where Yeoh shifted between an action star persona and the persona of a serious actress, alternating between roles in dramas and popular entertainment cinema. International recognition finally arrived when she was cast as Bond's sidekick Wai Lin in *Tomorrow Never Dies* (1997) at the age of 35—the oldest Bond girl ever—and as female sword fighter Yu Shu Lien in Ang Lee's martial arts drama *Crouching Tiger, Hidden Dragon* (2000).

Balls Like a Man

"The Bond woman is a new kind, she is a woman of the nineties, strong, intelligent, and equal with Bond mentally as well as physically," Yeoh commented in interviews when *Tomorrow Never Dies* premiered in 1997.[2]

However, Yeoh had played exactly this kind of woman from her first leading role in the cop action movie *Yes, Madam* (1985).

Yes, Madam opens with a comical scene in which a woman, who turns out to be police inspector Ng (Yeoh), is approached by a flasher in a bookshop. When he exposes himself, she slams a heavy book shut on his private parts with the man screaming in agony. Immediately after, a bank robbery takes place next to the shop and inspector Ng joins the action. She kills one of the robbers, and when the gun is empty she picks up a shotgun from a dead guard and causes an armed money transport to crash. "I am not sure there's any bullets," she echoes Dirty Harry as she aims at a bleeding robber on the ground. "Want to take a chance?" In just three minutes inspector Ng (we never learn her first name) is introduced as an equal to inspector Harry Callahan and also, like Harry, ready to kill rather than arrest criminals. Tough, merciless, agile, and literally throwing herself into the action, her body language is quick and unrestrained, reminiscent of the emerging fitness culture (underlined by her sporty outfits and sneakers) and the fact that she is twenty-three and not, like Eastwood in *Dirty Harry*, forty-one. *Yes, Madam* signals youth, energy, and eagerness.

In the next action sequence, inspector Ng leaps into martial arts when a suspect resists arrest at the airport. His female hostage turns out to be senior inspector Carrie Morris (Cynthia Rothrock) from Scotland Yard who is an expert in martial arts and in Hong Kong to help the police solve the murder of an English accountant, Mr. Dick. The thin plot revolves around inspectors Ng and Morris' attempt to retrieve a microfilm in which Mr. Dick had documented a gangster boss' fraud. The microfilm ends in the hands of three thieves, in the English subtitles named Aspirin, Panadol and Strepsil, who attempt to blackmail the gangster, Mr. Tin (Panadol is played by Hark Tsui, the famous director of *A Better Tomorrow III* and *Once Upon a Time in China*). In the final fight Morris and Ng break into Mr. Tin's house to retrieve the microfilm, save Panadol and Aspirin, and beat up the villains.

According to fight choreographer Craig Reid, Hong Kong's martial arts action films use three classical fight scenarios: MAMs (Many against Many), OHMs (One Hits Many) and triple Os (One on One).[3] The ten-minute-long fight sequence is a variation of the OHM, with Ng and Morris taking on an entire gang armed with sabres and knifes. Cynthia Rothrock is a world champion of several martial arts styles, and many of her movements are shown in full body frame and slow motion to document her ability to do the difficult moves: her signature *scorpion sting*, an over-the-head kick with a straight leg either forwards or backwards, hitting an opponent in the head with her foot, as well as back flips and running up walls to make somersaults in the air. Yeoh, at this time "just" a trained dancer, started picking up martial arts moves on the set from instructors and choreographers, and performed as many of her stunts as possible.

In her second action film, *Royal Warriors* (1986), Yeoh dislocated her shoulder when kicked by an opponent, the first of many injuries. Like Jackie Chan, Yeoh insists on doing her owns stunts if at all possible, attempting to fill a role completely and convincingly. In *The Stunt Woman* she landed on her head when jumping from a bridge and broke her hip and smashed sinews and muscles, and in *Crouching Tiger, Hidden Dragon* a knee injury required complicated surgery which took her away from the set for three months, almost making Ang Lee replace her with another actress. Broken ribs, torn arteries, smashed wrists. Fervor and dedication put Michelle Yeoh above other Hong Kong actresses and appealed to audiences.

Royal Warriors—which, together with *Yes, Madam*, was distributed in the European video market (in some countries as *Ultra Force 1* and *2*)—was even more successful than *Yes, Madam*. The plot evolves around four friends who during the war swear an oath to avenge each other's death. When one of them, a criminal accompanied by the police, is killed on a plane in a failed rescue operation, his death starts a chain reaction of killing and vengeance, with a new killer showing himself as soon as the police take down what they think is the only murderer. Yeoh again plays a Hong Kong police inspector, Michelle Yip, who happens to be on the plane where the first of the four men is killed. With the help of a Japanese policeman, Peter Yamamoto (Hiroyuki Sanada), and air company security guard Michael Wong (Michael Wong), Michelle kills the criminals.

As vengeance, Yamamoto's wife and daughter are killed by a car bomb, and the killer now targets Michael and Michelle. Michelle's boss tells her to watch Yamamoto, as "he is a hardboiled cop in Japan." Yamamoto goes on a private vengeance spree, and when Michelle covers for him, she is suspended from her duties. Michael, the security guard, is a comical figure who is inept at fighting and courts Michelle with flowers. The Hong Kong inspector—single and not the romantic kind—tells him, "You're so childish ... do you think this is all a big joke? Under better circumstances I don't mind playing along with you. But right now I'm not in the mood." At home the lovesick Michael repeats the words to his goldfish. Just as he rises to take action, he is kidnapped by the last killer. In a heroic move, Michael loosens a rope by which he is hanging from a building (he is being used as "bait" by the killer to catch Michelle) and falls to his death yelling, "Have a nice life, Michelle."

What starts as a light action movie with Michelle dancing in the street evolves into a mystery thriller and, with Michael's death, a dark revenge story in the "heroic bloodshed" tradition perfected by Tsui Hark and John

Woo in *A Better Tomorrow* (1986) and *The Killer* (1989). The killer sends Michelle and Yamamoto a videotape with information where to find him and images of Michael's coffin. The killer quickly pacifies Yamamoto and it is up to Michelle to take on the psychopathic villain. The final battle is an example of a triple O, One On One. Arriving in a small tank, Michelle rescues Yamamoto and runs down the pillars supporting the work shed, from where the killer shoots at her. When the shed crashes, they continue fighting in another work shed: The killer attacks with a chainsaw, a huge hammer, a mattock, steel poles, and Michelle takes a savage beating similar to the fights in *Kill Bill*. Slow motion sequences show Yeoh capable of martial arts stunts with high kicks and throws.

Yes, Madam and *Royal Warriors* made Yeoh the most visible and popular female action star in Hong Kong. "Michelle Khan's [Yeoh was billed Khan in the two films] second outing ... inspired countless Hong Kong production companies to cash in with a wave of femme fatale flicks," Rick Baker and Toby Russell write in *The Essential Guide to Hong Kong Movies* (1994). "Few could compete with her gutsy performance—she also did many of her own stunts ... [and] her first two pictures are still regarded as the cream of battling babe movies."[4] The films were retitled *In the Line of Duty* and *In the Line of Duty 2* and became the start of a series of seven films, with the last five featuring ex-dancer Cynthia Khan (whose name was created by combining the names of the two stars in *Yes, Madam*, Cynthia Rothrock and Michelle Khan). Yeoh's last film two films in this period are *Magnificent Warriors* (1987) and *Easy Money* (1987), the first a feminization of Steven Spielberg's *Indiana Jones* films, the second loosely based on *The Thomas Crown Affair*. When she married and retired from films, Cynthia Khan took over the crown as leading action queen.

Back in Action: Frustrated But Not Bitter

A divorce can be an excellent career move. It was for Nicole Kidman and certainly also for Michelle Yeoh, though she never complained about her absence from acting. "I did not believe it was possible to be married and have a career at the same time, that is how I am," she said in interviews after her return. "It was a natural choice for me to put aside my career. When I then divorced, many of my friends pointed out that there was still a place waiting for me in the film business."[5]

The divorce in 1992 sent Yeoh's career spinning faster than Trinity's breathtaking jump out the window in *The Matrix*. When Jackie Chan heard she considered returning to acting, he promptly invited her to co-star with him in *Police Story 3*, where she played Red China police inspector Jessica

Yang (still billed as Michelle Khan) opposite his Hong Kong super cop figure, Chia-chu. The result, according to reviewers as well as fans, was the only Jackie Chan movie where the female co-star outshone the protagonist.[6] By Hong Kong standards, this martial arts action movie about a Hong Kong cop teaming up with a Chinese colleague to catch a drug lord is thin on martial arts and the usual slapstick Chan humor. It is, however, packed with excellent scenes of Yeoh out-fighting, out-witting, and, most of all, *out-stunting* Jackie Chan.

Police Story 3 (1992) opens with a close-up of a painting of the English Queen in the room where Hong Kong and Chinese police superiors debate how to solve the drug problem. They want a "super cop," a wish granted with the arrival of Chia-chu (Jackie Chan) in China. However, as the painting indicates, it is not men but women who rule. This is the premise of the film, which is emotionally driven by the competition and bickering between Chan and Yeoh's characters. Chia-chu is undercover as a small-time criminal who helps the drug lord's second-in-command, Panther (Wah Yuen), escape from a labor camp. As they pass his home village (that is, the home village of Chia-chu's undercover role) Panther insists they visit Chia-chu's family. And now Chia-chu is quite surprised to find inspector Yang posing as his sister. Pretending to be playful he pinches her cheeks hard. Yang immediately punches her "brother" and yells, "You are squeezing me so hard!" The "sister" joins them on the run to Hong Kong and the bickering between the "siblings" continues for the rest of the film. On the ship Chia-chu complains he can't take care of her. "It's an order from above," says Yang, "they told *me* to take care of *you*." "You'll only be my millstone," Chia-chu responds. Yeoh's character immediately replies: "Don't be a male chauvinist!" When Panther appears behind her, Chia-chu slaps her in the face.

PANTHER: What happened?

CHIA-CHU: A womenfolk talks back and I can't stop her.

YANG: [slaps Chia-chu angrily in the face and waves her fist at him] What? Womenfolk? Chairman Mao said women hold half of the sky!

PANTHER: Stop quarreling, you siblings!

Police Story 3 elaborates on Yeoh's "new woman" star persona by casting her as fiercely professional and independent. This time without any trace of romance, her character never smiles to charm or please men, and she is only "girlish" and feminine when posing as Chia-chu's sister. What really knocked audiences out, however, was an action scene where Yeoh leaped a motorcycle from a hilltop onto a moving train. Jackie Chan is famous for choreographing complicated and spectacular action scenes where he performs his own stunts. Yeoh took this cue and the outtakes at the film's end titles showed her performing the motorcycle stunt three times without the aid of a stunt double or wires. Even by Hong Kong standards, this was highly impressive and we do not encounter similar images of female daredevilism in Hollywood. American fans commented on Yeoh's performance:

> She screams screen presence, and her beautiful face belies her hidden deadly martial arts skills. And more significantly she, like Chan, very rarely uses stunt-doubles. (Best example is her jump onto a moving train while riding a motorcycle. Previously a stunt-double tried to do this but failed, ending up with a broken leg. But then Yeoh tried it and hey, perfect jump!) ... we have a woman who is truly independent and can definitely look after herself, thank you very much.[7]

The year 1993 put Yeoh back on the throne of femme action with no less than six (!) films: *Project S*, a spin-off from *Police Story 3* without Jackie Chan but with Yeoh as inspector Jessica Yang; *The Heroic Trio* and *The Heroic Trio 2: Executioners*, two adventure-superhero movies shot almost back to back; and three kung fu period films, *The Tai-Chi Master*, *Butterfly and Sword*, and *Seven Maidens*. In 1994 two films followed: the kung fu period piece *Wing Chun* and *Wonder Seven*, an action film.

What is an absence in *Police Story 3* turns into frustration for Yeoh's future film characters and becomes integrated into her star persona: She is a single woman so devoted to her martial arts that love becomes a problem. A comic approach allows *Wing Chun* director Woo-ping Yuen to tackle the frustration of socially restrictive gender roles directly. Sex, marriage and martial arts are the main themes of the plot. Wing Chun (Yeoh) is a beautiful woman who as a young girl learned martial arts to avoid being forced into marriage. Kung fu, her mother told her, would scare men away and destroy any marriage. Wing Chun was in love with Leung (Donnie Yen), but when he left the village to study martial arts, she chose to become a fighter and can now beat the bandits who regularly attack the village. Because her father thinks she is a disgrace to her family, she lives with her aunt Fong (King-Tan Yuen), who grinds soya beans and sells soya milk and tofu produced from the beans. Then several things happen: Wing Chun rescues a young woman called Charmy (Catherine Hung Yan) from the bandits. When Charmy's husband dies she moves in with Wing Chun and Aunt Fong and becomes the "new sexy miss soya bean" wearing Wing Chun's women's clothes. Wing Chun dresses as a man—"Your muscles grow in all the wrong places" Aunt Fong comments—and when Leung returns he confuses her with a man, thinking she and Charmy are lovers. When he is caught peeping at the two women, he even insists Wing Chun has no breasts: "Why don't you admit it [i.e. that they are lovers], I couldn't see your breasts" "She is not hurt, just heartbroken," says the aunt to Leung when Wing Chun leaves.

Leung, however, has plenty of reason to be jealous as the film hints at

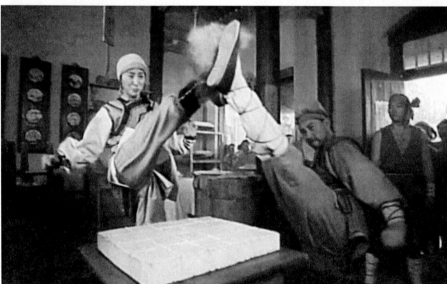

Top: You can't touch this! Wing Chun (Michelle Yeoh) tells a challenger in *Wing Chun* (Woo Ping Films Co Ltd, 1994) that he has won if he can touch her tofu cake, "tofu" being slang for female genitalia. *Bottom:* A fight between Wing Chun (Michelle Yeoh) and a challenger in *Wing Chaun* (Woo Ping Films Co Ltd.) takes place over the tofu cake with combatants kicking over, under, and through the table. The cake, however, remains untouched.

a lesbian love life unfolding in the home of the three women: Charmy gives foot massages that make Fong and Wing Chun groan and wriggle in delight, and in several scenes Charmy and Wing Chun help each other dress and undress. Clearly, the village men take Wing Chun to be lesbian. Maybe because she castrates men—quite literally when teaching the bandit Flying Monkey a lesson. His brother, Flying Chimpanzee, looks at his crotch as he returns bleeding from a fight with Wing Chun: "Now you can concentrate on your kung fu." Later, Monkey cries in frustration, "I have no dick. From where will the children come?" (Also, when she leaves for a fight, Leung yells, "Wing Chun, castrate him for me!") The bandits kidnap Charmy, and Wing Chun must battle Flying Chimpanzee who throws a mighty spear into a rock wall. "If you can get that spear out in three takes, then I'll release her. If not, then you will be here as my wife." The phallic pun on his "champion spear" (a heavy metal spear about three meters long) is intended. "Great, you're really somebody to fight with, don't say that I am not gentle," says Flying Chimpanzee when she wins the fight. Another sexual pun is the soft, white tofu—"tofu" being slang for female genitalia—which is eagerly consumed by the village men who flock to the shop to leer over Charmy.

Misunderstandings are cleared up in the end, women identified as women, and men as men. A female monk (played by famous action actress from the sixties, Cheng Pei Pei) advises Wing Chung to marry and settle down, an unconvincing ending in an otherwise truly gender-subversive film. Director Woo-ping Yuen would later choreograph the action scenes in *The Matrix* and *Crouching Tiger, Hidden Dragon*, and the film benefits from impressive and ingenious fight scenes, as when Wing Chun challenges a fighter to touch a tofu cake placed on a table between the two. Fighting over this cake, tossing it in the air and under tables, is an equilibrist feast of no less quality than anything seen in *Crouching Tiger, Hidden Dragon*.

In *The Tai-Chi Master*, also by Woo-ping Yuen, Yeoh played Siu Lin, a woman whose greedy husband has left her for a wealthy woman. She confronts the husband and his new wife in a restaurant, telling him she no longer regards him a man but a dog. The new wife immediately stars fighting to defend her honor, and the two women have a duel throwing tables and chairs at each other, smashing up the furniture, balancing on tables with only two legs left, and an amazing part with Yeoh using two table legs as stilts, kicking and somersaulting on her stilts. Yeoh's character teams up with the hero of the film played by rising Hong Kong star Jet Li (later making an international name with *Lethal Weapon 4*, 1998, *Kiss of the Dragon*, 2001, and *The One*, 2001) to help the villagers against corrupt Chinese government forces. There are plenty of martial arts, but no romance.

Produced the same year, *Butterfly and Sword* cast Yeoh as Sister Ko, the leader of a group of warriors called "Happy Wood" living in the forest. The plot revolves around Sister Ko helping Eunuch Li retrieve a letter from his enemy, Master Suen Yuk-pak, who is planning to kill the Happy Wood clan so he may rule the martial world. We are in a semi-magical world where Eunuch Li is a monstrous being and it is possible to jump *through* an enemy and use people as arrows shot off by silk bows. The action is impossible, poetic and aesthetically breathtaking, shot in slow motion and with takes from low and high angles, creating a sense of the surreal and mystery surrounding the warriors, who seem to live, fight, and float in the trees, although they have houses (there are several fight-and-float scenes in bamboo trees reminiscent of the later scenes in *Crouching Tiger, Hidden Dragon*). The action, making full use of wires, is graceful and balletic with most of it taking place at night in a dreamlike landscape. The drama is the tragic rectangular love story of three childhood friends who are now adult: Sister Ko is in love with warrior Sing-Wan (Tony Leung), called Sword. He, however, is in love with the young woman Butterfly (Joey Wong). And warrior Yip Cheung (Donnie Yep) is in love with Sister Ko.

Sister Ko is older than Sing-Wan, who regards her as his big sister. She commands the Happy Wood clan, and Sing-Wan accuses her of being selfish and heartless when a female warrior dies in the attempt to fulfill her orders and kill Master Suen Yuk-pak. "I haven't smiled since I was born," Sister Ko cries, "I know, deep in my heart, I don't feel happy. I am always scared." When he still rejects her, she drops her robe and, naked, asks, "Am I not like a woman? Am I not attractive?"

Sister Ko was a homeless child who struggled to become a great warrior and the leader of a clan selling their martial arts skills to those worthy of ruling China. She is a truly modern career woman living in legendary time. A merciless killer who without second thoughts beheads opponents. And a woman tormented by unrequited love. "From now on the world of martial arts belong to us. I hope you will stay by my side," she says to Sing-Wan. But he turns to Butterfly. The ending, due to last-minute decisions to change it in post-production, is unclear. Sister Ko, who is standing on a cliff when Sing-Wan rejects her, turns to the sea—and does she kill herself from sorrow?

Unlike Yeoh's previous films, *Butterfly and Sword* is purely tragic. Hong Kong cinema usually mixes emotions in ways that seem odd to modern Western taste (but is close to silent era movies). Thus, in *Tai-Chi Master* a heartbroken wife turns into a fierce warrior and when she suddenly stops fighting because her husband asks her to, he crashes a chair on her head rendering her almost unconscious. The hero then joins the fight to defend her honor and keep her—comically—on her feet while he returns kicks and punches from the other people fighting. Melodrama, slapstick humor, and action in one scene.

The Heroic Trio by Johnny To similarly mixes humor, tragedy, horror, action, and melodrama in the story of three female superheroes that do not have superpowers but, like Batman, are blessed with super *abilities* thanks to extreme training, the right equipment and—not least—dazzling outfits. Michelle Yeoh is Number 3, also called Invisible Girl, who kidnaps babies from a hospital and brings them to a monstrous Eunuch living in a lair underneath the city. Each baby is born on a lucky day and destined to become Emperor of China. Soon, the Eunuch will choose one of the children and then kill the rest. Wonderwoman (Anita Mui)—the wife of the policeman in charge of the case—is investigating the kidnapped babies case. And Thief Catcher (Maggie Cheung) is hired by the chief of police to find his kidnapped child, which is the last stolen baby.

Floating through the air, the mysterious Wonderwoman throws small, lethal metal wings, is dressed in black, and hides her face behind a silvery half-mask. She is elegant, calm, and kind to children and animals—a scene has her saving a child falling out a window as well as the child's kitten. The light-spirited and totally selfish Thief Catcher, on the other hand, only saves whoever pays well and rides her motorcycle wearing an outfit that is a youthful mixture of stockings, boots, skater gear, and a biker outfit. Humming and chanting, she steals yet another baby from the hospital to lure out the kidnapper. During the fight, however, this baby accidentally dies. Invisible Girl serves the monstrous Eunuch, who has erased her memory and tells her to clear all emotion from her mind. However, she falls in love with the young scientist whose invention—the invisible robe—she is using without his knowledge. She is dressed in a red catsuit and a long red robe. When they at last confront each other in battle, the three superheroes realize they have all been raised and trained by the Eunuch. They decide to unite forces and stop him.

In contrast to the *wuxia* films and the modern police movies there is no attempt at realism or any intention of "authenticating" the actors' martial arts skills. The action is cinematically spectacular and fantastic and is mixed with comic touches and cruelties. An example is when Invisible Girl fights with the Demon (Number 9) guarding the entrance to the lair and cuts off one of his fingers, which he then promptly eats. Another example is that the kidnapped babies are kept drugged in birdcages hanging in the air. Impossible in Hollywood would surely also be the scene where Wonderwoman and Thief Catcher discover a group of cannibal children kept by the Eunuch to become future servants like Number 3 and Number 9. Since they are no longer human Thief Catcher bombs them. The camera focuses on their twitching legs as they die and pee gushes from their crotches during the explosions.

The moral of the film is *not* Western: Invisible Girl is controlled by the Eunuch and has kidnapped the twenty babies (who, by the way, all die in the bombing of the lair), but the plot redeems her—perhaps because she loves the scientist and has found her childhood friendship? She attempts suicide twice but is saved by Wonderwoman and Thief Catcher. Yeoh's role is not as prominent as in her former films—partly due to her character being invisible in the first third of the film—but it is an interesting variation on her frustrated-in-love-but-not-bitter star persona. Again, love is not an option and the scientist is killed by the Demon. In the end Invisible Girl strolls with her friends towards the press to face the world, wearing a new cape and a new self-assurance. Its all about looking good for the cameras, as Thief Catcher concludes. (In fact, a good-looking action sequence between the three women in a warehouse was recycled in Olivier Assayas' meta film *Irma Vep* [1996], where a French director watches *The Heroic Trio* and promptly imports Maggie Cheung [playing herself] to star in his film because Hong Kong heroes is what the mainstream audience wants.)

The mood of *The Heroic Trio* (as well as its sequel *The Heroic Trio 2: Executioners*) is similar to the surreal comic-gothic world of Tim Burton's *Batman* (1989). Where *The Tai Chi Master* and *Butterfly and Sword* were in the *wuxia* tradition *The Heroic Trio* is pure fantasy/adventure inspired by Western movie tradition. This might explain why Hong Kong audiences were not impressed with the film and some of the Western reviewers familiar with Hong Kong cinema hated it. "[T]he film itself is almost defiantly unoriginal ... it pillages Japanese manga and four decades of Chinese pop culture to freshen up its countless borrowings from Hollywood. The result plays like an anthology: ideas and images from Walter Hill, Tim Burton and Luc Besson meet ... 'weightless' action choreography from the King Hu tradition..."[8] wrote Tony Rayns in his *Sight and Sound* review of the film. However, exactly this *mixture* of West and East may explain the cult success in the West: "...the film perfectly fuses the tried-and-true HK action formula (rousing choreography, colorful characters, unyielding camaraderie, fluid cinematography, humor and melodrama in equal portion) to Eastern and Western fantasy elements, creating an irresistible piece of entertainment," wrote *Video Watchdog*.[9] Rick Baker and Toby Russell concluded, "[D]espite some clumsy wire work and confusing plot, it's a fun film. The pace rarely slackens, the fighting femmes are a treat to watch and some of the action scenes are weird as hell..."[10]

Since neither the late pop singer and actress Anita Mui[11] (called the Madonna of the East) nor Maggie Cheung knew martial arts, the kung fu was sidestepped by weird and fantastic action and inventive camera work instead. Humor, Hong Kong cinematography, and Asian beauty united in a hit that, together with *Police Story 3*, familiarized the West with Michelle Yeoh.

Michelle Yeoh's makeup was altered in *Tomorrow Never Dies* (Metro Gold-wyn Mayer, 1997) to change her from Asian action babe to a more conventional international beauty. Still, at age thirty-five, she became the oldest Bond babe in history.

Finally, an International Star

When does one phase end and another begin in the development of an actor's star persona? When new layers or characteristics are consciously added to the existing persona, thus changing it in a career move? When yet unseen qualities are revealed through an actor's choice to take more risky roles that contribute to the growth of her persona? The star persona of Pam Grier proved incapable of development, perhaps, as also seems the case with Stallone and Schwarzenegger, because of a limited talent and the audience's rejection of changes in their star personas. In the case of Michelle Yeoh, however, such change took place when she made the choice to widen her star persona by playing the protagonist in the drama *The Stunt Woman* (1996) and to appeal to international audiences by starring in *Tomorrow Never Dies* (1997).

The Stunt Woman by Ann Hui is one of two Yeoh films directed by a female director (the other, also a realist drama, is *The Soong Sisters*, 1997, by Mabel Cheung). The story about stuntwoman Ah Kam falls in three parts: first she joins director Tung's (Sammy Hung) film production company as a day-to-day hired stuntwoman where she quickly rises to assistant director of action scenes. Then she falls in love with Sam (Jimmy Wong), a young businessman and bar owner, who convinces her to go to China and run his new Karaoke bar. When he falls in love with another woman Ah Kam returns to Hong Kong and her former stunt work. In the film's third part a member of the production company is involved with a gangster murder, Tung is killed when he tries to defend the man, and Ah Kam flees from the gangsters to save Tung's rebellious son, ten-year-old Ah Long (Lo Wing Hang), and takes on her shoulders the responsibility for the boy.

With slow takes and a calm camera which investigates the daily life and working conditions of the film production crew—we see the actors, the manuscript writer, special effects creator, director, the stunt crew, et cetera—*The Stunt Woman* creates a warm and convincing portrait of Ah Kam and contemporary Hong Kong. In a lowbeat realist tone we see her struggle to make a living as a single woman in modern Hong Kong, sharing a small rented room with a girl friend and hiding her job-caused bruises beneath t-shirts. She has no family and Tung wonders why she is single. "Are you married?" "No." "Got a boyfriend?" "No." "Are you gay?" When Ah Kam shakes her head he offers her his crew: "These are a bunch of good guys, you can take one of them and if it doesn't work out send him back, no questions asked." The warm feelings between the older and heavy Tung and the reserved Ah Kam are about to become romantic as Sam enters the scene.

The dramatic conflict with the gangsters disrupts the otherwise realist tone, yet the film showed Yeoh's skills as an actor, not just in the stunt and fight sequences, but also in low-key moments such as her irritation with Tung's nosey son Ah Long when the boy questions her in a taxi—"Whatever you do, don't sleep in my mother's bed." Or the bar scene, where Tung is beginning to make a pass at her as Sam interrupts. Ah Kam looks at them, and we understand this is the moment when she chooses between the men.

Ah Kam is afraid at her return to stunt work and to help her overcome her fear Tung simply pushes her off an eighteen-feet-high bridge where she is to jump down onto a moving truck. In an interview, Yeoh said the film was made as an homage to the Hong Kong stunt people and their hard work and, ironically, a failed stunt from this bridge left her with a fractured vertebra and in traction for a month, by miracle not breaking her back.[12] The outtakes during the titles show the fatal jump where Michelle Yeoh lands on her head and the crew carefully lift her on mattresses into an ambulance, in great pain, unable to move. The film can be read as a comment on Yeoh's dedication to stunt work and on her marriage, which led to retirement and, after the divorce, a return to the film industry. Ah Kam is thus warmly welcomed by Tung's crew who have missed her, and her character earlier explained that Sam didn't want her to continue stunt work. Most important, however, is the elaboration on her star persona which adds realism and intimacy to the portrayal of a woman's fear of commitment, her disappointment at love, and her final acceptance of life's unpredictability: as it is impossible to foresee every danger of the stunt and avoid injuries, so is it also impossible to foresee the dangers of love.

Reviewers agreed to read the film as an experiment with Yeoh's star persona; however, not all judged it a success: "...Ah Kam denies Yeoh's breadth. It ignores her breathtaking capacity simultaneously to span and inhabit such a wide range of gender-inflected personas [cross-dressing and homosexuality in *Wing Chun*, her super feminine role in *The Heroic Trio*, and her manly inspector in *Police Story 3*]. It attempts to squish her into a redefined and conventionalized all-around woman: professional/lover/nurturer. But this only manages to undermine the basis of her charisma."[13] I disagree. The film showed a Yeoh acting low-key in realist film material, radiating star quality in every scene, even those where she wears no makeup and mops a floor. It proved an actress able to span from the surreal, larger-than-life fantasy elements of *Butterfly and Sword* and *The Heroic Trio* to the low-key realism and unadorned life of a Hong Kong working woman.

Impressed with *Yes, Madam*, director Oliver Stone had back in the eighties called Yeoh "my all-time favorite actress."[14] Her international breakthrough in *Tomorrow Never Dies* (1997), however, is her least characteristic movie, glamorizing the star to look like a Bond babe. She enters the plot half an hour into the film at the villain and media mogul Elliot Carver's party. "I like a woman who takes the initiative," says Carver (Jonathan Pryce) hearing she sneaked in without an invitation. Later, when Carver discovers Wai Lin (Yeoh) is a colonel in the Chinese People's External Security Force, he handcuffs her to Bond (Pierce Brosnan), to whom she remains attached in a jump from the top of a skyscraper and on a motorcycle ride at full speed through Saigon. Again, performing many of her own stunts, she impressed the American film crew and made press material on release of the film. Her acting is convincing as the equal of and sidekick to Bond; however, scenes where they (for no reason) shower in the street and when he later rescues her from drowning with a kiss of air, provide a water-glistening, soft-focus Asian beauty uncharacteristic of the star Michelle Yeoh from her Hong Kong films. Makeup slightly changes her broad Chinese facial features into more conventional beauty, and of course she ends up in the arms of Bond. Even when she was married in *Wing Chun*, her character mounted her horse in one jump and, in a playful bedroom scene, her husband had to fight to part her legs. No easy surrender.

However, Yeoh still did a new take on the Bond companion. Where the "bad" Bond babe had been the professional fighter and the "good" Bond babe a feisty yet feminine beauty who relied on Bond's abilities, Wai Lin was an expert in martial arts and worked alone, investigating shipwrecks and mastering advanced computer technology—just like Bond. "Who is driving?" says Bond when they fight over the motorcycle, where Yeoh performed her stunt of crawling *over* Pierce Brosnan and *around* the bike while at full speed. "Are you trying to protect me?" she asks. Later, the action provides Yeoh with an MHO, Many-Hits-One, fight scene as a group of men attack Wai Lin. She eliminates everyone except one man that Bond knocks out. "I could have taken care of him," she coolly says. "But you didn't," Bond replies, eager to regain the upper hand. This action scene was done Hong Kong style with Hong Kong stuntmen and recorded in one take without a stunt double, as Yeoh was used to. Thus, the sound of kicks and hits was from the actual fighting, since Hong Kong stuntmen use no safety margin, but hit each other (though of course controlled and choreographed).[15] According to the film's press material, Pierce Brosnan came to the set especially to watch this scene and afterwards commented, "That was *so* sexy!"[16]

After *Tomorrow Never Dies* the incredible pace of Yeoh's film roles slowed down. She had a minor role in the thriller *Moonlight Express* (1999) before her biggest role to date as the warrior Yu Shu Lien in Taiwanese-American director Ang Lee's Oscar-winning *Crouching Tiger, Hidden Dragon* (2000).

The plot of the martial arts drama concerns three great warriors, two tragic love stories, one stolen sword and *wuxia* virtues: chivalric honor, revenge, martial arts. The story starts when the famous warrior Li Mu Bai

(Chow Yun Fat) retires and asks Yu Shu Lien (Michelle Yeoh) to take his sword, The Green Destiny, to Peking and give it to Sir Te, the protector of their monastery. In Peking, the 400-year-old sword is stolen. The thief turns out to be Jen (Zhang Ziyi), a governor's young daughter about to be married. She has secretly been trained in martial arts by her maid, whose real identity is Jade Fox. And a long time ago, Jade Fox (Cheng Pei-Pei) murdered Li Mu Bai's old master. The emotional center of the drama is the undeclared love between the aging warriors (in their forties). Li Mu Bai is about to declare his love to Shu Lien in a restaurant when they are interrupted, and the words must wait till the end of the film when he lies dying in Shu Lien's arms, shot by Jade Fox with a poisonous arrow:

> LI MU BAI: My life is departing. I have only one breath left.
>
> YU SHU LIEN: Use it to meditate. Free yourself from this world as you have been taught. Let your soul rise to eternity with your last breath. Do not waste it for me.
>
> LI MU BAI: I've already wasted my whole life. I want to tell you with my last breath I have always loved you. [Shu Lien cries and kisses him.] I would rather be a ghost drifting by your side as a condemned soul than enter heaven without you. Because of your love I will never be a lonely spirit.

As we well know from *Wing Chun*, martial arts and marriage are incompatible. The price a warrior pays for independence is love. And just when Li Mu Bai had renounced his warrior life so he could have love, Jen stole the sword.

"You are not married, are you?" Jen asks Shu Lien when they first meet. "What do you think?" "You couldn't roam around freely if you were," Jen concludes. Because she is misguided, Jen thinks she can use her martial arts skills to *escape* her social role as wife and *refuse* the responsibility of the warrior. When attacked by bandits in the desert she had earlier fallen in love with young bandit-hero Lo (Chang Chen) who "roams freely" in the desert. But once she has the sword, she refuses to leave even with him. Li Mu Bai can't bring himself to kill Jen, and when he attempts to convince her to become his pupil and find the path, he is killed. Jen repents. And Shu Lien tells her, "Promise me, whatever path you take in life, be true to yourself." Jen goes to the famous Wudan Mountain where she can be trained and her lover Lo awaits her. "Make a wish, Lo," she says. Lo closes his eyes: "To be back in the desert, together again."

Then Jen jumps from the top of the mountain. Or, rather, gracefully floats into the mist, because *Crouching Tiger, Hidden Dragon* suspends gravity and transforms emotion into movement. The first time it happens comes as a shock and a surprise; Jen steals the sword and Shu Lien attempts to keep the flying thief on the ground. Hong Kong swordplay always used wires and trampolines, but now martial arts are a magical state of mind. A scene where Jen and Li Mu Bai fight in the top of a bamboo forest a hundred feet above the ground, gracefully jumping and balancing on the delicate branches like birds, especially impressed audiences. In mythical Kung Fu, said photographer Peter Pau, "enlightenment is all about lifting, flying ... so we tried to fly with the action ... at human eye-level ... poetic and drama-driven, not action-driven ... not about doing high-flying kicks ... but about high-flying romance."[17]

In *Planet Hong Kong: Popular Cinema and the Art of Entertainment* (2000) David Bordwell describes the fascination of Hong Kong action through the formal analysis of motion. "In the best Hong Kong sequences, we rejoice in cinema's power over the physical world," he says and calls the action "a strategy of expressive amplifications."[18] Through its movement Hong Kong cinema turns emotions into exaggerated motion to capture the audience's attention and transfer emotion from the drama to our senses. "The clarity and rhythmic regularity of the Hong Kong style fulfill one goal of popular cinema—arousing and channeling emotion. Instead of an impassive, restrained realism, filmmakers present a caricature version of the action that aims to carry away the spectator. A fight or chase is given a distinct, vivid emotional profile—ferocity, panic, evasiveness, meticulousness..."[19]

Warrior Shu Lien (Michelle Yeoh) with double swords in Ang Lee's *Crouching Tiger, Hidden Dragon* (Columbia Pictures, 2000). The film borrows its theme and visuals from the Hong Kong action cinema.

In *Crouching Tiger, Hidden Dragon* the emotions relayed through motion are both *wuxian* and Freudian, in the sense that they both represent a person's inner strength or truth, *as well as* that person's repressed emotions, hidden abilities, and bottled-up hate and frustration. An example is the battle between Jen and Shu Lien in the monastery yard, a classical triple-O (One On One). At this point Jen still refuses to return the sword and go to Wudan Mountain. The battle is both Hong Kong and Western in style and content: Like Hong Kong action scenes it uses wires and special effects with the combatants spinning and swirling through the air, somersaulting off walls, smashing the furniture in the yard, using all kinds of weapons—luckily, posed on the wall is a selection of spears, swords, hatchets, et cetera. However, the space is oddly constricted to the square of the monastery yard, which symbolizes the restricted (repressed) space (emotions) of Shu Lien. Shu Lien wins the fight but, like Mu Bai, can't bring herself to kill Jen who floats/flies out of the yard. Jen represents youth's desperate urge for freedom, ecstasy, intoxicated with skill, strength, eagerness, but without the experience of the older woman. She does not have the responsibility which comes with *wuxia*; great skills call for great self-sacrifices—the dilemma and tragedy of the Eastern warrior.

Crouching Tiger, Hidden Dragon is homage to poetry and cinema rather than to love or *wuxia*. Why does Jen not choose Lo? Why did Mu Bai not choose Shu Lien? Because they love the beauty of martial arts, graceful floating, suspended in air. Because they prefer motion to emotion. "Fusion cinema" is the apt headline of an article by Peter Culshaw comparing *Crouching Tiger, Hidden Dragon* to fusion cooking and fusion music.[20] The film *is* a fusion of Eastern cinematography and *wuxia* with Western ideology. Its mixing of bits and pieces from East and West—wuxia and wirework with the two intertwined Romeo-and-Juliet-plots—is the result of a globalization of media which thrives on translocating national elements into new international products. Thus the film is in Mandarin, which neither Chow Yun Fat nor Michelle Yeoh speaks— but it felt more authentic, even if the actors had to learn every line by having them read out loud. Culshaw disliked the "California-isms" and "current liberal Hollywood world-view" of the film.[21] However, popular cinema has always renewed itself by taking inspiration from the spectacular and commercial. Motion and emotion sell. The grace of martial arts and the cinematography of Hong Kong reached a mass audience through Ang Lee's Oscar-winning film, which became the highest grossing foreign-language film released in the U.S.

Star Struggling

Like Western actresses, Michelle Yeoh wanted control over the development of her star persona and her future roles and therefore founded the

All grace, beauty, and wire motion in a femme one-on-one fight scene between older warrior Shu Lien (Michelle Yeoh) and the young thief Yen (Zhang Ziyi) in *Crouching Tiger, Hidden Dragon* (Columbia Pictures, 2000). (Courtesy of the British Film Institute.)

film production company Mythic Films. However, the first two productions (co-produced with Media Asia), the adventure film *The Touch* (2002) by Peter Pau and the science fiction action film *Silver Hawk* (2004) by Jingle Ma, lack the honest tone of Yeoh's Hong Kong movies as well as the quality of her international pictures. It is not always wise to let an actor control his or her star persona. Some succeed in handling their own star personas—like Clint Eastwood—but many fail—like Pam Grier, Geena Davis, and Demi Moore— misjudging the emotional match between a film, its audience, and the actor. What the audience likes about an actor does not necessarily correspond to what the actor wants to give the audience.

Michelle Yeoh is exceptional in Hong Kong cinema, which so far has provided Hollywood with new action choreography and with male actors and directors. Like most of her female colleagues, she entered the film business through a beauty contest. However, unlike them she developed a strong star persona based not on beauty or sexiness, but on female independence and strength, and on the ability to perform physical action. She gained a cult following by uniting the qualities of Jackie Chan and Chow Yun Fat: Physical action and a cool acting style. In Hong Kong one of her nicknames is Gang Tai Hua Ping, "beautiful vase made of iron and steel."[22] So far, she has lived up to that name. Her intense dedication to action and acting made possible her leap from the East to the West and has earned her a place in today's fusion action cinema.

Michelle Yeoh Filmography (Selective)

English titles are those under which a film is commonly known. Hong Kong movies are often retitled several times, like Wong ga jin si *(1986) known as* Royal Warriors, In the Line of Duty, Police Assassins, *and* Ultra Force. *Chinese titles are from the Internet Movie Data Base.*

Yes, Madam (Huang gu shi jie) (1985) Dir. Corey Yuen, filmed in Hong Kong. Inspector Ng, police action

Royal Warriors (Wong ga jin si) (1986) Dir. David Chung, filmed in Hong Kong. Inspector Michelle Yip, police action

Magnificent Warriors (Zhong hua zhan shi) (1987) Dir. David Chung, filmed in Hong Kong. Fok Ming-Ming, adventure

Police Story 3 (Jing cha gu shi III: Chao ji jing cha) (1992) Dir. Stanley Tong, filmed in Hong Kong. Jessica Yang, police action

Project S (Chao ji ji hua; Police Story 3 Part 2; Once a Cop; Supercop 2) (1993) Dir. Stanley Tong, filmed in Hong Kong. Jessica Yang, police action

The Heroic Trio (Dung fong saam hap) (1993) Dir. Johnny To, filmed in Hong Kong. Ching/Invisible Woman, fantasy/superhero

The Tai-Chi Master (Tai ji zhang san feng) (1993) Dir. Woo-ping Yuen, filmed in Hong Kong. Siu Lin, kung fu/period piece

Butterfly and Sword (Xiu liu xig hu die jian) (1993) Dir. Michael Mak, Dong-kit and Michael Mak, filmed in Taiwan and Hong Kong. Sister Ko, kung fu/period piece

The Heroic Trio 2: Executioners (Xian dai hao xia zhuan) (1993) Dir. Siu-Tung Ching and Johnny To, filmed in Hong Kong. Ching/Invisible Woman, fantasy/superhero

Seven Maidens (Wu xia qi gong zhu; also called Holy Weapon; Seven Maidens) (1993) Dir. Jing Wong, filmed in Hong Kong. Ching Sze/To Col Ching, kung fu/period piece

Wing Chun (Yong Chun) (1994) Dir. Woo-ping Yuen, filmed in Hong Kong. Yim Wing Chun, kung fu/period piece

The Wonder Seven (7 jin gong) (1994) Dir. Siu Tung-Ching, filmed in Hong Kong. Ying, action

The Stunt Woman (Ah Kam) (1996) Dir. Ann Hui, filmed in Hong Kong. Ah Kam, drama

The Soong Sisters (Song jia huang chao) (1997) Dir. Mabel Cheung, filmed in Hong Kong, Japan and China. Soong Ai-ling, drama

Tomorrow Never Dies (1997) Dir. Roger Spottiswoode, filmed in UK and U.S. Colonel Wai Lin, Bond movie

Crouching Tiger, Hidden Dragon (Wo hu cang long) (2000) Dir. Ang Lee, filmed in Taiwan, HK, U.S. and China. Yu Shu Lien, historical drama/kung fu

The Touch (Tian mai chuan qi) (2002) Dir. Peter Pau, filmed in Hong Kong, China and Taiwan. Yin Fei, adventure

Silver Hawk (Fei ying) (2004) Dir. Jingle Ma, filmed in Hong Kong. Lulu, action/adventure/sci-fi

Memoirs of a Geisha (2005) Dir. Rob Marshall. Mameha, drama

Failed Female Hero?
"Queen of Martial Arts"
Cynthia Rothrock

"The Biggest Star You Never Heard Of" was the headline of an article in *The New York Times* in 1994 illustrated by a photo of American actress Cynthia Rothrock smiling and doing a high kick above her head, dressed in a laced, black bodysuit.[1] I came across the article in 1998, when I was doing research on Sylvester Stallone at the Margaret Herrick Library in Los Angeles. In 1990, it turned out, he had broken a contract to do *The Executioner*, which would co-star the unknown Cynthia Rothrock. This was the closest Cynthia would come to Hollywood stardom.

The article wondered why fame had evaded Cynthia. Like martial artists-turned-actors Chuck Norris, Jean-Claude Van Damme, and Steven Seagal she was an expert in martial arts: from 1981 to 1985 she was an undefeated Karate World Champion in Forms and Weapons and held black belts in the Korean styles *Tang Soo Do* and *Tae Kwon Do*, in the Chinese style *Eagle Claw*, in contemporary Chinese style *Wu Shu*, and in the classical Chinese style *Northern Shaolin*. In 1985 she was the first Westerner to become a movie star in Hong Kong's cinema, and by 1990 she had made fifteen movies, eight of them in Hong Kong. Today, she has made more than forty-five movies, nearly all martial arts action movies. Numerous fan sites are dedicated to her on the Internet where she is known as "Queen of Video" and "Queen of Martial Arts." Her films are regularly programmed on American cable television and pay channels. And at the age of forty-eight she still does action movies. So why have most people never heard of Cynthia?

Cynthia Rothrock is an instructive example of the ambiguous pleasures, anxieties, and restrictions surrounding the female hero in a man's world. Her career demonstrates that women *do* conquer new territory. However, it also shows us the strategies deployed to contain them.

Hong Kong

Rothrock's movie career is the result of old-fashioned Hollywood "luck"—being in the right place at the right time—as well as of a series of misplacements and miscued representations, or, being in the wrong place at the right time and, later, in the right place at the wrong time.

She was born Cynthia Ann Christine Rothrock on March 8, 1957, in Scranton, Pennsylvania. At thirteen she started taking lessons at the private gym of her parents' best friends who recognized her talent and encouraged her to enter open karate competitions. In 1981, at the age of twenty-four, she was a World Karate Champion in Forms and Weapons and traveled around the US and the world to show her skills. Winning hundreds of trophies she was featured in newspapers and magazines and was on the cover of "virtually every martial arts magazine in the world," among them *Black Belt Magazine* (US), *Budo Karate* (Japan), *Sushido* (France) and *Kicksider* (Germany).[2] She performed with weapons such as the Chinese double broad swords, staff, Chinese nine-section steel whip chain, Chinese iron fan, and an assortment of Okinawan Kobudo and Japanese Bugei Weapons.[3]

Her film career was incidental. "At the time, I was on the first professional demonstration, the West Coast Demo Team. We were known all around the USA. One day, the then editor of *Inside Kung Fu* magazine called the team leader and said that a Hong Kong company [D & B Films] was looking for a new male lead to be like Bruce Lee. Since there were a few girls on the team he decided to bring everyone ... When my name was called I did some forms, weapons, and self defense techniques."[4] The producers were so impressed with the small, blonde fighter—Rothrock is five feet three—that they signed her on the spot and changed the role from male to female. It was for *Yes, Madam* (1985) co-starring Michelle Yeoh.

In Hong Kong, Rothrock turned out to be a unique combination: blonde, female, *and* a skilled fighter. Sammo Hung, the famous actor and director who produced *Yes, Madam* (and like Jackie Chan also a skilled fighter), said about Rothrock, "Cynthia made a tremendous impact in that film and in *Shanghai Express* and *The Inspector Wears Skirts*. It wasn't just that she was a Western woman doing martial arts, but that she was performing Chinese kung fu so well!"[5] Timing was perfect as Hong Kong's femme fatale action cinema was in the process of exchanging films set in a legendary or historical past with contemporary police stories.

Rothrock appeared in major as well as minor roles: While *Yes, Madam* would be her biggest hit in Hong Kong, she also starred in *Above the Law* (1986) and *The Blonde Fury* (1989), and had minor fighting roles in *The Millionaire's Express* (1986), *The Magic Crystal* (1986), *The Inspector Wears Skirts*

(1988), and *No Retreat, No Surrender 2: Raging Thunder* (1989). Production time is short in Hong Kong where film companies make the most of an actor's popularity. Foreign actors are fresh faces for half a dozen films after which the novelty has worn off. Also, cycles of similarly themed films are short-lived, encouraging a fast production rate.[6]

Rothrock was cast as a professional single woman who was always the equal of her male colleagues. Neither her gender nor her fighting skills had to be "explained," since female heroes and martial arts were common in Hong Kong action cinema. Rothrock would play a police inspector or special agent from Great Britain or the U.S. who had been invited to Hong Kong (a British colony until 1997) to investigate some crime with international ties (drugs, mob crimes, counterfeit money). As typical of Hong Kong cinema, plot and character development were secondary while action was the main attraction. Here, Rothrock's talents were showcased with impressively choreographed fights. Thus, in his book *Planet Hong Kong: Popular Cinema and the Art of Entertainment* (2000) David Bordwell analyzes a scene from *Above the Law* (1986) as representative of Hong Kong action: Using just twenty-four seconds and eighteen shots, Rothrock is shown fighting and handcuffing four opponents to a chair using one set of handcuffs.[7] American action films will often employ the technique of filming a punch with several cameras, then editing together several takes of the same movement

Cynthia Rothrock (right) and Michelle Yeoh (left) were teamed as British and Chinese police inspectors in the Hong Kong action film that made them both stars, *Yes, Madam* (D & B Films, 1985).

(the MSSQUE method—pronounced "misque"—Many Shots, one Strike, QUick Edit) to create the impression of speed.[8] This is typical of scenes with a fighter like Van Damme. Hong Kong also uses image manipulation to convey speed—slow motion, fast motion, fast editing—however, action choreography strains to stage inventive fights in new ways. In *Yes, Madam* Rothrock did the split ups up against walls and flashed her signature kick, *the Rothrock sting* or *scorpion sting*: immobilized by a larger opponent she kicks her leg straight above her head, thus hitting the opponent in the head with her foot while standing erect, a difficult kick which demands agility.

Skill was essential in the marketing of Rothrock. In *The Magic Crystal* (1986) the villain Karov comments on his opponents' fighting techniques, telling a victim, "You're using Chinese spear Yun Chun boxing, but you're not proficient enough. Now your ribs are broken." During his duel with the heroes Karov asks Cindy (Rothrock), "Eagle claw?" Indeed, Rothrock *did* use the characteristic Eagle Claw style in which she had a black belt—and Richard Norton, the actor playing Karov, was also a karate black belt who had fought Norris several times on screen. The fighting—even if unrealistically staged to showcase the fighters' skills and entertain audiences—was thus based on *real* abilities. In *The Blonde Fury*, where Rothrock played the film's protagonist and best fighter and was the first Westerner to single-handedly open a film in Hong Kong, she did an MHO (Many Hits One) fight scene on a bamboo scaffold swarming with opponents attacking her from the windows, from behind and from the front. Her character, Cindy, runs down the scaffold's aisles, climbs down ladders, and when she is completely surrounded by men with weapons, hacks the bamboo with an axe thus causing a large section of the scaffold with the attackers to fall, then uses the long bamboo sticks to gracefully jump down from the tall building and land in the street below. Another impressive scene in *The Blonde Fury* was a fight on a huge rope-web, hanging down from the ceiling and reaching the floor, like a spider's web. Years later, Rothrock singled out this scene: "We did a week of fights on the ropes. It was very difficult. The ropes were hard and would burn your legs when you bounced off them. All the bruises were worth it though, because I thought the fight scene was brilliant."[9]

Authenticity, skill, and difficult stunts performed by the actress were characteristic of Rothrock, just as they also were with Michelle Yeoh, as I discussed in the previous chapter. Often Rothrock was cast as *tougher* than her Asian colleagues. Thus in *Yes, Madam*, Ng (Yeoh) must restrain Carrie (Rothrock) from beating an arrested criminal and in *The Inspector Wears Skirts*, Lo (Rothrock) is called in to aid in the training of a group of police-women. Rothrock's character has them run through fire to teach them to run faster and jump through real bullets and bombs to move quicker!

Cynthia Rothrock impressed audiences with her martial arts in *Yes, Madam* (D & B Films, 1985), where she did her scorpion kick and—here—split ups against the walls.

In 1989 Hong Kong film company Golden Harvest decided it was time to launch Rothrock as an action star in the US.[10] *China O'Brien* (1990) and *China O'Brien II* (1991) were co-produced by Raymond Chow, founder of Golden Harvest, and directed by Robert Clouse, who had earlier directed Bruce Lee in *Enter the Dragon* (1973) and Jim Kelly and Gloria Hendry in *Black Belt Jones* (1974).

A Female Martial Arts Hero in America

The relocation from Hong Kong to America can be read as a theme of misplacement in Rothrock's American movies: First, her *martial arts skills* are now a problem which is addressed, explained, and often toned down. Down toning was done, for instance, by pairing her with a male (never female) fighter, often the tall, Australian actor Richard Norton with whom she did ten films. An English magazine even aptly dubbed Rothrock and Norton the "Fred Astaire and Ginger Rogers of Martial Arts movies."[11] Second, Rothrock's *star persona* was Americanized, softened, and naturalized by uniting her Hong Kong type—the professional single woman—with a female stereotype: She was now both a professional *and* a daughter raised by a father figure—in *China O'Brien*, *Rage and Honor*, and *Lady Dragon*—or a *Death Wish*-style vigilante avenging the death of a relative, often a husband, as in *Lady*

Dragon, Guardian Angel and *Outside the Law*. Third, the films would address the "problem" of her *masculine* skills colliding with a *female* body using strategies of narrative explanation, erotization, and marginalization.

The Exotic Skills

China O'Brien (1990) is representative of what happens when East meets West. As Yvonne Tasker has pointed out, even the female hero's name is composed to link opposites: the Asian "China" meets the immigrant-Irish "O'Brien."[12] Immediately addressed in the opening scene are the female hero's skills: China teaches a martial arts class and when a student drinks water during training she corrects him (as I know from my daughter's karate, visits to the bathroom and drinking must be done before or after class). "All this fancy shit don't mean nothing on the street, I'd like to see you enter

Transferring action stardom from Hong Kong to Hollywood would prove difficult for Cynthia Rothrock. In *China O'Brien* (Golden Harvest, 1990) martial arts champion Rothrock starred as a sheriff's daughter taking on her father's murderers. *China O'Brien* was combined with a sequel in 1991. The box office of the two films did not convince Hollywood Rothrock was destined for stardom. (Courtesy of the British Film Institute.)

the blood," he dares her. She instructs him—and the audience—that "martial arts is an art form, it's not just about kicking and punching," yet agrees to meet his gang to prove the efficiency of her "art form." As she later fights attackers in the dark alley, she comments on each of her moves.

> [two guys attack China who throws them to the ground]
>
> CHINA: Now, that was *aginake*.[13]
>
> ATTACKER: Hey, wanna play rough, bitch?
>
> CHINA: [twists the third attacker's arm] *Sogate*—with a little pressure you can break the fingers. [A fourth guy attacks and is immobilized by China] *Shionage*—can cause dislocation of the shoulder or the elbow. [A fifth attacker is taken down] *Hokinake*—with perfect timing an opponent can be thrown off-balance. [A sixth attacker is kicked] That was a *lotus* attack. If you have any questions, please see me later. [China hits a seventh attacker with a metal fence] Use all available weapons, a simple right cross ...

A karate teacher enters the alley and interrupts, "China, this fight is for real, these aren't Termite's gang!" The opening scene introduces her as exceptionally skilled in an exotic combat style and relocates her to an American setting, where men will attack a woman simply because she is alone in a dark alley, tapping into Western fears of women as targets of sexualized violence in the male urban space of the big city. China's defense proves that women need not be passive and helpless (as the helpless women in dark alleys saved by RoboCop and Catwoman—"You make it so easy for them, don't you?" Catwoman sneers at the woman). Yet, the scene also shows that the urban streets *remain* male territory since a woman without China's skills would have become a victim.

Inexplicably, the men attack one at a time instead of all together. When an attacker has no fight skills, a fight will last only as long as it takes one person to knock out the other. In Hong Kong, everyone is skilled and fights are meticulously choreographed to be long and visually stunning. In *China O'Brien*, the martial arts are basic (China "demonstrates" the moves) and serve only to introduce Rothrock's skills. The American audience is "instructed," like China's student, to pay attention and be impressed.

Good Girl or Bad Girl?

If Rothrock were unique in Hong Kong, she was even more so in Hollywood. There had simply never been a woman like her. After having made the mistake of rejecting mega star Bruce Lee, Hollywood had learned to "cope" with the martial arts skills of male heroes through strategies of *Americanization* (the outspoken nationalism of Chuck Norris),[14] *erotization* (the masochistic beating scenarios in Van Damme's films), and *naturalization*

(Seagal's successful incorporation of Eastern fighting techniques into Western settings). This, however, was in relation to men for whom violence was considered "natural." What about a woman?

In Hong Kong, women would fight against men as well as women, but in America the symmetry of male heroes confronting male villains became the asymmetry and cross-gender scenario of a woman—Rothrock—confronting men. Could fighting skills be presented convincingly without masculinizing her in the process? Would and could a male audience identify with a female hero who beats up men like a male hero would? When men fight, such scenes were ripe with homophobic and homoerotic elements. When women fought women—as occasionally happens in the action cinema (*Cleopatra Jones*, *Red Sonja*, *Charlie's Angels: Full Throttle*)—such scenes were also ripe with homophobic elements (villains were butch or lesbian) as well as using the female hero as erotic spectacle. The questions of spectacle and sexuality were complicated further by the fact that Rothrock did not remove her clothes for the camera. This was in contrast to (female as well as male) colleagues in the American action cinema where undressing became a key to success. However, Rothrock did not want her body to be an erotic spectacle in the Mulveyan sense, but wanted to focus on her martial arts skills. And she wanted fights to be realistic, which was why she preferred fighting men. "When I fight women, I have to go pretty easy. So it doesn't look as powerful—and as realistic."[15]

Where Rothrock fighting men had been a natural thing in Hong Kong, it became a sensitive issue in America. In 1990, four years after Sigourney Weaver returned as a Rambo-esque Ripley in *Aliens*, but still on the brink of femme action cinema, the question was: is the female martial arts hero a real woman? "I bet you like beating up on men, don't you?" a scared guy accuses China in *China O'Brien II* (1991). "It's tough, sometimes, being a woman," China responds enigmatically, neither confirming nor denying his allegation that she takes pleasure from "beating up on men."

Rothrock's entire production of films, however, is extremely careful about linking pleasure to her martial arts. The specter of "unnaturalness" was countered by various strategies of which the first was *stereotyping*. Let us return to the fight in the alley, which ends with China shooting an attacker, who turns out to be merely a child. Vowing never to touch a gun again, she resigns her police job in the big city and returns to her mid–West hometown, where her father is the sheriff. When he and a deputy are killed by local crime lord Barlow (Stanton Davis), China runs for sheriff and is elected. With the help of old friend and ex-special forces Matt (Richard Norton), China confronts Barlow and his gang in what is essentially the same plot as in *Black Belt Jones* and *Sheba Baby*, where daughters also avenge killed fathers.

Aware that Rothrock's skills would place her in-between conventional gendered bodies and identities, the producers cast her as an archetype (the daughter) and provided her with a boyfriend (Matt). China is not a stranger in this town; she is its daughter and welcomed by the citizens who in the beginning of China O'Brien II award her a medal for making the town "one of the safest in America." At the public ceremony a little girl tells her, "When I grow up I want to be like you."

Of the archetypes—the dominatrix, the rape-avenger, the Amazon, the daughter, and the mother—the daughter is the least threatening to men. I have not seen every American Rothrock movie, but am basing this discussion on China O'Brien, China O'Brien II, Rage and Honor, Rage and Honor II: Hostile Takeover (both 1992), Lady Dragon (1992), Guardian Angel (1994), Sworn to Justice (1996) and Outside the Law (2001). Here, Rothrock is never cast as a mother and there are no children to be saved, as otherwise is the trend after Ripley rescues little girl Newt in 1986. Neither was Rothrock cast as an Amazon or as a dominatrix, the most independent and erotic of the archetypes. Instead, she was essentially always a good girl. If not in the archetype of the daughter, then as a policewoman or agent whose husband or fiancé is killed. Her characters are "educated" and trained by the law, and their skills developed to serve and protect an institutionalized, patriarchal system. This is a naive and uncritical version of the daughter, who does not question the law or the jobs to be done. Unlike rebellious daughters like Foxy Brown, Nikita, Nina, or Lara, Rothrock's characters never oppose the system and when they become vigilantes, they don't turn the system's shortcomings into a critique of the system as such. They are, like Chuck Norris' heroes, loyal to friends, society, and nation.

Low budget action cinema, however, is based on action and pleasure, and it is revealing how this "pleasure" is defined erotically in contrast to Rothrock's Hong Kong action movies. Thus, because Rothrock's Good Girl stereotypes do not provide much erotic pleasure, a pack of Bad Girl and Bad Boy stereotypes are written into the plots as villains, sidekicks, and minor characters. These prostitutes, strippers, evil femme fatales, lesbians, as well as well-hung male villains function as erotic and kinky eye candy. Where Rothrock's characters are "good and decent," the Bad Girl characters are "bad and sexualized." In China O'Brien the good-bad dichotomy is found in the bar scene where a woman, who is drinking with the boys, challenges China to a fight. Another Bad Girl character is Barlow's wife, who seems to endure his beatings because he has power and money, but kills Barlow in the final confrontation. She serves to underline Barlow's perverse character and provide erotic frisson as a beaten and sexualized spectacle (she is twice seen tied to the bed with Barlow threatening her). A long stripper scene in

China O'Brien II has the same visual function; appearing in the opening of the film, a woman strips to music in front of a man, then pulls out a gun and shoots him. Such images of beautiful and aggressive women—here a blonde in black underwear and high heels—are obviously contrasted to the decently dressed China who only uses her skills for self-defense.

When the *China O'Brien* movies failed to attract mainstream cinema audiences, Rothrock's future movies were aimed at the video market, and the erotic dimension was noticeably developed. In *Rage and Honor* and *Lady Dragon*, both from 1992, Bad Girls and Erotic Boys are prominent. In *Rage and Honor* Rothrock plays a daughter and a sister—the plot has her and a brother, Conrad Drago (Brian Thompson), raised by a Chinese *sensei* (teacher). When Conrad kills their parents' killers, the sensei rejects him. In return, Conrad kills the sensei and becomes a corrupt person who now uses his skills to torture and kill. Kris (Rothrock) uses her skills to help and protect. Surrounding female hero Kris are a number of erotic stereotypes: Evil Boy Conrad, fit and with naked torso; Good Boy Preston (Richard Norton), also fit and fighting without his shirt; the Evil Femme Fatale Rita with a gun, Conrad's lethal girlfriend in red dress and high heels; and finally Evil Lesbian Hannah and her gang of sexy lesbians who fight, steal, and kill for money. "This gotta be a gag!" hero Preston moans, when he first encounters a flock of killer women in jeans-rags and black underwear a decade before *Sin City*'s (2005) similarly dressed lesbian criminals. Later, Hannah puts him in a cage, removes his shirt, and orders him to fight Kris. "The Gutless Wonder from Down Under versus The Blonde Banshee," she announces the fight to her laughing gang. It may be a gag, but it is also a convention of low budget action films that evil women function as sexy dominatrixes, who are allowed to cross conventional borders of gender because they function within sexual role-playing. We shall return to the theme of sexual role-playing in chapter 9 dealing with the Amazon.

Hannah (Alex Datcher) is an example of crossing traditional borders of gender in the frame of sexual role-playing. Hannah is a lesbian and a well-proportioned mulatto, sexy, and playful ("Hannah *likes* this," she purrs when watching a fight, referring to herself in third person). She acts "butch" (that is, masculinized), but is visualized as a "femme" lesbian (that is, in feminine terms). Judith Halberstam refuses to speak of good and bad stereotypes per se, but singles out the "true" type as "a type, in other words, that does exist within the subculture."[16] "Stereotypes," Halberstam says, "are not in and of themselves right or wrong. Rather, they represent a particularly economic way of identifying members of a particular social group in relation to a set of quickly recognizable characteristics."[17] Hannah is an example of the evil sexy lesbian, who is not "true" in the sense of referring to a social type within

Promotion still of Cynthia Rothrock and Australian co-star Richard Norton in *Rage and Honor* (IRS Media, 1992). During the nineties, Cynthia Rothrock adjusted her no-sex-only-action image to suit American taste: softer, sexier, and exposing more skin, quite a different figure from her characters in her Hong Kong films. (Courtesy of the British Film Institute.)

society, but is an erotic type from sexual role-playing. A role-playing, that is, where men look at or have sex with women as part of heterosexual, not homosexual, desire. Like Barlow's beaten wife, Hannah is a "bad" and "sexualized" woman, here cast as dominatrix instead of victim. Hannah orders killings, stages fights, and takes pleasure in watching. But she functions on behalf of the male audience as part of sadomasochistic pleasure.

The villain's girlfriend, the sexy Susan (Bella Esperance) in *Lady Dragon* (1992), is another example of an evil lesbian. When Ludwig has Kathy's husband killed on the stairs of the church just after their wedding, Kathy leaves the CIA to get vengeance. She infiltrates Ludwig's organization by befriending Susan. Clearly, this is a sexually charged friendship; Susan picks up Kathy in the street and invites her to live in Susan's home, she provides Kathy with clothes and a job. Late at night Kathy tucks a drunk Susan into bed. Susan is unhappy, because Ludwig prefers beating younger prostitutes to having sex with her. When Kathy reveals her true identity, Susan is furious about her "lies" and sends her a message from Ludwig with the words, "Paybacks are a bitch, aren't they, Sugar?" Three times Susan attempts to plant a kiss with a finger from her lips on Kathy's, with Kathy each time blocking her hand. This is the closest I have seen Cynthia Rothrock come to fighting a woman in her American films.

Another erotic stereotype in Rothrock's movies is the evil sadist. He is physically strong, evil, and takes pleasure in causing pain. In American film he is also an erotic spectacle, whose body is as fit as the hero's. This figure belongs to the scenario of male masochism. In the action cinema the hero will eventually rise to the occasion, return an opponent's blows, and make an impossible comeback from having been broken to winning the fight. This is the recurring scenario of underdog-heroes Stallone and Van Damme, who are matched with bigger opponents who have equally fit and strong bodies. (In Van Damme's movies the opponent is often black as a further sign of perversion.) Villains Conrad in *Rage and Honor* and Thor in *Rage and Honor II* are such figures. The archetype of the evil sadist originates from Leopold von Sacher-Masoch's novel *Venus in Furs* (1870), where a figure called "The Greek" whips the masochistic protagonist with such efficiency that he "cures" him of being a masochist.[18]

The evil sadist is a common stereotype in the action movie where he represents homoerotic pleasure as well as homophobic unease. Because he so obviously addresses a male audience, he is rare in mainstream femme fatale action cinema. In low budget femme action cinema he still addresses a male audience, however, sometimes in two versions. The blonde and gigantic Thor (Ron Vreeken), who fights Preston three times in *Rage and Honor II* but is not pitted against Kris (Rothrock), represents homoerotic and masochistic pleasure. Ludwig in *Lady Dragon*, who beats, rapes, and later is pitted against Kathy in a fight, is an attempt at modifying the evil sadist from representing male masochism to representing the more traditional male sadism. "I could give you pains the likes you have never imagined," Ludwig threatens Kathy and then rapes and beats her: "So since you like to act like a whore, I'll be happy to accommodate you."

The Action Body and the Problem of Gender

"Plot? What plot? ... 'Martial Law' has some nice fight scenes, although none stand out as being anything special. It is entertaining, and all that really matters is we get to see Cynthia Rothrock and Chad McQueen in plenty of butt-kicking action."[19] As this comment on the Internet makes clear, fans do not enjoy Rothrock movies because of their plots but because of the action scenes. Martial arts movies are, like the action genre as such, about able bodies. Their mission is first and foremost to facilitate the *performance* of the body and to demonstrate the fighters' *abilities*. Another fan commenting on the film *Tiger Claws* (1992) laments that "this genre is plagued by production values, acting and direction, which puts it only one peg above porn, if that ... Cynthia Rothrock's abilities are accomplished, but her acting is limited. Bolo Yeung still doesn't seem to have mastered English, although I always enjoy his performances."[20]

The references to porn and performance in the latter quote indicate that the body is a sexual spectacle. However, this spectacle *is* at the same time a story. Linda Williams in her essay "Film Bodies: Gender, Genre, and Excess" (1991) examines the body in porn, horror and melodrama, calling these "body genres" because they display bodies "jerking" in a strong affect which we—the audience—are supposed to mimic (to "jerk off" to a porn movie, the melodrama as "tear jerker," and the horror movie as "fear jerker"). Williams links each of her body genres to a psychological "question," which forms the nucleus of the genre as well as of the audience's fascination, "There is a link, in other words, between the appeal of these forms and their ability to address, if never *really* 'solve,' basic problems related to sexual identity." In horror, says Williams, the question or "enigma" is that of "sexual difference," in melodrama it is that of "the origin of the self," and in porn the enigma is "the origin of sexual desire."[21]

The action movie—and within this genre especially the martial arts movie—is a body genre, where audiences enjoy the performances of bodies and share their excitement. English film scholar Richard Dyer has called the viewer situation a "surrender to pleasure" and compared this to sex. "The favoured position of hardcore fans for watching action movies in the cinema is slumped in the seat with legs slung over the seat in front. This is an excellent position for anal sex as well as for cunnilingus and fellatio. Come to think of it, for the male viewer action movies have a lot in common with being fellated."[22] Elsewhere, I have discussed the action movie as a body genre and described its "enigma" or "basic problem" as the fantasy of a Utopian masculinity which escapes Oedipal castration.[23] Or, in other words, the action hero's masculinity is that of an adolescent who refuses to "grow up" and enter adulthood. The action hero is fixed in *pre-Oedipal desire* (he wants love and recognition from a "good" father, that is, a pre–Oedipal and dyadic father) and *Oedipal conflict* (he keeps having conflicts with "bad" fathers, villains, "evil" systems, that is, the castrating Oedipal father). To put it simply: the action hero embodies the fantasy of remaining all-powerful, almighty, and invincible despite suffering castration and despite entering adulthood, experiencing the reality principle, and operating in society. The action movie, like Schatz's genres of rites of orders, tells of a hero's rites-of-passage which do *not* result in a passage into adulthood. The hero remains a hero—and as Robert Warshow has phrased it in relation to the hero in the western, "What could he 'get ahead' to? By the time we see him, he is already there."[24]

In the action cinema, this story of a Utopian masculinity comes in two versions. First, it can be *physical* as in Van Damme's films where the hero overcomes obstacles (villains, bombs, problems) by using his body. The male body is tested to the limit of death, resurrected, and (miraculously) proves victorious. Or, second, the story can be both *mythological* and *physical*, as is often the case in the films of Stallone and Norris, whose heroes save the nation with physical (and miraculous) performances. Thus, the male action hero may save his honor (*Bloodsport*, 1988), the nation (*Invasion U.S.A.*, 1985), or the Earth (*Armageddon*, 1998)—but in either case his resource is his body.

This is where the female action hero is a problem. Heroes will save the day, the nation, and the Earth, but (with Ripley as an exception) women do not make mythological heroes. They are demoted to minor missions: saving a child (*Aliens*), a family (*Outside the Law*), themselves (*Nikita*), avenging a personal injustice (a popular motive across genres from rape-revenge to action), or, if the tide is high, saving a child plus a family plus themselves plus a small town (*The Long Kiss Goodnight*). If they save more than that, it ceases to be personal. Thus, Lara Croft does not want to be thanked, in contrast to Rambo, who furiously demands that his nation recognize him. Despite their training and fancy outfits, women retain this aspect of serving as "angels of the threshold" rather than roaming warriors. We will return to the issue of narrative and body in the next section of this study, "Into the Action." At this point in our inquiry into female heroism, mythology is not yet an issue, since Cynthia Rothrock belongs to the first narrative of Utopian masculinity: the story of an invincible body.

In *Spectacular Bodies* Tasker describes the female version of the male rites-of-passage in action movies as "the heroine's transformation through the body" which is accomplished through "changing appearance" (which can be a change of clothes as well as pose) and "the women's increasing ability to 'handle themselves'," as when Ripley becomes a soldier even if she earlier in *Aliens* claims, "I'm not a soldier." Or Thelma and Louise's transformation from rape victims to killers, robbers, and feminist fugitives. Tasker is right in pointing out transformation as central to the female hero. Cynthia Rothrock, however, is different from other female heroes. Why? Because, like the hero in the western, she is already "there." Like her male colleagues she does not need to learn anything, only to show her abilities. And it is exactly in these situations that the *performance* of the action body collides with the *gender* of the female hero. "[R]ather than swapping a biological identity for a performative one, she personifies a unity of disparate traits in a single figure," Jeffrey A. Brown writes about the female action hero.[25] However, this "unity of disparate traits" is not at ease in the figure of Rothrock. "At a fundamental level every action heroine, not just those who are explicitly sexualized, mobilizes the specter of the dominatrix," Brown further claims.[26] But again, in Rothrock's case issues of spectacle, performance, and body are complexly coded.

First, the *way* Rothrock applies her martial arts is defensive rather than aggressive. An example is when Hannah wants Kris and male sidekick Preston to fight each other in *Rage and Honor*. Preston refuses and Kris starts attacking him—"Are you afraid to fight me because I am a woman? You are tough. Show me how tough you are. Fight! Fight!"—to prevent Hannah from killing him. Rothrock's characters thus often fight to *protect*. We rarely see Rothrock's opponents bleed or die, in contrast to the male sidekicks and their opponents, who bleed and die spectacularly. Rothrock's world championships are in the categories Forms and Weapons, categories where the fighter doesn't actually fight but performs sets of movements. This "soft" version of martial arts is again in stark contrast to the presentation of the skills of a star like Seagal, who claimed the fights in *Above the Law* (1988) were "more real than any action ever seen on film, the techniques are exactly what would be used in these situations—very simple, very street, very lethal moves."[27] Rothrock never made claims of reality or of being invincible (like Bruce Lee who supposedly was never beaten in a fight). The authenticity of her skills is folded back into her body (Rothrock *has* the physical abilities), rather than aimed at other bodies (as are Seagal's physical abilities; significantly, his signature martial arts scene is breaking an opponent's bones with a loud "crack"—the sound underlining that Seagal has the ability to *hurt* opponents). This way, even if Rothrock has masculine qualities (her fighting skills), those qualities are presented and used in a "softer" way than her male martial arts colleagues. When she fights Preston in the arena, Kris performs "spectacular" moves (somersaulting high over him and using ropes to rebound) to distract the audience, while Preston uses simple, direct moves. The martial arts element in Rothrock's American films plays to both readings; her character can beat any man, yet her fights are less aggressive than the men's.

Also, Rothrock's body offers another example of the unease about the "unity of disparate signs" and in-betweenness. Usually, the action hero's body is an erotic spectacle, whether the hero is male or female. When male, such spectacle is ripe with homoerotic and homophobic tension ("You're kind of pretty. I don't know if I wanna fight you—or fuck you," says a villain to Van Damme in *Lionheart*). When the hero is female, the narrative is often twisted to legitimize showing as much skin as possible (supermodel Milla Jovovich's strap costume in *The Fifth Element* is a particularly revealing example, but short dresses, torn clothes, or underwear will also do the job). Rothrock, however, would not remove her clothes for the camera.[28] She would not be a sexual spectacle, not even in terms of the "musculinity" which Tasker discusses in relation to Linda Hamilton's trained body in *Terminator 2* and Sigourney Weaver in *Aliens*. "In order to function effectively within the threatening, macho world of the action picture, the action heroine must be masculinized. The masculinization of the female body, which is effected most visibly through her muscles, can be understood in terms of a notion of 'musculinity.' That is, some of the qualities associated with masculinity are written over the muscular female body. 'Musculinity' indicates the way in which the signifiers of strength are not limited to male characters."[29] Rothrock's movies *never* draw attention to her muscles.

The female hero's body becomes a paradoxical object: Female, yet not a sexual spectacle, fit for fight, yet not aggressive. The in-betweenness can be traced in the customizing of the female hero. In the above scene, Hannah tears off Preston's t-shirt and turns him into a male pin-up (naked torso showing his taut muscles glistening with sweat). The big-breasted Hannah is herself also a traditional sexual spectacle: tight black corset, torn shorts, stockings, black gun. And evil red-haired Rita, bitching with Hannah, is yet another spectacle. Amidst all these erotic bodies, Kris is dressed conservatively in long pants and a polo neck sweater, as if refusing to be any kind of female object for the male gaze. Indeed, customizing Rothrock seems a bigger challenge to producers than coming up with a plausible plot or good acting.

Her costumes in *Guardian Angel* (1994) sum up the basic dilemma of Rothrock's career: What story is there to tell of a woman who already *has* the perfect skills? What kind of woman is the fighting female hero—is she a "real" woman? And how can she be eroticized if her body cannot be used as a spectacle? Rothrock plays police officer Christine McKay investigating counterfeiting. When her police fiancé is killed by female villain Nina (Lydie Denier), Christine quits the police and works as a bodyguard. A new client, playboy Lawton Hobbs (Daniel McVicar), wants protection from his psycho ex-girlfriend Nina (the same Nina who killed Christine's fiancé), and Christine protects Lawton, kills Nina, solves the counterfeiting, becomes Lawton's new girlfriend, and is reinstated in the police. This development can be traced over her costumes: In the beginning, costumes are either gender neutral—tight sweater, loose trousers, heavy shoes—or butch femme—black, tight pants and short-sleeved tight, black top. After the fiancé's death, her

The changing costumes of Cynthia Rothrock in *Guardian Angel* (PM Entertainment Group, 1994) reflect the gender ambiguity of her martial arts hero, oscillating between butch, masculine, and feminine. Here bodyguard Christine McKay (far right) meets millionaire client Lawton (far left) in baggy jeans, cap, and heavy shoes, a stark contrast to the dozens of bikini-clad babes Lawson surrounds himself with.

From butch to feminine. McKay (Cynthia Rothrock) ends in a costume signaling high-class elegance with a slightly masculine touch (the black trousers) in *Guardian Angel* (PM Entertainment Group, 1994). She's dressed for fight *and* for a millionaire boyfriend.

costumes become masculine: bulging shirts, heavy boots, badly fitting jeans, cap. Christine's personal crisis results in defeminization and men begin to question her skills. "I didn't think a bodyguard could be a girl—do you think you can handle it?" a potential customer asks and is promptly kicked out of her trailer. Playboy Lawton, surrounding himself with bikini-clad babes, also questions her choice of job:

LAWTON: How does a woman as attractive as you get to be a cop?

CHRISTINE: Now see, that's charming. A bit sexist ...

LAWTON: [interrupts] A little sexism keeps a woman on her toes.

CHRISTINE: Typical male statement.

LAWTON: Typical female reaction. Men and women are different. Why do you want them to be the same?

CHRISTINE: Who said I want them to be the same? You know, I didn't want to be a cop forever. I thought some day I'd raise a family. It just didn't turn out like that.

Ironically, Lawton and Christine agree that for a woman to be a cop and have a family are choices excluding one another. A corrupt cop voices the same opinion to Lawton, "I've got to ask you something: Why would a man want a female bodyguard? Shit, where's your pride?" As Christine falls in love with Lawton, her costumes are refeminized and even promoted from working class to upper class (a white, two-piece suit, a riding outfit). This is an ambiguous statement on the linking of biological gender and social gender: Domesticated through love, Christine is allowed back in the police force, and domesticated through "proper" feminine clothes she makes it into Lawton's bed.

Rothrock's characters often operate in this psychological space of loss and promise; a family has not yet been instated, but when or if it is, it will surely change the female hero. Until then, she remains a woman in a vacuum.

"Queen of Video"

In 1985, *Time* wondered about Chuck Norris, "Norris is not magnetic ... his popularity, all in all, is curious. The hard-core audience does appreciate his athletic bona fides ... But the question remains: Why is Chuck Norris a movie star?"[30] The answer at the time was that Norris possessed the fighting abilities a Western audience was eager to see. Once competition got tough and the star older, he was demoted from film star to television star.

Why, then, is Cynthia Rothrock *not* a movie star? After almost fifty films, she remains unknown outside the connoisseur circles of low budget martial arts movies. When I searched shops in Los Angeles nobody knew her name, and I had to mail order her films. I believe two factors worked against her. The first was unlucky timing. In 1985, the twenty-eight-year-old Rothrock was unique in Hong Kong where no competitors were blonde or had her skills. In 1990, however, she was thirty-three and trying to enter a film industry with heavy competition: Norris had starred in karate movies since 1977; Van Damme had just entered Hollywood with *Bloodsport* (1987), *Cyborg* (1989), and *Kickboxer* (1989); and Seagal made his first action movie, the successful *Above the Law*, in 1988. Also, as we will explore shortly in the next section, women had just entered the adventure and action film with Brigitte Nielsen in *Red Sonja* (1985) and Sigourney Weaver in *Aliens* (1986).

The second and perhaps more important factor was that in Hollywood different rules apply for the two genders. Clint Eastwood, squinting and with crooked teeth, could become a movie star. Stallone with a speech defect, an unmagnetic Norris, and a Schwarzenegger with heavy accent. All were laughed at by film reviewers, yet made it due to either acting skills (Eastwood) or unique bodies (Stallone, Norris, Schwarzenegger). Rothrock, who is not a trained actress, did not possess a natural acting talent. With male actors, such a lack was compensated for by their physique. In such case, the star would shamelessly exploit his body as an erotized spectacle, which Rothrock didn't. Linked to the issue of spectacle is that of beauty. "Beauty" is a normative judgment, yet a physique which adheres to certain aesthetic and social norms is institutionalized as a necessary quality of the female star. Even Michelle Yeoh was a beauty queen before becoming an actress, and Meiko Kaji was praised as a classical Japanese beauty.

With a long nose, small eyes, and a slightly stocky body, Rothrock is no classical Hollywood beauty. Furthermore, her body is trained for fight and not for show, as were the "hardbodies" of Hamilton and Weaver. Rothrock's physique is not built according to aesthetic norms, like today's female stars who go through exhausting fitness programs to "shape" their bodies. Later, Rothrock would compromise about being an erotic spectacle. Comparing earlier and later films, Rothrock's breast size changed and in the mid-nineties she tried "softening" her image by undressing almost nude for a photo session in *Femme Fatales Magazine* in 1995. *Sworn to Justice* (1996) promised audiences the star as they had never seen her; in one scene Rothrock performs martial arts movements in a negligee and her character is much more erotic than earlier. At this point, however, Rothrock was thirty-nine, an age where undressing becomes risky. Fans disagree whether it was a good idea. "It's obvious they wanted the character to come off as sexy but it doesn't work. Dressing a wholly unattractive dumpy 40 year old woman in short skirts and heels certainly isn't fooling me," was one reaction to *Sworn to Justice*.[31] Another blamed her co-star: "Not only is he [Kurt McKinney] a very bad actor, but also too much time is devoted to their unbearably cheesy 'romance' ... as if we rented this to see a no-name moron in the fight scenes instead of Cynthia Rothrock."[32] Some fans found her irresistible. "Cynthia is unbelievably sexy in this and the film overall stands out as one of her best achievements." Many of her "serious" fans dedicating time to her Hong Kong films as well as her martial arts career were skeptical as to sexing up the star. "...I was a bit dismayed that a woman who has resisted gratuitous nudity in her films for ten years posed for some fairly cheesecakey pictures. She says she's trying to soften her image a bit. My only question: why?"[33]

Stallone offered no explanation why the contract to do *The Executioner* was cancelled. Also, we can only wonder why Rothrock was not paired with another martial arts star (would it be too overwhelming with two star fighters in one film? Van Damme thus chose to star with himself in *Double Impact*, where he played twins). "There hasn't been a real female action star yet, so I think at this point the studios don't want to put a whole lot of money into someone like me," said Rothrock in 1994. "They'll say: 'Oh, I don't know.

Can she be the hero's girlfriend?'"[34] The two *China O'Brien* films failed at launching Rothrock as a new female action hero to cinema audiences, and judging from Internet sites and comments on her films, Rothrock has been unable to attract a female audience. Men, however, accept her for the very same reasons they accept other martial arts stars: convincing performances, authentic skills, and impressive fights. In 1993 Rothrock told *Newsweek*, "I get lots of letters from young men. They say I make Jean-Claude Van Damme look like a wimp."[35] Even people who dislike her films like her fighting: "Her acting skills are almost laughable ... still her fighting scenes are awesome. This movie seems as if it was written just for her, due to the martial arts scenes. But I would definitely say Cynthia has to stick to her martial arts and not her acting career."[36]

In a postfeminist age, Cynthia Rothrock offers an intricate case of in-betweenness, intended as well as unintended. She is muscular, yet refuses to be "musculinized." She is a woman, yet not a conventional Hollywood beauty and for many years refused to be erotized. And when she was rejected as a female hero by mainstream Hollywood, she in turn rejected roles as "the hero's girlfriend." As "Queen of Video" she invented her own brand and refused to be domesticated by Hollywood as well as by the men in her films. And male fans love her this way.

Cynthia Rothrock Filmography (Selective)

Yes Madam (Huang gu shi jie) (1985) Dir. Corey Yuen, filmed in Hong Kong. Inspector Carrie Morris, police action

The Millionaire's Express (Foo gwai lit che) (1986) Dir. Sammo Hung Kam-Bo, filmed in Hong Kong. Bandit, multi-genre adventure

Above the Law (Zhi fa xian feng) (1986) Dir. Corey Yuen, filmed in Hong Kong. Cindy Si, action

The Magic Crystal (Mo fei cui) (1986) Dir. Jing Wong, filmed Hong Kong. Cindy Morgan, adventure

The Inspector Wears Skirts (Ba wong fa) (1988) Dir. Jackie Chan, filmed in Hong Kong. Special agent Madam Lo, action comedy

No Retreat, No Surrender 2: Raging Thunder (1989) Dir. Corey Yuen, filmed in Hong Kong and the U.S. Helicopter pilot, action

Blonde Fury (Shi jie da shai) (1989) Dir. Hoi Mang and Corey Yuen, filmed in Hong Kong and the U.S. Cindy, action

China O'Brien (1990) Dir. Robert Clouse. Sheriff China O'Brien, action

China O'Brien II (1991) Dir. Robert Clouse. Sheriff China O'Brien, action

Honor and Glory (Zong heng tian xia) (1992) Dir. Godfrey Ho, filmed in Hong Kong and the U.S.

Tiger Claws (1992) Dir. Kelly Makin, filmed in Canada and the U.S.

Rage and Honor (1992) Dir. Terence H. Winkless. Kris Fairfield, action

City Cops (Miao tan shuang long) (1992) Dir. Chia Yung Liu, filmed in Hong Kong and the U.S.

Martial Law II: Undercover (1992) Dir. Kurt Anderson

Angel of Fury (1992) Dir. Ackyl Anwary, filmed in Indonesia.

Lady Dragon (1992) Dir. David Worth, filmed in Indonesia. CIA agent Kathy Gallagher, action

Rage and Honor II: Hostile Takeover (1992) Dir. Guy Norris, filmed in Indonesia and the U.S. Kris Fairfield, action

Lady Dragon 2 (1993) Dir. David Worth, filmed in Indonesia.

Irresistible Force (1993) Dir. Kevin Hooks. Television movie

Undefeatable (1994) Dir. Godfrey Ho, filmed in Hong Kong.

Guardian Angel (1994) Dir. Richard W. Munchkin. Police officer Christine McKay, action

Fast Getaway II (1994) Dir. Oley Sassone

Portrait in Red (1995) Dir. T.L. Lankford

Eye for an Eye (1996) Dir. John Schlesinger

Sworn to Justice (also called Blonde Justice) (1996) Dir. Paul Maslak

Deep Cover (1996) Dir. Nicolas Celozzi

The Dukes of Hazzard: Reunion! (1997) Dir. Lewis Teague

Tiger Claws II (1997) Dir. J. Stephen Maunder, filmed in Canada.

Night Vision (1997) Dir. Gil Bettman

The Hostage (1998) Dir. Bryan Tod (no information)

Tiger Claws III (1999) Dir. J. Stephen Maunder, filmed in Canada.

Manhattan Chase (2000) Dir. Godfrey Ho, filmed in Hong Kong.

The Untouchable 2 (2001) videogame, produced in Canada and the U.S.

Never Say Die (also called Outside the Law) (2001) Dir. Jorge Montesi. Television movie, filmed in Spain.

Bala Perdida (Lost Bullet) (2003) Dir. Pau Martínez, filmed in Spain.

Redemption (2003) Dir. Art Camacho

Sci-Fighter (2004) Dir. Art Camacho

PART THREE

Into the Action

Sigourney Weaver:
The Alien Series and
the Mother Archetype

Ripley is a heroine like no other. She thrills you. Her powerful
presence and unstoppable soul will always live on in the minds
of movie-goers. She and Newt form a surrogate mother-daughter
relationship that is more touching than anything I've seen before
in the "Alien" series ... She's the perfect action hero.
—Fan on the Internet[1]

The striking image of a sweat-glistening Sigourney Weaver as Ripley
dressed in military outfit with an M.41A pulse rifle held high in one arm
and a ten-year-old girl clutched tightly in the other arm became an instant
icon of female heroism in 1986. Critics were divided as to whether James
Cameron's blockbuster hit *Aliens* was feminism or not but audiences were
ecstatic, unanimously concluding "Ripley is the template for the modern
action heroine" and that she was "one of the greatest heroines of all time."[2]

Lieutenant Ellen Ripley from the *Alien* series is the origin of what I
call the mother archetype. She is the prototype after which later mother
heroes—Sarah in *Terminator 2: Judgment Day*, Charly in *The Long Kiss Goodnight*, Mace (played by Angela Bassett) in *Strange Days* (1995), and Beatrix in
Kill Bill—are fashioned. A unique combination of masculine and maternal
qualities made Ripley the first female hero to initiate a film series and reach
mythic proportions. As we will see, the maternal holds a paradoxical position: A mother figure generates the haunting scenarios which made *Alien*
an acclaimed horror film; but she is also the hero turning *Aliens* into a blockbuster hit praised by fans as the best action movie ever.

The series, consisting of *Alien* (Ridley Scott, 1979), *Aliens* (James
Cameron, 1986), *Alien 3* (David Fincher, 1992), and *Alien: Resurrection* (Jean-
Pierre Jeunet, 1997), is unique for several reasons: First, if we define a series

as more than two films, it is the only Hollywood film series with a female hero. In 1973 and 1975, Warner tried to market black model Tamara Dobson as agent Cleopatra Jones but cancelled a planned third film, and in 1990 and 1991 a series with martial arts champion Cynthia Rothrock as sheriff China O'Brien was abandoned. Second, after the success of *Alien*, the ambition was not "merely" to entertain but also to produce films by auteurs of popular genre cinema (David Fincher was not an auteur at the time; however, he replaced action director Renny Harlin who left *Alien 3*). Finally, the series was able to cross genres. Unlike the Bond films or series like *Halloween*, *Alien* took its ensemble cast—Ripley, the alien, an android, the Company—from horror to action movie, to drama, and to fantastic cinema. Like the alien adapted to new environments, so Ripley proved herself capable of adapting to new genres and new conceptions of the female hero.

Monster, Mother, Other

What we can call the "origin story" of the mother archetype starts with Ridley Scott's science fiction and horror movie *Alien* from 1979. Both science fiction and the horror genre offer metaphorical narratives of Otherness in the form of aliens and monsters, and at first glance *Alien* did indeed look like the science fiction tales from the fifties, which was what most critics saw. "*Alien* ... is, of course, our old friend the fifties monster movie all dressed up in posh new clothes."[3]

The plot starts as the crew on the commercial towing spaceship the *Nostromo* has their hypersleep interrupted by "Mother," the ship's computer, who has intercepted a transmission of unknown origin from planet LV-426. The crew consists of seven people: Captain Dallas, pilot and lieutenant Ripley, co-pilot Lambert, science officer Ash, Kane, and engineers Brett and Parker. When Dallas, Lambert, and Kane investigate the transmission on the planet, they find a crashed spaceship with a fossilized pilot. The pilot's chest looks as if it, mysteriously, has exploded from within. At the *Nostromo* Ripley (Sigourney Weaver) deciphers the transmission and discovers that it is not an SOS, but a warning. When the astronauts return, one of them, Kane (John Hurt), is infected with an alien life form and Ripley denies them access to the ship due to quarantine regulations. Ash (Ian Holm) overrules her and opens the doors. During dinner before takeoff, an alien life form suddenly bursts from Kane's chest, killing him and escaping in front of the eyes of the shocked crew. With uncanny speed the small alien grows into an adult monster with molecular acid for blood, killing off the crew one at a time. As they desperately attempt to kill the monster, they discover Ash is an android carrying out Mother's secret order: "Bring back alien life form

... Crew expendable." As the last survivor with the cat Jonesey, Ripley abandons and blows up the *Nostromo*. When she discovers the alien has followed her aboard the rescue vessel, she flushes it into space through the air lock and finally enters hypersleep.

On the surface this looks like a traditional bug hunt narrative. However, on closer inspection, another figure hides inside the monster plot. Not an alien life form, but a familiar figure: Mother. From the computer operating system Mother to the perverse male "pregnancy," and to the organic alien design, *Alien* was saturated with images of conception, birth, bodily fluids, phallic and vaginal forms, and offspring. Most striking was the birth of the alien in the "chestburster scene," which was the scene that convinced 20th Century Fox to invest in Dan O'Bannon and Ron Shusett's script. "[T]hat was the one scene, the pivotal scene, that made everyone sit up and take notice," said associate producer Ivor Powell.[4] Everyone imagined the pregnant astronaut as a man; in the script every character was meticulously written as gender neutral to underline that gender was unimportant in the future, but on page one was noted that "one or two characters could be female to reach a broader audience."[5] Thus, the script did not suggest two characters be *male*, which underlines that "neutrality" be read as "male."

The chestburster scene was the seed from which the idea to *Alien* had sprung and around which the plot had been developed in collaboration between Dan O'Bannon and Ron Shusett. The chestburster idea originated from one of nature's dramas, which had haunted O'Bannon for years: He had heard how a female wasp paralyzed a spider, laid her eggs on its body, and then buried her victim alive in the ground to serve as food for her hungry larvae once they hatched from the eggs. What if this were to happen to a human? In *Alien*, astronaut Kane is the only human host. But excised from the film were scenes where Ripley discovers two crew members, Dallas (Tom Skerritt) and Brett (Harry Dean Stanton), in a storage room where they had been paralyzed by the alien and glued, or cocooned, to the walls with sticky residue to serve as hosts for future aliens. The paralyzed spider from O'Bannon's vision had become paralyzed *men*.

The chestburster scene and the vision of the wasp laying her eggs on a spider were deeply disturbing images of procreation. Barbara Creed in *The Monstrous-Feminine* points out that a "mother" body must be responsible for producing the alien eggs. The alien spaceship which Dallas, Lambert (Veronica Cartwright), and Kane find on LV-426 was designed organically in the form of a horse shoe with two protruding "legs" between which were vagina-shaped openings. The astronauts enter down tunnels with walls made of huge bones and organic tissue, a dark, vaginal abyss leading to a circular room where the floor is covered with three-feet-tall eggs waiting to be "activated." Kane enters this symbolic uterus and when he touches an egg, a creature inside it with a long tail, a probe in the middle, and a vulva-like body smashes his helmet screen and orally rapes and impregnates him with its alien life.

The connection between Freud's conception of *Das Unheimliche* and the family as monstrous is well established in psychoanalytic film theory. The real monster in *Psycho* is the mummified Mother who, when alive, in cannibalistic fashion had swallowed her son. The uncanny—*das Unheim-liche*—is the once familiar which is repressed and returns as alien and unrecognizable. The uncanny is the once homely (*heimlich* meaning both homely and secret) returning to us in monstrous form. That which we repudiate is that which is most intimate to us. Rhona Berenstein in "Mommie Dearest: *Aliens, Rosemary's Baby* and Mothering" (1990) points out that Otherness is relational as well as oppositional. The boundary between us/them and between "I/it" is blurred, because Otherness "points to the 'defining' subject—as a mechanism for defining subjectivity in relation to an/other—and as it stands in opposition to that subject—Other than the 'I' at times connoting an object of fear, derision, hatred."[6] In patriarchy, argues Berenstein, "Mother ... serves as a conspicuous signpost of the blurred division which stands between the western Self and its projected other."[7] In patriarchy, man conceives of himself as the Father, "the ultimate creator and social progenitor." But "being of woman born he must, if not deny that fact, then transcend it."[8] Men fear the maternal body because they are born from it—the female body as uncanny—and because patriarchy is unable to duplicate its generative qualities. "[N]o matter how hard patriarchal culture tries, it still can't reproduce without mothers."[9] At least not in 1979 and in 1986. In *Alien: Resurrection* (1997) the clone returns as man's attempt at duplicating Mother's generative ability.

"Mother" lurks in *Alien*'s conception of maternal places and images of birth. We find not one but two wombs: one is the alien spaceship with its dark uterus, its organic design, and the pulsating eggs; the other womb is the inside of the *Nostromo*. "Mother" gently wakes up her "children" in a circular room, where sleep pods are placed in a circle forming a white, technological "womb" that is both parallel to and in contrast to the organic, alien "womb." "In outer space, birth is a well controlled, clean, painless affair. There is no blood, trauma or terror,"[10] says Creed of *Alien*'s first birth scene when the crewmembers emerge nearly naked from the sleep pods, stretching and slowly moving their limbs to make the blood circulate in their bodies. The second birth—the alien bursting through Kane's chest in splashes of red blood—is the repressed "bloody" version of this first "anemic" birth.

Corresponding to the two maternal places and births—the alien and the human-made—are two images of a Mother and of Motherness as Otherness. The first is Mother, the man-made operating computer system. The second is the absent alien mother, a figure we do not see but whose existence is indicated by her eggs and by the alien design by Swiss artist H. R. Giger, famous for his dark and sexually evocative "biomechanical world," as he called it.[11] This design combined male and female genitals in the various stages of a hermaphroditic alien: first a female egg; next, the "facehugger" combined a phallic tail and probe with a vulva-shaped body and spider-like fingers evoking the snakes on Medusa's head; third, the infant alien looked like an erect penis with teeth; and, fourth, the adult alien had two sets of jaws, a small jaw sliding in and out from inside a larger jaw, evoking a penis (this is especially obvious when Ripley undresses to enter a spacesuit, while the alien moves its inner jaw in and out, salivating and hissing in excitement). The deleted scenes with the two cocooned men indicate that the alien was meant to be a hermaphrodite that could reproduce itself from just one specimen. Without the deleted scenes, it is less obvious that the creature is a hermaphrodite; however, the subversive design of its biology is clear. The male (Kane) is a passive host to life, not an active participant, but a recipient and a container. Man is without control over conception, birth, and offspring, he is not even a Father and genetic supplier.

Psychoanalytical theory, says Creed, imagines the figure of the woman/mother in opposition to the man/father and as part of the patriarchal family. The mother can be a pre–Oedipal *dyadic* mother with whom the child has an intimate relationship. The dyadic mother is "good" when she feeds, caresses, and protects her child, and she is "bad" when she weans it or suffocates it with too much attention. Or the mother figure can be an Oedipal *triadic* mother who is part of the father-mother-child triad. In psychoanalytic theory, the Oedipal mother is a castrated "object of sexual jealousy and desire"[12] who is controlled by the father. The Oedipal mother is "good"—that is, castrated—when she accepts her place as object, and she is "bad" when she takes the father's place as castrator. In fiction, the mother is often composed of several "mothers"; thus the mother in *Psycho* is both a dyadic mother "swallowing" her son and an Oedipal mother killing the son's love objects.[13]

In *Alien*, says Creed, we find traces of an *archaic mother*, which various cultures have imagined as existing before patriarchy. She is "the generative, parthenogenetic mother—that ancient archaic figure who gives birth to all living things ... [I]f we posit a more archaic dimension to the mother—the mother as originating womb—we can at least begin to talk about the maternal figure as outside the patriarchal family constellation. In this context, the mother-goddess narratives can be read as primal scene narratives in which the mother is the sole parent. She is also the subject, not the object, of narrativity."[14] The archaic mother is an oceanic mother, the life-generating force of nature we find in various religions. This is the Greek Gaia, in China called Nu Kwa, in Sumer named Nammu. Within patriarchy, says Creed, she is imagined as a primeval black hole "which threatens to reabsorb what it once birthed."[15] Patriarchy is terrified of the archaic mother because she signifies a generative femininity *outside* the masculine. "[T]he primeval mother does not need the male as a 'father', only as a host body, and the alien creature murderously gnaws its way through Kane's belly. Its birth leads to the male mother's death."[16]

The two mothers are inversed versions of maternity: To the "safe" technical design of the *Nostromo* corresponds the "dangerous" organic design of the alien spaceship. To the "safe" bright world ruled by Mother corresponds the "dangerous" and desolate LV-426 with howling wind and eternal night. However, from the first sign of the alien—the transmission—borders between alien and human, good and bad, male and female, dissolve. The alien mother is fertile where Mother is sterile. And the alien protects its species where Mother sacrifices the crew for profit. "They must have wanted the alien for the weapon's division," Parker suggests. The alien is an archaic mother uncontrollable by patriarchy, Mother is man-made and controlled by The Company, a Father substitute that turns out to be much more deadly than the alien ("You don't see them fucking each other over for a percentage," Ripley will later say in *Aliens* when the Company representative Burke tries to have her impregnated with an alien and returned to Earth).

While borders dissolve between alien and human bodies, other borders are restored. The absence of gender returns in perverse forms when the android Ash attacks Ripley by rolling a pornographic magazine into a tube and forcing it down her throat—reminiscent of the alien probe down Kane's throat. And when the alien kills the other female astronaut, Lambert, the camera shows a long black tail with a nasty-looking hook reaching up between her legs. In perverse fashion gender is restored to normal: Women rapable and Ripley vulnerable when she faces the alien in her underwear.

Ripley is not a hero in *Alien*. The horror genre has victims and survivors, not heroes. She is instead a typical example of Clover's Final Girl who is "watchful to the point of paranoia; small signs of danger that her friends ignore, she registers. Above all she is intelligent and resourceful in a pinch ... The Final Girl is boyish, in a word. Just as the killer is not fully masculine, she is not fully feminine..."[17] Ripley was originally conceived as a male character and it was Fox that suggested the lead character could be female. Dan O'Bannon and Ridley Scott immediately agreed to the idea. A woman as protagonist in a science fiction film was a novelty. However, a woman confronting a monster in a horror film would soon become a convention: Laurie killed Michael in *Halloween* in 1978, Alice killed Jason's mother in 1980 in *Friday the 13th*, and from then on Final Girls would be everywhere. The fact that Ripley had been conceived as a male character made her stronger than the usual Final Girl. She is older (Weaver was thirty) and a skilled pilot and second-in-command after Dallas. She is also intelligent (she deciphers the alien transmission), alert and rational (refusing Kane entrance due to danger of infection), angry when overruled by Ash, courageous when hunting the alien, levelheaded when flushing it out through the air lock. She is completely without feminine fear or softness.[18]

Vulnerable yet resourceful. Astronaut and officer Ripley (Sigourney Weaver) in Ridley Scott's *Alien* (20th Century Fox and Brandywine Productions, 1979) is no female hero, but an example of the Final Girl who kills the monster in the horror movie.

Clover insists there are no feminist potentials in the Final Girl. "To applaud the Final Girl as a feminist development, as some reviews of *Aliens* have done with Ripley, is, in light of her figurative meaning [as symbolic male], a particularly grotesque expression of wishful thinking."[19] I shall return to feminism later in this chapter; however, at this point I want to note that even if the Final Girl does not *represent* feminism, her figure does reflect a change in society's view of women. The often noted strength of Rip-ley owes its existence to the *possibility* of imagining a woman in a man's place without her being first drawn in stereotypical fashion as femme fatale, dom-inatrix, or rape victim. Ripley does not *enter* a man's place; she *is* in it from the outset.

The Mother Archetype

James Cameron's blockbuster hit *Aliens* with the tagline "this time it's war" transformed Ripley from Final Girl to mother archetype. Cameron had just written and directed *The Terminator* (1984) and written the screenplay for *Rambo: First Blood Part II* (1985), and his take on Ripley was fueled by the high-octane masculinity of these two films.

Aliens opens with Ripley's rescue after drifting fifty-seven years through space. The computer holds no records of any alien and The Company charges Ripley with destroying the *Nostromo*. Planet LV-426 has been colonized with sixty or seventy families for over twenty years. When communication with LV-426 ceases, Ripley accepts to join a rescue mission of colonial marines. On the planet aliens have invaded the colony and used the colonists as "hosts." A ten-year-old girl, Newt (Carrie Henn), is the only survivor. When the inexperienced commanding officer in charge of the mission, Gorman (William Hope), panics, Ripley takes over and pulls the marines out of the buildings. She orders a vessel to come and pick them up but it, too, has been invaded by aliens and crashes. The survivors must return to the alien-infected buildings and send the android Bishop (Lance Henriksen) out to remote control a second vessel down from the mothership. On top of the problems of invading aliens and a nuclear power plant about to explode is added internal betrayal: Company man Burke (Paul Reiser) exposes Newt and Ripley to aliens in an attempt to bring the species back to Earth. Soon Ripley, the wounded marine soldier Hicks (Michael Biehn), and Newt are the only survivors and just before they reach the ship, Newt falls into an air vent. At the ship Ripley arms herself so she can return and save Newt, and confront an alien queen in a nest full of eggs. Like the alien in *Alien*, the queen also follows Ripley aboard the vessel and after a *mano a mano* fight with Ripley in a mechanical power-loader, she flushes it out the air lock and enters hypersleep with Newt, Hicks, and android Bishop at her side.

In 1985 *Rambo* was the number two top-grossing movie, and the affinities between Ripley clutching a rifle and Newt, and Rambo holding a machine gun and a POW, did not go unnoticed.[20] The link between Ripley and Rambo go beyond weapons, victims, and white tops; it is also in their psychological profile and status as misfits. When penning *Rambo*, Cameron

Sigourney Weaver as Ripley with ten-year-old Newt (Carrie Henn) in *Aliens* (20th Century Fox and Brandywine Productions, 1986). Male audiences cheered and feminists complained as Ripley united maternal plight with Ramboesque action. Balancing pulse rifles and little girls made Ripley the prototype for the mother hero archetype.

combined the heroic templates of the outsider and the outcast, the first a lone(ly) figure who is the best at something (*Shane*), the second a wrongly accused person who must clear himself (*The Fugitive*). In *Rambo*, war veteran Rambo is presented as innocent of the crimes he committed in *First Blood* (1982) and for which he has been sent to prison. In the beginning of *Rambo* he is given "a second chance" and offered "reinstatement in the corps" if he accepts a mission to look for POWs in Vietnam. "Why me?" he asks. A good question, since he is a violent, unstable, and criminal ex-green beret who is unfit for a society that rejects him. However, Rambo is also presented as wrongly accused and must demonstrate that he is, as his superior puts it, "the best" soldier there is.

Cameron cast Ripley in the same mold as outsider-and-outcast hero. The corporate board members consider her hysterical and sentence her to a "six-month-period of psychometric probation" and they suspend her fly certificate. On offering her the mission, Burke comments on her work in the cargo docks where she runs loaders: "I think it's great you're keeping busy. And I know it's the only thing you could get." Final Girl Ripley from *Alien* has been reduced to a chain-smoking bleak existence with nightmares about giving birth to an alien. "What would you say if I could get you reinstated as a flight officer? ... Come on, it's a second chance, Kiddo," Burke tells her. Like Rambo, Ripley must return to the scene of "trauma": Rambo returns to the very same camp where he was a prisoner, and Ripley returns to the same planet where her ship picked up an alien. Rambo was instructed to take pictures and not engage the enemy; Ripley is to act as "advisor." "You wouldn't be going in with the troops," promises lieutenant Gorman (William Hope). "I can guarantee your safety." Ripley at first refuses: "I am not a soldier." In interviews Cameron said Ripley was an average person. "It's more interesting to see a normal person in abnormal circumstances than a highly trained person like Superman or James Bond."[21] But surely Cameron knows better: Ripley is *not* average and she accepts the mission.

Aboard the *Sulaco*, she is the outcast of a new social group, the marines. Inspired from his research on Vietnam for *Rambo*, Cameron came up with the idea of "grunts in space."[22] If images of birth serve as horror in *Alien*, memory of Vietnam is the setting in *Aliens*: The exterior design of the *Sulaco* looks like a machine gun and the interior like a military base with poster pinups, machine guns, missiles, and sleep pods in a row like a military lineup.[23] In contrast to *Rambo*, however, the macho attitude is presented ironically with the black sergeant Apone (Al Matthews) putting a cigar in his mouth the moment he wakes up, and marine Hudson (Bill Paxton), bragging: "Check it out, I'm the ultimate badass. State of the badass-art. You do not wanna fuck with me. Check it out. Hey Ripley, don't worry, me and my squad of ultimate bad-asses, we'll protect you." Ripley will soon protect *their* asses, but first she must win their respect. "Is there anything you *can* do?" Apone asks when she offers her help. To his surprise, Ripley can operate the power-loader, wrapped as a child inside the huge robot-like machine in which she will later fight the queen. Following the conventions of the war movie, the soldiers cannot win the war because wars are not "winnable" events but horrifying circumstances "fought from day to day."[24] In *Aliens*, the war is even fought from hour to hour with the stay on the planet lasting just a few hours. Ripley was right when she said, "I am no soldier." She is no soldier; like Rambo she is a larger-than-life hero.

Sex and gender were never verbally thematized in *Alien*, but banter is lively in *Aliens* with Gorman calling his marines "tough hombres," sergeant Apone calling them "sweethearts," and private Vasquez telling private Hudson "fuck you, man." "Anytime, anywhere," he replies. Vasquez (Jenette Goldstein) is the tough female marine with short hair and red bandana who does push-ups after coming out of hypersleep. "Hey, Vasquez, have you ever been mistaken for a man?" Hudson teases. "No, have you?" Hudson will turn coward and "feminine" when the going gets tough. But not Vasquez. She is the most masculine of the marines, who immediately discard Ripley as some "Snow White" not to be reckoned with. Vasquez is muscular, big-breasted, aggressive, phallisized ("I only need to know one thing: where they are," she says and takes aim with an imaginary gun), sexually provocative, and uses macho lingo. "You always were an asshole, Gorman," are her final words when Gorman pulls a grenade, holding her in his arms and saving them both from a fate worse than death. Rhona Berenstein reads Vasquez as the stereotypical lesbian and masculinized woman, who makes Ripley (without makeup and in gender neutral clothing) appear androgynous rather than masculinized. "It is thus as an androgynous figure that Ripley has her pregnancy nightmares and as an androgynous figure that she adopts Newt."[25] Vasquez' sexual preferences remain unsaid but her looks and behavior employ stereotypical butch and lesbian conventions. Susan Jeffords in "'The Battle of the Big Mamas': Feminism and the Alienation of Women" (1987) reads Vasquez as "overt masculine" and sees her as the (sterile) woman who "allow[s] Ripley to appear nurturing, sensitive, and demur by contrast."[26] In Jeffords' view, Ripley is not really nurturing but in the service of "corporate masculinism." And Harvey R. Greenberg in "Fembo: *Alien's* Intentions" (1988) suggests that "the characters of Vasquez and Ripley constitute different versions—one naked, the other veiled—of the same distorted vision of feminine power ... compounded out of that bellicose phallocentricity..."[27] Interestingly, no critics read Vasquez as a positive female character offering a new feminine role model. Such rejection of her character has over the years been contested by many of my students, male and female, who in their papers ask why Vasquez must be rejected just because she is portrayed as butch.

Vasquez is the "ball-buster," a phallic woman who stands at one end of a gender scale, where feminine overlaps with masculine. Vasquez is never in a frame with little girl Newt and exchanges no words with her. The marines are unable to interrogate the mute girl, because their approach is too "masculine" and insensitive. Ripley, on the other hand, uses "feminine" tactics and cleans Newt's face with a tissue. "Hard to believe there's a little girl under all this. And a pretty one. You don't talk much, do you?" Ripley's emotional behavior is initially a "lack" ("that could have been better" says Burke after Ripley loses her temper and yells at the board members). What is "hysterical" in a peace situation will be a life-saving reaction in war. "Pull your men out of there," Ripley screams and pushes Gorman from the driver's seat. What is an unfit response (screaming at a meeting) becomes a rational response (saving the soldier's lives), and finally a maternal and fitting response when confronting the queen ("Get away from her, you *bitch*"). This development is parallel to Rambo's unfit reaction in *First Blood* (maiming American civilians), which becomes a healthy response in *Rambo* (killing enemy soldiers). In *Rambo* the female soldier Co Bao softens a traumatized Rambo and makes him promise to bring her with him back to America; in *Aliens* Newt also softens Ripley and makes her promise to bring her back to Earth:

RIPLEY: I'm not gonna leave you. I mean that.

NEWT: Is that a promise?

RIPLEY: I cross my heart.

NEWT: And hope to die?

RIPLEY: And hope to die.

In the original 137-minute theatrical release of the film, Ripley had no family. No husband or children. In the extended version aired on television in 1987 (available in an English distribution) Ripley had a daughter.[28] In 1999, a 154-minute director's cut showed Cameron's conception of Ripley's character as a mother with a loss: On Earth Ripley cries over her daughter Amy, who has died at the age of sixty-two. "I promised I'd be home for her birthday. Her *eleventh* birthday." In the director's cut, the ten-year-old Newt fills in for Ripley's ten-year-old daughter, and Ripley makes a new promise, which will not be broken.

As I discussed in the Introduction, the mother archetype is not about transforming from "good" to "bad" mother and back to "good" mother again; it is about constructing a third position from which can be articulated a new notion of motherhood. The "good" mother in the first position is the traditional mother as "beneficent, sacred, pure, asexual, nourishing."[29] She symbolizes the patriarchal family and raises her children in a self-sacrificing manner. She is almost a Pietà. The bad mother abandons her post as "mother" and "family." Across male film genres, this is her fall from grace. Whether a daughter raped in *Eye for an Eye*, a daughter is lost in *Aliens*, or a daughter is abducted in *Long Kiss Goodnight*, the missing mother is at "fault." She is a quitter, or worse, a deserter. The explanation—which is never an excuse—is her desire to do what men do: work.

The queen is a different figure from the archaic mother in *Alien*. Berenstein notes that the queen is Ripley's monstrous double. A double represents those qualities we internalize to become psychologically "complete." An identity needs balance. "So who's laying these eggs?" Ripley asks when they discuss the nature of the alien. Hudson suggests it is some kind of insect, like a bee: "There's like, one female that runs the whole show." "Yes, the queen," says android Bishop. Hudson: "Yeah, the mama. And she's badass, man. I mean *big*." When Ripley stumbles into the alien nest, the "badass" queen is lit from behind to give her body a halo. The light has connotations of a religious revelation and the queen is an awe-inspiring image of maternity. A gigantic external uterus produces the eggs before our very eyes. Monstrous, yes, but also a rational matriarch ordering her "soldiers" to back away when Ripley threatens to destroy her eggs. When Ripley later has armed herself by mounting the huge powerloader which gives her a stature equal of the alien, she is similarly lit from behind and the camera pauses to contemplate Ripley as an awe-inspiring mother-warrior. The twin mothers are mirror images, protecting their offspring, ruling armies, and commanding troops.

Just as the attitude to children is clear—*never* leave a child behind—the attitude to family is simple: It is a revered object to be rescued and when the "sixty to seventy families" are lost on LV-426, a new family emerges: Ripley, Newt (calling Ripley "mummy"), and Hicks. Hicks, played by Michael Biehn who was the savior in *Terminator*, is a father/soldier with compassion and emotion. "Don't touch that, it's dangerous, honey," he tells Newt who is fingering a pulse rifle. Their exchange of first names (Dwayne and Ellen) indicate a future romance. But this is no simple return to the patriarchal family. Mother has compassion and operates pulse rifles and powerloaders; Father is saved by Mother; the Innocent Child is enlightened about babies and monsters ("Is that how babies come? I mean, people's babies?" and "My mummy always said there were no monsters, no real ones. But there are"); and the family even has a repairable nanny, Bishop.

Cameron molded his female hero as a Pietà with a pulse rifle and a girl-child, a hero who unites the Final Girl's masculine qualities with those of a protective mother. As so many of cinema's female heroes, Ripley is an ambiguous product of in-betweenness: both "not a soldier" and of Ramboesque proportions, both a nervous wreck with nightmares and a strong mother defending her family. In the theatrical version, Ripley was not a biological mother, but later maternal heroes became biological as if biology guarantees maternal instincts.

Feminists and left-oriented intellectuals did not welcome Cameron's revelation. Lynda K. Bundtzen in "Monstrous Mothers: Medusa, Grendel, and now Alien" (1987) found *Aliens* "a profoundly disturbing allegory about contemporary feminism" because it split the maternal into nature and body (the alien) versus culture and the mechanical (Ripley) and rejected the first. "I want to ask why the female body must be represented with such primal terror, such intense repugnance, and why it needs to be so resoundingly defeated," Bundtzen asked and concluded, "despite a wish to praise this revision of mothering as a cultural choice ... I cannot."[30] The uncanny alien design—the mixture of phallic and vaginal biology—and the alien's status as purely monstrous made it impossible for Bundtzen to accept—and thus access—Ripley's strength and heroism. Susan Jeffords in "'The Battle of the

"Get away from her, you *bitch*." Wrapped inside a power-loader, Ripley challenges the alien queen in *Aliens* (20th Century Fox and Brandywine Productions, 1986). Feminists, however, criticized the lack of bonding between the two female characters.

Big Mamas': Feminism and the Alienation of Women" (1987) was provoked by the portrayal of women as unable to bond with each other (Ripley and Lambert in *Alien*; Ripley and the four female marines in *Aliens*; Ripley and the queen) and rejected Ripley as a feminist figure because "Ripley's 'feminism' ... is victorious only because it accepts the point of view of a corporate masculism at the expense of relations between women."[31] Feminists discarded Ripley because she used masculine violence, a view with which even male feminists like Harvey Greenberg (1988) agreed: "[T]o become a competent woman one must learn to manipulate the tangible or verbal instruments of aggression, which patriarchal society formerly reserved for men alone."[32] The critique focused on Ripley's body (with its lack of clear feminine signifiers), her use of masculine violence, and her lack of bonding with women.[33]

This rejection strikes me as being almost as aggressive as the rejection of the alien, "sucked into the vacuum of space as if thrown back into whatever imaginative void could have germinated such horror."[34] Rebecca Bell-Metereau—the only positive feminist critic—suggested that reviews of *Alien* overlooked that the protagonist was strong *and* female because "our perceptions are formed by what we expect to see" and Ripley was "a heroine who is so foreign as to be unrecognizable to most popular critics."[35] Berenstein's analysis is interesting because she locates her own perception of the film as caught in-between two positions:

> ... I am left with a mass of contradictions in theme, character portrayal, style and structure which suggest that the binarism is at once intact and irrevocably collapsed. Just as nature and culture do (paradoxical) battle in these texts, so too are these films balanced along a tightrope which divides a progressive from a reactionary reading of them ... *Aliens* challenge us to recognize popular film and the horror film in particular, as being able to simultaneously embody both politically progressive and regressive elements.[36]

What are we to make of *Aliens*? Is Ripley a "Rambolina"[37] or a "Fembo" as Greenberg calls her? Is this merely women behaving like men in an effort to access male power, and is the film thus a sign of patriarchy's attempt at transforming men *and* women into prototype macho warriors? "If women can see no future beyond joining the masculinist elite on its own terms, our civilization will become more destructive than ever," laments Germaine Greer.[38] From this feminist perspective, a woman who masters the masculine world (driving a tank, reading digital maps, using a pulse rifle and a powerloader) is no longer a woman and not a positive role model. It is in this line of argumentation that Clover concludes, "It may be through the female body that the body of the audience is sensationalized, but the sensation is an entirely male affair." I disagree. Role reversal may not always

lead to subversion but it opens up the *potential* for subversion by calling attention to existing gender roles. I agree with Berenstein that we tend to overlook alternative images because we do not expect to find them and when
we find them, we are unable to determine their significance.

Postmodernism and cultural studies show that popular culture, rejected
by modernism as aesthetically repetitive and morally dangerous, offers aesthetically original and thematically rich texts as "high art" culture. According to Hans-Georg Gadamer and Edmund Husserl, we meet the world with
a "horizon of expectation" formed by our pre-judgments and prejudices.
When we "see" the world, we fuse our horizon of expectations with the
world, able to see only what our "frame" permits us to see. Our understanding of any object is determined by our pre-understanding of objects, our pre-
knowledge of the world, which is related to what Heidegger calls our
being-in-the-world. We are not simply beings, but specific beings in a specific
world under specific historical circumstances. Our consciousness is historically determined, as our mental schemata are shaped by experience, knowledge, and intention. It is impossible for us to "see" the world with "an open
eye" unhindered by a frame; all we would see would be what Wilhelm Dilthey
calls the random-next-to-each-other-ness of things, a chaotic world with a lim-
itless number of elements in it, an experience similar to the stressful view
of the schizophrenic.[39] No. We sort according to our pre-judgments and
prejudices.

By feminist standards, *Aliens* may not be a feminist film. But it provided
new roles for women, which were rejected by a feminist critique unable to
"see" or acknowledge the mother archetype as a new hero. Judith Halberstam in *Female Masculinity* thus calls Vasquez "a surprising source of butch
imagery" but misreads her behavior and fate. "Vasquez proceeds to cruise
Ripley and whispers 'ché bonita' as she walks by. Of course, Vasquez's studly
appreciation for the rather asexual Sigourney Weaver does not save the latina
from being one of the first victims of the voracious aliens ... this butch meets
a gory and untimely end."[40] But Vasquez' remark is ironic, meaning that she
distances herself from Ripley and the fact that she once saw an alien
(to assure the audience that Ripley is not the possible object of butch or
lesbian desire). Vasquez does not "cruise" Ripley, and Vasquez is the *last*
marine to die. Halberstam overlooks that Vasquez is butch, heroic, *and* last
to die.[41] Perhaps because in Halberstam's horizon of expectation a blockbuster hit like *Aliens* cannot show a strong butch figure? Another example
of misreading is Greenberg who interprets the queen as "the ... Bad
Mother of infancy, she who binds so closely that one strangles in her clutches,"
as well as "an overdetermined symbol of the Company's Bad Mothering," and
finally the aliens as "fit objects for exploitation, slavery, or slaughter."[42] In his

reading, the queen stands for the Bad Mother, the bad Company, and the slavery of Western society. This psychological, ideological, and political interpretation is an analysis vacuum-packed around its object to prevent outside interpretations from corrupting its "content." Greenberg regrets "Cameron's sexism, racism, and jingoism" and rejects *Aliens* as "a noisy, empty, but ideologically dangerous 'bug hunt'"[43] while ignoring the film's *intentional* ridicule of macho masculinity and Reagan tactics.

I also find Jeffords' analysis of the nuclear family problematic. She argues that since Ripley defeats the alien with the help of corporate war equipment (weapons and help from corporate created/trained android Bishop and marine soldier Hicks), the new family is "restructured then not only *with* but *by* the corporate" and that the new feminism/family "can now afford to stop fighting the corporate because it *is* the corporate." This is reading against the grain. Clearly, Cameron does not endorse either the Company, or its use of families to conquer new terrain, or its use of marines to solve unsolvable missions (the allegory of Vietnam as "lost mission"). Greenberg and Jeffords "see" Cameron replacing Ridley Scott's critique of capitalism/Company with one individual, Burke. However, company man Burke does not replace The Company; he *represents* it. "They can bill me," Ripley tells him when he argues with "dollar value" against her decision to nuke the colony from orbit. "They" is a reply to Burke *and* the Company. *Aliens* may not provide an alternative to the nuclear family, but it provides a critique of aggressive patriarchy and an *alternative* nuclear family with mother as matriarch, father as postfeminist, daughter as able to handle herself, and technology as the lifesaving support of the future family.

The feminist response to *Aliens* did not "see" a new female hero who was strong, intelligent, and maternal. Feminists discarded the representation of a woman in a man's world in charge of soldiers and technology, and they chose to ignore the representation of a maternal body, which was a source of heroic strength instead of "uncanny."[44]

Clover wonders about the audience for horror films. "Do females respond to the text (the literal) and males the subtext (the figurative)?"[45] That is, do men "read" the Final Girl as a man and do women read her as a woman? Such speculation ignores what audiences *do* respond to. Of the series' four films, *Aliens* is the most popular with 667 fans on the *Internet Movie Data Base* almost unanimously praising the film as "a perfect 10,"[46] "the best sequel ever made in movie history"[47] and "a true example of greatness."[48] It is revealing to compare such audience reactions to critics' reactions. Where no critics elaborate on Hudson (Bill Paxton), the bragging marine who is a coward when it comes to killing aliens, Hudson is again and again singled out as "the show stopper in this flick" and the real stand-in for the male audience. Not Hicks the hero, but Hudson the coward. ("My favorite character is the cocky marine Hudson ... I even wanted him to die the first time I saw it but he really grows on you. He's the most realistic of the characters").[49] Also, Vasquez is welcomed as a figure of female strength (I have not found a single comment reading her as fake, phallic, or a representative for patriarchy). And above all, Weaver's Ripley is embraced as a new hero:

> Her character is one of the greatest heroines of all times. Sigourney really does pull it off. No one else could have done it like her. Ripley's maternal connection with the young girl Newt is amazing to watch ... but the ultimate scene is her final battle with the galaxy's most deadly creature—set to a pulsing military score ... Quite possible my favorite fight scene of all time.[50]

Comments on the Internet Movie Data Base are anonymous, so there is no knowing which authors are male or female. However, the frequent positive evaluation of, for instance, Hudson indicates that many could be written by men. It would be academic arrogance to ignore this warm reaction to Ripley as woman, mother, and hero. As I have just demonstrated in the former chapter on Cynthia Rothrock, often audiences see what critics for many reasons overlook. I believe it is a mistake to discard such enthusiastic responses (as Greenberg does) as "serious misreadings" which do not understand the "Neanderthal politics" and "bellicose phallocentricity" of *Aliens*.[51] One of postmodernism's central insights is that a text is a bundle of voices and there is no such thing as one authoritative reading of it.

Into the Fire and Out of the Ashes

In her ever-changing incarnations, Ripley is the perfect postfeminist hero and Sigourney Weaver is an exception to the rule that the actress playing the female hero must be young and botoxed. Weaver traverses space and time as a true pioneer: She is a Final Girl in *Alien* before that concept hardens into stereotype, in *Aliens* she is the prototype for the mother archetype, and in the nineties she will become posthuman in the series' fourth and last film, *Alien: Resurrection* (1997).[52]

The third film in the series, *Alien 3* (1992), is the least popular and has the least number of comments on the Internet Movie Data Base.[53] The production was problematic: Renny Harlin quit because of disputes over the script and David Fincher, a director of music videos, was called in to complete the film without a finished shooting script. The production company, however, disliked his version as too depressing and re-cut the film, and Fincher was furious about the theatrical release.[54] The plot is simple as usual: After a fire on the *Sulaco*, a rescue vessel with Ripley, Newt, Hicks, and

Bishop crashes on the planet Fiorina "Fury" 161. The only habitation is a former correctional work facility whose 5,000 prisoners are reduced to twenty-five ex-prisoners—all "double y chromosome"—who have chosen a life of celibacy. They run the mineral ore refinery and operate the furnace. Ripley is the only survivor from the crash and she is also the only woman on the planet. In her ship were an alien egg and a facehugger, which impregnates a dog that gives birth to a new alien. There are no weapons on the planet so the men must use one another as bait to lure the alien into the furnace. Impregnated with an alien, a queen, Ripley is about to throw herself into the furnace when Company representatives enter the facility. "You still can have a life," says the leader (Lance Henriksen), who is the designer of android Bishop. "Children. And most important: you'll know it's dead." But Ripley does not believe him and throws herself into the fire, holding the newborn alien close to her breast as it bursts from her body on the way down. Final words are, "Work Prison Fury 161. Closed and sealed. Custodial presence terminated. Remaining refining equipment to be sold as scrap. End of transmission."

The visuals were as bleak as the plot. "Keep it dark!" Fincher constantly repeated during filming and the result is a Gothic scenery with dark tunnels connecting huge vaults in an atmosphere of decay and death. The living quarters are in a grey color scale and the work facility is in a burning yellow, metaphorical of human existence as a choice between living death or hell. Everyone is shaved (because of lice) and with her bald head and grey clothes Ripley resembles the grey ex-prisoners as well as the black alien.

Death is everywhere: From the deceased Newt, that Ripley asks prison doctor Clemens (Charles Dance) to perform an autopsy on in the morgue, to the corpses that facility leader Andrews (Brian Glover) speaks a sermon over. "...They have been released from all darkness and pain ... ashes to ashes, dust to dust." In the same moment that the leader, the Afro American ex-prisoner Dillon (Charles S. Dutton), says, "Within each death there's always the promise of a new life, a new beginning," an alien is born from the dog's body. However, this time there *is* no new beginning, no hero, no broken promise to be kept, no surrogate family. The inhabitants are neither fit for society ("You don't wanna know me, Lady. I'm a murderer and a rapist of women"), nor for family romance. Ripley's affair with Clemens is a matter of physical need rather than pleasure. In an intimate moment after they have had sex, Clemens confesses to being a drug addict and a murderer (and, we understand, a rather unfit father), but is brutally interrupted as the alien penetrates his head. So much for intimacy.

The shaved heads, the syringes (three times we see a person being given an injection), and the deadly organism infecting an all-male society made

David Fincher went for the gritty, downbeat, dysfunctional look in his take on female hero Ripley in *Alien 3* (20th Century Fox and Brandywine Productions, 1992). Some critics interpreted this as a comment on HIV.

critics read *Alien 3* as an allegory of AIDS ("They think we're scum and they don't give a fuck about one friend of yours who's died," Ripley tell them).[55] The central symbolism, however, is martyrdom. The men practice some kind of "apocalyptic millenarian fundamentalist Christianity" and when they attempt to rape her, Ripley forgives them. Ripley is no rape-avenger but a martyr throwing herself into the fire in the hope of a human future without the alien. "They just want it for their bioweapon division," she tells "85" (Ralph Brown), who clings to the illusion that the Company will rescue them.

Maternal imagery is present in two perverse forms: In Ripley's handling of Newt's corpse—pretending to say goodbye, but examining the body and insisting it be cut open in a grand guignol scene—and in her tender clutching of the screeching alien infant. "A most complicated gesture, and quite unlike any other I've ever seen in movies," comments Amy Taubin.[56] The latter is the film's signature scene, equivalent of the chestburster scene in *Alien* and the battle of the big mamas in *Aliens*. Ripley holds her arms out in a crucifixion gesture and gracefully falls backwards into the abyss, quoting the heroic suicides in *Thelma and Louise* (1991) and the furnace termination/suicide in *Terminator 2*, films by Ripley's two "fathers," Ridley Scott and James Cameron. In *Alien 3*, Ripley's suicide is self-sacrificial with a choir on the soundtrack and the camera circling in slow motion. The Company man who promises Ripley "children" is the devil tempting the believer, because Ripley *does* believe in maternity. However, the clock is ticking (actress Weaver was forty-three and not made to look younger) and maternity is irredeemably lost, the surrogate daughter cut open, the sexual partner a murderer, the scan images of her fetus a perverse pregnancy.

From a budget of eight million dollars in *Alien* to eighteen million in *Aliens*, *Alien 3* jumped to fifty million, and *Alien: Resurrection* (1997) by French director Jean-Pierre Jeunet reached seventy million dollars.[57] Despite the budget, however, this fourth and last sequel was as unpopular as its predecessor. *Alien 3* flirted with family ties between the alien and Ripley ("Don't be afraid, I'm part of the family"). The alien did not kill Ripley because it sensed her "pregnancy" and the film's tag line, "The bitch is back," had referred to Ripley/the alien as one figure, M/other. In *Alien: Resurrection* Ripley literally becomes the monster's mother when scientists on the military medical research spaceship *USM Auriga* two hundred years later produce a clone from her blood and extract an alien fetus from the womb of a resurrected Ripley. When the pirate ship the *Betty* docks with an illegal cargo of human "hosts" for the alien, things get out of control. A pirate, Call (Winona Ryder), turns out to be an auton (an android made by androids) sent by renegade androids to kill Ripley and the alien. During the fight between the military and the pirates, the twelve cloned aliens escape from their cages. Of the six pirates and forty-nine military crew members only four survive: clone Ripley, android Call, the crippled pirate Vriess (Dominique Pinon), and not-too-smart pirate Johner (Ron Perlman). Once again, the alien is a blind passenger aboard an escape vessel, this time sucked out in liquid form through a small window.

Alien: Resurrection took the mother archetype into the area of techno-bodies and ARTs, Assisted Reproductive Technologies. The film asked the question: What right do we have to produce life? And if we produce life, what is our responsibility towards this life? The techno-body is a technologically enhanced body, "a boundary figure belonging simultaneously to at least two previously incompatible systems of meaning—'the organic/natural' and 'the technological/cultural'," Anne Balsamo writes in *Technologies of the Gendered Body: Reading Cyborg Women* (1997).[58] Clone number eight, Ripley, is a techno-body. Ripley is no longer just human; her blood melts metal and she has superhuman strength and agility, qualities crossed over from the alien DNA to her human DNA.

A distinction that is *not* blurred is between male and female. Balsamo points out that "the gendered boundary between male and female is one border that remains heavily guarded despite new technologized ways to rewrite the physical in the flesh."[59] As boundaries go, some are more easily crossed than others and gender remains a naturalized sign of who we are. The "who" is defined according to categories of race, class, gender, and species, which are constructed through discourse. "[T]here is no 'natural' approach to the female body that is rooted in an essentialist female nature ... the 'cultural significance' of the body is a matter of its symbolic construction, not its 'natural femininity.'"[60]

Throughout the series Ripley is a female hero with explicitly "masculine" elements: in *Alien* she has masculine character traits (intelligence, resourcefulness), in *Aliens* she appropriates macho behavior (Rambo-tactics), and in *Alien 3* she has a masculine appearance (shaved head, prison clothes). However, she always remained a non-sexualized woman and a caring character. In *Alien: Resurrection*, not only Ripley's DNA changes, but also her femininity. She is dressed in a costume that sets her apart from the soldiers: a tight, dark purple, designer outfit of leather with high boots and a vest. The costume has connotations of corset and dominatrix gear, and its "darkness" and leather material resembles the alien. For the first time in the series Ripley wears makeup and has long hair, and with her tough language ("So who do I have to fuck to get off this boat?") and S-M costume, Ripley has become an image of the monstrous-feminine. When a scientist trains her to say "fork" and indicates his fork, Ripley replies "fuck," an exchange that evokes deep-rooted notions of the female as erotic, dangerous, and uncanny. Fans complained, "I missed the Ellen Ripley from the first three films. She was a caring person: someone the audiences liked. In this film, she's a cold, steely I-don't-give-a-crap clone."[61]

The portrayal of a mother hero shifts focus from biology and gender (good mother versus bad mother) to biology and ethics (good parent versus bad parent). In "(M)other Discourses" (2000) Dion Farquhar divides maternity into three components "genetic/chromosoval, uterine/gestational, and social/legal.[62] That is, the genetic code, the physical pregnancy, and the social upbringing. Farquhar argues that ARTs, Assisted Reproductive Technologies, denaturalize maternity by offering insertion of donated eggs and donated sperm and thus opens a debate about which body is the "real" maternal or "real" paternal body: is it the owner of the genetic code, the individual who carries the pregnancy, or the person bringing up the child?[63] "By definitively separating sex from reproduction, reproductive technologies break the naturalized assumption that reproduction is heterosexual and

Boundaries between monster, mother, and human are blurred in *Alien: Resurrection* (20th Century Fox and Brandywine Productions, 1997), when Ripley (Sigourney Weaver) returns as a clone whose human DNA has blended with that of the alien fetus in her womb. Here Ripley wakes up in the alien "nest."

heterosocial."[64] This opens possibilities for patriarchy as well as for feminists: Men can reproduce without women, and women, on the other hand, can reproduce without men.

Who is responsible for a techno-child (and here we must not forget that the alien and Ripley are both techno-children)? The army scientists who cloned Ripley fail at raising techno-children. "Roll over? Play dead? Heel? You can't teach it tricks," says Ripley. "Why not? We're teaching *you*," is the insensitive response. Military technology is "evil," not because it is male and patriarchal, but because it is immoral. It can create techno-life, but it cannot raise techno-children because it goes against basic ethics by treating this life as an object. Thus, it fails to recognize both the animal nature of the alien as well as the human nature of the clone Ripley.

ARTs and their "product"—the techno-body or posthuman body—are ambigiously coded. The alien is "bad" (not "evil") because it is a predator with an instinct to kill. Ripley, on the other hand, has an instinct to protect. "We can't trust her," Call says about techno–Ripley. But it is *men* and *male* nature which cannot be trusted. Men are egoistical, irresponsible, and greedy whereas women—here in the form of techno-women—are humane, self-sacrificial, and responsible. Thus, android Call risks her existence to save Earth ("I should have known," says Ripley when she finds out Call is an android, "no human being is that humane"). Ripley's humaneness is presented in maternal terms: She has a "motherly" talk with Call to convince the android to override the system (called "Father") and open a pathway through the spaceship to reach the *Betty*. "Father's dead, *asshole*," Call yells to the general over the communication system. Call and Ripley connect in a mother-daughter relationship which puts mother before father and daughter before son. In the alien nest Ripley witnesses the birth of the Newborn that has mixed human and alien DNA. The Newborn kills it's alien mother (the uterine host) and turns to Ripley as its "real" mother (the genetic code). "I'm the monster's mother," Ripley earlier said. She must now choose between raising an adoptive "daughter" or a biological "son," the android or the alien. "[P]erhaps a unique situation in film (mother killing son and being a hero for it)," a fan commented about the final confrontation, where Ripley says "I'm sorry" as the screeching creature is sucked out the window like an abortion. Ripley catches Call's arm and embraces her adoptive "daughter" as they enter Earth's atmosphere.

Where the former three films operated with taxonomies of human versus monstrous and good mothers versus bad mothers, the taxonomies in *Alien: Resurrection* are diffuse. There seem to be two: the theme of human versus inhuman, which is no longer cast as human versus monster, but as human/male versus posthuman/female (the latter being the artificially created life of clones and androids); and, second, the theme of ethics. Clearly, to be human ought to mean one behaved morally, which is tantamount to having *humane* ethics. Beings are presented as "good," "bad," or "evil" according to behavior. Thus, the cloned alien is "bad" (not "evil") because it is genetically coded to be a predator and kill. It is *a*moral, not *im*moral, because it is an animal. The military crew and the pirates are "evil" because they treat life and techno-life as an object. Apart from one female scientist and one female pirate, the humans are men, and male nature is consistently presented as immoral and "evil."[65] Clone Ripley and android Call are located in-between human and technological, right and wrong, good and bad; on the one hand, their genetic codes were created by humans (in Call's case a program invented by androids who again were invented by humans) and could be said to position them as human and "good." On the other hand, their uterine/gestational origin is artificial and could thus be seen as "wrong." Ultimately, behavior settles ethics. Those who behave in a *humane* and *morally responsible* way (Call and Ripley) are "good," those behaving *beastly* (the alien) are "bad," and those being immoral (the military crew, the pirates) are "evil."

The film's humane ethics are located in techno-bodies that are composed as female and compassionate. We see this in the film's signature scene, which is when Ripley finds a room with the seven "failed" clones that were created before her. "Kill me," clone number six begs from an operating table. The clones are failed techno-bodies. They are artificial life, which it will be difficult to raise. Ripley is a good techno-body, because she is humane *and* fully functional. But her fore-clones are biological freaks. Ripley responds to their misery by killing them (it seems only one is alive and the rest dead). "What a waste of ammo," Johner comments, "must be a chick thing." Now, if we again ask if it is ethical to produce artificial life, the film is confused. Its first answer seems to go along the line that it is unethical to create techno-children, but if they can share our humane values, they must be accepted and may even turn out to be more humane than humans (as Ripley). Techno-children incapable of sharing our values must be exterminated (as the alien). The film's second answer, however, lies in Ripley's flamethrower. The clone on the operating table is clearly a deformed human, a woman, who can talk and feel pain. To kill her is presented as an act of compassion and "a chick thing." How are we to read this scene? Is it female is to be compassionate and kill those who suffer? Or is it "a chick thing" to terminate deformed techno-life that does not fit our physical standards? If the first is a return to gender essentialism, the latter could only be understood as antifeminist (that is, that women with "wrong" female bodies are not allowed to live).

Reading Ripley

It is the nature of a film series to resurrect its characters and it is the nature of Ripley to return in new versions of the mother archetype. This archetype was born from the dystopian *angst* of Otherness in *Alien* and the Utopian spirit of Rambo in *Aliens*—a strange match indeed. As we saw, feminists did not welcome Ripley as a role model for women. She was a "fake" feminist who had crossed over to the enemy, patriarchy. I think, however, that if we are to read her we must open our eyes for a broader horizon. Speaking in the context of technology, Dion Farquhar points out how postmodernists and feminists disagree:

> Within a postmodern politics, there are no guaranteed outcomes, no train of victory narratives to hop on for the ride to glory. Instead, there is a range of strategic responses to subjections including the multiplication of resistances, the scrambling of master-codes, and the nurturing of new and hybrid forms ... New representations of uncertainty and ambiguity, toleration of differential receptions and constructions of these technologies, and multivalent potentials are not acknowledged, or decried as anti-feminist, by fundamental feminists.[66]

Farquhar is looking for a "third way" which is neither "uncritical endorsement or out-of-hand dismissal." I wish to join her endeavor and enter the terrain of in-betweenness where Ripley epitomizes one of the "new and hybrid forms." When they see Earth at the end of *Alien: Resurrection*, Call asks, "What happens now?" "I don't know," Ripley replies, "I'm a stranger here myself." Ripley was always a stranger whether as Final Girl, as mother archetype, as martyr and savior, or as posthuman techno-mother. She has always crossed borders between genders, between gendered behavior, and between species. There *are* no given answers, no biological essentialism, no "real" mother. What does it mean to be male or female, masculine or feminine, father or mother? In the *Alien* series, this question is an ongoing dialogue between gender stereotypes, prejudices, and new perceptions. "Not foundations but horizons," Farquhar wants. I agree.

Like a Phoenix, Ripley keeps rising from the ashes. A female hero, a mother, and a monstrous Other. We might not agree with the answers, but her questioning has challenged essentialist views of what it means to be a woman ... or, rather, a human ... or, better yet, *humane* in a man's world.

Alien Filmography

Alien (1979) Dir. Ridley Scott. Lieutenant Ellen Ripley, horror
Aliens (137 minutes, director's cut is 154 minutes) (1986) Dir. James Cameron. Horror/action
Alien 3 (114 minutes, Special Assembly Cut version is 145 minutes) (1992) Dir. David Fincher. Horror/drama
Alien: Resurrection (1997) Dir. Jean-Pierre Jeunet. Horror/fantasy

Daddy's Action Girl: *Nikita* and the Daughter Archetype

Meanewhile, in ivory with happy art
A Statue carves; so gracefull in each part,
As women never equall'd it: and stands
Affected to the fabrick of his hands.

—Ovid *Metamorphosis*[1]

The female archetype I call *the daughter* found its prototype in 1990 with Luc Besson's French action thriller *Nikita*. Nikita is a young junkie who shoots and kills a policeman. She is sentenced to life imprisonment and her suicide is faked in prison. The government now presents her an ultimatum: be terminated for real or be trained as an agent serving the nation. Nikita undergoes an extreme makeover and a renegade junkie is transformed into a reliable and beautiful assassin. After four years of training the young woman is released into a double life as a secret agent. In the end, however, Nikita is unable to kill. She abandons the agency and, reluctantly, her new fiancé.

Reviewers called the character "deep as a puddle,"[2] but Nikita caught the attention of audiences across the world. The film was remade in Hong Kong as *Hei Mao* (*Black Cat*, 1991) and *Hei Mao II* (*Black Cat II*, 1992), an American remake appeared in 1993 with John Badham's *Point of No Return*, and the television series *La Femme Nikita* based on Besson's film ran five seasons with ninety-six episodes from 1997 to 2001. Today, the young-woman-trained-as-assassin-by-the-state has become a common archetype in film and television. We find the daughter in different versions; however, Luc Besson must be credited with creating the most widespread and popular prototype. However, whether the daughter is trained by an older experienced criminal as Beatrix is in *Kill Bill*, by her own father as Lara Croft is in *Lara Croft:*

Tomb Raider, by a Grandmaster as in *Red Sonja*, or by an agency as is Sydney Bristow in the television series *Alias* (2001-), a number of features recur in such conspicuous fashion as to constitute what I call the archetype of the daughter.

The daughter has three themes: the first, *education*, is about an older man or a "male" system teaching a young woman to "behave"; the second, *masquerade*, is concerned with her performance of stereotypical masculinity and femininity; and the third, *prostitution*, is about her relation to her employer and the job. From a poetic perspective, the daughter archetype is, of course, a modern update of the Pygmalion myth. The sculptor Pygmalion carved his ideal virgin from ivory and infatuated with his perfect maid, he kissed and caressed the statue, dressed it, hung jewelry around its neck, and took it to bed as his wife. At last Venus took pity on his prayers and turned ivory into flesh, "a perfect Virgin full of juyce and heat."[3] From a gender perspective, the daughter archetype is the fantasy of a man teaching a woman how to be a "real" woman. The daughter's femininity is thematized as a role she performs to please her teacher. Femininity is a socially learned behavior and not a biological instinct. Finally, from a psychological perspective, the daughter is an incestuous archetype. Her teacher is an older man who molds a young woman into his desired shape. She is Daddy's girl, not Mummy's. Psychologically speaking, they are father and daughter (sometimes they are also biological father and daughter). However, symbolically speaking, they can also appear to be lovers or a man with a mistress. The narrative can be almost pedophiliac, as Besson's *Léon* (1994) where the twelve-year old orphan Mathilda (Natalie Portman) moves in with an adult killer to learn the trade.

Educating the Daughter-Agent

The daughter differs from my other archetypes by a striking disjunction between her actions and her appearance. She does not *look* like the type you would expect to tripwire bombs, handle oversize guns, and assassinate people in cold blood. Where the dominatrix and the Amazon are sexualized creatures who promise a certain (sexual) type of violence, and the rape-avenger has a clear-cut motive and the killer-look to carry out her vengeance, the daughter is often slight, flatchested, and with an air of adolescence. She looks like a "sweet girl" and fools her opponents by her looks alone. In contrast, the mother archetype doesn't "fool" anybody and never hides her capacity for action.

Our fascination with the daughter lies in this linking of sweetness with violence and of demureness with sexual masquerade, character traits and

The daughter-father theme is almost pedophiliac in Luc Besson's action film *Léon* (Gaumont and Les Films du Dauphin, 1994) where assassin Léon (Jean Reno) falls in love with his young apprentice Mathilda (Natalie Portman).

demeanors that are usually taken to exclude one another in a person. Yet, in the daughter they form a union, which, as I shall argue shortly, is neither natural nor normal. In his essay "Gender and the Action Heroine: Hardbodies and the *Point of No Return*" (1996) Jeffrey A. Brown has argued that the female hero in *Nikita* and *Point of No Return* constitutes "a new action heroine" who signals "a growing acceptance of nontraditional roles for women and an awareness of the arbitrariness of gender traits."[4] His argument is that the action films of the early nineties (he gives as examples *Blue Steel* 1990, *Silence of the Lambs* 1990, *Nikita*, *Thelma and Louise*, *Terminator 2: Judgment Day* 1991, and the films by Cynthia Rothrock) "challenge both cinematic and cultural assumptions about what constitutes natural or proper female behavior."[5] Drawing on the theoretical work of Joan Riviere and Judith Butler about gender masquerade and gender performance, respectively, Brown finds "the modern action heroine confounds essentialism through her performance of traditionally masculine roles ... she is in full command of the narrative, carrying the action in ways that have normally been reserved for male protagonists."[6] From this point of view the female hero is *free* to choose between feminine and masculine behaviors, her body has become a "a functional body, a weapon" that wields muscles and guns with the same naturalness which has so long empowered men. Though she must fight and suffer, "the trials she is forced to endure are all brought about by her pleasurable appropriation of masculine power."[7]

Since I find Brown's article exemplary of a postfeminist tendency to read the female hero as a gender bender and a subversive figure, I shall use it as a reference point for a discussion of this line of argument. Brown's article is—as is often the case with popular cultural criticism—a combination of insightful as well as misleading analysis that leads to what I think is a sympathetic but mostly wrong conclusion. Speaking from a postfeminist and *pragmatic* rather than optimistic position, my intention is not to critique Brown's article but to point out the variable positions at play in the construction of the daughter archetype who—which I agree—is a new figure in the nineties. In chapter seven I explored what I saw as a too *negative* feminist reading of Ripley in the *Alien* series. In this chapter my intention is the opposite: to contest an overly *positive* postfeminist reading of the daughter archetype.

The recurring question with the daughter is always "How did she become this way?" A question implying that her actions are unnatural for a *woman*. Thus, in establishing this archetype the narrative always provides us with a reason, some sort of explanation, a motive. Girls do not naturally grow up to become secret agents (as boys do according to the logic of films with male heroes that *never* question why he has chosen this line of work). Daughters need strong motivations which usually are provided by their fathers. Therefore, it is misleading when Brown calls Megan Turner's (Jamie Lee Curtis) choice to become a policeman in *Blue Steel* "her *pleasurable* appropriation of masculine power" (italics mine).[8] Megan tells her police lover that her motive for becoming a policeman was not that she "wanted to shoot people" (which was her first answer), but that the experience of growing up with an abusive father taught her the necessity to be able to defend oneself ("Does he still hit you, Mum?"). The daughter's reason for becoming an agent or a warrior is often related to family: a missing mother, a dominant father, or an entirely dysfunctional family. Cynthia Rothrock sometimes played a daughter archetype in her martial arts action films, in which case murdered husbands, fiancés, brothers, and fathers provided motive for revenge. Charly in *The Long Kiss Goodnight* was raised by her father, a Royal Irish Ranger, and after his death Mr. Perkins, head of the CIA, adopted her.

Little black cocktail dress, big shiny gun, French stylish action film. Anne Parillaud, heroine of Luc Besson's *Nikita* (Gaumont and Cecchi Gori Group Tiger Cinematografica, 1990), is the prototype for the female-assassin-working-involuntarily-for-an-agency plot now found in television shows *La Femme Nikita* and *Alias*.

Sidney Bristow, too, has been raised by a CIA father because her mother (a KGB agent) abandoned the family.

To correct the daughter's malfunctioning it is necessary to reeducate her. It was by taking his cue from *education* that Besson proved his genius. As the promotional material for the film informed, he was inspired by the Pygmalion myth and Bernard Shaw's famous play *Pygmalion* (1916) about a linguistics professor who makes a bet that he can transform a simple flower girl into a convincing society lady. The first half of *Nikita* is dedicated to the transformation of primitive and aggressive Nikita (Anne Parillaud) into the beautiful, professional, and sophisticated Marie. In the opening scene Nikita and three friends break into a pharmacy to steal drugs. During the gun battle with the police she indifferently listens to music on her headphones and when a policeman lifts them off her ears, she sticks a gun to his face, smiles vaguely, and pulls the trigger. "Nikitaaaa," she rasps at the police station when asked her name. The police chief calls her "cutie" and slaps her off the chair. Nikita asks for a pencil. The policeman again asks her full name. She stabs the pencil through his hand and screams, "My name is *cutieeeee...*"

With her unkempt hair, running makeup, emotional numbness, and dirty punk clothes Nikita is the prototypical "dysfunctional" young woman. "Maggie's initial rugged aggressiveness is tantamount to the action heroine's performance of masculinity,"[9] says Brown about the female hero Maggie (Bridget Fonda) in *Point of No Return*, the American remake of *Nikita*. However, this is not "masculinity." It is the cliché of a young criminal wearing precisely the outfit stolen by Schwarzenegger from a punk at the beginning of *The Terminator*. The punk clothes signify adolescence and rebellion, the unkempt exterior signals inner "disturbance," and the emotional numbness calls for reeducation or reprogramming (which the terminator is subject to in *Terminator 2*).

The film has three scenes of rebirth. The first is after the faked suicide when Nikita wakes up in a white room. "Is this heaven?" she asks agent Bob (Tcheky Karyo), who is dressed in black like a priest.

BOB: I work ... let's say, for the government. We've decided to give you another chance.

NIKITA: What do I do?

BOB: Learn. Learn to read, walk, talk, smile and even fight. Learn to do everything.

NIKITA: What for?

BOB: To serve your country.

A new Nikita is born under the scrutinizing gaze of Bob. First, she must be tamed. "Used one before?" the shooting instructor asks as she shoots a target into two pieces. "Never on paper!" And when the karate instructor tells her to hit him, she slaps him in the face, an unexpected move that takes him by surprise. She is a "natural" with the instincts of a predatory animal (kill or be killed) and not limited by social conventions. Nikita bites the karate instructor in the ear and dances a mock ballet. The instructor in feminine behavior and social manners, Amande (Jeanne Moreau), turns Nikita's exterior into beauty, but Nikita removes the wig and reverts to trashy appearances. "In three months she's screwed up everything," the chief complains to Bob, "lost your touch?" As I shall return to in the next section, Amande represents femininity. However, Nikita lacks *paternal* guidance, and progress only comes when Bob advances from watching her to engage in a more personal relationship with her. On her twentieth birthday he brings a cake with lit candles and says they have two weeks. Or else. On her television screen a kiss is exchanged between lovers in an old movie. "Who are you?" the man asks. "I don't know," responds the woman.

The gesture of the cake initiates the process, which three years later results in the beautiful woman Bob takes to an expensive restaurant and hands a gift wrapped in gold paper. A pistol and a test: Eliminate the target behind her. The scene is visualized as a man with a mistress: she is in a short, black, sleeveless evening dress, Bob has the manners of a gentleman and offers champagne, and Nikita is almost clapping her hands in anticipation (what wife would do so?). Now, Brown claims, "there is no underlying natural state" and the female hero as "biological female is free to enact either or both of the most stereotypical of masculine or feminine behaviors."[10] His example is when Maggie in *Point of No Return* is trapped before a small bricked-up window which Bob had told her would be open. When she pretends to surrender, the bodyguard lowers his gun and she shoots him. He is fooled by her looks and would have (perhaps) shot a man without hesitation. The French original has no corresponding scene. Nikita kills the target, seeks an alternative exit when the window is a dead-end and escapes through a garbage chute in the kitchen.[11] In both versions Nikita/Maggie returns crying and furiously attacks Bob, then kisses him: "I will never kiss you again." Is there an "underlying natural state" in her behavior? Her frustrated crying when she is cornered in the kitchen, her crying upon her return to the agency, and her kissing Bob? To me this is all abundantly "feminine" in the context of action. Does—and we now speak in the logic of action genres—a man cry and kiss his superior and instructor?

In short, once the daughter has learned to "behave" she becomes quite a conventional woman. Judging from her apartment she likes interior decoration. She goes shopping after her first successful mission, and she jumps happily on beds with shrieks of delight. When Nikita is ordered to eliminate a target on what she thinks is a vacation gift from Bob for her and fiancé Marco (Jean-Hugues Anglade) to go to Venice, she is crying while killing. And at the end Nikita sobs and implores Victor The Cleaner (Jean Reno) to abandon the mission. "I cannot take it anymore." She is no longer a callous killer, but has become a caring person. "My poor love. They'll wear you out," Marco whispers in her ear that night. "The job's too tough for you. Look at your tiny hands. They need protection. They mustn't get old. Stop before it's too late." The daughter is not "free" to perform the social role of "killer." She has appropriated the "proper" social and emotional role of a woman, and now wants to be able to accept Marco's marriage proposal in Venice rather than deny him access to the bathroom because of an ongoing assassination from the bathroom window. "You've gotta help me, I can't do this. I can't live like this anymore," Maggie begs Bob (Gabriel Byrne) in *Point of No Return*. "I know that you like [the fact that] you made me into something different. But you're not looking close enough. I *am* different. Help me be better. Please, Bob, let me go."

A gendered binary is firmly in place: a woman is gentle and not violent, she cares rather than kills, and she is emotional and not numb. This is not compliant with being a secret agent and a killer, which is why Nikita and Maggie quit their jobs. The agents in the series *La Femme Nikita* and *Alias* also repeatedly express their aversion to the work and their desire to leave it. There is no "free will" in the daughter's life as an agent. She is constantly "abused" by a creator infatuated with his product. "I miss the time when I had you to myself every day," Bob (Karyo) tells a furious Nikita. "Listen: Which word do you not understand? There is no 'through'! There is no "out'!" says the American Bob (Byrne). The fathers will not let the daughter go.

Gender: Performance, Masquerade, Essence

You could almost think Besson had written his plot in homage to Joan Riviere's famous essay about masquerade. However, I doubt he has heard of the English psychoanalyst who in 1929 analyzed how a female patient would follow her speech in public with a most unsuitable flirt with the older men in her audience. "The exhibition in public of her intellectual proficiency, which in itself carried through successfully, signified an exhibition of herself in possession of the father's penis, having castrated him."[12] The patient was married, respectable, yet compelled to use feminine coquettish behavior to avert what she unconsciously feared would be men's reprisals for her entrance into "their" territory—public space. Flirting was not her usual behavior but her employment of a standard "feminine" behavior. She "acted" feminine when she entered the "role" of woman and used femininity as a "mask."

The widespread fame of "Womanliness as a Masquerade" in feminist criticism is primarily due to Riviere's bold description of the relation between womanliness as masquerade and genuine womanliness in this famous passage:

> Womanliness therefore could be assumed and worn as a mask, both to hide the possession of masculinity and to avert the reprisals expected if she was found to possess it—much as a thief will turn out his pockets and ask to be searched to prove that he has not the stolen goods. The reader may now ask how I define womanliness or where I draw the line between genuine womanliness and the 'masquerade.' My suggestion is not, however, that there is any such difference; whether radical or superficial, they are the same thing.[13]

Two things are central: First, Riviere concludes that the patient has stolen the penis from the father; she has not renounced the penis and thus not accepted castration. She hides her masculinized status by trying to please and appease men with overly feminine behavior to make them think she does not have the penis and is without "guilt." In fact, she *has* stolen the "penis"—a term I will substitute with "traditional male behavior" (which in this case means being intellectual and displaying one's ability in public)—and she wants recognition for her proficiency in "male" affairs; "[the fantasy's] weak point was the megalomanic character, under all the disguises, of the necessity for supremacy."[14] Today we would hardly call the patient "megalomanic," but say she wished for the same recognition granted men. Bearing in mind the violent rites of the rape-revenge movie, we know well that recognition of "having" the penis (or "phallus" as the organ's imaginary concept is called in psychoanalysis) is not something automatically granted men. Men's recognition of each other's accomplishments rests on acts of violence, precariously gendered behavior, and anxiety for reprisals. There is no "natural" manliness which has the authority to grant or deny recognition. There are only acts of masculine display which constitute temporary male identities. The behavior of the male rapists in the rape-revenge film testifies that being a "man" is not an essence but something which must constantly be tested and proved by, for instance, raping women.

The second point is essentialism. If femininity is a mask, then what is behind the mask? Riviere's answer is that femininity is a set of social behaviors that women learn during childhood development. "Normal" women employ this behavior unproblematically. "[W]omen who wish for masculinity" may use the *very same set* of social behaviors to "cover up" their masculine features. Thus, femininity is not seen as a biological essence but as a behavior. And this behavior is, in the case of Riviere's patient, used pathologically as a masquerade.

The concept of femininity as a behavior which can be "performed" by a woman while *at the same time* be part of her psychological identity—worn like a costume in a play or at a masquerade ball—has been appropriated by feminist and postfeminist theory. Feminist criticism sees masquerade as a concept which *exposes* the social constructedness of femininity and in this exposure, supposedly, lies a potential to subvert our naturalized hierarchical gender binary, where male is opposed to female as active to passive, hard to soft, strong to weak, aggressive to empathic, and so forth. By using femininity women may distance themselves to the gender roles provided by society. Postfeminist criticism, on the other hand, finds in the masquerade theory an apt metaphor for how women may use gender roles to pursue individual goals by freely choosing among gendered behavior according to one's need, "...the masculinized heterosexual woman reveals the arbitrariness of gender in a way that is not easily discounted ... her performance, her narrative function, and her very body emphasize the artificiality of gender roles," says Brown and concludes, "the growth of cinematic images of women kicking ass helps push the envelope of culturally appropriate gender traits."[15]

Let us now turn to Nikita. She is familiar with the masculine skills of killing and fighting, skills which need only be controlled and directed into their proper outlets (shoot the bad guys, not the good guys) to serve the nation. But she is a stranger to femininity. Amande's classes take place in a boudoir with a makeup table and a mirror lit by light bulbs in the fashion of a theater's dressing room. To become a woman is to become an actor, learn to apply makeup, and choose the appropriate costume. "Smile when you don't know anything. You won't be any smarter, but it's nice for those who look at you," is lesson number one. Is this femininity genuine? In a mesmerizing tone Amande says, "Allow yourself to be taken over by the faint fragility which will make your face beautiful. A smile. A smile, its surface sweetness. Gentleness. Almost a mood." The soft music creates an atmosphere of intimacy and of the protagonist trying to reach inwards to search for long forgotten sensations and emotions. Looking into the mirror Nikita manages only a poor imitation of a smile.

Nikita and *Point of No Return* differ in their thematization of femininity as performance. In the French version Amande *is* feminine. When she enters her room through a secret door, a coffee cup held delicately in her hand, the aging woman moves with the seductive grace she will teach Nikita. In the American version Amanda (Anne Bancroft) alternates between soft and hard stances. "Smile a little smile, say something off-hand, it doesn't have to fit the situation really. Say, 'I never did mind about the little things.'" When Maggie refuses, Amanda snarls, "Say it! Arrgh!" Then softly with a smile, "Please, dear: a smile and the sentence." Amanda's use of soft-spoken words and smiles is an act, a masquerade. It is not her "own" personality, and when Bob three years later takes Maggie out for the first time and compliments Amanda on the beauty of her student, Amanda responds with a radiant smile. The smile is wiped from her face and replaced with a sad expression when Bob and Maggie are gone. Amande (Moreau) is a role model of feminine behavior. Amanda (Bancroft) is an instructor in femininity as a masquerade. The two, says Riviere, are one and the same thing.

The element of performance in the masquerade theory has directed both feminist and postfeminist critics to use Judith Butler's theory of gender as performance. In *Gender Trouble* from 1990 Butler analyzes gender as the exterior product of performative acts done by and written over the body, rather than springing from an interior identity. "Gender ought not to be construed as a stable identity or locus of agency from which various acts follow; rather, gender is an identity tenuously constituted in time, instituted in an exterior space through a *stylized repetition of acts*."[16] In Butler's view, one *is* not a woman; one *becomes* a woman through "acts, gestures, enactments [which] are *performative* in the sense that the essence or identity that they otherwise purport to express are *fabrications* manufactured and sustained through corporeal signs and other discursive means."[17] She focuses on drag as subversive because it emphasizes gender as a fabrication and thus destabilizes the safe and recognizable hierarchical and binary categories of "man" and "woman." The notion of having a "true" gender is a "fantasy" created by our conviction that such a thing as a "true" gender exists in the first place. The idea of gender as inner identity and an essential sex is "a regulatory fiction ... constituted as part of the strategy that conceals gender's performative character..."[18]

This view of gender as *performance* instead of essence is taken up in regard to the female action hero's use of male and female skills and character traits. Brown thus slides from a résumé of Butler's theory—"drag subverts and destabilizes gender essentialism from within the system"—to applying her theory to the action film. "The gender-destabilizing work performed by the modern action heroine poses a direct challenge to one of the key perspectives of film theory ... The action heroine is an obvious contradiction to the woman-as-image theory typified by Laura Mulvey."[19] Another example of combining Butler's theory with the female action hero is Laura Ng's postfeminist analysis of the television series *La Femme Nikita*, an analysis that identifies "the power of ambiguity on the designation of the female warrior and the resistant agency these gray areas grant the woman warrior."[20] In the series Nikita is tall, blonde, and innocent of the crime of which she is convicted. Like Brown, Ng argues that the female hero's use of her body as spectacle and weapon signifies control over gender roles and over the male gaze. In Ng's example Nikita uses her body to seduce a man. "She controls what he sees and how he sees. In constructing herself in a specific way and by carrying out the alternative agenda of attempted murder, Nikita clearly is the one using the power of the gaze, not Michael or the audience. Her body is no longer a potential hazard; it is a tool she presents and utilizes for her own designs."[21]

Now, let us look at Nikita's ability to use gender and her body as a "tool" or, in Brown's words, "a weapon."[22] In the French and American films Nikita/Maggie carries out four assignments involving murder: (a) The initial test in the restaurant, (b) passing as a maid in a hotel, (c) assassinating a target in Venice/New Orleans, and (d) retrieving stolen data. On the last mission a "cleaner" arrives to fix problems and kill survivors. The point I want to pursue is whether gender is performative without an essence (Butler), or whether there is an essence "behind" the performative acts which are used as masquerade (Riviere) and, if this is the case, how this essence is constructed. On the first mission the daughter wears a black cocktail dress, a conspicuous costume gracing posters for *Nikita* as well as *Point of No Return*.

Brown goes to some length to argue that Maggie's dress is linked to the undershirt she wears at the start, and that the undershirt belongs to the male action heroes. "The same type of black undershirt is worn by Stallone in the *Rambo* series, Bruce Willis in *Die Hard* and such muscular/masculine women as Linda Hamilton in *Terminator 2* ... Her [Maggie's] black cocktail dress appears in the film and in the promotional stills to be a frilly version of the undershirt."[23]

To set records straight: just as there are different kinds of dresses, there are different kinds of men's undershirts. The one worn by Bruce Willis in the *Die Hard* movies is a tight, white, anonymous cotton undershirt similar to the ones my husband wears. Stallone wears different undershirts in the *Rambo* series: In *First Blood* he wears a sleeveless brownish shirt which is not very tight or revealing and not really an undershirt at all; in *Rambo: First Blood Part II* and *Rambo III* (where Stallone's body was much more muscular than in *First Blood*) he wears a black muscle shirt of the kind bodybuilders wear to reveal as much muscle as possible. The undershirt worn by Linda Hamilton in *Terminator 2* is a black tight cotton top rather than an undershirt; it combines the color of Stallone's costume with the design of Willis' and reconfigures the eighties undershirt as "top"—significantly it *is* her top in the warm desert and not her undershirt (this could be DKNY or Armani). And to be pedantic: Nikita in the French film never wears a man's undershirt. Her black cocktail dress refers back *as contrast* to her trashy punk clothes. Maggie wears a grey loose shirt, which looks more as if the sleeves have been cut off rather than it being a man's undershirt. Brown uses Hamilton's black top to link Maggie's dress to the undershirt of the action hero in the eighties. My objection to this reading is, first, that the top in *Terminator 2* is from 1991 and Nikita's cocktail dress is from 1990. To my knowledge female heroes *before* Linda Hamilton did not wear men's undershirts (Weaver, for instance, wears an anonymous white t-shirt in *Aliens* and the tiny white undershirt she wears in *Alien* in 1979 is no relation to the action hero's costume in the eighties). The black dress is thus *not* a reference to the white undershirt. One could argue that the cocktail dress has become a reference in *Point of No Return* from 1993 where it now pays respects to Hamilton's top from 1990. But—and this is my second objection—the dress in the American remake is *less* like an undershirt than the French dress; Nikita's tight dress is made of a soft stretch material with straps around her shoulders intertwining on the back, while the American dress is made of chintz material and a slingback neck, leaving the back bare. Maggie's dress is a feminine design with a fitted cut and a fluttering skirt.

I see no resemblance between Maggie's dress and a man's undershirt, and there is no man's undershirt in *Nikita*, only a black cocktail dress. Yet

Female assassin Maggie (Bridget Fonda) fools her opponents with her feminine costume in John Badham's American remake of the French film *Nikita, Point of No Return* (Art Linson Productions and Warner Bros., 1993).

Brown concludes "this heavily coded signifier of the black undershirt is incorporated into Maggie's initial feminine disguise."[24] I think this is an example of postfeminist wishful thinking. To argue for the "destabilizing resonance of this image" Brown quotes reviews which focused on exactly this scene, "[A] big gun and a killer miniskirt," "little black dress, great big gun," and "a slight woman deftly handling big guns" (in *Maclean, New York Times,* and *Wall Street Journal*).[25] However, it is no surprise reviewers notice this image since both film production companies singled it out for press material, lobby cards, posters, and so forth.

To stay in this admittedly pedantic train of thought, we must ask if this image was chosen because the film companies believed it *destabilized* gender? Put another way, does the female hero destabilize gender because she wears a dress and has a gun? Does the bringing together of opposites destabilize them? In this case I will argue the opposite: Bringing them together *stabilizes* feminine and masculine *as* each other's exact opposites which meet only in the exceptional case of a "pathological" girl who is "re-educated" by the system. The fascination is built on the premise that the female hero is one of a kind. Again and again she is the only female agent surrounded by men. Thus, even if we see other young women at the training facility where Nikita spends four years, we see Nikita interacting professionally with men. Charly in *The Long Kiss Goodnight* is up against dozens of male CIA agents. And when Sydney in *Alias* meets female agents, they are *enemy* agents typecast as evil Amazons (as Sydney's K-directorate rival, Anna Espinoza), as femme fatales (as her mother, KGB agent Irina), or as bitches (as Ariana Kane, the Alliance counterintelligence investigator). After an initial "pathological" display of masculine traits (her violent behavior and random killing of a police officer) the daughter's future use of feminine and masculine traits is highly coded *as* feminine and masculine. There is nothing destabilizing about her use of gender. She performs the conventional gender roles in her professional life (posing as a maid in her second assignment) and has internalized them as essence in her personality and her private life (crying while killing in her third assignment).

The "private" Nikita, Maggie, Sydney, and other daughter-agents do not confound gender expectations. They acquire an essence, a gendered "I" which is every cliché of a "woman": in France she is enigmatic, childish, seductive, charming, and sometimes melancholic (all mixed together in paradoxical fashion), and in the U.S. she is childish, sweet, uninhibited, independent, energetic, and light-humored (also a paradoxical mix which nonetheless is meant to convince us she has become a "real" woman). The daughter enjoys love, intimacy, sex, and partying and does not want to devote herself to work. This "essence" or "I" is a problem, because it conflicts with her professionalism: Nikita/Maggie are in tears when they discover the dinner with Bob is a mission to kill; in Venice/New Orleans the conflict between performing a job and pretending to be on vacation leaves them heartbroken; and during the last mission they become almost dysfunctional. They did not enter a man's world voluntarily, but were forced to do so. When we look closer, we see that a woman's world is defined as the *private* sphere of fiancé, family, friends, and home—the space where Nikita jokes childishly with Marco, where J. P. (Dermot Mulroney) proposes to Maggie, and Sydney invites friends for dinner and has Halloween parties. Unlike Rambo for whom hell *is* home (the famous tagline for *Rambo: First Blood Part II* was "what you call hell, he calls home") the daughter's home *was* hell, which is why she ended up as an agent in the first place. Her biggest wish is to create a home that is a paradise, not hell.

In her analysis of *Batman Returns* Jacinda Read compares Catwoman to the vampire-bitten Mina in the novel *Dracula*. Read argues they are both a mixture of vamp(ire) and New Woman, both lethal femme fatales and independent females. "I want to suggest that *Batman Returns* represents an attempt to reach a similar compromise between the demands of feminism and the increasing call in the 1990s for a return to more traditional models of gender (otherwise known as the backlash)."[26] The killed and resurrected Catwoman combines traditional masculine and feminine character traits—fighting and flirting, catching criminals and defending society—into the uneasy balance of the female superhero. This figure, says Read, is not subversive, since Catwoman defends the values of a capitalist and patriarchal system and, furthermore, because her construction as a melancholic single career woman desiring a partner (like Batman) operates in a plot whose "narrative moves do implicitly suggest that the solution to this crisis lies in the reinstatement of the family as the primary institution through which conventional and stable gender identities are produced and secured."[27] Superheroes and arch villains share warped childhoods. So, too, does the daughter.

Speaking of superheroes, we must clarify what status the costume has in the daughter's world. Here, we must differentiate between "masquerade," "disguise," "costume," and "cross-dressing." "Masquerade" refers to the masquerade ball where men and women use costumes and masks. Riviere uses "mask" and "masquerade" in the sense of *hiding* one's identity—that is, as a "disguise." Feminist criticism has used Riviere's terms as *revealing* society's gender roles and, in the postfeminist approach, as a voluntarily *playing with* identity and gender—that is, as "costume" rather than "disguise." The cross-dresser uses the mask not to "hide" but to display a part of his or her identity. Thus, in queer theory cross-dressing reveals, which explains the subtitle of Judith Butler's book *Gender Trouble: Feminism and the Subversion of Identity*. Drag subverts by exposing gender as performance and situating alternative identities in-between the binary of masculine and feminine. Brown calls Maggie "a double-cross-dresser" and "a dual drag"[28] because she "enacts femininity as a disguise for her symbolically masculine role," thereby showing that "all layers of identity are performed, that there is no underlying natural state."[29]

Maggie is a professional agent, which sets her apart from Riviere's patient and Butler's drag. One could say the daughter in her pathological state shares with the patient and the drag an alternative relation to gender, but once she is "cured" (that is, educated) she transforms from "sick" to "normal" and can no longer access masculine gender traits without this being painful. What, then, is her relation to gender, identity, and masquerade? I want to return to Riviere's lack of distinction between womanliness as genuine behavior and masquerade. Is this a refusal of essentialism—or can it be taken as Riviere's consent to a womanliness which can be *both* an essence and an act? She does not explicitly deny the latter and even if she does not construct womanliness as a *biological* essence, she certainly sees it as a social essence. By "social essence" I intend an essence, which according to Butler is "discursively produced and circulated by a system of significations,"[30] that constructs the subject as a gendered individual while growing up. We cannot evade this process and later subversion, fragmentation, or rejection will always come *after* this gendering.

The "starting point" of the daughter is a lost essence due to a disturbed childhood. The emotionally numb Nikita and Maggie are short on empathy but have plenty of aggression to spare. Speaking of the cross-dressing tomboy, Yvonne Tasker says she "is typically explained and contained in terms of her relationship to her father. Her 'masculine' qualities stem from a distorted upbringing in which she has had to rely on herself, whether this is expressed in terms of the loss of the mother or an identification with the father deemed excessive for a woman."[31] The daughter also has a "distorted upbringing." Maggie and Nikita do not mention their fathers and cry because their mothers did not attend their funerals. Megan in *Blue Steel* has an abusive father, and Sydney in *Alias* was abandoned by her KGB mother at the age of six and brainwashed by her CIA father, so that she would make the perfect spy as an adult. Understandably, Sydney has a complicated relationship with her father (with whom she works as a double agent in the criminal agency SD-6 and the CIA) and to her mother (who shoots her at the end of the first season). Upbringing is presented as a failed "imprint" on the daughter. This imprint, which is thematized as the ability to have intimate relationships, is regained through Sydney's secret agent work in the first and second season. Here, Riviere is relevant: The daughter's education to become an agent is *both* thematized as finding an essence (womanhood) and memorizing a role (femininity), it leads *both* to her discovery of a genuine gender and to her use of gender as an act. The agency cures the daughter, but with her newfound essence she is unable to be both a professional killer and a woman. Unlike James Bond, she is not satisfied with bedding beautiful women and killing criminals. She wants a *real* life with a *real* fiancé and *real* emotions.

The ambiguity of the daughter lies in her relation to gender: she is a trespasser and a traditional woman, a rebel and a conservative, a victim and a survivor, a private person and a professional. In this respect she stands in stark contrast to the male agent. Not her life, but her identity is at stake when she points her gun, which is why Nikita breaks down next to Victor the Cleaner, why Maggie quits the agency, and why Megan is carried lifeless from the crime scene. They are not fit for the job. The serial format prevents the protagonists of *La Femme Nikita* and *Alias* from quitting. However, all they can dream of is a "normal" life with a mother, a father, and a fiancé. A happy moment for Sydney in the second season is when she, her father, and mother in unison gun down a group of terrorists in "Passage, Part II"— the perverse image of a real family. Or when she in "The Abduction" for the first time since childhood embraces her mother. This happens under police surveillance on the rooftop of the prison where Irina is locked up. As Irina and Sydney affectionately embrace, heavily armed guards draw machine guns and order them to part, "Back away, back away!" The happiest moment, though, is when Vaughn and Sydney kiss for the first time, similarly dressed in Kevlar vests and black assault uniforms after the successful raid on SD-6 in "Phase One."

In her 1999 introduction to *Gender Trouble* Butler admits, "Gender can be rendered ambiguous without disturbing or reorienting normative sexuality at all. Sometimes gender ambiguity can operate precisely to contain or deflect non-normative sexual practice and thereby work to keep normative sexuality intact."[32]

Initial Transformations and Mission Masquerades

When Brown claims the action heroine is "an obvious contradiction" to the "woman-as-image theory," he is wrong. She may or may not have a female audience, but she always appeals to men by fitting Hollywood conventions—slim, beautiful, and young. (Sigourney Weaver, Geena Davis, and Michelle Yeoh who play heroes in their forties are exceptions). When beautiful women age they become villainesses as Sharon Stone in *Catwoman* and

Faye Dunaway in *Alias*). Beauty and body are constantly on display in the daughter's narrative, first as a surprise revelation in her transformation from misfit to fit, then in the missions requiring costumes that can hardly be called inconspicuous.

I want to distinguish between two types of transformation: *initial transformations* and *mission masquerades*. The first, the initial transformation, works like reality shows such as *The Swan* and *Extreme Makeover*, whose participants with the aid of plastic surgeons, fitness instructors, dentists, dietitians, psychologists, and personal stylists are turned from "ugly ducklings" into "swans." The daughter is styled into a "revelation" of beauty, grace, and social skills. "Are you an ugly duckling or a swan? Because the choice is yours, you know," says Amanda. As with the reality programs, the initial transformation is not a reconstruction of a "true" identity hidden within, but a Pygmalion *construction* of a new ideal femininity. In *Working Girls* (2000) Tasker points to two dynamics at play in scenes of cross-dressing. "[T]he first is to do with *transformation*, whilst the second concerns a desire for *knowledge*" (italics mine).[33] The transformation comes at the exhilarating moment of "'becoming something other'":

> Typically represented through montage sequences with an upbeat soundtrack, transformation is offered as cinematic spectacle that takes place, like the numbers in Hollywood musicals, in a space to one side of the narrative ... These are moments when words will simply not suffice, because what is offered seems unspeakable (in whichever sense) or because only clichés are available.[34]

Transformation is central to the daughter archetype. It is tied to a new identity, a new future, the opening of a door to a new world of choices. This is cross-dressing in the sense of crossing *back* from a (wrong) "masculinized" identity into feminine identity and at the same time class cross-dressing in moving the agent *up* to a higher level, metaphorically as well as professionally and socially. "Still as ambitious," the chief comments, as Bob wants an S1 classification for Nikita: the perfect killer and perfect woman.

Initial transformations release different elements in the archetypes: In the rape-avenger it often signifies a release of sexuality (such as Thana turning increasingly sexy as she kills); in the mother it releases "masculine" capabilities (Ripley learning to use the pulse rifle and Slim learning martial arts); the dominatrix has no initial transformation since she *is* like "that"; and if an initial transformation happens to the Amazon it releases her "true" Amazonian self. Thus, Catwoman's transformation from ordinary to superhero is her initiation into her true personality. "In my old life I longed for someone to see what was special in me," Catwoman (Halle Berry) writes in her goodbye letter to Tom (Benjamin Bratt) in *Catwoman* (2004), "but what I really needed was for me to see it. And now I do. You're a good man, Tom.

But you live in a world that has no place for someone like me. You see, sometimes I'm good. Oh, I'm very good. But sometimes I'm bad. But only as bad as I wanna be. Freedom *is* power. To live a life untamed and unafraid is the gift that I've been given and so my journey begins."

Initial transformations change the daughter irrevocably. There is no going back. Initial transformations take the daughter "out" of her old "self" and "into" a new "self." Looking into the mirror Nikita asks Amande, "Did you go through this once?" Amande smiles and hands her a lipstick. "Let your pleasure be your guide. Your pleasure as a woman. And don't forget: There are two things that have no limit: femininity and the means of taking advantage of it." The mirror as metaphor invokes the Lacanian mirror phase where the imaginary is constituted after the recognition of oneself as "Other" in the mirror (another connotation of the mirror is, of course, an entrance to another world). Identification comes from shaping oneself after the image of the Other. Daughter narratives constantly return to this process of initiating a new "I." The image of the old Nikita fades to a new Nikita applying mascara in preparation for her dinner with Bob.

The outcome of the initial transformation is a daughter-agent—a second self—who performs missions for the agency and is handed assignments by a mentor or a father figure. (In *Alias* Sydney's contact in the CIA is called her "handler.") Where initial transformation has to do with *interior* change the secondary transformation scenes are about *exterior* changes. They are masquerades in the sense that they are intended to have the agent pass for someone else. Mission masquerades involve all kinds of roles and outfits from art dealer and male diplomat (*Nikita*) to mental patient ("Color-Blind"), corpse ("Passage, Part I"), or old lady ("Firebomb"). They are often traditional Mulveyan scenes of woman-as-spectacle with the agent in disguise as prostitute, girlfriend, or escort. With Bob, Nikita looks *exactly* like a mistress with an older lover; Maggie poses as a gangster's girlfriend with a French accent, red boots and red, short outfit; and Sydney in "So It Begins" tells her partner Dixon "don't panic," and in a matter of seconds transforms from a Russian blonde maid to a Russian blonde prostitute, now wearing a short, blue latex dress. The image of the prostitute or kept mistress recurs throughout the television series, which has Sydney in disguise at parties, discos, and in bars, places where a "nice girl" is excluded. Sydney's costumes are always ultra-tight to show her figure; her hair changes from brown (Sydney's natural color) to red, white, or purple, from straight to curly, from loose to elaborately set hair styles. Her entire body is constructed as costume and spectacle. Thus we see her dressed and in makeup as a Japanese geisha ("The Counteragent"), as an Indian woman in sari ("Passage, Part I"), or simply as a prostitute in black underwear with a whip ("Phase One").

The female hero's ever-changing costumes in the television series *Alias* (Touchstone Television and Bad Robot, 2001–) constitute a central appeal of the show. Jennifer Garner plays double agent Sydney Bristow.

Riviere's patient had stolen the father's penis and, says Riviere, normal heterosexual womanhood is founded on renunciation of the penis and on acceptance of castration and of the knowledge that, "I must not take, I must not even ask; it must be *given* me."[35] "It" is the penis/the paternal signifier of the Law. The gun is such a phallic signifier of the Father, an overdetermined object that was stolen by the pathological daughter. She is then captured, punished, and reeducated after which the gun is forced back into her hands by a father figure. The choice to use the gun as daughter-agent is not *her* choice but *his* choice, and the use of the gun is now painful and not pleasurable. The narrative construct of "unethical services performed by a young woman kept against her will" connotes prostitution with the father as a pimp and sometimes also a pedophile. Thus a bored twelve-year-old Mathilda in *Leon* tells the concierge at the hotel that Leon (Jean Reno), the adult assassin and her reluctant savior, is both her father and her lover (they then have to change hotels again). Nikita and Maggie both kiss Bob, whose symbolic father role is underlined in *Point of No Return* where J.P. wants to know Bob's age—"I am thirty-seven"—which makes him thirteen years older than Maggie—"fourteen, her birthday is coming up in three months," says J.P.[36] "What exactly is your point?" Bob asks, irritated.

The point is that the father (and, behind him, the agency) is abusing the daughter-agent. Any lack of services will result in termination. "I can't stand you," the chief tells Nikita, "I'd have let you die. So toe the line. You won't be warned." The American chief tells Maggie a joke to test her, "You'll love this. A woman goes into a bar with a duck under her arm, right. Orders a couple of beers. The bartender says: 'What are you doing in a bar with that pig?' She says: 'I beg you pardon, it's a duck.' He says: 'I beg *your* pardon, I was talking to the duck.'" When Maggie doesn't laugh, the chief adds, "I think you're dangerous. Real loose cannon. If it had been up to me I'd have put you down, so don't make any mistakes. Cause I'm telling you, if you cross on a red light you are worm bait." In *Alias* Sydney is under constant suspicion for not being loyal to SD-6 and its chief, Archie Sloane, who had her fiancé murdered. If her loyalty is questioned she, too, will be worm bait. The joke (which does not figure in the French film) reveals uneasiness. Megan Turner in *Blue Steel* must also listen to a dick joke from her superior about a prostitute sewing a client's penis, which she accidentally bit off, back on. But backwards.

Dick jokes reveal male uneasiness about handing the daughter the gun/phallus. Will she behave and accept her castration? Does she know how to handle it? Or will she turn it against the father and "castrate" him? Can she tell the difference between a dick and a duck, as the joke goes in *The Long Kiss Goodbye*, where agent Waldman mistakes the picture of a duck for a dick and immediately afterwards loses his life in the water, where Charly takes the gun hidden in his crotch and saves her life. "Other agents are often reluctant to feel up another man's groin," he said earlier. The daughter, in her capacity as professional, isn't. She is trained to handle groins and guns, men and missions.

The Third Self

The desire for knowledge, which Tasker locates within the cross-dressing and transformation scenes, involves a "discovery or revelation ... [which] is at least potentially more sinister, and to some extent sadistic ... associated as it is with a fear of discovery and exposure, but also with a loss of identity."[37] Our fascination with the daughter is (a) in the *initial transformation* which thematizes our identity as a changeable part of our self, if not completely free then at least something we can develop under proper guidance; (b) in having her perform *mission masquerades* where the audience can enjoy the voyeuristic spectacle of "woman-to-be-looked-at-ness"; and (c) in providing suspense as to whether she will "pass" as a cross-dresser or be "made," which will result in severe punishment. Thus, when Sydney is "made" in the mental hospital in "Color-Blind" she is subjected to water torture. This is the sadistic version of the spectacle (or, if one identifies with the tortured, the masochistic version).

Riviere's patient feared men's reprisals if she revealed her "masculine" character trait (the stolen penis). In the daughter's case it is the other way around; she is afraid of the reprisals if she fails to perform her masquerade and lowers her gun (the penis/phallus). "I never did mind about the little things," says Maggie when Victor the Cleaner (Harvey Keitel) is about to terminate her because she is failing to function as a secret agent. The repetition of the studied phrase signifies submission to the agency and her acceptance of the masquerade as daughter-agent. However, the phrase also signifies her sudden realization that if she fails, she will be terminated, and that she has no choice but to leave the agency if she wants to be free. The punishment inflicted on the daughter when her masquerade fails is severe. In *Nikita* and *Point of No Return* the punishment is emotional suffering: Nikita and Maggie cry because they cannot be honest with their fiancés or have a private life out of reach of the agency. After completing their education they develop *a third self*, which is the intimate, private, or "real" self with the fiancé at home. In the end, Nikita and Maggie quit their jobs to pursue this third self, which will become their future "I." Sydney in *Alias* also has multiple selves: Her private self (her identity with friends) is a student who works at a bank; the secret agent self trained by SD-6; and when

SD-6 kills her fiancé she joins the CIA to bring down Sloane and SD-6 and develops her third self: the angry double agent. This third self—the double agent—is the only self where Sydney can be truly intimate with people (her father, mother, her fiancé Vaughn, her friend Will). And even this third self is invaded by the agency. The punishment when the masquerade fails can also be literal pain. Connected to the question "Who are you?" is always the threat of death. Samantha reverts into the spy Charley when she is tortured. Torture is recurrent in *Alias*, where Sydney loses several teeth under torture in the series' first episode "Truth Be Told" and later suffers electro-shock, beatings, being shot, and almost having her kneecaps broken with a hammer.

The daughter's third self, as Read concludes about Catwoman, negotiates between feminism and patriarchy.[38] The result is a postfeminist female hero with a multiple personality that consists of an old self, a new professional self, and a new private self. She prefers to be intimate rather than professional and prioritizes emotions and feminine essence over her masculine profession. Nikita, Maggie, and Charly are not willing to serve their countries if this means compromising their third selves. Thus, even though they are *able* to perform gender as masquerade, they are not free to do so but forced to, and eventually choose to live gender as essence. That is, they quit their agent jobs. This conservative equality and choice postfeminism, where private is prioritized over professional, becomes ambiguous in the new millennium where the daughter does not quit but is trying to administer her multiple selves. Sydney in *Alias* thus remains a professional and struggles to have a private love life, and *La Femme Nikita* ends with Nikita as the new head of Section One. However, in contrast to the mother figure who is untamable, the daughter always operates *within* the rules of patriarchy.

Daughter Action Filmography

Nikita (1990) Dir. Luc Besson, filmed in France and Italy. Secret agent and assassin Nikita/Marie

Black Cat (Hei Mao) (1991) Dir. Stephen Shin, filmed in Hong Kong. Secret agent and assassin Erica/Catherine

Black Cat II (Hei Mao II) (1992) Dir. Stephen Shin, filmed in Hong Kong.

Point of No Return (UK title: The Assassin) (1993) Dir. John Badham. Secret agent and assassin Maggie/Claudia

Léon (1994) Dir. Luc Besson, filmed in France and the U.S. Child, avenger, and apprentice Mathilda, action

Cutthroat Island (1995) Dir. Renny Harlin. Daughter and pirate queen Morgan Adams, adventure

La Femme Nikita (1997–2001) filmed in the U.S. (96 episodes). Secret agent and assassin Nikita/Josephine

Charlie's Angels (2000) Dir. Joseph McGinty Nichol. Detectives Natalie, Dylan, Alex

Alias (2001) ABC television series (98 episodes, still running in 2006). Secret agent Sidney; "Truth Be Told" 1:1, September 30, 2001; "So It Begins" 1:2, October 7, 2001; "Color-Blind" 1:7, November 25, 2001; "The Counteragent" 2:7, November 10, 2002; "Passage, Part I" 2:8, December 1, 2002; "Passage, Part II" 2:9, December 8, 2002; "The Abduction" 2:10, December 15, 2002; "Phase One" 2:13, January 26, 2003; "Firebomb" 2:16, February 23, 2003

Lara Croft: Tomb Raider (2001) Dir. Simon West. Adventurer Lara Croft

Charlie's Angels: Full Throttle (2003) Dir. Joseph McGinty Nichol

Lara Croft Tomb Raider: The Cradle of Life (2003) Dir. Jan de Bont

Kill Bill: Vol. 1 (2003) Dir. Quentin Tarantino. Assassin Black Mamba/Beatrix Kiddo/The Bride/"B"/Mummy

Kill Bill: Vol. 2 (2004) Dir. Quentin Tarantino

Elektra (2005) Dir. Rob Bowman. Assassin Elektra

The Warrior and the Wardrobe: The Amazon Hero

> Feminism and misogyny at the same time. I honestly don't know
> if I love this film or hate it with a passion. It has Thelma and
> Louise appeal, but also appeals to male sexual fantasies by mak-
> ing womyn [sic] objects.
> —Fan comment to *Amazons and Gladiators* (2001)[1]

> 31 breasts. 67 corpses. Nipple painting. Acid-washed horndog.
> Gratuitous blind fortune teller. Face biting. Amathea brazenly
> declares her quest, "I'll be no man's slave and no man's whore!
> And if I can't kill them all, by the gods, they'll know I've tried!"
> —Fan comment to *Barbarian Queen* (1985)[2]

On the one hand, the Amazon embodies strength and independence of men with her "Thelma and Louise appeal" as a viewer calls it. She is a woman in a man's world who is fully capable of kicking men out of their territory. On the other hand, when she does her kicking she is visually rendered as an erotic spectacle clad in strategically placed leather strings or some other sexy costume. Thus, the second quote is about *Barbarian Queen* (1985), a Roger Corman release with model Lana Clarkson as Queen Amathea. "No man can possess her. No man can defeat her" ran the tagline on the film's poster with five silicone-enhanced beauties in impossible string bikinis, holding phallic spears and swords and casting sultry and angry glances at the audience. Such exploitation, obviously, is a far cry from feminism. Yet, the television series *Xena: Warrior Princess* (1995–2001) was embraced by a homosexual audience who interpreted the long legged and armor-clad Xena and her red-haired sidekick Gabrielle as a butch-femme couple. The producers picked up on this response and added a lesbian subtext to the series, which divided critics between those praising the show as groundbreaking and feminist and those who found the show merely simulating feminism.

The Amazon from Greek mythology is an ambiguous figure. She is not a heroic character but a monster like the Gorgon and the Sphinx. To prove himself a worthy hero, an Athenian warrior should defeat an Amazon, who was considered the most dangerous adversary. Her mixture of female biology and male character traits evoked erotic *frisson* and fear, and there were two ways to deal with her: kill her ... or marry her. Either way—as corpse or wife—the Amazon part disappeared. When he looked down at Penthesilea lying dead at his feet, Achilles thus bitterly regretted he had killed the beautiful Amazon queen instead of making her his wife. The "pure" Amazon is a rare protagonist in modern cinema. In *Amazons and Gladiators* (2001) Sabrina discovers she is an Amazon by birth, but most of the time "pure" Amazons function as side characters.[3] What I call "the Amazon hero" is, strictly speaking, a female warrior who is Amazonian in psychology, in exterior (her costume, weapons), or is placed in a narrative using Amazon elements (hatred of men, love of war and so forth). Thus, Xena frequently fights alongside Amazons, Gabrielle is adopted by Amazons in the show's second episode, the fierce Guinevere in *King Arthur* (2004) has an Amazonian personality, and Abigail in *Blade Trinity* (2004) uses Amazon equipment.

The Greek Amazon

Who were the Amazons? The Greek historian Lysias (440–380 B.C.) writes, "For their bravery Amazons used to be considered men rather than women for their physical nature. They seemed to surpass men in their spirit instead of falling short of them in appearance. They ruled many lands and enslaved their neighbours. Then, hearing of the great reknown of this land, they gathered their most warlike nations and marched against the city. A glorious reputation and high ambitions were their motives. But here they met brave men and came to possess spirits alike to their nature."[4]

In Greek mythology Amazons are female warriors who love war. "Amazon" means "those who have no breasts" since Amazons reportedly cauterized the right breast of infant girls to be better able to shoot the bow (however, Amazons were never depicted without a breast but always with two breasts).[5] They hated men, bred once a year, and raised only girl children. According to different accounts, boys were either mutilated or killed. Amazons entered Attic history as black-figure vase paintings in 575 B.C. and became popular as *Amazonomachies*—depictions of battles between Greeks and Amazons. Their first written account is by Euripides in *Heracles* (c. 417 B.C.) where Heracles steals a girdle from the Amazon Andromache. In a later myth the hero Theseus rapes and abducts an Amazon, which cause the Amazons to attack Athens.[6] This myth of the vengeance of a rape evolved into the myth that Lycias told about Amazons attacking Athens for no reason and being (justly) annihilated.

William Blake Tyrrell in *Amazons: A Study in Athenian Mythmaking* (1984) points out that the idea of a civilization of woman warriors is a patriarchal fantasy. There is no historical evidence as to their existence. The myth simply inverts the social order of ancient Greece. "If one was to remove everything Western from Japanese culture, for example, much that is authentically Japanese would remain. In the case of the Amazon myth, however, this process will show that apart from Athenian patriarchy the Amazon has no substance. The attempt to separate fact from fancy failed because without the reversal there is nothing."[7] The Amazon originates from men's fantasies about women. Social order required men to go to war and women to marry and raise children. Men were "civilized" while women's nature was "bestial" and had to be tamed in marriage. The boy's initiation rite was to go to war and the girl's initiation rite to marry and bear children. Marriage placed her within patriarchy. Without marriage she was outside social order. She became "a daughter in Limbo"[8] and an androgyne, neither man nor woman. Outside marriage she could not even be a mother, since the uterus was merely considered a container for the male "seed." Only a father contributed to a child's genes and a woman could only be mother in her capacity as *wife*.

In ancient Greece men represented human order, civilization, and culture while women represented the bestiality and savagery of nature.[9] Between the male and the female pole, the Greek inserted a third category, the feminine, denoting "those aspects of the female pole which are similar to the male pole and therefore valued by men."[10] When women marry, they share in the male pole and become part of civilization. "Woman" is divided into "female" and "feminine," which is respectively negative (as the negation of "male") and positive (because now subordinated to "male"). "The negative side of the construct Woman, the female pole, represents in fact no more than the capacity of women to act on their own for their own pleasure and purposes," concludes Tyrrell.[11] Thus, the Amazon myth is structured in binary opposition to a male order which it inverts by combining "male" and "female" elements in the Amazon, and by having her refuse the "feminine." Amazons do not behave like women, but like men: They live outside the home, use weapons, are dominant, and go to war. They refuse to marry and when they need to breed, they abduct and rape men and later raise the children without fathers.[12] Genetic value is inverted; where the Greeks value the boy Amazons value the girl, and where the Greeks value the father

Amazons value the mother. The Amazon conquers lands, enslaves men, rapes, fights, is dominant, aggressive, and has sexual desires.[13] She is the contrast to a well-behaved wife, as is clear from Plutarch's description of a proper wife in *Advice to the Bride and Groom*:

> [The wife] ought to be most conspicuous in her husband's company and stay in the house and hide when he is away ... The wife ought not to have any feelings of her own but join with her husband in his moods whether serious, playful, thoughtful, or joking ... Should a man in private life be without control or guidance in his pleasures and commit some indiscretion with a prostitute or servant girl, the wife should not take it hard or be angry, reasoning that because of his respect for her, he does not include her in his drunken parties, excesses, and wantonness with other women ... She ought to speak to her husband or through her husband and not be disgruntled if, like the fluteplayer, she utters sounds through the tongue of another.[14]

The Amazon is no fluteplayer. Like the single women in *Sex and the City*, Amazons are "sexual, not virginal, and they desire men while rejecting male babies."[15] As daughters of Ares, the god of war, and the nymph Harmonia, they were associated with savage war and uncontrolled eroticism. Ares represented "war as murderous fury and savage bloodthirstiness,"[16] and Harmonia was linked to the goddess Aphrodite who again as the patron of courtesans represented untamed eroticism. It was thought that Amazons worshipped Ares (representing war), Artemis (goddess of the hunt), and Cybele (goddess of the fertile earth and wild animals). The Amazon therefore had a dual nature; she was *bestial* like women because she was not controlled by men and marriage, and she was *masculine* because she behaved like a man. "The result is a sexual hybrid. Amazons are not women in male armor but are androgynes—apparitions composed of male and female elements which confuse the distinctions between the sexes and the values and categories of thought assigned to each."[17]

Tyrrell links the Amazon myth to transition rites between adolescence and adulthood. The Amazon is what would happen if the daughter refused marriage and instead took the place of the young man, the *ephebe*, as he is called in his two-year training to become a warrior. If girls refused to be women and chose to be men, the result would be "the topsy-turvy world of the Amazon."[18] Tyrrell does not comment on the sexual aspects of the myth: the sado-masochistic fantasy of aggressive women killing or raping men and mutilating boys, and the fantasy of men reversely killing or subduing beautiful and aggressive women. The confusion of categories was obviously charged with sadomasochistic sexuality as when, for instance, the cults of the goddess Cybele held orgies where men performed voluntary castration. Clearly, the Amazon is related to the dominatrix.

The Amazon in Greek mythology was a woman who behaved like a man: she went to war, loved fighting, and hated staying home with a family. Who says postfeminism is a new concept? Brigitte Nielsen as Sonja in *Red Sonja* (Dino De Laurentiis, 1985). (Courtesy of the British Film Institute.)

The Amazon Costume

Like the dominatrix, the Amazon in modern popular culture is an iconic archetype whose costume marks her as a non-realist character. She is a fantastic and fictional figure in contrast to, for instance, the mother, the daughter or the rape-avenger. You wouldn't notice them in a crowd, whereas most people would look twice at Zula or Xena or Red Sonja. Talking about the woman's costume in silent cinema, Jane Gaines says it "should place a character quickly and efficiently, identifying her in one symbolic sweep."[19] In silent cinema the costume filled in for missing dialogue, "like decor, [it should] provide iconographic cues related to typage, and narrative conventions; in the absence of sound it was seen as a substitute for speech." A woman's costume was a one-line statement that said, "I am the vamp" or "I am the straight girl," thus communicating a film's narrative in a single image. So, too, does the costume in Amazon cinema. It says, "I am the Amazon," thus identifying this female archetype in one symbolic sweep. There is no mistaking Corman's babes with their pointy swords and string-bikinis for vampires, action heroines, or, say, single career women.

In ancient Greece, Amazons dressed like men: heavy or light coats of war with fringes on the thighs, bare legs, sometimes just a dress in a light fabric. Men were occasionally depicted fighting in the nude; however, Amazons were depicted dressed or half-dressed. In classical European paintings the Amazonomachies became popular with Amazons in Greek clothing and armor (helmet, shield, sword, spear, and bow). However, when the Amazon crossed the Atlantic and arrived in Hollywood she left her Greek costume behind. Films such as *Tarzan and the Amazons* (1945) and *Queen of the Amazons* (1947) place her in a jungle and in a swimsuit-style costume without armor.[20] In the popular American cinema the Amazon costume is no longer Greek but combines Western lingerie with various styles of "tough," male, or adventurous clothing signaling to the audience that this is an Amazon in a man's world. *Conan the Barbarian* (1982), which marks the return of the Amazon to modern popular cinema, is an example: On the film's poster Conan takes a step forward on a mountain top and raises his mighty sword above his head with a glowing fire in the background. Before him, facing us, the female warrior Valeria squats in an impossible pose with her long legs spread wide apart and the fringes on her leather body-suit forming a dark shape between her thighs, her long blond hair blowing as if touched by a light breeze, her hands holding a sword between the legs. Her tight leather costume is the shape of a teddy and held together in the front with strings. The male warrior is just as sexualized a spectacle as the female warrior: Conan wears a loincloth, which leaves most of his impressively muscular body naked, and like Valeria he has loose hair and long boots. The weapons, the boots, and the heavy metal bracelets signify armoring and war, while the tailoring of the costumes as underwear signifies erotic fantasy and sexual role-play.

With sound cinema, says Gaines, a star's costume should signal everyday life *and* the extraordinary. Such a complicated message is usually not necessary in the case of the Amazon, where everyday life *is* the extraordinary. We are in the realm of the fantastic, both in the generic sense of fantasy as well as in the psychological sense of fantasized as opposed to real. The changed costume signals the Amazon's move from the realm of myth to the realm of erotic fantasy. The underwear part can be more or less outspoken: Valeria's costume is cut as a teddy as are many later Amazon outfits, including Red Sonja's brown leather teddy; Zula's costume in *Conan the Destroyer* (1984) is a string bikini in black leather; Xena's armor is a Victorian style corset in heavy black leather with an exterior metal bustier; Sabrina in *Amazons and Gladiators* and Gabrielle both wear the more "girlish" camisole; and Guinevere wears an empire-style brassiere in *King Arthur*.

We could ask why the Amazon would wear such an skimpy costume that cannot possible stay in place during her horse riding or fighting and provides no protection whatsoever from the cold weather or possible enemy attacks. How come, for instance, that Arthur and his knights as well as the Saxons and the Romans are all dressed in heavy armor, fur, and skin for their protection and comfort, whereas the Toad women (the English resistance fighters) fight in long pants and brassiere (!). This is because the Amazon's costume, like Ilsa's outfits, is an erotic outfit.[21] In the context of female superheroes in the comics, Scott Bukatman notes about their costumes that:

> the fetishism of breasts, thighs, and hair [is] so complete, that the comics seem to dare you to say anything about them that isn't just redundant. *Of course* the female form has absurdly exaggerated sexual characteristics; *of course* the costumes are skimpier than one could (or should) imagine; *of course* there's no visible way that these costumes could stay in place; *of course* these women represent simple adolescent masturbatory fantasies (with a healthy taste of the dominatrix).[22]

Unlike the daughter, the mother, and the rape-avenger, who change in and out of different costumes to stress different parts of their personality (being, for example, vulnerable, sexy, professional, private), the Amazon has one costume because she is a one-dimensional archetype. Whether Xena fights or has beers with Gabrielle at an inn, she wears exactly the same black armor. It only changes when the narrative requires a change of clothes for some specific reason, because if she had a closet it would contain (like Batman's closet in his Batcave) one row of identical armors. The Amazon is less a person than an icon and a fantasy. Her costume should not interpret a

Hard in all the right places: a phallic weapon, phallic look, phallic body, and revealing costume made Grace Jones a convincing Amazon warrior in *Conan the Destroyer* (Dino De Laurentiis, 1984). (Courtesy of the British Film Institute.)

personality or trace any psychological development, because she does not develop and her personality is fixed in the mythic soil. It shows her character with an exact match between exterior and interior. Like the gunfighter who is already "there," as Robert Warshow formulated it in "Movie Chronicle: The Westerner," where should she possibly move on to? The gunfighter had his gun, his hat, his horse, and his mentality. He need change neither clothes nor personality. He is already "there." The Amazon has also reached her destiny, or rather, never left it, because like the queen in a game of chess may move and attack, the wooden piece never hides or changes. It *is* the queen, as the Amazon *is* the Amazon.

In the former chapter I discussed the daughter's use of male and female costumes and of masculine and feminine behavior, and argued that it did not subvert traditional gender roles or refuse gender essentialism. Her costume was used in a "realist" mode and her development from "ugly" and "masculinized" to "beautiful" and "feminine" was a victory for the development of traditional, stereotypical femininity. When the daughter disguised herself (as bimbo or prostitute or whatever required) it was as part of her job; this second-order costume was a "pretense" intended to fool people. The Amazon costume is already a second-order costume. It is not a "realist" element but like Ilsa's Nazi uniform an indication of the fictional. We should not read this costume literally. It is a make believe, a game. Thus, to read Ilsa as a historical figure would be to read against the grain. She is a figure from S-M role-play, a dominatrix out of the erotic imagination and she masquerades in the literal sense of the term. Where the realist female archetypes use costumes like we use everyday clothes, the dominatrix and the Amazon are at a masquerade ball. Their costumes explicitly play with gender and sexual behavior.

Discussing dominatrix pornography, Thaïs E. Morgan in "A Whip of One's Own: Dominatrix Pornography and the Construction of a Post-Modern (Female) Subjectivity" calls the dominatrix "both masculine and feminine, off-balance and firmly upright, sexually available and impenetrable ... all at the same time."[23] Morgan reads the dominatrix in an epistemological perspective as belonging to playing and as part of a semiotic system of difference (strong/weak) rather than a "real or absolute, sexual difference" (male/female). Thus, in playing, the woman can be female/strong and the man male/weak, thus upsetting traditional gender hierarchy and establishing another. "This invitation to treat gender semiotically—as a set of freely playing signifiers that can be renegotiated and even altered depending on the subject and the context—is an exhilarating one."[24] Morgan admits that the play mode only allows the ordinary codes to be switched around temporarily because they are framed by a hypercode where the "play" is limited to certain situations (such as sex or masquerades). Thus, women may dominate men when this is part of male S-M play and fantasy.

Like the masquerade theory used in feminist and postfeminist theory, Morgan links this *playing* with gender codes (roles) with a *dislocation* of the borders between traditional gender roles. Thus, she believes the momentarily upsetting of codes opens for a re-reading of gendered behavior, "...a typical dominatrix 'scenario' from a hard-core pornographic magazine, can be read in two ways: as confirming the hypercode of sexual difference, or as challenging it."[25] In postfeminist fashion, Morgan points out that the hyperbole of signifiers, the mocking of male strength, and the exposure of gender roles as gender masquerade may be read as a critique of sexual difference. "Thus, through her self-conscious role playing—acting 'like a man' and 'like a woman" at the same time—the dominatrix breaks the frame of sexual difference, transgressing the prescribed limits for Woman ... In sum, with her phallic whip, her phallic high heels, her phallic hair, her phallic tongue, and her phallic clitoris, the dominatrix icon produces a monstrous hyperbole of phallocentricism, whose effect is to dislocate and destroy rather than to relocate and affirm the hypercode of sexual difference."[26] This is essentially the same argument used in queer theory. We find an example of such monstrous hyperbole and "dislocation" of the hypercode of sexual difference in two scenes from *Barbarian Queen*. In the first scene, the group of warrior women come upon a house where men torture and rape women. They kill a man who is raping a woman strung up on a fence. This scene is paralleled when Amathea later is captured and strung up on a rack. But when her tormentor rapes her, Amathea locks her pelvic muscle around his penis and squeezes. "Wait, wait," he screams, "stop squeezing, too tight." Amathea forces the man to set her free and then kills him. The film thus dislocates the codes of the female rape-victim as weak and helpless and relocates them (much as in rape-revenge cinema) as a rape-victim being dangerous and lethal.

But, as in the case with the daughter, we should pause and ask ourselves if this is a pleasurable playing with gender codes within clearly defined and agreed-upon rules aimed for male pleasure, or whether it is feminist dislocation of them. The postfeminist answer would be that it is both. From a male point of view, however, there is no doubt as to where pleasure resides in this scene, which many male fans on the Internet Movie Data Base single out as their favorite, "Nudity and bondage and fondling yes, but I have to say the most memorable scene occurs when Queen Amethea uses a unique method of escape after she has been captured and tied up in the warrior camp and is being fondled by one of her captors."[27] Men have no problem identifying with men as victims and women as castrators if this happens in an erotic context where it is obvious that the women are there *to be looked* at. "The actress shows her best asset several times—they are real, boys, no silicone in them!"[28] is a comment for *Barbarian Queen II: The Empress Strikes Back* and about *Red Sonja*, "[i]t was nice, however, to see Nielson without implants and sorta decent hair."[29] This leaves two questions: First, can women identify with the female/strong/sexual position of the Amazon and, second, when is the dislocation of gender codes merely "play" and when does it have the potential to become feminism? There is no simple answer to such questions. As we shall see shortly, *Xena: Warrior Princess* divided feminist critics on exactly this issue: Can popular culture employ and break with gender stereotypes at one and the same time?

Like with the dominatrix, the Amazon costume signals an aggressive and angry eroticism. It is designed to evoke the man's world of war and fighting, yet at the same time tailored to reveal the female hero's "natural" feminine physique. Long legs, cleavage, loose hair. As in all femme fatale cinema, there is never any mistaking the female hero for a man. Writing about fashion, Sherrie A. Inness comments on "toughness" in fashion. "One way to assure readers of the femaleness of a subject is to include a touch of femininity to limit the toughness of men's clothing or mannish clothing worn by women. As long as the femaleness and the femininity of the models is evident, then the cross-dress attire becomes nothing more than a costume."[30]

Lately, a negotiated version of the Amazon has appeared in popular cinema. The costumes of female warriors like Zula, Sonja, and Amathea explicitly signal a mixture of Amazon (untamed by men), warrior (weapons), and dominatrix (aggressive eroticism). Guinevere and Abigail are examples of a softer, "negotiated" Amazon who is strong and able to fight, yet submits to men. In *King Arthur* the native Celt woman Guinevere (Keira Knightley) is rescued from a torture dungeon by the Roman Commander Arthur (Clive Owen). Her costumes change from the Roman dresses Arthur gives the young woman to cover herself in the cold (long, feminine dresses) to her native Celtic clothes, which she wears in the final battle against the Saxons. The contrast between Guinevere and the Roman and Saxon warriors is striking: they are in heavy armor and coats due to the cold winter and need for protection. But the Celtic warriors (both men and women) are in light costumes that look like North American Indian leather clothes, with bare torsos in war paint. Guinevere wears tight leather pants, a braided leather brassiere with loose strings and straps in a quadratic empire cut (blending French empire with Indian style), and her body and face are painted blue with black ornaments. This costume is clearly no defense against axes and swords but a spectacle elaborately composed to make Guinevere look like a ballet dancer gracefully presenting studied moves with her knife and marked as female, feminine, and fragile.

The female hero Abigail (Jessica Biel) in *Blade Trinity* (2004) is another example of a negotiated Amazon. She is the leader of the Nightstalkers, a group of vampire hunters who liberate Blade from prison and help him defeat the vampires. Abigail and her friend Hannibal King (Ryan Reynolds) become two sidekicks Blade reluctantly accepts. The three are featured on posters and advertisement stills with protagonist and hero Blade (Wesley Snipes) in the middle flanked by the two young heroes. In mythic terms, the three can be interpreted as the adult Athenian warrior flanked by two *ephebes*. He uses heavy weapons fitting for a warrior (Blade's trademark sword and a number of guns, throwing stars, et cetera), while the ephebes use lighter long-range weaponry: Abigail has an elaborate technological bow with explosive arrowheads and Hannibal uses small handguns. Abigail has three costumes that each elegantly mediate Amazon conventions with modern ladies' fashion: Her first costume is black, low-cut tight leather pants and a leather corset laced in the front and cut above the navel. This is the modern designer-style Amazon with her bow and arrow holster carried on the back. She wears this costume when she hunts with Blade and Hannibal King. The second costume is a black and red figure-cut outfit in synthetic fabric, black pants and zipped jacket in a fitness design. This costume is worn at night and links her to Blade through its fabric, cut and the colors black and red; it interprets vampire hunting as "sport." The third costume, which was featured on film posters, has Abigail in brown low-cut leather pants and a grey cotton top with print on the front (of, among other objects, angel wings). The top is without sleeves, cut above the navel, and is worn with a second red top underneath. This is "underwear as outerwear" as Kim Walden notes.[31] On the back two strings wrinkle the fabric to simulate the lacing and wrinkling of a corset, and on the poster the top looks like a modern corset. Abigail is a postfeminist image of the Amazon turned designer-retail. With a slim figure held in place *without* a corset, just wearing a cotton top, she is fit for fight. Her flesh—like her clothes—stays in place.

Hypercode Framing: The Amazon Narrative

> Don't see this movie for the plot. Don't see it for the dialogue. You'll want to see it because the 4 main actresses in the film eventually have nude scenes in this order: rape, nipple play, wrestling, woman on the fence topless, rape, stripped topless, Lana's torture scene ... Me, I saw it for Lana Clarkson.[32]

As the above quote underlines, the visualization of the Amazon "tames" her aggressiveness by making her a stereotypical Mulveyan spectacle. It is up to the audience to decide whether this aggressive/erotic woman should be read as being within the gender code or breaking with it, depending on whether

Together, hero Blade (Wesley Snipes) with vampire hunters Abigail (Jessica Biel) and Hannibal King (Ryan Reynolds) offer different points of identification in *Blade Trinity* (New Line Cinema, 2004): old-fashioned masculinity flanked by a postfeminist woman and a metrosexual male.

we enter the "play" position or not. Narratively, however, a woman who is aggressive always breaks with the gender hypercode and her behavior needs an "explanation." The realist archetypes (the mother, the daughter, and the rape-avenger) are spun into specific events, which serve as "origin narratives" in terms of plot and psychology to explain why they choose to behave like a man. The Amazon, coming from Greek myth, already has an "origin narrative." It is necessary to "tame" this narrative so the Amazon becomes less intimidating. To this purpose, modern popular cinema replaces her original narrative as man-hating Amazon with a new narrative as helpful Amazon. This is done by giving her a new mission, a new social context, and a different Amazon character.

Wonder Woman is an early example of how the Amazon is reinterpreted and placed in a patriarchal context: psychologist and feminist William Moulton Marston invented Wonder Woman, the first of the many female superheroes in the comics, in 1940. She is an Amazon princess who leaves her native island and Amazon tribe to join Superman in his defense of America. Marston intended her as a role model who was "tender, submissive, peaceloving as good women are" and who combined "all the strength of a Superman plus all the allure of a good and beautiful woman."[33] He speculated, "Not even girls want to be girls so long as our feminine archetype lacks force, strength, and power." Marston designed Wonder Woman in a swimsuit-style costume the colors of the American flag and with a "magic whip." In Marston's comic stories, her whip was extensively used to tie men, and in his professional writings Marston addressed bondage as a key to break with the stereotypical gender roles. Later, when Wonder Woman was no longer written by Marston, this dominatrix aspect was toned down (but is of course retained in the visualization of female superheroes such as *Catwoman*, *Shi*, and *Vampirella*).[34]

The New Mission

In the new narrative, the Amazon society disappears and is substituted by a group of people representing the good forces in patriarchal society. The group is composed of diverse characters which represent the different character traits necessary to function in society. Thus, in *Red Sonja* the group consists of Red Sonja, hero Kalidor, a child-prince and his chubby servant; and in *Blade Trinity* the Nightstalkers count in their numbers an Afro-American, a blind single mother, her daughter, a chubby technical nerd, and Abigail and Hannibal. The new social context demonstrates that the Amazon's mission is not to conquer patriarchy and destroy the family, but to defend it against evil.

Valeria (Sandahl Bergman) in *Conan the Barbarian* (1982) is not the best example of the helpful Amazon. She is a warrior and a thief who feels responsible only for herself until she meets Conan. She gives her life for the man she loves, rather than for a sense of justice. She is, however, an example of the Amazon tamed by love. The second Conan film, *Conan—the Destroyer* (1984), uses the Amazon more consciously in the character of the barbarian Zula (Grace Jones), who is chained and used as amusement for warriors when Conan passes her with his group:

Princess Jehnna: Conan—they are six against one!

Conan: One, two, three ... I think you are right.

Princess Jehnna: And she is tied to the stake—do something!

Conan rides up to the woman—and cuts her chain. She needs no man to defend her, but turns with a huge grin and outfights her attackers. Zula—as played by black model, singer, and actress Grace Jones who was an icon of femme fatale cool in the eighties—is a savage and bestial woman (she even has a tail) who fights with a primitive weapon, the stick, and like an animal is driven by her instincts. "What would you do to attract a man?"

princess Jehnna (Olivia d'Abo) asks her. "Grab him! And *take* him!" is the response. The barefooted Zula is almost non-verbal with wide-opened eyes, wild grins, and bestial screams, and her black bikini with strings up both her thighs evokes leashing rather than armor. This savage warrior, who had been captured when she attacked a village with her tribe of female warriors, is tamed through the social fabric of Conan's group, where she learns friendship and loyalty. In the end she becomes Jehnna's captain of the guards. "Zula. I need a captain of the guards. I see no reason why a woman wouldn't do as well as a man," Jehnna says. The tamed Amazon looks at Conan, and after he nods approvingly, she accepts the position. Thus, what starts as a leashed and savage creature is turned into a civilized soldier serving a white virgin Queen (not breaking with class and race stereotypes).

Similarly, *Red Sonja* (1985) also essentially tells the story of an Amazon tamed by love and friendship. Sonja has sworn "no man may have me unless he has beaten me in a fair fight." When she rejected the sexual advances of the evil queen Gedren, the queen in response killed Sonja's family and had her soldiers rape Sonja. After this, a spirit in the forest gives Sonja magic strength. "Vengeance shall be yours. Vengeance on Queen Gedren who wanted you for herself. Your disgust was clear ... [I]n your quest for justice and vengeance you will need great strength. For your sword arm must have no equal. I give you that strength." The rape victim Red Sonja is thus pitted against a *female* rapist, Gedren, who (like the mythic Amazons) is a conqueror and hates men. The negative Amazon traits (hating men, conquest) are given to a lesbian, and the positive traits (strength, beauty, erotic attraction, the Amazon costume) to a heterosexual woman. To make the difference clear, Gedren has a hideous scar and wears a mask and a costume that covers her entire body. Sonja is initially trained to fight by an elderly sword master who praises her for being "the master of the master" but also warn her "in life all is not swordplay. Hatred of men in a lovely young woman; it could be your downfall." To tame the helpful Amazon, the plot gives her a male love interest, Lord Kalidor (Arnold Schwarzenegger), who insists on courting her even if it be over his dead body. "So, the only man who can have you is one who has tried to kill you," Kalidor says with a smile. Two other companions are a child prince and his servant Falkon, who serve to let Sonja tap into her "feminine" and "motherly" side. The end leaves Sonja and Kalidor dueling; however, this is done with a smile suggesting that they will be lovers when they tire from fighting.

In this fashion, the Amazon "mission" is turned into narratives of justice, democracy, and even, as in *Blade Trinity*, the survival of mankind. In *Barbarian Queen* Amathea and her female warriors join forces with peasants suffering under the tyrant Lord Erika and convince them to revolt. "We were brave once," their leader says, "we were warriors. Now it's time to fight again." "Until there is freedom enough for all of us," adds Amathea. And in *Amazons and Gladiators* Serena leaves the arena with the threat, "If you hurt any more slaves or Amazons, or I hear about any more women being abused, then I shall return and kill you all!" The camera lingers on her armored figure, then pans to a woman in the crowd and zooms in on her fist clenched in shared anger.

The idea of justice and democracy evolves into an Amazon character trait, and is the central theme in *King Arthur*. Guinevere convinces Arthur, who is half Briton and half Roman, that he is more Briton than Roman and ought to fight *against* Rome. Arthur already knows equality—"Arthur says that for men to be knights, they must first be equals" one of his knights comments about the round table where no one sits at the head—but he needs to be educated about freedom. Only when he saves the beautiful Guinevere does he understand that equality is also for "Toads" (the name for the Celts rebelling against the Romans). "It's a natural state of any man to want to live free in their own country," Guinevere tells Arthur. "I belong to this land. Where do you belong, Arthur?" She is the daughter of Merlin, the leader of the Celts, and Merlin tells Arthur that his motivation should be "love." Armed with love and freedom Arthur finally has a cause worth fighting for. "The Romans have left," Saxon king Cerdic says to Arthur, "who are you fighting for?" "I fight for a cause beyond Rome's and your understanding."

Before the battle with the Saxon army, Arthur speaks to his knights, "The gift of freedom ... is in our acts and in us ... If this be our destiny, then so be it. But let history remember: That as free men we *chose* to make it so." Guinevere is the person who has opened his eyes and sharpened his ethics. She is the symbol of freedom and justice.

The Amazon Spirit

In myth, the Amazon's nature is dual, bestial/female and masculine. In modern popular culture this ambivalence changed according to modern Western dichotomy. Here, the bestial belongs to the masculine/primitive/ aggressive and the civilized belongs to the feminine/cultural/tamed, the two poles still paradoxically combined in the Amazon. We find the two poles in Guinevere, who, on the one hand, is the civilizing figure teaching Arthur and becoming his wife in a demure white dress, and, on the other hand, is a bestial warrior in blue war paint jumping the Saxons with savage screams.

This idea of a masculine/feminine female warrior who helps men

A postfeminist version of the Amazon. Celt princess Guinevere (Keira Knightley) in the adventure film *King Arthur* (Touchstone Pictures, Jerry Bruckheimer Films, 2004) is fiercely independent, yet loyal to her father and an inspiration to her future husband and king, the Roman knight Arthur. (Courtesy of the British Film Institute.)

has a mythic correspondence in the figure of the valkyries from Norse mythology. They, similarly, were perceived as contradictory creatures. "[T]here are essentially two distinct and antagonistic perceptions of valkyries: they are seen both as fierce, elemental beings and as benevolent guardians."[35] Helen Damico writes of the duality, "Variously called *skjaldmeyjar* 'shield-maidens' and *hjálmvitr* 'helmet-creatures,' terms that describe their appearances as armed warriors bearing shield and helmet, they possess a physical beauty that is emphasized by epithets dealing with gold ornamentation of helmet and bright byrnie ... Although their attitude regarding the hero is not ambivalent, their relationship with him is. They are simultaneously the force that propels him into the action that will ensure immortal fame and the agency that brings about his destruction."[36]

In her tamed version, the Amazon has a function similar to the valkyries. She, too, motivates the hero and guides him in moments of weakness, but she also loves him and fights with him on the battlefield. Eowyn in *The Lord of the Rings: The Return of the King* (2003) is related to the valkyrie (rather than the Amazon) when she, dressed in heavy armor, kills the Nazgûl Master who says, "No man can kill me," to which she responds, "I am no man." Eowyn has no hatred of men, she fights to protect her father and mankind, and she is in love with Aragorn.

Another way to tame the Amazon spirit is to team her with a bigger male warrior. From Arnold Schwarzenegger in the Conan films and *Red Sonja* to martial arts fighter Richard Norton playing Lucius in *Amazons and Gladiators*, we find a muscular male whose "proper" masculinity ensures the Amazon's heterosexuality. Thus, Arthur marries Guinevere (not the original ending but the one preferred by a test audience), and *Blade Trinity* also has a huge male warrior, Blade. Here gender is reworked over three figures: First, Blade is the "proper" masculine hero who is saved by the Nightstalkers. Contrasted to him is Drake, an excessively muscular and aggressive Dracula, who is killed. The second figure is Abigail, Whistler's daughter (Whistler is Blade's helper, who is killed in the beginning of the film). In her looks and costume, Abigail represents "proper" femininity. Her natural beauty is contrasted to the female vampire Danica Talos, who in her business dress and high heels, her tied back hair and heavy makeup is a vampire fleshed out as evil vamp-and-single-career-working-woman (she even, reportedly, has a fanged vagina). Like Drake, she is killed. The third figure is Hannibal King, who represents a postmodern, metrosexual masculinity that incorporates "feminine" sensitivity. "I date older men," he jokes when Blade ask how they finance their operations and calls himself a "David Hasselhoff fan." "You should get in contact with your inner child," he tells Blade, "also, you might consider blinking." Abigail is a rare Amazon hero *not* erotically engaged with any character, but an independent tomboy. "When I came of age I tracked down my dad and told him I wanted in. I've been doing it ever since." She leads the vampire hunters with a relaxed attitude, listening to music on her MP3 player while killing. "You're kids. You're not ready to go into this," Blade argues, "look at the way you *dress!*" But Blade is last year's model and the Nightstalkers the new look. Abigail can calmly respond, "Like it or not: We're all you've got."

Untamed, But Bound by Love: *Xena: Warrior Princess*

I want to end this chapter about modern Amazons with a look at Xena from the television series *Xena: Warrior Princess* (1995–2001, 134 episodes). She is a striking example of the carefully constructed ambiguity of femme fatale action and of the contradictory readings such ambiguity creates.

Xena appeared in the series *Hercules: The Legendary Journeys* (1994–1999, 116 episodes) as a villain that Hercules had to defeat in the episode "The Warrior Princess" from 1995. The evil warlord Xena (Lucy Lawless) proved so popular that the show's producers, Sam Raimi and Rob Tapert (who created Xena), wanted to create a spin-off series. MCA Universal, who distributes *Hercules* and *Xena*, told them to "get her turned around so that she's good."[37] Thus, in the episodes "The Gauntlet" and "Unchained Heart" (1995) "evil" Xena became "good" Xena. "We changed the end of the third episode because, originally, Xena was slated to die," Tapert said.[38] In "The Warrior Princess" Xena schemed to kill Hercules (Kevin Sorbo) so she could rule Arcadia. In "The Gauntlet" she was conquering territory with her army ("she was like a demon from Hades," a woman sobs), but disagrees with her second-in-command, Darphus (Matthew Chamberlain), as to whether they kill women and children. When she rescues an infant from a village that Darphus has burned down, he takes over her army and forces her to walk the "gauntlet." Nobody has survived the gauntlet before and a stripped Xena is mercilessly beaten by her former soldiers. She survives and flees to a cave (symbol of healing and rebirth). Joining forces with Hercules, Xena kills Darphus and renounces being a warlord. "Killing isn't the only way of proving you're a warrior, Xena," Hercules earlier said. The third episode, "Unchained Heart," has Xena and Hercules killing Darphus again (he has been resurrected by Ares) and becoming lovers. With his unselfish heroism Hercules shows Xena how a true warrior behaves:

> XENA: You know, I've been in a hundred other battles, and the only thing that's ever come over me before them was a cold rage. But now ... Is this what it feels like to be you, Hercules?
>
> HERCULES: I think you're just finding out how good it feels to challenge the forces of evil.
>
> XENA: I wouldn't be doing it if you hadn't given me the chance.
>
> HERCULES: Whatever I did doesn't count. You made the decision on your own.

Amazons and valkyries are tamed by love and marriage. The valkyrie-bride Modthrytho converts "from evil to virtuous queen after her marriage," a change of temper which "parallels ... the progression of the fierce war-demon to gold-adorned warrior-queen."[39] To be precise, Xena can love only *after* she has been turned around to be "good." After they make love she leaves Hercules and starts on her quest.

> HERCULES: Xena! (they embrace and kiss)
>
> XENA: Let me go. There's so much in my life I have to make amends for. I've got to get started.
>
> HERCULES: I wish you'd let me help.
>
> XENA: You already have. You unchained my heart. Goodbye, Hercules.

Xena is reformed within a patriarchal and heterosexual frame and begins a journey, which would soon prove more legendary than Hercules' journey.

The duality of Evil and Good, however, would remain in her as an eternal battle.

Evil Xena	Good Xena
kills	saves
conquers	defends
not a mother	saves a child/later becomes mother
emotionally crippled	emotionally unchained
unable to love	able to love
independent	independent
single	friends
has male partners	finds love
refuses marriage	refuses marriage

Xena is constructed as a feminized version of the traditional heroic quest, which has a tainted hero making up for past sins.[40] The first episode, called "Sins of the Past," returns Xena to her village and mother and provides her with sidekick Gabrielle (Renee O'Connor), a peasant girl who decides to follow Xena as her bard. Xena, like Wonder Woman, upholds American values of freedom and justice; opposes tyrants and protects small societies (which often resemble the settlers on the American frontier); and respects the family unit, yet also treasures individualism. Xena thus represents traditional hero qualities.

Coupling Xena with Gabrielle provided a radically different narrative than earlier Amazons had been given. Because of its serialized form, the show was able to incorporate audiences' reactions in its future character and plot development. With a "self-conscious campiness" and "cheap special effects, slapstick humor, anachronisms, and cartoon-like fight scenes,"[41] the show was postmodern camp: At one and the same time "just fun," yet able to engage in all aspects of the emotional from friendship, love, and jealousy to loss and death as well as freely raiding history for events worthy of retelling. The show's tone alternated between camp, tragedy, drama, and slapstick comedy, employing usually separate modes of narration.

Like the Amazon, Xena is female, yet masculine in spirit. Her appearance is the Amazon aesthetic: a light black leather teddy, over this a heavier leather teddy, then metal armor, accentuating her long legs and cleavage, on which the camera often lingers. As played by five feet ten-and-a-half inch tall and agile actress Lucy Lawless, the black-haired Xena is strong and aggressive, and even though her heart has been unchained, she still finds it difficult to express emotions. Gabrielle is her opposite: slight, girlish, a red-blonde with green eyes, dressed in pastel colors and long skirts, traveling on foot next to a Xena on horse.[42] Gabrielle believes in love as the way to solve

Just another Amazon in armor or a lesbian in disguise? Many fans inter-preted the friendship between hero Xena (Lucy Lawless, shown here) and her faithful sidekick Gabrielle (Renee O'Connor) in the television series *Xena: Warrior Princess* (MCA Television, Renaissance Pictures, Studios USA Television, Universal TV, 1995–2001) as a butch-femme relationship.

conflicts, where Xena has faith in violent action. In their relationship Xena is the active hero and Gabrielle the nourishing partner, "doing all the emo-tional work for the couple," as Elyce Rae Helford phrases it.[43] The friend-ship, says Helford, can be interpreted as that of a butch-femme lesbian couple, and Helford reads Xena as a "stone butch" with "serious difficulty revealing any emotional or physical vulnerability."[44] After the first season a lesbian interpretation was incorporated into the show as subtext. "Xena and Gabrielle share intimate experiences; they sleep on the same blanket or take a bath together, for example. They also engage in displays of affection, such as hugs, kisses, and shared tears. And they exchange ambiguous dialogue, including sexual innuendo and *double entendre*, as well as overt and direct declarations of love."[45] The lesbian subtext is known among *Xena* fans, the so-called *Xenites*, as "The Subtext" and is intensely explored and elaborated on by fans on the Internet.[46]

In *Xena*, the dichotomy between violence and love is not between the masculine and the feminine. Rather, it is an internal duality haunting Xena as well as an external thematic played out in the relationship between Xena and Gabrielle. Numerous fans interpret their relationship as one of master and slave with hints of S-M. An early trace of such subtext appears in first season's second episode, "Chariots of War," where Xena is chained in a barn and charged with murder when she protects a group of farmers against a mysterious attacker who disappears (but turns out to be Ares). When some of the farmers come at night to get "payback" by beating her up, Evil Xena takes over. Beating the men Xena also knocks Gabrielle unconscious. Later, when Gabrielle has acted as her lawyer and Xena is cleared of charges, Xena asks, "How could you come back after what I did to you?" "It wasn't you, I know that," Gabrielle replies.[47] Xena's violence against Gabrielle returns occasionally. Thus, in an often quoted third season episode, "The Bitter Suite," Xena drags Gabrielle behind her horse trying to kill her in revenge for Gabrielle's evil daughter Hope having killed Xena's son Solan. Also, Gabrielle is repeatedly referred to as an object *belonging* to Xena. Helford quotes the second season's episode, "A Day in the Life," where Gabrielle has traded Xena's whip for a frying pan to a woman, Minya, whose fiancé Xena has set her eyes on. An angry Minya refuses to return the whip to Xena, "No, it belongs to me. You don't get that concept real well, do you? The whip is mine. The frying pan's yours. Hower [the fiancé] is mine. *She's* [pointing at Gabrielle] yours."[48]

Whether we read Xena and Gabrielle's relationship as lesbian, bisexual (both women have numerous love interests), or as a heterosexual friendship, the traditional dichotomy of male/female, strong/weak, violence/love, is constantly de-essentialized and challenged. Xena grows into a "softer" character, while Gabrielle turns more Amazonian (riding horses, fighting alongside Xena, dressing in light armor), and both grow stronger, fiercer, and more clarified about their feelings towards each other. They put their friendship above other relations and only leave one another for heroic obligations.

The sixth season tri-part episode, "The Rheingold," "The Ring," and "Return of the Valkyrie" is an example of the show's reworking of gender roles. The three episodes use (among several sources) three Norse sagas. One is of Danish king Roar plagued by the troll Grendel, who is killing his warriors. The warrior Bjowulf travels to Denmark and kills Grendel and its mother, an evil giantess. Another saga is that of the valkyrie Brynhilda, whom Odin returned to Earth to be a mortal and marry, because he was discontent with her service. She swore to marry only a man without fear, and her father surrounded her with a ring of fire; he who dared cross the flames could marry her. Sigurd rides through the flames, but Gunnar marries her due to a magical confusion of identities. An evil Brynhilda conspires to have Sigurd murdered, then commits suicide.[49] The last saga is of Fafner's cursed gold that brings death to its owner and ends at the bottom of the river Rhine.

The three episodes reverse the narrative function of men and women. In "The Rhinegold" an Evil Xena battles the valkyrie Grinhilda (Luanne Gordon) over a ring melded from the Rhinegold. Possession of the Rhinegold corrupts those who have *not* forsaken love, which Evil Xena has. However, Grinhilda loves Odin and when she puts on the ring trying to defeat Xena, she becomes a monster (called Grendel) and is caged by Xena. Thirty-five years later, Beowulf (Renato Bartolomei) seeks the help of Xena to stop the monster from slaughtering people, and Xena parts from Gabrielle and leaves with Beowulf. Convinced that Xena will need her help, Gabrielle follows her trail to Denmark. She hears the legend of an evil valkyrie, Xena, who made Odin forsake love. Gabrielle is befriended by a warrior, Bruunhilda (Brittney Powell). In the next episode, "The Ring," Gabrielle, Xena, Bruunhilda, and Beowulf kill what turns out to be Grendel's son. As they take on Grendel, Odin arrives with his valkyries—who are evil because they have forsaken love—and demands the ring, threatening to kill Gabrielle. Xena refuses to give it to him and instead puts it on. The Good Xena (who has not forsaken love) now suffers amnesia. Bruunhilda gives Gabrielle the ring to hold because she is "pure," and transforms herself into an eternal circle of flames that surround Gabrielle, who becomes a Sleeping Beauty in a white dress. Only Gabrielle's "soul mate" may cross the flames. In the third episode, "Return of the Valkyrie," Beowulf finds an amnesiac Xena about to marry Danish king Hrothgar. He brings her back to the woods where she convinces Grendel to again have faith in love. Grendel's faith transforms her back to her human shape as Grinhilda. Xena enters the flames and wakes Gabrielle with a kiss. They return Grinhilda to Odin (who becomes "good") and Xena returns the Rhinegold to the Rhinemaidens, from whom she had stolen it.

An intricate re-structuring of the sagas has taken place: Xena acts as both Beowulf slaying the monster Grendel and its mother, and as Sigurd crossing the fire to marry Brynhilda. Gabrielle takes the place of Brynhilda, who became evil and caused a tragedy in the sagas. Tragedy is replaced with the Sleeping Beauty theme and a happy ending for Xena/Sigurd and Gabrielle/Brynhilda. Bruunhilda, who sacrifices herself so she can save Gabrielle, is added to the narrative. Her love is lesbian:

BRUUNHILDA: Is Xena all you think about?

GABRIELLE: Xena is my family, she's the most important thing in my life.

BRUUNHILDA: Gabrielle, listen to me: I bring to Valhalla the bravest warriors slain in battle. Heroes. But your heart has more truth, more courage, than any I've seen. The beauty inside you burns like a star, Gabrielle. I was supposed to betray you and Xena—but I couldn't. Not now. You've changed me. You've opened my eyes and you've changed me, the way you changed Xena.

Gabrielle: I don't know what to say. I'm sorry.

BRUUNHILDA: [desperately] I defy my God for you, Gabrielle!

When Gabrielle turns to leave, Bruunhilda exclaims, "I can see your heart lies with Xena—but I'll prove to you which one deserves your love," and sacrifices herself. It is striking that where Bruunhilda must die, her sister-valkyrie Grinhilda survives thirty-five years as a monster and can return to Odin. On the one hand, female love is depicted as strong and everlasting— Gabrielle and Xena's love for each other, Bruunhilda's love for Gabrielle, Grinhilda's love for Odin, not forgetting Grendel's love for her son (a reworking of the alien mother in *Aliens*). Even Odin is counting on female love and thinks Xena will not put on the ring—"Your love for Gabrielle prevents that!" On the other hand, a lesbian love is "mastered" narratively by killing the trespasser, which is why Bruunhilda must die. Female sensations of love and friendship and motherhood are depicted as stronger than corresponding male sensations. Men who are in love are dominant, selfish, and greedy. When Xena rejects king Hrothgar he hisses, "*you* are a fucking queen and your duty is to fulfill your master's desire." Later, on the way to Grendel, Beowulf assures Xena who still does not remember her past, "You will do more good with this sword than a hundred Viking queens." Also, Odin prefers a scheming Xena to his faithful Grynhilda, and does not care about the death of Grendel's son, who was also Odin's son.

Helford finds *Xena* is "an excellent example of a polysemic text" which explains "why a series some may see as revolutionary may be identified by others as reactionary or even as a complex blend."[50] Looking at the representation of female strength and lesbianism in *Xena*, it is clear that both are invoked and restrained at the same time. Bruunhilda's love for Gabrielle is impossible—not, says the show, because it's lesbian, but because Gabrielle is involved with somebody else. Narratively, however, Bruunhilda's fate is death instead of the other female characters' resurrection. Only hinted at can lesbianism be tolerated. "Friendship" is constantly confused with "love" as when Brynhilda says, "I wish I had a friend like you" (by "friend" she intends "lover") and Gabrielle replies, "You do" ("friend" meaning "friend"). The term "lesbian" is not used; however, the "subtext" is clearer than any "text." When manipulating the Rhinemaidens Xena says, "Come on, show it to me." "You wanna become a Rhinemaiden?" they ask, swimming in the Rhine. "Sure. Then I can play with you all day." The lesbian subtext of "it" and "play" is supported by Xena's flirt with the maidens. When she returns the gold they coquettishly ask, "What magic has made Xena such a noble creature that she would give up the power of the Rhinegold?" "It wasn't magic," Xena responds, looking intensely at Gabrielle who smiles at her, bathed in a soft, golden light.

It may have been Hercules who unchained Xena's heart but it is Gabrielle who binds it with love.

Feminism, or, "Strong Independent Bimbos With Anti-Gravity Bodies"

Sexually speaking, the Amazon is the most transgressive of the archetypes. She is independent of men, has equal strength to them, is neither daughter nor mother, and is free of family obligations. Whether she surrenders her heart to a man or to a woman or to no one is her decision. Valeria gives her heart to Conan but Zula prefers to "grab" a man. Guinevere is tamed by marriage but Abigail remains single. Amathea marries Argan but she also liberates him from the tyrant's castle. Also, the Amazon is the only archetype to flirt with homosexuality. Xena and Gabrielle love numerous men, but their hearts belong to each other.

The Amazon's unchained behavior makes her a role model to some. On CNN on August 3, 1998, Secretary of State Madeline Albright "identified Xena as one of her heroes"[51] and female critics praise that "[t]oday, girls who enjoy play-acting do not have to compromise their developing intellects to find worthy heroines to impersonate, enjoy and respect. Today, instead of Charlie's Angels, girls play Xena and Gabrielle."[52] Especially in the culture of lesbian, gay, bisexual and transsexual (LGBT), Xena was welcomed as a hero (along with idols like Linda Hamilton in *Terminator 2*). Her entrance into these areas was made possible by producers' willingness to play along with audiences' interpretations. The show's openly gay producer, Liz Friedman, replied to questions of lesbianism, "I don't have any interest in saying they're heterosexuals. That's just bullshit—and no fun, either,"[53] and said about the show's subtext, "I've always been a big believer in the power of popular culture. The best way to convey more challenging ideas is to make something that functions on a mainstream level but that has a subtext that people can pick up on—or not."[54] *Xena* leaves many clues to be "picked up" and Walter Alesci describes producers' use of the show's characters as "permanent contradiction." "We hadn't planned it, but we love the positive feedback we get and, yeah, we play on it and have fun with it," producers Tapert and Stewart said.[55]

Ambiguity makes it difficult for critics to categorize *Xena* as feminism or non-feminism. Joanne Morreale notes, "*Xena: Warrior Princess* is overtly feminist, yet its discourse, the way the story is told, remains traditionally patriarchal," but decides to read the series as camp *and* feminism.[56] Helford, on the other hand, is "not convinced television can give us truly progressive feminist or queer visions," and reluctantly rejects *Xena* as promising but not *really* feminist, because the show uses butch and femme stereotypes. Exactly the same stereotypes make Helen Caudhill welcome the series because it "reclaims the [female] quest and presents the reality of women wielding violence and power and loving whom they choose ... an image that is changing forever the way popular culture looks at women."[57] To her, the image of female-to-female aggression is subversive and pleasurable, because such an image is suppressed by both a politically correct feminism as well as by patriarchy. Such difficulty in "judging" takes us back to Thäis E. Morgan and her call to read the dominatrix as a liberating figure on the ground that "the moral/mimetic approach to pornography is a dead-end for feminism."[58] She appeals to allow for contradictions between pleasure and politics. Thus, an image or fiction may be liberating to one user and suppressive to another. "It allowed me to know a world of lesbians that I didn't know at that time. My life is a 'before Xena' and an 'after Xena'," a lesbian fan said on a television show.[59] Such statements are in contrast to a heterosexual interpretation, "I have never seen anything that would give the impression of them being lesbians. In my opinion this whole idea is just wishful thinking on your part. I find it to be an extreme insult that you would try and degrade their close, FRIENDLY [sic] relationship by thinking of them as gay."[60]

Carefully constructed as a polysemic sign, Xena is both hero *and* sex symbol to both men *and* women. Originally a female villain, the Amazon today is a sexualized and ambiguous hero voicing feminism while pleasing both sexes. In the setting of fantasy and adventure she blurs gender boundaries, while at the same time appealing to old-fashioned pleasures. Thus, a female customer rejects the strong independent women in comics as "[s]trong independent bimbos with anti-gravity bodies," while a male customer finds, "[these portrayals are] exploitative of the female body; however I don't find this objectionable."

Lost in the postmodern maze of plural readings and open signs it may help to look at who *creates* these archetypes. As always, men create strong women according to their pleasures and psychological needs. "People are tired of these overblown male characters with bulging muscles and no brains," says the creator of female superhero *Shi*, and the creator of female superhero *Mantra* speculates, "to some extent, it could be considered a feminist issue ... It might come down to something psychological; a lot of readers today were raised by [single] mothers ... so they might be more willing to see a female in a position of leadership."[61] Dominating women are everywhere—to be enjoyed, to be used as role models, and to be tamed. The question, yet to be answered, is if choosing one kind of identification, one point of view, excludes a viewer from entertaining other kinds of identification and gaining other kinds of pleasures. Can we enjoy and transgress simultaneously?

Amazon Filmography (Selective)

Conan the Barbarian (1982) Dir. John Milius. Swordfighter and thief Valeria, fantasy/adventure

Conan the Destroyer (1984) Dir. Richard Fleischer. Amazon Zula, fantasy/adventure

Amazons (1984) Dir. Paul Michael Glaser. Television movie

Red Sonja (1985) Dir. Richard Fleischer. Swordfighter Red Sonja, fantasy/adventure

Barbarian Queen (1985) Dir. Héctor Olivera, filmed in the U.S. and Argentina. Barbarian queen Amathea, fantasy/adventure

Amazons (1986) Dir. Alejandro Sessa, filmed in Argentina.

Barbarian Queen II: The Empress Strikes back (1989) Dir. Joe Finley, filmed in the U.S. and Mexico. Princess Athalia, fantasy/adventure

Hercules: The Legendary Journeys (1994–1999) 116 episodes, television series; "The Warrior Princess" 1:9, March 13, 1995; "The Gauntlet" 1:12, May 1, 1995; "Unchained Heart" 1:13, May 8, 1995.

Xena: Warrior Princess (1995–2001) 134 episodes, television series. Female warlord/reformed warrior Xena, fantasy/adventure; "Sins of the Past" 1:1, September 15, 1995; "Chariots of War" 1:2, September 22, 1995; "A Day in the Life" 2:15, March 2, 1997; "The Bitter Suite" 3:12, February 14, 1998; "The Rheingold" 6:7, November 18, 2000; "The Ring" 6:8, November 25, 2000; "Return of the Valkyrie" 6:9, December 2, 2000

Amazons and Gladiators (2001) Dir. Zachary Weintraub, filmed in the U.S. and Germany. Half-Amazon Serena, drama/adventure

The Arena (2001) Dir. Timur Bekmambetov, filmed in Russia and U.S. Druid maiden Bodicia, slave girl Jessemina, adventure

Boudica (2003) Dir. Bill Anderson, filmed in UK and Romania. Celtic warrior queen Boudica, historical drama

King Arthur (2004) Dir. Antoine Fuqua, filmed in the U.S. and Ireland. Celtic warrior (later Queen) Guinevere, adventure/drama

Blade Trinity (2004) Dir. David S. Goyer. Vampire hunter Abigail Whistler, horror

PART FOUR

Age of Ambivalence

10

Disturbing Creature:
The Female Soldier
in the War Film

This idea of female marines? It's a bunch of bull, man. They cause
trouble and they can't do the work. It's why we call recruits girls.
You ever see a woman try to change a tire on one of those big
trucks? Or hike 30 miles with all the gear? With my black buddy
it's different. He can carry that 100-pound backpack and when I
wake up next to him in the field I don't want to sleep with the
dude.

—American marine[1]

JORDAN O'NEIL: I'm not here to make some kind of statement.
All I care about is completing the training and getting operational
experience. Just like everyone else, I suspect.

CHIEF OF STAFF: If you were like everyone else, Lieutenant, I suspect we wouldn't be making statements about not making statements. Would we?

—G.I. Jane (1997)

"Let me see your war face," Senior Drill Instructor Hartman tells
Private Joker during inspection of the recruits in Stanley Kubrick's *Full Metal
Jacket* from 1987. Private Joker screams the best he can. "Bullshit, you didn't
convince me. That is not a war face. I am not scared. Let me see your
real war face!" Private Joker then screams and grimaces like a homicidal
maniac. Another recruit comes from Texas. "Do you suck dicks?" Hartman
asks the soldier. "I bet you're the kind of guy that would fuck a person
in the ass and not even have the goddamn common courtesy to give him
a reach-around. I'll be watching you!" Welcome to the strange universe
of the war film where men learn to suck dicks and kiss ass, are humiliated,
mutilated, and trained to kill. This is where Nick gets sick in *Deer Hunter*
(1978) and Kovic is castrated in *Born on the Fourth of July* (1989), where
lieutenant colonel Willard is traumatized in *Apocalypse Now* (1979) and

captain Miller gets his uncontrollably shaking hands in *Saving Private Ryan* (1998).

How about women in war films? Do they learn to suck dicks and kiss ass, are they traumatized, mutilated, nicknamed? No, because this only happens to men. Men do this in the name of *honor* and *brotherhood*. *Honor* is tied to glory and defeat, to victory and victimization. It is related to nationalism and ideology, politics and power. *Brotherhood* is about male initiation rites, becoming one of the boys and a man, finding one's war face and learning to kick ass or else suck dicks. "It's all about the man next to you," a soldier says in *Black Hawk Down* (2001), a remark intended as an answer to the movie's question: Why are American soldiers in Somalia? Not because they care about Somalia but because they care about *each other*. War films are not so much about actual wars as they are about national history and male socialization. Women do not belong here. First, because only men can have honor (women can have *pride* which is different; where honor is public, pride is private), and, second, because she cannot be one of the boys.

Most male film genres are at some time in their development "feminized" as Jeanine Basinger calls the replacement of male heroes with female heroes. This almost never happens in the war movie. Women can be nurses, enemies, prostitutes, or soldier's wives but not soldiers.[2] That is, not until the mid-nineties, where the female soldier made her entrance in *Courage Under Fire* (1996), *G.I. Jane*, and *A Soldier's Sweetheart* (1998). When women become combative soldiers in the war film three things happen: First, the war film transforms into a war drama or what I call "the female war movie." Second, everything becomes a question of gender from where she sleeps and showers to the disturbing scent of her perfume, from the length of her hair to her menopause and body weight. Third, just when she has succeeded in entering the male arena of war, she disappears from the plot.

From Male Tragedy to Female Drama

To understand the full extent of the havoc female soldiers bring to the war film we must first look at the structure of the genre.[3] In my definition, the war film is constituted by three elements: First, the *iconography* is realist and set in modern time. War films are about the real wars in the twentieth century with its modern technology of tanks, automatic weapons, airplanes. Films set in the future belong to the science fiction film and films set before World War I are historical dramas. Second, as Kathryn Kane discusses in "The World War II Combat Film" (1988), the *narrative* of a war film has two uniformed military forces of different nationalities meet in combat.[4] Finally, also pointed out by Kane, *two themes* are central in war films: the theme of victory or defeat, and the theme of the integration or disintegration of a group of soldiers into a team. The first theme is ideological; the second is social. "The movement toward victory or defeat is depicted in scenes of combat. The movement toward integration and disintegration is depicted in scenes of general behavior in and out of battle. One aspect of each axis appears and forms the action of all the films."[5]

We can visualize the two themes as a diagram whose two axes "map" the ideology of the war movie: Victory is based on the successful integration of individual soldiers into a *team* and not on a single heroic figure. Thus, values such as cooperation, duty, loyalty, respect, authority and team spirit replace the usual American lone wolf heroism. In their "positive" outcome, the ideological and social themes form a war film where soldiers are integrated into a team and win the war, an endorsement of conservative nationalism and male bonding. In their "negative" outcome, the two themes result in an anti-war movie: soldiers fail to become a team and the war is lost or portrayed as futile. In general, the harder a movie is to place on the two axes, the more interesting the plot: Soldiers can be almost integrated into a team yet lose the war as in *Black Hawk Down* or they can win the war yet fail to emerge as a team as in *Platoon* (1986). In some movies, victory and team remain unclear—are the three soldiers in *Three Kings* (1999) a team and is their liberation of Iraqi prisoners a victory? War films show audiences the culturally constructed nature of nationalism, male identity, and men's social roles. The soldiers learn to accept the chaos of war and if they become heroes this is incidental rather than instrumental to the final outcome. "Nobody asked to be a hero. It just sometimes turns out that way," says Sergeant Eversmann in *Black Hawk Down*.

Let us now turn to women. Audiences do not need an explanation for why men join the army. They are drafted or volunteer because they "get to blow shit up" (*G.I. Jane*) or want to be "the first kid on the block with a confirmed kill" (*Full Metal Jacket*). War is simply considered a "natural" part of male experience. Different with women. According to war films, war is not a natural female experience and the audience needs a clear reason why they join the military. The motivation to fight is therefore now anchored within the individual as a *personal* choice for *personal* reasons. Thus, in *Courage Under Fire* where Lieutenant Colonel Nat Serling (Denzel Washington) carries out an inquiry to establish if helicopter pilot Karen Walden (Meg Ryan) should be given the Medal of Honor in combat posthumously for courage under fire, he asks her parents, "It was unusual wasn't it, for Karen to want to be a helicopter pilot?" The father takes full responsibility, "I guess that's my fault. I took her to the fair when she was eleven." At the fair Karen had a ride in a helicopter and "when she came down ... well, I don't think she ever came down, really." Karen fell in love with helicopters, and this is why she joined the army. To make it clear that Karen does not enjoy war, her helicopter is not for combat but is a small medical unit helicopter.

Neither does intelligence officer Lieutenant Jordan O'Neil (Demi Moore) in *G.I. Jane* choose combat. She is chosen by senator Lillian DeHaven (Anne Bancroft), who is using a debate over sexism in the military to push her personal political agenda. In the Senate, the role of military women in combat is debated: Can they perform as well as men? Or is there discrimination against women? To settle the argument, the Navy allows a woman to enter SEAL training, the hardest elite military program with a drop out rate of sixty percent. The ambitious Jordan accepts DeHaven's offer because active duty is the key to advancement. And, as Jordan tells her boyfriend Royce (Jason Beghe), who has passed her in ranks because of his combat experience, "Honey, this is just a career opportunity. You don't want me sleeping my way to the top, do you?" No, he doesn't. But neither does he want her to move to the top, which makes her angry. This is a career opportunity and the risk of a broken relationship does not stop her.

War movies are embedded in contemporary social and political debates and discourses. In the case of female war films, these are about gender and domestic politics rather than the economics of war or questions of foreign politics. Female war movies work hard to establish a motive for their cross-gender plot—what Amy Taubin has coined "a gender-fuck film"[6]—but they work even harder to ensure us that this "gender-fuck" motive has nothing to do with feminism. Jordan tells Royce, "The only thing that scares me are the sexual politics. I'm just not interested in being some poster front to women's rights." "Women's rights" and "feminism" are swearwords in war films, and of *Courage Under Fire, A Soldier's Sweetheart* and *G.I. Jane*, only the latter film explicitly addresses these issues. The way this is done is highly interesting: Feminism is invoked in the opening scene where DeHaven in a public hearing accuses the Navy of sexual harassment and discrimination against women. In the next scene, the political issue of women's status in the Navy is turned into the *individual drama* of Jordan's ability to complete the SEAL program. Neither DeHaven nor Jordan cares about women's (or any other group's) rights. In true postfeminist spirit, the two career women fight for themselves. "It was never meant to happen," DeHaven later tells Jordan, "we never expected you to get this far."

The war movie's social theme is about integrating the men into a team. For such integration to take place, military training must transform the men into soldiers and teach them the value of obedience, solidarity, bravery, perseverance, fighting skills, and the ability to kill. This transformation or education can be portrayed positively as in *An Officer and a Gentleman*, whose antihero becomes a (gentle)man, or in *Saving Private Ryan*, whose soldiers finally come to understand and accept the sacrifices America must make to defend democracy in the world. The transformation can also be valued negatively as "destroying" rather than "building" a soldier's character. Thus, Gomer Pyle has the happy smile wiped eternally from his face as he voluntarily leaves the army's "world of shit" when he kills Senior Drill Instructor Hartman and commits suicide in *Full Metal Jacket*. In his study of the German Freikorps soldiers after World War I, German sociologist Klaus Theweleit describes the German soldier as "a man whose physique has been machinized, his psyche eliminated—or in part displaced into his body armor ... a man with machinelike periphery, whose interior has lost its meaning."[7] Transforming men into soldiers erases their personality and reduces sensitivity to mere primitive sensations. "I feel pain, therefore I am. Where pain is, there 'I' shall be."[8] The soldiers become functional killing machines but dysfunctional human beings.

Whether films take a "positive" or "negative" stance one thing is certain: war irrevocably changes men. They can win their "red badge of courage" (the "honorable wound" as Hemingway called a wound achieved in combat) and they can lose their limbs, their sanity, their lives. But war does *not* change women.

When women enter the military, they come fully equipped with "adult" personalities. Military training may transform their bodies but not their characters. To underline this point, *G.I. Jane* repeats the same crisis situation at the beginning and the end: In the beginning intelligence officer Jordan outbets her superiors by guessing the correct position for extracting a group of elite soldiers who have missed their original point of extraction. At the end of the movie she guesses the route taken by Master Chief Urgayle (Viggo Mortensen), who is pursued by Libyan soldiers. In both scenes she saves the soldiers' lives with her last minute calculations. SEAL training has made no difference; she was a winner from the beginning. Likewise, *Courage Under Fire* has parallel but reverse combat scenes at beginning and end: First we see Serling accidentally killing his best friend in friendly fire when he mistakes the American tank for an enemy tank. Towards the end we see Karen using her fuel tank as an improvised bomb to save the crew of a Black Hawk crashed on Iraqi territory, and later she protects her crew by laying cover fire as the men are extracted by helicopters. Karen succeeds where Serling fails.

War movies let women to step *into* character, a character they had all along. Thus, we understand from the interview with Karen's parents that she is a determined person; as a child she wanted to fly helicopters, she raised her five-year-old daughter as a single mother, and she was a resourceful and brave officer making the right decisions during combat. And when it comes to pain, it is not her training as a soldier but her personal experience as a mother that has taught her to handle pain. "I gave birth to a nine-pound baby, asshole. I think I can handle it," she says when shot in the stomach. Likewise, Jordan radiates iron will and intelligence from her first scene in *G.I. Jane* where she extracts the lost crew—a face similar to when she saves Urgayle.

Where the military force a new identity onto and into the male soldier, it frees a repressed identity in the female soldier who was not allowed to express herself fully before. Nowhere is this as clear as in the barbershop scene, a standard trope of the genre: Stanley Kubrick's *Full Metal Jacket* opens with the soldiers having their heads shaved. This is presented as stripping the young men of their individual identities and turning them into (anonymous) soldiers, the camera panning across their blank faces accompanied by a happy war song as an ironic comment on the Vietnam war. Women in combat—Jordan, Jeanne in *The Messenger: The Story of Joan of Arc* (1999) and Mulan in *Mulan* (1998)—also cut their hair. This is a voluntary act which liberates them from the restrictions of female biology and allow them to enter

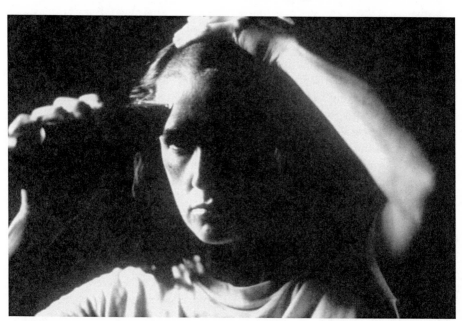

Long hair is a sign of abominable femininity and weakness in the war film. Female soldier Jordan O'Neil (Demi Moore) voluntarily cuts her hair to prove she is "one of the boys" in Ridley Scott's *G.I. Jane* (Hollywood Pictures, Largo Entertainment, Trap-Two-Zero Productions, 1997).

the world of war. The women cut their hair by their own hand in scenes of triumph accompanied by jubilantly rising music in music video style sequences. "The bitch is gone" goes the song text as Jordan—and actress Demi Moore—shaves off her long hair. Yvonne Tasker has pointed out that gender cross-dressing signifies moving *up* the social hierarchy for women.[9] If men lose identity in the army, women retrieve theirs. When the "bitch" is gone the "real" person can step out.[10]

What, then, about the two thematic axes of war movies? How does the female soldier perform here? The answer is, as always when women enter male territory, ambiguous. She wins on one axis but loses on the other and destroys both sets of values on her way. On the victory-defeat axis, modern female war films are careful to present women with foreign enemies: Libyan soldiers in *G.I. Jane*, Iraqi soldiers in *Courage Under Fire*, Viet Cong soldiers in *A Soldier's Sweetheart*. We must not doubt the female soldier's ability to fight and kill. The real enemy, however, does not come from abroad but from within. It is society's male institutions and the real battle is with the gender boundaries separating men and women. This explains why the enemy in female war movies is faceless and nameless, a transparent ghost rather than a physical presence. In effect, all men have replaced the foreign enemy: fellow recruits, drill sergeants, boyfriends, chief of staffs.

The grandiose tragedy of men dying in war transforms into a postfeminist drama of women winning access to that last male stand: the military. "No chick is gettin' through this program," a soldier mutters as Jordan walks into the mess. "That's bull shit, they can't do what we can do," another comments, and a third soldier adds, "Just give me one night with her and I will show you." Female soldiers must fight for their right to be in what is presented as an inappropriate place for a woman. A black soldier even comments on female soldiers being today's "niggers." They assert their right to be on male territory by being smarter (Karen and Jordan has better judgment than the male soldiers), faster (Jordan becomes fastest at assembling her rifle), braver (Jordan convinces her team to wait for Urgayle although they are in enemy country) and more resilient (Jordan completes the SEAL training which sixty percent of the men quit). The female soldier proves herself to be competent and in the case of Mulan, Jordan, and Jeanne, also a brilliant leader.

However, the idea of a single soldier winning a battle dissolves the two axes of the war movie. On the social axis, heroism distances the female soldier from the team. She is not one of the boys, but their leader and savior (it is not incidental that Marianne in *A Soldier's Sweetheart* takes her name from the French national icon Marianne). And, on the ideological axis, war ceases to be chaos and becomes instead a rational environment to be analyzed and mastered by intelligence officers and their computer software. In the war film this is *wrong*. It is cheating. Where are the lost limbs picked up in the streets in *Black Hawk Down*? In female war movies war is a sanitized affair.[11] Off-screen casualties, no close-ups, merely decorative blood and minor injuries replace broken soldier bodies. But war is not "losses"—it is hell. And you can neither calculate nor control hell. Why else would Nick be sick and Willard a borderline psychotic?

Body Politics

An early scene in *G.I. Jane* has DeHaven choosing the appropriate female body for the Navy SEAL program. Her staff laughs as she comments on the photographs, one of a marathon runner—"They should do a chromosome check"—another of a power lifter—"Is this the face you want to see on the cover of *Newsweek*? She looks like the wife of a Russian wheat farmer" (the woman looks like Bev Francis, the bodybuilder made famous by documentary *Pumping Iron II: The Women*). Third is Jordan's body which is pretty, petite, and slim compared to the earlier women, yet still fit. DeHaven is pleased, "Now, this really is top drawer. With silk stockings inside." The scene locates Jordan's body in a "safe" place within feminine territory. And this is the point of departure from which the film sets out to investigate a central fear of war movies: That of the female body and of femininity.

In action movies the hero's body survives falling sixty feet from a bridge or walking through bullet rain. Not in war movies. The soldier's body is sensitive, penetrable, and mortal. Limbs fall to the ground, internal organs are ripped from their proper places, men desperately tend wounds. In vain. Although trained to be a lean, mean killing machine, the soldier is made of soft flesh. But softness and sensitivity are sensations a soldier cannot afford. In the cultural imagination, softness and sensitivity are linked to femininity and women. Repressed from men's bodies, sensitivity is projected onto women from where it is regarded as a mortal threat.

War movies have two images of women: The American woman and the enemy woman. American women—mothers, sweethearts, wives—are the sentimental images of family and nation, "emblems of love and home" as they "see their men off and welcome them home again, and appear in memory or flashbacks in chastely romantic scenes or caring for children."[12] Thus, at the end of *Black Hawk Down* a letter from a dead soldier to his wife is read as the end credits role over the screen, "My love, you are strong and you will do well in life. I love you and the children deeply ... So in closing, my love, tonight tuck my children in bed warmly. Tell them I love them. Hug them and give them a kiss goodnight from daddy." Daddy's woman is maternal, warm, loving. Enemy women—prostitutes, guerrilla warriors, anonymous civilians—are the opposite. Where American women represent the stable ground, enemy women are the abyss into which soldiers fall. "It is a dread, ultimately, of dissolution—of being swallowed, engulfed, annihilated. Women's bodies are the holes, swamps, pits of muck that can engulf," Barbara Ehrenreich writes in her introduction to Klaus Theweleit's *Male Fantasies*.[13] Think of the sniper in *Full Metal Jacket*—a young Vietnamese woman with braids. Or the only Vietnamese attacker in *Apocalypse Now*, a young woman who suddenly throws a grenade into a helicopter. The mere movement of a hand will turn enemy women into the abyss.

Psychologically, the American and alien woman are part of the same concept of femininity, the *heimlichness* of the good woman against the *unheimlichness* of the bad woman. Female sensitivity is "safe" when it is tied to home and separated from the soldier's universe, and it becomes "dangerous" when it enters and "pollutes" his world of war.

The plot of the female war film establishes the female soldier as heroic. But her body invokes fear and terror. The softness, sensitivity, and penetrability linked in our imagination to the female body remind the soldier of the repressed fact that his body, too, is soft, sensitive, and penetrable. Therefore she must prove that she is *not* sensitive, *not* soft, *not* penetrable. Three issues that are at the heart of *G.I. Jane*. In the opening scene Theodore Hayes (Daniel von Bargen), a soon-to-be Secretary of the Navy, explains to the Senate, "The Navy has instituted special sensitivity courses for all its male recruits demonstrating even more progress..." However, "sensitivity" is an unpopular issue as the Chief of Staff at the SEAL training camp makes clear when Jordan enters his office to complain about being treated differently from the men:

> CHIEF OF STAFF: What I resent is some politician using my base as a test tube for some grand social experiment. What I resent is the sensitivity training that is now mandatory for my men ... But most of all, what I resent, is your perfume, however subtle it may be, competing with the aroma of my fine 3 dollar and 59 cent cigar, which I will put out this instant if the phallic shape of it happens to offend your goddamn fragile sensibilities. Does it?
>
> JORDAN: No, Sir.
>
> CHIEF OF STAFF: No, Sir, *what*?
>
> JORDAN: The shape doesn't bother me, Sir. Only the sweet, goddamn stench.

The female soldier must prove she is *not* sensitive, *not* soft. Sensitivity is for women. Not for soldiers. The phallic cigar does not offend Jordan; only its sweet (feminine) smell. By this logic, she enters a category outside both male and female. New rules must be instituted; Urgayle orders schedules for the use of showers to keep male and female bodies apart. The soldiers object when Jordan enters their sleeping quarters, "Look, tampons! You can't sleep here." Like bullets and penises, tampons penetrate the female body. They are the bloody reminders of physical disorder, of the breakdown between bodies and genders. But Jordan doesn't need her tampons; her menses cease due to the physical training, a biological response that is "not at all unusual for female athletes" a female doctor explains.

Jordan's survival of "hell week" proves she is neither sensitive nor weak. But is she penetrable? In war movies every body is penetrable. By bullet or knife. Penetration is also when two soldiers jerk their arms up a comrade's injured leg to grab a severed vein in *Black Hawk Down*. Penetration is the risk a soldier takes. *G.I. Jane* links penetration to sexual penetration and rape. Heroines are raped in a variety of film genres, from action films such as *Foxy Brown* and *The Long Kiss Goodnight* to rape-revenge and action films such as *I Spit on Your Grave* and *Kill Bill: Vol. 1*. Men, too, can be raped and are so in dramas such as *Deliverance* and *American History X* (1998). But soldiers are never raped in war films; instead they rape enemy women as in *Casualties of War* (1989). When a woman becomes protagonist, the issue of rape lingers in the perimeter of threats she faces, not only from men in general but from soldiers in particular. The female soldier operates in a one-sex world of macho masculinity where control and protection are vital if she is to survive with her body intact. Weapons, sex, and protection are linked when the soldiers are instructed in capping their rifles with condoms to avoid the intrusion of fluid. Ironically, the female soldier is taught to protect her weapon against the dangers of the "feminine" seawater.

To be soft means to be penetrable. And for a woman that spells rapable. During SERE training (Survival, Evasion, Resistance, Escape, a simulation of capture and torture by the enemy) Jordan defends herself with her hands tied behind her back against Urgayle's abuse and attempted rape. If she quits, he says, the violence will cease immediately. She kicks him in the groin. "Don't start something you can't finish," he says and knocks her to the ground. The men in the compound turn their backs on Urgayle and side with the woman they until now resented. Her will *not* to be soft, *not* to be sensitive, and *not* to be penetrable convince them she is one of them. "Her presence makes us *all* vulnerable," Urgayle explains when the bleeding Jordan gets up behind him and yells, "Suck my dick!"[14] She will not be raped, and she will not be positioned as a "woman" who makes the men "vulnerable." According to Jordan biology is not the issue and her body should not be treated any different than the men's. She will accept the beatings, yes, but not rape.

The message is confusing: *G.I. Jane* positions its heroine as non-rapable

Demi Moore as female soldier Jordan O'Neil is beaten, tortured, and nearly raped during SEAL training by Master Chief Urgayle (Viggo Mortensen) who is determined to rid his all-male group of her dangerous presence in *G.I. Jane* (Hollywood Pictures, Largo Entertainment, Trap-Two-Zero Productions, 1997).

because she insists on "taking it" as a man. But because Urgayle is not charged with assault and rape after the incident, the movie indicates that rape is a "natural" and thus forgivable part of male aggression, which Jordan could have avoided had she not placed herself in the "wrong" position.[15] Also, the rape attempt is not reported and is thus condoned and forgiven. Confusion surrounds the body of the female soldier. Is it feminine or masculine? At the outset, Jordan's body was approved by DeHaven. But as Jordan advances in the SEAL program the "silk stockings" disappear. Hair is shaved off and her face bruised, new muscles spring from doing one-armed push-ups, amenorrhea sets in. What was once a simple duality between "right" and "wrong" female bodies becomes a scale with feminine at the bottom and masculine at the top. As Jordan advances in the program, her body moves towards the top. And this is where the body politics of the female war film turns ambiguous.

Two scenes in G.I. Jane illustrate the ambiguity surrounding pain and gain. The first scene consists of five short sequences showing Jordan doing push-ups accompanied by music on the soundtrack, low angle shots and close-ups of her body in top and shorts. The visual aesthetic is that of a body-builder documentary such as Pumping Iron or Pumping Iron II: The Women with low angle shots to make the body appear larger and more impressive. Like the posing bodybuilder, Jordan's body has been oiled to make her muscles glisten and stand out. The provocative effect is the same as in Pumping Iron II: The Women, where the male judges debate the limits of femininity in response to the masculine body frame of Australian bodybuilder Bev Francis. There are limits the female body cannot go beyond, and even if Bev has the most impressive muscles, she ends third in the competition. Close-ups of Jordan's behind and breasts when she does push-ups accentuates her gender characteristics, yet frame them within a (male and inappropriate) physical activity. Jordan does her push-ups in a dark machine room, leaning on two chairs, and in the fifth sequence she masters push-ups with one arm behind her back. The five push-up scenes salute female strength, but the choice of camera angle, music, and editing shows a female body out of balance, grotesque rather than strong. In the scene following the last push-up sequence, Jordan is unable to pull herself out of the water and into a raft boat during training. The push-ups, it seems, were for show and not for effect.

In the second scene the battered female body is first included in, then excluded from the male world: After SERE training, Jordan's crew invites her for a drink in the bar. The scenario is cozy, the bar lit in a warm light, the music comforting, the atmosphere filled with laughter and celebration. "Jordan, you are really *okay*," says the soldier Flea. Then, in the women's restroom, a woman approaches Jordan who is examining her facial bruises in the mirror: "Ain't really none of my business, but I'll say leave the bastard." The woman leaves and Jordan smiles confidently to herself in the mirror. A husband does not beat her; her bruises are of a different kind. Not the martyr-wife's, but the hero-soldier's. The bruises are not from the violence men inflict on women, but from the violence men inflict on men. Jordan's smile signals victory. She has succeeded in taking a man's place. Almost. Her body can still be read in "feminine" terms and when she returns, the bar has become dark and claustrophobic, the music noisy, fat men shoot darts. A man's world after all. Jordan leaves the bar and drives to the beach where a group of military women (nurses, doctors, clerks) earlier invited her to a barbeque.

As the female soldier moves up the body scale, she gains masculine ground but in the process loses feminine status. Every breaking of gender boundaries is shot through with confusion and ambiguity. Every move up the scale of masculinity also means a move *down* the scale of femininity.

Reviews and comments linked Jordan's training to drag performance. "Jordan has been conceived as a kind of male action toy in female drag," with the director "transposing the most stereotypical male action traits onto women and, in the process, reaping kudos for being 'liberated,'"[16] wrote Peter Rainer in *New Times L.A.*, reading Jordan as a speculation in pseudo-liberation. Others criticized *G.I. Jane* for performing the standard macho-military masculinity with the variation that the soldier now was a woman instead of a man. "Instead of subverting old strategies to aim at a fresh target, *Jane* re-ups for a familiar mission. The result isn't a different perspective; it's drag ... If military women cannot separate America's perceptions of power from the masculine, women cannot hope to lead anywhere," Terry Diggs argued in "G.I. *Jane* Is Such a Drag" and concluded "we have allowed the military to dress up like a guy for long enough."[17] Most responses to the movie were negative and denied that it had any liberating, subversive or feminist content. Only one feminist comment argued differently. Amy Taubin saw Moore's "sculpted body—the product of work, will, and surgical enhancement" as the means "to play a character who's not a boy toy" and found the movie "a genuinely feminist depiction of a woman who pushes gender to the edge."[18] To the edge—or over? In *Female Masculinity*, Halberstam defines "female masculinity" as "a biological female who presents as butch, passes as male in some circumstances and reads as butch in others, and considers herself not to be a woman but maintains distance from the category 'man'."[19] Female masculinity is when women do not feel comfortable with traditional "femininity" but neither with the category "men" or traditional "masculinity." Women experimenting with sexual and social gender traits—dykes, drag kings, butches, cross-dressers, tommies—are examples of female masculinity. When female soldiers fall outside the categories of masculine and feminine, they enter Halberstam's category of female masculinity. The cross-dressing, the hair-cutting, the swearing, the will to enter a man's place, are presented by these narratives as *unusual* and *unfitting* for a woman.

Thus, it comes as a shock to Serling that the soldier whose death he is about to investigate is a woman. "What did you think the hoopla was about?" the army's public relations advisor replies (the "hoopla" being a ceremony with the President in the Rose Garden and Mary Anne, Karen's daughter, receiving her mother's Medal of Honor—"there is not going to be a dry eye from Nashua to Sacramento"). But like Jordan, whose body is increasingly thematized as troubling, Karen's femininity is also "disturbed." When Serling talks to Karen's co-pilot Rady (Tim Guinee), Rady's wife calls her "butch" to which Rady says, "Honey, shut up." Then, to Serling, "She was, you know." From Serling's inquiry into Karen's life we get the picture of a tomboy child, a butch woman, a single mother whose marriage according to her parents was "no picnic." Ambivalence surrounds Karen, who is "a good mother" and "a soldier," two things which the plot demonstrates cannot co-exist. Karen's commitment as a soldier got her killed and as a result her daughter will be "mothered" by grandparents.

The female soldier is caught in-between gender categories. She can prove herself the equal of men, even superior to them, but in the end Urgayle is right. The female soldier makes the men "vulnerable." Her body pollutes their male world and must therefore be cast out.

The Symbolic Weight of Gender

Since the draft ended in 1972, women account for a still growing part of the US military. In 1972 there were 45,000 female soldiers or 2 percent. In 1997 there were 14 percent in the army, 17 percent in the air force, 5 percent in the marine corps and 13 percent in the navy.[20] With the arrival of an all-volunteer corps, gender weight started to shift towards a gender-integrated army with women becoming commanding officers (but women did not serve in combat infantry and front-line artillery). The *symbolic* weight of gender, however, seems frozen. Our culture finds it difficult to visualize women as warriors, and in our cultural and mythological imagination women remain where they have always been: at home.

In war mythology, warrior women can be represented in two ways: either as Amazons, the Greek race of female warriors, or as a national icon like Germania, Britannica, and Marianne. According to historian George L. Mosse the warrior woman as national icon enters bourgeois mythology as "the guardian of the continuity and immutability of the nation, the embodiment of its respectability."[21] This woman is not linked to aggression or combat but "was assimilated to her traditional role as woman and mother, the custodian of tradition, who kept nostalgia alive in the active world of men."[22] She "ruled without force ... and was usually seated, a figure of quiet strength." Even when she was clad in armor and holding weapons she was not a warrior but a symbol; her "feminine virtues held society to its moral goals, while man was the soldier, the heroic figure who translated theory into practice."[23]

Between woman as sexualized Amazon and woman as maternal and national icon there is, it seems, not space for a contemporary female warrior. In today's culture—news media, war movies—the combat soldier is predominantly male. Images in the news of battle, conquest, and losses are of *male* soldiers. Thus, a resonant image in the European news at the time of Operation Freedom in Iraq, March 2003, was a photo of American soldiers, all men, in one of the many living rooms in Saddam Hussein's palace.[24] In the center a soldier reclined in a rococo armchair, smoking, his legs widely spread, an image of conquest and a metaphor of the American "rape" of the Arab country and the "feminine" palace, his cigarette the symbolic equivalent of an after-sex-cigarette. Male soldiers can embody such symbolism because like war movies they are at one and the same time images of war, masculinity, and nationalism. According to historian Martin van Creveld, "men have made war their special province because they cannot reproduce" and "war is the theater in which men prove their masculinity and in which masculinity is a prerequisite for success."[25] Likewise, war is the theater where nations prove their status. Judging from their lack of representation in the media, female soldiers cannot bear the weight of nationalism and war.

The case of Jessica Lynch, the real life American teenage soldier who was captured, wounded and rescued in Iraq in March 2003, makes an interesting example.[26] "No politician can afford to let women come home in body bags," says DeHaven at one point in *G.I. Jane*. DeHaven is behind the false accusations against Jordan of being a lesbian which result in Jordan being pulled from the SEAL program. Threatening to expose DeHaven, Jordan is reinstated. DeHaven is a manipulating politician, but the audience nonetheless knows she is perfectly right. American politicians cannot afford to have dead female soldiers. Jordan asks if "a woman's life is more valuable than a man's." No, not more valuable. But of different value, one that the nation cannot afford to lose: American women are "emblems of love" by mythic standard. Men signify the strength of a nation and women signify home ground, regenerative forces, eternal values. Killing women will signify the loss of home ground. This is why Jessica Lynch was represented in Danish newspapers by her senior prom photograph, childhood snapshots, and her innocent-looking army portrait.[27] Lynch became front-page news across the world when she was missing in action. A few days later she was rescued from an Iraqi hospital and the American military declared her a combative female war hero who had killed several Iraqi soldiers before she was captured. Two months later, the English media deconstructed the military's story and revealed that Lynch never fired her weapon and that her alleged bullet and knife wounds were from RTA (Road Traffic Accident). However, the Lynch story had served its purpose: Not to show the female soldier as a combative soldier, but as the all–American blond teenager with blue eyes and the innocent victim of savage capture. The spin story drew (perhaps unconsciously) from the classical seventeenth century myth that historian Richard Slotkin calls "the captivity narrative."[28] In this myth a white woman representing Christian virtues is kidnapped by Indians and held in "spiritual darkness" and "madness" until American men rescue her. In her autobiography *I Am A Soldier Too: The Jessica Lynch Story* (2003) Lynch was portrayed as an innocent teenager, a daughter, and a rape victim with amnesia, and *not* as hero, a woman, or a soldier (despite the title of her book saying otherwise).[29]

In contrast to the safe and comforting image of all–American Jessica Lynch, who symbolized home ground rather than American invasion, another news story circulated in the newspapers in the summer of 2003: It was an interview with a young African female soldier called Black Diamond, a colonel in the guerilla forces in Liberia. Images of the beautiful Black Diamond who pointed her AK-47 at scared men, dressed in tight jeans and a red top wearing a wig and with blood-red, long fingernails, were the very epitome of female *unheimlichness*.[30] However, in-between the American *heimlichness* and African *unheimlichness* there is no room for the "ordinary" female soldier.[31]

Writing about *G.I. Jane* and *Courage Under Fire*, Yvonne Tasker says, "whilst the central female characters are tough and masculine-coded ... these images of military women are normalized precisely *through*, and not despite or against, discourses of masculinity."[32] She argues for "a more flexible model" that understands gender "as a set of discourses that are contested, accepted and resisted within networks, rather than binaries" (209, 215). Reading Karen and Jordan as figures who are complexly coded feminine as well as masculine through their physical performances and social roles, Tasker suggests we talk about "gendered discourses" rather than gender binarism. It seems obvious to read the female soldier as a break away from gender binarism. However, the unease, fear and ambivalence that surround the female soldier contradict such a reading. Let us look at the consequences her heroism has for the men around her.

In *G.I. Jane*, Urgayle tells Jordan the Israelis stopped using female soldiers in combat because the men "couldn't get used to the sight of women blown open. They'd linger over the wounded females, trying to save those that obviously couldn't be saved, often to the detriment of the mission." Jordan asks how Urgayle got the Navy Cross. By pulling a 240-pound man out of a burning tank. Could she have done that, he asks her. During the operation in Libya, Jordan pulls Urgayle out of enemy fire (but then, he weighs closer to 140 pounds). Afterwards, Urgayle gives Jordan his Navy Cross. With a wounded leg and on crutches, his eyes lock with Jordan's in mutual recognition of true soldier spirit: someone willing to risk one's life for a fellow soldier. "It's all about the man next to you," as *Black Hawk Down* says. It is forgotten that Iraqi soldiers pursued Urgayle because he gave away his position when he shot a Libyan soldier that Jordan hesitated to kill with her knife. Like the Israeli soldiers, he, too, was afraid to see Jordan's body wounded in combat. He shot the soldier and risked his life because he was uncertain if Jordan could kill. She compromised his life and the mission.

A soldier with a limp and without his Navy Cross is a castrated soldier. The consequences gain wider proportions in Thomas Michael Donnelly's television movie *A Soldier's Sweetheart* (1998). Here, a team of medics work in a camp located on the border between enemy country and friendly territory where they patch up the wounded soldiers' bodies before sending them by helicopter back to the hospital. One medic, Fossie (Skeet Ulrich), imports his girlfriend from America. When Marianne (Georgina Cates) arrives in Vietnam she is "a piece of home": innocent and girlish with feminine clothes and a Samsonite beauty box. But as time passes, the symbolic piece of homeland is attracted to the green jungle and the "greenies," the green berets, which she joins. Soon, she leaves even them to fight alone and barefooted in the mountains. Again, this is a tale of male castration. When Marianne embarks on her nightly missions with the greenies, Fossie desperately tries to locate her. He reproaches the other medics because they filled her with "crap about Amazons" and instructed her in the use of an M-16. Instead of representing "home" she has turned *unheimlich*, unpredictable, unlocatable, beyond gender categorization. She has become, as the film's narrating soldier Rat played by Kiefer Sutherland tells us, more bloodthirsty than the greenies. Fossie goes mad from her "betrayal" and at the end she leads Rat to his (and her) death in a white explosion obliterating them from the screen. *A Soldier's Sweetheart* is a feminized version of Joseph Conrad's *Heart of Darkness* which transfers "the horror, the horror" from the hearts of men to the nature of woman. The film should be read as a psychological drama about an American masculinity castrated by the Vietnam war, symbolized by the innocent Marianne who turns into a corrupted national female icon and an image of woman as abyss.

A castration fantasy—several, in fact—is also at the heart of *Courage Under Fire*. The film has three military crews: Serling's crew, the crew of the crashed Black Hawk, and Karen's crew. The first two represent an ordinary masculinity with men that are neither gun crazy nor trigger happy but simply serve their country and are happy to survive despite losses and amputations. Men who trust their leaders. Serling's crew even understands and forgives that he by mistake took out an American tank with friendly fire. This is the risk in war. Karen's crew, in contrast, is a picture of shattered masculinity. From co-pilot Rady with his haggard face, in a wheelchair, nursed by his bitter white-trailer-trash-wife, to Altameyer in a hospital high on the morphine he administers to himself to ward off the guilty memories of how the crew left Karen to die. Ilario (Matt Damon), the young helicopter nurse, thin, wasted, lost, chain-smoking, shooting morphine between his toes, about to commit suicide before he reveals the truth about Karen's

Will male soldiers trust female officers to lead them in battle? Gender ambivalence and castration anxiety are at the heart of *Courage Under Fire* (Fox 2000 Pictures, 1996), where officer Karen Walden (Meg Ryan, center) is shot by friendly fire during the Gulf War.

death to Serling. And, finally, Monfriez (Lou Diamond Phillips), Hispanic and tattooed with taut muscles and underwear that mark him as slightly deviant (perhaps gay?), obsessed with macho masculinity, poker, expensive cars, becoming a professional boxer. Johnny "Night Train" Monfriez he calls himself. He commits suicide by driving his car onto the train track, screaming, "I was a good soldier. A *good* soldier!" as the train rams into his convertible.

But Monfriez was *not* a good soldier. He was a coward, which we learn in Ilario's flashback that takes the audience back to the past. When they discovered the crashed Black Hawk under enemy fire, Monfriez suggested they call for backup and head home. Karen improvised, using her gasoline tank as a bomb, and was shot down. She refused to leave the wounded Rady behind and involuntarily cried. "Oh, great, the captain is crying," says Monfriez. "It's just tension, asshole, it don't mean shit," Karen responds angrily. At the sight of her female sensitivity or "tension" Monfriez talks the crew into mutiny. "She is trying to get us killed! Do you want to die?" The men silently agree, and Karen then demands that Monfriez hand over his SAW (Squad Automatic Weapon) to her. "There's no way you're taking away my weapon, *cunt*." Karen responds by drawing her gun. "Section 28-J, code of military justice: Mutiny. An offense punishable by death." At this moment an Iraqi soldier appears behind Monfriez. Karen shoots the soldier, Monfriez instinctively returns fire and shoots Karen. During the night they wait and when a rescue team arrives in the morning Karen provides cover fire for her crew. When the rescue team asks if there are any more left, Monfriez says the wounded Karen is dead. Rady is unconscious and the rest of the men accept the lie.

The plot in *Courage Under Fire* is about female strength and male weakness. I have suggested that the female soldier cannot be integrated into the male team because her gender marks her as other. We can now add that if war movies are about the construction of men's masculinity—how perverse or compromised this may be—female war movies are about the construction of a heroic female identity, which reconfigures feminine and masculine traits in the female soldier. This, however, is at the expense of men's masculinity. Where war movies play out scenarios of national struggle and control, female war movies play out scenarios of female struggle and male loss of control.

Contrasting Karen to Serling, it is clear that had she been a man the crew would have respected her judgment of the situation. She fails to function as commanding officer simply because she is a woman and therefore cannot initiate the men into manhood. She cannot be a symbolic "father" like sergeants Barnes and Elias in *Platoon* who function as Private

Chris Taylor's two fathers. And because we identify with Serling, and not Karen, we share his concern with the men, rather than her loss. "As an effect of this audience positioning, the film generates considerably more concern about the potential damage to young men in the gender-integrated military than about how women such as Walden—or her young daughter—might survive and succeed in that world," Susan E. Linville says in "'The *Mother* of All Battles': of *Courage Under Fire* and the Gender-Integrated Military."[33]

Women in war movies are disturbing creatures. They insert themselves between genders that usually are kept apart. Refusing to be spectacles, to be weak or sensitive or penetrable, they collapse gendered hierarchies. Jordan, who was initially "silk stockings," becomes a drag soldier and a hero leaving Urgayle with a limp but without his Navy Cross. *G.I. Jane* ends with an image of Urgayle and does not indicate whether Jordan continued her service in combat and lost her boyfriend or whether she returned to her former work in Intel. She disappears from the plot and her future is unknown. Karen, constructed as butch and sensitive, a single mother unable to lead her crew, may be able to create children but was unable to create soldiers. Her death in friendly fire is the result of male collapse, a gender disorder for which she—in the film's logic—is responsible. Marianne slips from home-like to unheimlich, turning into the lethal figure of the undominated and untamed Amazon.

In today's cultural imagination, a woman cannot represent the nation as a combat soldier. On a narrative level, the female war movie presents protagonists who break gender barriers.[34] On a visual, psychological, and thematic level, however, she disturbs the gendered rules on which war, as well as the war film, rests. Shifting from a feminist to a postfeminist perspective will not lift the mythological weight in the war film. Here, images of combat women during war exist as one of two: either heimlich (woman as safe ground) or unheimlich (woman as abyss). It may be that our social possibilities change, but our cultural visions of gender lag hopelessly behind.

Female Soldier Filmography

Private Benjamin (1980) Dir. Howard Zieff. Private Judy Benjamin, comedy
Aliens (1986) Dir. James Cameron. Lieutenant Ellen Ripley, science fiction/action
Courage Under Fire (1996) Dir. Edward Zwick. Captain Karen Walden, drama/war film
G.I. Jane (1997) Dir. Ridley Scott. Intelligence officer Lieutenant Jordan O'Neil, drama/war film
Starship Troopers (1997) Dir. Paul Verhoeven. Pilot Carmen and female ground soldier Dizzy Flores, science fiction/war film/comedy

Mulan (1998) Dir. Tony Bancroft, Barry Cook (animation). Female soldier Mulan, animated drama/war film

Soldier's Sweetheart, A (1998) Dir. Thomas Michael Donnelly, television movie. Female soldier Marianne, drama/war film

The Messenger: The Story of Joan of Arc (also called Joan of Arc; Jeanne d'Arc) (1999) Dir. Luc Besson, filmed in France. Female soldier Joan of Arc, drama/war film

Basic (2003) Dir. John McTiernan. Investigating officer and Captain Julia Osborne, drama/thriller

War Films in Chapter 10

All Quiet on the Western Front (1930) Dir. Lewis Milestone
From Here to Eternity (1953) Dir. Fred Zinnemann
Bridge on the River Kwai, A (1957) Dir. David Lean, filmed in the UK.
Patton (1970) Dir. Franklin J. Schaffner
The Deer Hunter (1978) Dir. Michael Cimino
Apocalypse Now (1979) Dir. Francis Ford Coppola
An Officer and a Gentleman (1982) Dir. Taylor Hackford
Rambo: First Blood Part Two (1985) Dir. George P. Cosmatos
Heartbreak Ridge (1986) Dir. Clint Eastwood
Platoon (1986) Dir. Oliver Stone
Full Metal Jacket (1987) Dir. Stanley Kubrick
Hamburger Hill (1987) Dir. John Irvin
Born on the Fourth of July (1989) Dir. Oliver Stone
Casualties of War (1989) Dir. Brian De Palma
Saving Private Ryan (1998) Dir. Steven Spielberg
The Thin Red Line (1998) Dir. Terrence Malick
Three Kings (1999) Dir. David O. Russell
Black Hawk Down (2001) Dir. Ridley Scott
Hart's War (2002) Dir. Gregory Hoblit
We Were Soldiers (2002) Dir. Randall Wallace

11

The Action Star Persona
of Milla Jovovich

One afternoon, when I was in Tokyo in 2004 to do research on Japanese actress Meiko Kaji, I visited the Sony building. Outside the futuristic building hung a forty foot long banner featuring Milla Jovovich as female hero Alice in the action-horror movie *Resident Evil: Apocalypse* (which, incidentally, is also distributed by Sony). Inside, Milla again greeted me in the hall from several oversize posters advertising the film, and on the next floors an interview with her played on flat television screens, which the audience could sit down and enjoy in comfortable chairs. Capcom's computer game *Resident Evil*—one of the most popular computer games in the world—had sold more than seven million copies in Japan and Milla Jovovich was clearly a popular film star here. In Europe she had also managed to create a name for herself with *The Fifth Element* (1997) and *The Messenger: The Story of Joan of Arc* (1999) by French director Luc Besson who is considered by Europeans a significant film auteur. In the US, however, Milla was not a star. In fact, she was hardly considered an actor. As she fought and kicked her way through aliens, English soldiers, monsters, and medical experiments, audiences stayed away from her films and critics turned increasingly nasty. The model-turned-actress was discarded as a bad actress whose "inadequacy as an actress strikes the viewer like an arrow to the heart" (*Entertainment Today*), suitable only as "a great Vanity Fair photo spread" (*San Francisco Examiner*).[1]

The critique is understandable, yet unfair. Understandable, since Milla cannot be called a "good" actor in the sense of playing convincingly, as actor Dustin Hoffman, for instance, can pass as an autistic, a single father, a cross-dressing out-of-work actor, a hippie, or a conscience. But then actors whose star personas were based on their physical appearance have always been rejected as "bad," from Marilyn Monroe to Sylvester Stallone. Unfair, however, as I believe there is more to Milla than merely a body. Especially in *The Messenger: The Story of Joan of Arc*, critics panned "the disastrous choice" of a model to play the martyr Jeanne, "a character too important and complex for model-cum-actress Milla Jovovich."[2] Milla was rejected as "just" a body unable to fill a character and as an annoying actor giving a "neurotic and shrill" performance.[3] The two things—on the one hand, a lack of substance and, on the other hand, neurotic presence—are central to Milla's action star persona.

My interest in Milla began when she beat the English army at Orleans in The Messenger, screaming and rolling her eyes like a madwoman. Quite a different Joan from the saintly Maria Falconetti I knew from Carl Theodor Dreyer's La Passion de Jeanne d'Arc (1928). I cannot recall a female hero as neurotic and insistently passionate as Milla's Joan, or "Jeanne" as the character is called with a French pronunciation of the name despite the English "Joan" in Besson's title. I remembered Milla as "the supreme being" Leeloo in The Fifth Element, a weird performance in impossible costumes by French haute couture designer Jean-Paul Gaultier. The star, which I earlier had found annoying, I now found fascinating. In appearance, acting style, and star persona Milla differed from anything I had seen. The female hero is usually caught in a state of in-betweenness where she must choose between two positions presented as excluding one another and gendered respectively "feminine" and "masculine": she can be a mother or have a career (but not both); be a feminine desk soldier or a butch combat soldier (but not both); a natural woman or an invincible fighter (but not both). The conflict erupts when she tries to be and do both: a mother with a career, a feminine combat soldier, a natural woman and a killer. Uniting separate positions creates a state of in-betweenness where "normal" gender roles become in flux. Such in-betweenness can be fraught with tension as in the films of Meiko Kaji and the rape-revenge film, or it can be presented as "just" entertainment to be enjoyed in play mode by a male audience who relocates the aggressive female hero to the "safe" position of spectacle.[4]

Milla Jovovich represents a new version of in-betweenness. Where most female heroes have a traditional femininity—sexy, seductive, and unmistakably female—Milla's characters appear almost ugly with marked features, an androgynous appearance, and a hysterical behavior. Where the female hero alternates between female and male positions, Milla is caught in constant emotional high-strungness, a symptom of intense repression. Her in-betweenness manifests itself in a thin, flatchested body shaking manically in anger and hysteria. A body stripped not only of clothes (Milla has a scene where she is naked in all her action films) but also of large breasts, broad hips, round bottom. Milla's body is that of an adolescent who can pass as boy or girl, but neither man nor woman. In-betweenness is also in her acting style with vibrating nostrils, wide-open eyes, a shrill voice which trembles and cracks at the height of a scream.

In *The Messenger* the French officers ask what Jeanne thinks. "I don't think, I leave that to God. I'm only the messenger," is her reply. This was laughed at by critics who found the actress Milla Jovovich all form and no content. I think, however, that there *is* a message in Milla, whose protagonists are social outsiders saving the world, whose model body is rejected as "empty," and whose acting style may be "bug-eyed" over-acting but carries the marks of hysteria and repression. What is the message? Let us see.

Model Milla

Milla is not just a model, she is a *supermodel* who has been on the covers of more than a hundred magazines worldwide and in the late nineties became the spokesmodel and face of L'Oreal. In 1987 Richard Avedon from Revlon voted her one of the fifty most unforgettable women in the world, and in the late eighties she was one of the Eastern European models that launched the anorexic look that in the nineties spread to Hollywood.

Milla Jovovich was born in 1975 in Ukraine and came to the U.S. when she was five. Her mother left a career as an actress to become the house-keeper for director Brian De Palma, and she passed on her movie ambitions to Milla who became a child model and started taking acting lessons at nine.[5] When she was twelve, Milla was the youngest model to appear on the cover of a women's fashion magazine. Before, fourteen-year-old Brooke Shields had been the youngest model to grace the cover of a fashion magazine. Milla's first leading film role was in *Return to the Blue Lagoon* (1991), a remake of *The Blue Lagoon* which in 1980 had featured fifteen-year-old Shields. However, Milla's appeal is different from Shields'. Milla's look was sensual and challenging. In 1988, Jeffrey Dash, the owner of Prima Model Management, explained to the *L.A. Herald-Examiner*, "Europe and Asia fell easily; it was America that put up the most resistance ... Her look might have been too scary for the Americans." The look was reworked for the U.S. to look "just like a kid."[6] "Brooke and I have completely different images," Milla told *Playboy* in May 2002, "she's always been very much America's sweetheart, and I am not. I'm an alien. I'm Russian."[7] The "alienness" of Milla's look and personality is repeated in interviews which present Milla as an international star of personal taste, sophistication, and independence ("Hollywood's high-brow babe" who plays "contemporary roles doused in panache and exudes a natural air of going-slightly-mad Hollywood diva").[8] Besides being a model and an actor, Milla is a singer who has recorded three albums and several singles, among them two songs on the soundtrack of Wim Wender's *The Million Dollar Hotel* (2000) where she plays a tenant.

Brooke Shields was a pretty model like Geena Davis, Michelle Pfeiffer, Cameron Diaz, and Demi Moore, to mention a few of Hollywood's famous models-turned-actresses. But Milla's look and body are different. Maybe because she is not an American model but an international supermodel with a weird, androgynous look skipping along the borders of beauty and ugliness, of thinness and anorexia, of masculinity and femininity, of adolescence and womanhood. Hers is not a natural-looking body, but rather a human frame, which appears to be digitally constructed with its ideal thinness, almost a sick body, an investigation of postmodern femininity rather than an image of feminine beauty. "Our fathers may fawn over Liz Hurley—but Milla Jovovich is surely thinking man's crumpet for the digital generation," *Arena* commented.[9] In the advertisements for DKNY Milla looks cool and classic, she is androgynous when posing for Cerruti, confused and boyish in advertisements for Alberto Biani and she looks like a decayed, hungry vampire posing in clothes for Anna Molinari. On the covers of *Arena* (July 2002) and the Russian *GQ* (August 2002) she looks like a young drag queen with impossibly thin thighs, red boots, and protruding ribs. The anorexic look is evident in images for Neuman Marcus at Bloomingdale's, and Milla resembles a teenage prostitute in her photograph from the top hundred sexiest women.

In interviews Milla Jovovich expressed ambitions beyond modeling. "The joke is, 'Oh, from L'Oreal to Joan of Arc,'" she told the magazine *W* in 1998. "Well, you know what? I *can* do L'Oreal and then play Joan of Arc."[10] Where fashion magazines were positive, critics picked up on the fact that Milla had married Luc Besson after *The Fifth Element* and divorced after *The Messenger*. A lawsuit from director Kathryn Bigelow against Besson for breach of contract and of stealing her research for the film project "Company of Angels" about Joan of Arc because Bigelow refused to cast Besson's wife in the leading role was settled; however, such behind-the-scenes stories became a subtext in the reception of both *The Messenger* and, retrospectively, *The Fifth Element*.[11] *Resident Evil* was directed by Paul W.S. Anderson who was Milla's fiancé in 2002 and in 2004 produced *Resident Evil: Apocalypse.*

The Action Star Persona

After Besson had cast Milla, her future star persona coalesced around an action star persona, which in costumes and framing underlined her androgynous figure rather than make it more womanly. Besson used low or high angles rather than full person shots to focus on limbs and close-ups of her face. Also, his films established her acting style with nervous tics, body spasms, awkward body movements, a shrill and uncontrolled voice, and the emotional intensity of an imminent nervous breakdown. Her performances in minor roles also exhibited an awkward and nervous but simultaneously strong persona, but were toned down and often positively noticed by critics (who seemed surprised that she could act). "As the awkward, introvert Eloise falling for Tom Tom and coming out of her shell, the beautiful Milla Jovovich convinces. She has a rare ability to appear at the same time immensely fragile and very strong."[12] Since her debut in the drama *Two Moon Junction* (1988), Milla has tried her hand at romance in *Return to the Blue Lagoon* (1991); drama in *Chaplin* (1992) and *He Got Game* (1998); avant-garde film with Wim Wender's *The Million Dollar Hotel* (2000); comedy in *Dazed and Confused* (1993), *Zoolander* (2001), and *You Stupid Man* (2002); and thriller in *The House on Turk Street* (2002). Since 2002, however, she has focused on the genre that made her a film star in Europe and Asia: action films.

Even if *The Fifth Element* is an action-science fiction film, Milla's role as Leeloo can hardly be stretched into that of a female action hero. But the seeds are here for the future action persona. The flimsy story, based on Besson's script written when he was sixteen, has Absolute Evil return each five thousand years to try to destroy the Earth which must be defended by a fifth element, a supreme being who unites the four elements earth, air, fire, and water. In 2259, Evil arrives in the shape of a planet-sized fireball in New York where Korben Dallas (Bruce Willis) is a retired-elite-soldier-turned-cab-driver, Zorg (Gary Oldman) is the villain doing business with Evil, and Leeloo (Jovovich) the fifth element sent by Mondoshawans to protect Earth. Albeit a divine creature, Leeloo is a naive woman who learns about human life from a computer. On the brink of destruction Leeloo hesitates to save Earth because she has learned about the evil that the human race creates. With a kiss Korben demonstrates the value of love and in the fraction of a second before Earth is destroyed a white light shoots out from Leeloo's body and destroys Evil.

Critics discarded the film as a postmodernist failure where pastiche and form overpowered content and emotion. With costumes by designer Jean-Paul Gaultier, designs by comics illustrators Jean Giraud and Jean-Claude Mezieres, and special effects blending digital effects with miniatures and studio models, critics deemed *The Fifth Element* "a decadent fashion show without human content," or, as a Danish review summed up, "like something strange, perhaps a UFO, passing quickly before your eyes to make you exclaim, 'hey, what was that?'"[13]

Three elements become characteristic for Milla's action persona: a body designed, examined, or experimented on by scientists and doctors; a naive

Milla Jovovich as Leeloo in Luc Besson's science fiction film *The Fifth Element* (Gaumont, 1997), dressed in an eye-catching costume created by haute couture designer Jean-Paul Gaultier and nicknamed the Band-Aid by the film crew.

childlike innocence; and a hysterical body language. A running comment is that the divine being is "perfect." Leeloo is reconstructed from a few cells which have survived from the crash of the Mondoshawans' space ship. "It's almost like this being was engineered," a scientist tells a general as they wait for the reconstruction to finish, "the cell is, for lack of a better word, perfect." The supreme being turns out to be a young woman with red rag hair who the machine dresses in white "thermo bandages" leaving little to the imagination. The scientist smiles, "I told you: perfect." "I'd, uhm, like to take a few pictures for the archives," says the general. When the flash of his camera hits her virgin body, the supreme being has what looks like an epileptic seizure: her body bends over in an arc as she beats the glass ceiling of the reactor and screams inarticulately. The men try to reason with her, "If you want out, you've got to learn to develop them communication skills!" Leeloo scans the room, the general, and the identity tag he dangles in front of her eyes, the camera zooms in on a close-up of her eyes, she growls like a feline animal, then breaks the glass and jumps right through the walls of the room.

Leeloo is a character of contradiction: sent to protect yet crying over human violence, thousand of years old yet in the body of a young woman, learning martial arts from watching Bruce Lee on a computer yet fainting when catastrophe is imminent. The critics' response was to ignore the actress and notice the body. And as long as they thought Milla was "just" a body, they were condescendingly positive: "Jovovich, dressed by Gaultier and shot by Besson (who handles camera operation) and DP [director of photography] Thierry Arbogast to maximize the scruffy-nymphet qualities Besson seems to favor in his female leads, does a good job melting certain Sil and Nikita qualities, although the mix is hardly as existential as either of those previous female protagonists."[14] Milla is "dressed" and "shot" to maximize "scruffy-nymphet qualities" in a strap costume reportedly nicknamed the Band-Aid by the film crew.[15] Another reviewer offered this judgment of her performance: "Jovovich's long-limbed beauty is exploited fully. Her first 10 minutes on screen leave us little to wonder but what she must look like with clothes on."[16] Again, her body is "exploited" which (male) reviewers found compensated for an otherwise failed film: "Leeloo is clad in a garment that looks improvised from Ace bandages but gets no complaints from me."[17]

At this point in twenty-one-year-old Milla Jovovich's film career, no one noticed the trembling lips, manic facial expressions, tears, fainting fits, and nudity. Backed by male co-star Willis, she was more sidekick than female hero and such a behavior perhaps found "natural" for a woman. This, too, perhaps explains why many critics didn't bother to mention her name in their reviews of The Fifth Element.[18] This changed with The Messenger: The Story of Joan of Arc (1999). What in retrospect can be seen as a hysterical subtext of Milla's action star persona that is already present in The Fifth Element is explicitly thematized in Besson's interpretation of the medieval French martyr Joan of Arc as a delusional teenage peasant girl.

In 1928 Carl Theodor Dreyer had chosen to focus on Jeanne's trial and her faith in La Passion de Jeanne d'Arc. Jeanne's tears on the fire were shared by the crowd, close-ups of her face crosscut with a cross, her last word is "Jesus" and as she dies the crowd yells, "You have burnt a saint" and riots. In Besson's version saintliness is replaced with insanity and tremendous faith with tragic fate. The film opens with eight-year-old Jeanne (Jane Valentine) confessing to a priest in church and on her way back to her village laughing that everything is "wonderful." She finds a sword in the field, clouds suddenly gather ominously as she has her first vision, and on her return English soldiers attack the village. When her older sister Christine gives

Jeanne her hiding place in a closet, Jeanne watches Christine defend herself with the sword from the field. "A woman with a sword," the soldiers laugh and spear Christine with Jeanne's sword and rape the dead body. This memory haunts Jeanne, who at seventeen convinces the Dauphin of France (John Malkovich) to give her an army that she uses to take back the city of Orleans on May 8 in 1429. She is, however, defeated at Paris and captured at Compiègne, after which the French king refuses to pay her ransom. During her trial at Rouen, Jeanne has conversations with her Conscience, a figure she has seen in her visions as respectively a boy, a young man, and an old man (the latter played by Dustin Hoffman). The Conscience absolves her when the French Bishop refuses to do so, and Jeanne is burnt at the stake without any apparent sympathy from the crowd on May 30, 1431.

Spreading his story over more than ten years, Besson paid attention to the dramatic life and personal development of Jeanne with emphasis on her youth and innocence. Dreyer had chosen the thirty-five year old actress Falconetti because of her serene facial features, and in his direction and filming she was visualized as a female Christ. Falconetti's tear-filled eyes turned towards heaven and her expression of dignified masochism echoed how

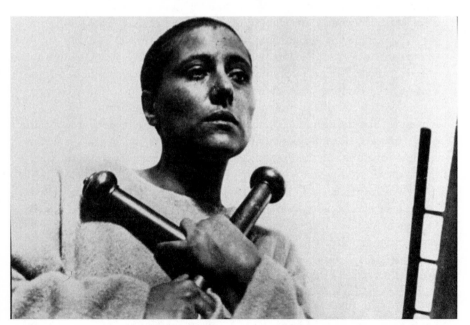

Danish director Carl Theodor Dreyer chose the thirty-five-year-old actress Maria Falconetti to play Joan in *La Passion de Jeanne d'Arc* (Société générale des films, 1928) and made her look like a female version of Christ, passively suffering and clutching the cross.

classical art had pictured a crucified Christ and the holy virgin in Marian iconography. There is nothing serene or dignified about Milla's Jeanne. She is driven by her "voices" and high-strung emotions, and her repeated answer to comments about not being so impatient is "sooner is better than later." The youth and androgyny of her appearance can be seen in her male armor that, in contrast to the outfit of the Amazon archetype, does not enhance her as a feminine spectacle. In contrast to earlier film versions and visualizations of the martyr, Jeanne's armor is not designed to fit a female body; there is no room for breasts and no skirt. Her makeup is natural and boyish, and in the film she cuts her hair in men's fashion. Also, her hair changes from light blond to dark brown during the two-year period of fighting and capture. The change of hair color indicates her loss of innocence and the darkening of her conscience.

Milla's warrior martyr is both a hysteric and a typical teenager. Hysteric when she casts herself at the feet of the Dauphin, crying and shaking, and when she is furious with her officers for ignoring her. When they discuss strategies for attacking the English Jeanne paces back and forth talking still louder to herself: "And why is there nothing to see? Because I haven't done anything. And why haven't I done anything? Because none of you WILL LISTEN TO ME!" She shouts the last words and the camera zooms in on her sweaty, agitated face. When they launch an attack without her, she rushes to the battle where soldiers are retreating and reopens the attack against her officers' advice. "But the drawbridge is closed," Dunois (Tchéky Karyo) objects. "Not for long!" she says and charges her horse towards the besieged castle. With a handheld camera Besson uses an ultra close-up of Jeanne screaming like crazy and her eyes wide open. Her horse leaps over the walls of the fortress, she gallops past the English soldiers and in the confusion cuts the rope holding the drawbridge. Jeanne's untraditional and unconditional warfare has begun.

Hysteria, unchecked emotions, anger, fear, fury, impatience, impulsiveness. These are associated with hysteria as a clinical diagnosis and with women in general. Milla's Jeanne *is* hysterical and even borderline schizophrenic. We excuse hysteria in teenagers because of their age; we expect them to be irrational, angry, rebellious, and hypersensitive. "Why are you so angry? Calm down," the captain Aulon (Desmond Harrington) tells a furious Jeanne, when her officers find it difficult to take orders from "a girl." "I'm calm, it's GOD THAT'S ANGRY!" However, her conscience has been with her since childhood, before the rape of her sister. He is not a construct of traumatic memory, but a sign of psychic disturbance. He does not deliver a believer from evil, but places further guilt on the shoulders of a delusional. When asked what she thinks, Jeanne responds, "I don't think; I leave that to God. I'm only the messenger." The message, however, is not clear to Jeanne who dies with a lost and helpless expression on her face. Her fidgeting feet in chains are reminiscent of her fidgeting with hands, mouth, and eyes during the trial and signify continued delusion. The final song text adds to the psychodrama.

In contrast to Dreyer's film, *The Messenger* is not homage to faith. Jeanne's officers—Dunois, Gilles de Rais, La Hire, and her captain Jean—put their lives in the hands of a peasant maid because they admire her spirit, not because the believe in her voices or visions. *The Messenger* is homage to a feminine "spirit" refusing to calm down. The film's press material refers to modern interpretations of Joan of Arc's visions as "the result of neurosis, hysteria or illness" and Jovovich says about the real Joan, "It was a story I never believed in. It's strange to play her, because I just never took it seriously. There's not a person there. It's just an icon. It's a phrase, it's an adjective. Everything except a human being."[19]

Ironically, this was exactly how reviewers felt about Milla's performance as Jeanne. In *The Fifth Element* Milla's performance had been received as yet one more model being used as enjoyable and not-to-take-serious eye candy. In *The Messenger*, however, the model played a "real" character and

Warrior virgin with a tomboyish look. In Luc Besson's *The Messenger: The Story of Joan of Arc* (Gaumont and Europa Corp., 1999), the famous saint Joan (Milla Jovovich) becomes a stubborn and hysterical teenager throwing herself into battle against the advice of her officers. Behind Joan is her faithful captain Aulon (Desmond Harrington).

wanted to be a "real" actor. This was not welcome. *The San Francisco Examiner* saw her as "an annoying, sometimes ridiculous cipher at [the movie's] heart," and found that her "interpretation of the part, and acting ability, begin to trip things up. [She was] screechy and unstable, overwrought and unconvincing as a leader who could rally a discouraged army." The review concluded, "[Besson's] Joan would make a great Vanity Fair photo spread."[20] Milla is reduced to a "spread," not a character. Also, it might not have been a wise move to point out a "very smoky, very strange" fashion photo of Milla Jovovich as the inspiration to the make the film and create the character Jeanne, as the film's press material did.[21] *Boxoffice Magazine* found "her performance becomes wildly erratic, vacillating between tremulous indecision and fearless confidence, often coming off as a maniacal, bug-eyed crazy person who exhibits none of the qualities that would inspire her army..."[22] *Sight & Sound* concluded, "Jovovich just seems neurotic and shrill,"[23] and in Denmark female reviewers were sarcastic: "Besson's choice of a bland model is a disaster," nothing but "naked ass."[24] In *Information* another female reviewer wrote, "Milla Jovovich has a certain chic model-like appearance, but unfortunately she masters just two expressions: She can be sorrowful and shed tears, and she can do a trick with her eyes so they shine with sheer madness ... under no circumstances, however, is this enough to carry an entire movie."[25] (However, in stark contrast to their American colleagues, several Danish male reviewers were positive: "Milla Jovovich is a new superstar. She brings the more than five hundred year old myth of Joan of Arc to life with a surprising contemporary actuality, sexuality, spice, and power.")[26]

Milla's breakthrough as a female action hero did not come about as a result of her movies with Besson, which were received as Besson vehicles and not Jovovich vehicles, but came with the two filmatizations of Capcom's computer game *Resident Evil*, *Resident Evil* (Paul W.S. Anderson, 2002) and *Resident Evil: Apocalypse* (Alexander Witt, 2004), with yet a third movie, *Resident Evil: Extinction*, planned for 2007. The *Resident Evil* films may not do well in cinemas in the US and Europe, but they are popular with computer players and as rentals and have secured Milla status as a female hero with a male audience.

In Paul W.S. Anderson's *Resident Evil* a future company called the Umbrella Corporation carries out experiments with biological weapons in an underground facility called the Hive. When the deadly T-virus escapes, the Hive responds by closing down and killing everyone inside. The female hero (credited as Alice[27] but never called by her name in the film) wakes up with amnesia as a team of special soldiers enters the Hive to investigate the security break. The soldiers bring Alice and two more amnesiac survivors with them into the Hive, where they are killed off one at a time by either the facility's security system (laser rays, deadly gas, traps) or by the humans that the T-virus has transformed into zombies. On the way they encounter the Zombie Dogs, the Crows (experimental tissue creatures), and the Licker (a monster with a long tongue), all creatures from the game. Since players would be familiar with the outcome of the female hero's quest, Anderson wrote his script as a prequel to the first game which thus lets the audience guess at who will survive and who will die. The result is an action/horror/science fiction film, which works efficiently as a "standalone action film," as the Constantin Film Production called it. In the end, everyone except Alice dies. Classic zombie problem.

As written by Anderson, Milla's character Alice continued her action star persona.[28] This time, amnesia explained why the female hero was a "blank" personality who responded instinctively with martial arts moves and professional shooting before she recalled that she was in fact a security guard assigned to protect the Hive. With less talk and an explanation for a bewildered expression, Milla convinced as the game's female hero. Interestingly, even if Milla this time played an adult woman (Alice is married and has a job) her body still carried a hysterical and adolescent subtext which broke out in what we can call Jovovich's "signature scene": a scene where her body is naked, subject to experimentation or hospitalization, and caught in invol-

Hysteria, mental illness, and medical examination are part of Milla Jovovich's action star persona. Screaming and shaking with pain, female hero Alice (Jovovich) wakes up on the operating table in an abandoned hospital in *Resident Evil* (Constantin Film Produktion GmbH, New Legacy, Davis-Films, Impact Pictures, 2002).

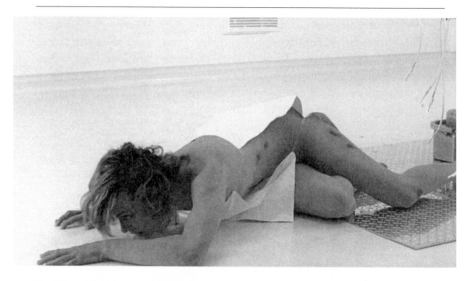

Is this a hero or a mental patient? Like Jovovich's Band-Aid costume in
The Fifth Element, the two pieces of paper in *Resident Evil* (Constantin
Film Produktion GmbH, New Legacy, Davis-Films, Impact Pictures, 2002)
form an unusual costume constructing a "sick" action body covered in
bloody wounds and evoking the self-mutilation of young girls.

untary spasms. In *The Fifth Element* this is when Leeloo is born in the reactor. In *The Messenger* it is the public examination of Jeanne's virginity. And
in *Resident Evil* this happens towards the end where Alice wakes up on the
operating table in an empty hospital in Raccoon City, screaming and gasp-
ing for air. She tears off the dozen of syringes that connect plastic tubes to
her head, thighs, arms, and sides, and falls from the operating table and
crawls backwards in the white room like a terrified animal. Her trembling,
white body is decorated by little bleeding wounds from the syringes and covered by two pieces of white paper held together with metal clips. Her genitals, we see, are shaved. Outside everything is chaos with overturned cars
and a newspaper headline, "THE DEAD WALK!" Alice grabs a shotgun
from a police car and faces the world with a grim look, and the camera
zooms backwards and up, leaving her as a solitary white spot in an otherwise red and black hell.

Paradoxically, with *Resident Evil* nobody except fashion magazines
thought of Milla as a movie star, at least not in the US and Europe. Maybe
because the film was regarded as "just" entertainment and not about
"real" emotions. The fleshing out of a pixel computer game character raised
fewer concerns than that of a martyr (but we shall see in the next chapter
that the most well-known computer-game-turned-film, Eidos' *Tomb Raider*,

would see debates over the "correct" body and personality). If reviews mention Jovovich at all, this is hastily, passing on applause to her co-star Michelle Rodriguez who played the tough female soldier Rain. Thus the *New York Times* concluded, "it is Ms. Rodriguez's job as Alice's tough, streetwise cohort to do the feeling for both of them," and the *Los Angeles Times* praised Rodriguez as "a tough-talking, attitude-throwing veteran of 'The Fast and the Furious' who is working overtime for the title of the 21st century's first true B-movie queen."[29]

Virginity

Virginity plays a part in the shaping of Jovovich's action persona, thematically as well as psychologically. Thematically, virginity is central in *The Fifth Element* where Leeloo threatens Korben with a gun the first time he wakes her with a kiss ("not without my permission") but saves the world the second time he kisses her. And in *The Messenger: The Story of Joan of Arc*, virginity is what convinces the Dauphin that Jeanne is sent from God. In *Resident Evil* and *Resident Evil: Apocalypse*, virginity is not an explicit theme. However, Alice has no romantic relationships and her body is uniquely resistant to the T-virus, two elements that can be read as celibacy and a body resisting "intrusion."

Virginity has always been read and used as a sign. When the parliament at Poitiers in *The Messenger* ask Jeanne to show them a sign that she is sent by God, she replies, "Give me an army. Take me to Orleans. There you will see the sign that I was sent to make." Divinity is not easy to test—but virginity is. It is historically correct that Joan's virginity was tested, not publicly as in *The Messenger*, but in private by Charles' stepmother, the Queen of Sicily, and her maids. Two years later, the Duchess of Bedford, wife of the ruler of England and France, ascertained her virginity during her trial at Rouen. It was intact and the Duchess gave orders that she was not to be abused. Virginity saved her from the rape and torture common in heresy trials. But not from death.[30]

Today, virginity is still overlaid with significance. Once lost it cannot be restored (although it is increasingly popular to have virginity surgically restored), and when it is lost the body is no longer "whole" or "unblemished." Virginity is taken as a sign of purity and truth; like a blank page, it cannot lie. Virginity is also a state of in-betweenness. A virgin is suspended in a sexualized-but-not-yet-adult-gendered realm. In Christianity, virginity was used as the path to an "ideal androgyny" where the eradication of sexuality made women progress to the "pure" manhood of Christ. Marina Warner in her study *Joan of Arc: The Image of Female Heroism* (1981) describes how Christianity links virginity to holiness. "Saint Jerome had proclaimed that faith abolished sexual difference and wrought a new asexual state, an ideal androgyny, which transcended gender and represented Christian virtue." Saint Ambrose wrote that "[s]he who does not believe is a woman, and should be designated with the name of her sex, whereas she who believes progresses to perfect manhood, to the measure of the adulthood of Christ."[31] About the female martyrs in the Middle Ages Warner notes how "sexlessness is virginity's achievement and a metaphor for martyrdom" and that the "transcendence of gender in most of these cases heralds ... a rebirth into an exalted state of original wholeness, where sex did not obtain."[32]

Christianity may interpret virginity as "sexlessness," but sexuality and eroticism are overwhelmingly present in the suffering female martyrs as they also are in the images of a suffering Christ in Renaissance art. Like a virgin, Jesus founds his faith on celibacy and the sublimation of desire. The ideal is not the male gender or a generic neuter but the repression of sexuality into a state of virginal in-betweenness that leads to "perfect manhood."

Dreyer did not dwell on Jeanne's virginity in 1928. To Dreyer, faith was central. In his adaptation of the legend, Besson turned things around. Faith was secondary. In fact, faith results from a virginity that Besson links to trauma, suggesting that Jeanne became a martyr and a saint due to her need to repress and sublimate rather than the other way round (that is, the view that she suffered because of her faith). Besson provides the childhood trauma of the older sister Christine being killed and raped with Jeanne's sword. This memory haunts eight-year-old Jeanne: "Why didn't he pick my life instead of hers? It was my fault, I was late, she gave me her hiding place," Jeanne asks a priest. "Perhaps he chose you because he needs you for some higher calling, so as long as you answer that call your sister will not have died in vain," he replies. Rape, death and woman-with-a-sword make sense if Jeanne is chosen, and the traumatic childhood experience provides a motive for guilt and repression. The historical Joan, in contrast, claimed to hear voices at thirteen and then vowed her virginity to God. Her sister was not raped and she did not have a traumatic childhood.[33]

If the Christian interpretation of virginity is purity, the psychological interpretation of virginity complements this purity with its "dark side": a traumatic fear of coitus, repression of desire, and hysteria. Freud thought virginity was a dangerous state. In "The Taboo of Virginity" (1918) he speculates that in prehistoric time the two sexes were equally strong until one day men subjugated women into the weaker sex. "The feelings of bitterness arising from this subjection still persist in the present-day disposition of women,"[34] Freud writes, and suggests that the memory of this prehistoric battle lingers in women's biology: "...defloration has not only the one, civilized consequence of binding the woman lastingly to the man; it also unleashes an archaic reaction of hostility towards him..."[35] Thus, much like classic Greek society thought about the conquest of an Amazon (rape her and marry her), Freud sees the conquest of a virgin as a "civilizing" but dangerous act. Freud uses the Apocrypha of Judith beheading Holofernes as evidence of a virgin's wish to decapitate—symbolically castrate—the man who deflowers her. Besson evidently knows his Freud: As the Dauphin (Malkovich) contemplates Jeanne, who is walking in the grass and swinging her stick in the flowers, the camera zooms in on her from a low angle. Suddenly, in a few frames, flowers and stick becomes a sword decapitating a man in close-up—a scary sight. "Let's find out," Charles then replies to the question of her virginity and the next shot shows the instruments for the examination: A long row of black pairs of forceps. The public examination of Jeanne is a virgin-rape: Men intrude on the virgin body to ascertain its purity.

There are two kinds of virginity: One is *eternal* virginity as represented by the Virgin Mary and by Queen Elizabeth I (the latter became known as "The Virgin Queen"). In western culture, eternal virginity is linked to serenity, maternity, and the idea of mercy. This eternal virgin is a gentle and holy mother who cares for her children, an image we find in religious imagery and in national icons like Germania and Britannica. The other kind is *nubile* virginity. A nubile virgin chooses virginity to avoid the transition from adolescence to maternity. She is not a caring, maternal figure, but a woman refusing to be a woman. Her rejection to being deflowered is a provocation in patriarchal society because she does not fit into the roles of stereotypical woman, wife, and mother. The nubile virgin is dangerous because she is in-between the female and male roles as they are constituted by society, and because she questions the gendered hierarchy upon which social order rests. Nubile virginity can only be excused as an adolescent's experimentation with gender, such as being a tomboy.

Cross-dressing as a man is one way to reject ordinary womanhood, and Joan's male dress and short hair were the subject of five of the seventy articles of condemnation brought against the historical Joan at her trial. "Cross-dressing was forbidden," Marina Warner writes in the introduction to *The Trial of Joan of Arc* (1996), "the Bible calls it an abomination, in Deuteronomy 22, and St. Paul had expressly forbidden women to cut their hair."[36] During her trial Joan repeatedly defended her male attire and refused to put on women's clothing. The judges concluded, "you have continually worn man's dress ... you have also worn your hair short, cut *en rond* above your ears, with nothing left that could show you to be a woman ... As for these points, the clerks say that you blaspheme God in His sacraments; that you transgress divine law, the Holy Scriptures and the canon law..."[37]

Again, where Dreyer's Jeanne is depicted as enduring an archetypical *feminine* and *passive* suffering at the hands of men, Besson shows a Jeanne who *actively* enters the male world in defiance of the limitations put on her because of her gender. Thus, Dreyer's Jeanne has her hair cut by men mocking her, whereas Besson's Jeanne cuts her own hair to gain respect from her officers. Like the female combat soldiers we examined in chapter ten, she cuts her hair to disavow the limitations of femininity. It is a voluntarily phallization of the female hero's body, which turns it into a weapon instead of a woman. This cross-dressing is not intended as a disguise but used to tap into male qualities. The female hero does not want to be a man; she wants *not* to be a woman. "Joan was using male apparel to appear sexless, rather than male, to appear not-female, rather than female. She was not in disguise—everybody knew that she was Joan la Pucelle, the magic virgin. Female in body, but not in spirit—her dress signified her abjuration of the weakness of femininity, both physical and spiritual."[38]

Hair cutting and cross-dressing are central elements in the legend of Joan of Arc. They are connected to virginity, to "perfect manhood," and to the liberation of a female hero's potential. In the Middle Ages women were forbidden to cut their hair in men's fashion; as the war films with female combat soldiers demonstrate, the act still holds magical powers.[39]

The Essence of Milla

In-betweenness is rarely welcome when it challenges the beliefs of a society. It was three hundred years before Jeanne got her surname d'Arc. In life she was called Jeanne la Pucelle, Joan the Maid. The French *de* signifies nobility and *arc* came from the bow (*arc*) used by the Amazons. Joan was not canonized a saint until 1920, almost five hundred years after her death. Critics judge Milla Jovovich to be an inessential actress, untalented, and appropriate for the cover of *Vanity Fair*. I think, however, that they miss the essence of movie star Milla.

This essence is not easy to pin down. It is in her body and acting style, not in the traditional sense of "beauty" and "good" acting, but in her ability to function as a blank page and an empty sign. Milla's female protagonists are not characters with stable personalities. They are either innocent like Leeloo, who was born as an adult in a soundproof reactor; or borderline schizophrenics like Jeanne, who speaks to her visions and herself, which turn out to be the same thing; or amnesiac like Alice, who is unable to remember her past and wins back bits and pieces of her memory during the plot, but is lost in a world gone zombie. The end of *Resident Evil: Apocalypse* (2004) has Alice once again subject to biogenetic experiments against her will, when she is kept naked and unconscious submerged in a container filled with water. Milla Jovovich's protagonists appear as blank as the white undershirt Jeanne wears in her medical examination or the paper covering Alice on the operating table. Rather than being women with personalities of their own, these roles reflect a society's conception of femininity as ideal, blank, and without stable personality.

The physical purity of Milla's protagonists is linked to virginity and idealized biology. But this purity comes through the repression of self and gender. The female hero's body is a paradoxical site of innocence and aggression.

With its extremely thin frame, the action body of actress and supermodel Milla Jovovich borders on the anorexic and androgynous. Here is Jovovich in *Resident Evil: Apocalypse* (Constantin Film, Davis Films, Impact Pictures, 2004), the second of four planned films based on Capcom's computer game *Resident Evil*.

Thus, the warrior skills of Milla's heroines are not something they are master of, they erupt instinctively, almost automatically, as an expression of
uncontrolled anger or repressed memory. Fighting is not a willed action but
a spontaneous reaction (as when Alice discovers the martial arts abilities she
didn't know she possessed until she comes face to face with the Zombie
Dogs) or a hysterical symptom (when a hysterical Jeanne attacks the English).
Milla's action body does not appear strong and healthy, but hysterical and
hospitalized. The tics, spasms, screams, and outbursts read like hysterical
symptoms which according to Freud are "substitutes, produced by 'conver-
sion,' for the associative return of ... traumatic experiences." The symptoms
"serve the purpose of sexual satisfaction and represent a portion of the subject's sexual life..."[40] Milla's heroines differ from the female archetypes in
the man's world because they are androgynous, virginal, and alien images
of a female hero, whose desire is expressed through hysterical symptoms.
Come to think of it, it is wrong to say that Milla's body is naked on the
operating table in *Resident Evil*; rather, it is "covered" with the bloody wounds
from the syringes, wounds that look suspiciously like the self-mutilation of
many young women today.

Kurt Wimmer's science fiction film *Ultraviolet* (2006) continues an
action star persona balancing in-between savior and sickness, the supernatural and the irrational. As the vampire-killer Violet Song jat Shariff, Milla
is again subject to bio-examinations with blood tests and scannings. The
order to "please remove all articles of clothing and proceed into the scan-
ner" reminds us of similar nude inspection scenes in *The Fifth Element* and
Resident Evil. Fixed by a male gaze scrutinizing her perfect body for infection
and betrayal, this is less the nightmare control of a future totalitarian state
than it is the fantasy of our present. Critics were, again, critical. "It's never
clear whether the rail-thin Jovovich actually performed in the film or just
consented to full-body digitization," *The Village Voice* remarked.[41] Milla's
frame lends itself to digital aesthetics, not just as a spectacle but as a human
spectre as well. The spectre of a female sensitivity struggling to come to its
senses, just like the vampire Violet struggles with her own nature and
repressed emotions.

I think there *is* a message in Milla. In the nineties androgyny and
anorexia became trendy and culminated in the character Trinity in *The
Matrix* (1999) and in the actress Calista Flockhart from the television series
Ally McBeal running from 1997 to 2002. As a model, Milla conveys cool
androgyny and enviable body control (with her thinness which could be mistaken for anorexia). As a movie star, however, her action star persona reveals
the dark side: repression, hysteria, and the lack of a "real" person. In-between
these two is where women find themselves today.

In *Ultraviolet* (Screen Gems Inc., Ultravi Productions Inc., 2006), based on a fictitious comic book, female hero and vampire Violet Song jat Shariff (Milla Jovovich) can change the color of her costume and hair, freeze time, pull hand weapons from her flesh, and cheat bio-examinations.

Milla Jovovich Filmography (Selective)

Return to the Blue Lagoon (1991) Dir. William A. Graham. Lilli, romance

The Fifth Element (French title: Le Cinquieème élément) (1997) Dir. Luc Besson, filmed in France and the U.S. Alien savior Leeloo, action/science fiction

The Messenger: The Story of Joan of Arc (also called Joan of Arc; Jeanne d'Arc) (1999) Dir. Luc Besson, filmed in France. Martyr Joan, drama

Resident Evil (2002) Dir. Paul W.S. Anderson, filmed in the UK, Germany and France. Action hero Alice, action/science fiction

The House on Turk Street (2002) Dir. Bob Rafelson, filmed in Germany and the U.S. Girlfriend Erin, gangster drama

Resident Evil: Apocalypse (2004) Dir. Alexander Witt, filmed in Germany, France, the UK and Canada. Action hero Alice, action/science fiction

Ultraviolet (2006) Dir. Kurt Wimmer. Action hero Violet Song jat Shariff, action/science fiction

12

High Trash Heroines:
Lara, Beatrix, and Three Angels

"Oh, it's a breast question!," says a beaming Jolie, cutting to the chase. "No, that's fine because personally ... I wouldn't want those breasts. But she's one cup size bigger than me," she says with a smile, "I'm a 36C, [in the movie] she's a 36D, in the game she's a DD."
>   —Angelina Jolie about *Lara Croft: Tomb Raider*, 2001[1]

JOURNALIST: Drew, what are your favorite body parts of Lucy's and Cameron's?

BARRYMORE: Lucy's tushie and Cameron's boobs. Not that I don't love Cameron's butt and Lucy's boobs.

DIAZ: Lucy has great boobs. They're so firm [grabs her own breasts]

JOURNALIST: Lucy?

LIU: It's so hard, because I've seen both of these girls–
>   —Liu, Barrymore and Diaz about
>   *Charlie's Angels: Full Throttle*, 2003[2]

Watching Uma fight Vivica A. Fox's character, that's hot. When you see two beautiful women, and they're hurting each other— punching each other in the face, bashing each other's head against walls, slicing each other's hands—that hurts, more than with two guys. There's just a naughty aspect to seeing women fight.
>   —Quentin Tarantino about *Kill Bill Vol. 1*, 2003[3]

The "High Trash" in the title of this chapter does not refer to any notion of "quality" (or lack thereof) in regards to aesthetics, gender politics, or otherwise. It refers to a postmodern strategy popular in Hollywood's blockbuster action films in the new millennium: that of raiding low budget films and genres until now relegated to the status of obscure trash or cult. With *Star Wars* George Lucas revived the fifties' Sunday matinee movie as blockbuster cinema for the seventies. Similarly, films like *Charlie's Angels*

(2000), *Charlie's Angels: Full Throttle* (2003), *Lara Croft: Tomb Raider* (2001), *Lara Croft Tomb Raider: The Cradle of Life* (2003), *Kill Bill Vol. 1* (2003) and *Kill Bill Vol. 2* (2004) have demonstrated the economic success of recycling low culture media products—computer games, old television series, exploitation genres, Asian cinema—into blockbuster cinema boasting Hollywood's highest paid female actors.

What makes high trash heroines unique is not that they, like Frankenstein's monster (as one review called *Kill Bill Vol. 1*), are patched together from quotes and odes and homages to every possible cinematic geek pleasure from la Nouvelle Vague to spaghetti westerns and Sonny Chiba. Exploitation cinema has always done this, the only difference now being that mainstream movies rip off exploitation (and, again, neither is this new). No, unique is the *explicitness* of the exploitation, the hyper-ironic tongue-in-cheek approach disarming any critique of the producers of being antifeminist, speculating in profit or speculating about anything at all. Unique is the sheer amount of artistic energy channeled into deliberately thin plots and the increasingly high budget ventures. The attitude is "we just want to have fun" and the female heroes are "girls" not to be taken seriously in contrast to "Geena Davis and Kathleen Turner [who] got mired in post-feminist self-consciousness."[4]

Three elements define high trash heroines action films: Everyone agrees they are merely "fun" and that plot and content are irrelevant; the only thing which matters is the female hero and her *body*; and the portrayal of the female hero is related to an unspecified and unpoliticized empowerment of women.[5] The chapter is divided into three sections dealing with these three elements: *fun*, *body*, and the question of *empowerment and identification*. Let us first look at the "fun."

The Wink of an Eye

Charlie's Angels (2000), the first of the High Trash Heroines action films, is based on the television series *Charlie's Angels* (1976–81) featuring Jaclyn Smith, Kate Jackson and Farrah Fawcett-Majors as three private detectives working for anonymous millionaire Charlie, whose face is never seen. The angels receive orders from Charlie's voice heard over a speakerphone and through his assistant Bosley. Whereas the television actresses were unknown before the series (Farrah later becoming famous for her long blond hair), actresses Drew Barrymore, Cameron Diaz, and Lucy Liu were major Hollywood stars who from the outset marked the movie as a high profile star vehicle. The plot of *Charlie's Angels* had Eric Knox (Sam Rockwell) hire angels Dylan (Barrymore), Alex (Liu), and Natalie (Diaz) to retrieve software stolen from him. He turns out to be a villain using the angels to steal software that he needs to use to locate and kill Charlie, whom Knox believes murdered his father. In the end the angels kill Knox and defeat his lover and second-in-command, Vivian Wood (Kelly Lynch), and a creepy hired hand nick-named The Thin Man (Crispin Glover). In the sequel, *Charlie's Angels: Full Throttle* (2003), the angels had to retrieve two rings that contained secret information about people in a government witness protection program. The rings were stolen by ex-angel Madison (Demi Moore) who was selling to the highest criminal bidder, among these Dylan's former Irish boyfriend Sea-mus O'Grady. The angels retrieve the rings, kill Seamus, defeat and kill Madison, and go to the premiere of an action movie featuring Alex's boyfriend Jason at Mann's Chinese Theatre on Hollywood Boulevard.

The *Charlie's Angels* films didn't have coherent plots with "deep" char-acters but consisted of loosely connected scenes providing ample opportu-nities for the angels to travel, change costumes, do action scenes, and perform undercover gigs as masseuses, Swiss folk singers, race car drivers, strippers, motorcycle drivers, forensics experts, et cetera. Reviewers found the plot "a hyperactive hodge-podge of pop video and video game. It's a fizzy, caffeine-rich cola for teenage eyes, offering a quick, disposable blast of pop-culture wham-bam-buzz that's forgotten in five seconds."[6] Some liked this "potato chip of a movie," which the review in the *Los Angeles Times* found to be "[t]asty and lightweight, it's fine for a cinematic snack ... Making it an entire meal, however, really isn't advisable."[7] Others praised the film like *Variety*, who enjoyed "the sheer visual and visceral pleasure of watching Cameron Diaz, Drew Barrymore and Lucy Liu strut, slink, kick, dance and vamp their way through this splashy femme empowerment fantasy."[8] And then there were those who just gave up being intellectual and surrendered to playful irony like the *Wall Street Journal*: "The story has to do with ... but do you really care what the story has to do with? The main thing is that the Angels get to wear bikinis, stiletto heels, motocross outfits..."[9] Indeed.

Director McG (Joseph McGinty Nichol) developed a new style that was "cooler, sillier, more cartoonish ... not so 'high style'," defined by "fun" and "color" and a heightened reality. "This isn't reality, this is Angel World ... we just went for as much impact and punch as possible."[10] The film was intended as "a fantasy, an escape," "an ode to fun" and "to California," mix-ing different elements and styles which the director liked; "I like split screens, the great MGM musicals," hence the film's split screen effects and the dance sequences with Natalie, one in her dreams (on stairs as in an MGM musi-cal), another at the Soul Train discotheque, and a fight scene with The Thin Man in a set built in imitation of the back alley in *West Side Story*. When Drew Barrymore, who was co-producer and had taken the initiative to make the film, chose McG, he was known for commercial videos and music videos, and his feature film debut reflected the same sample approach to style and content as we find in video-shop-clerk-turned-director Quentin Tarantino. McG wanted each scene "to be like turning the pages of a book" with the audience remembering a scene for its distinct set and color, like a scene with a stunning red bathroom which is an exact copy of the bathroom in *The Shining*. This kind of intertextuality is not an intellectual challenge to think of themes, styles, periods, or genres, but to indulge in memories of past pleasures. Umberto Eco's postmodern "quote" became an explicit credit, as in the beginning of *Charlie's Angels* where *T.J. Hooker—The Movie* is playing on an airplane and a character comments, "Another movie from an old television show."[11]

A famous quote by Bruce Lee is, "I am no style, but I am all style."[12] Lee was referring to his fighting technique, Jeet Kune Do, which he composed by taking the best moves from every fighting style and combining them into a single system. Rather than limit himself to one style, he went

Charlie's Angels (2000) pays homage to earlier television series and films. Here, the "babe bonding" of angels Dylan (Drew Barrymore), Natalie (Cameron Diaz), and Alex (Lucy Liu) as chained prisoners on the run is a reference to Pam Grier and Margaret Markov chained together in *Black Mama, White Mama* (Columbia Pictures, 1972) (see photograph on page 44).

for every style. "Use no method as your method, have no limitation as your limitation."[13] Similarly, high trash heroines are "all style," using every conceivable camera effect (high speed zooms, split screens, freezing the image), the dumbest jokes ("You have good hands. I could use someone like you in my staff," Corwin tells Alex, who works undercover as masseuse and replies, "My hands are not going anywhere near your staff"), the hottest action (copying the martial arts wirework of *The Matrix*) and the silliest detective work yet (from the sound of a bird chirping behind Bosley, who is pleading the angels to come rescue him, Natalie concludes the bird is a *Sitta Pygmaea* living only at Carmel, which is then where the angels look for Bosley). With a style uniting television, commercials, and films, McG hit the formula of success: More *is* more.

The year after *Charlie's Angels* came *Lara Croft: Tomb Raider* (2001), the first film to be based on a computer game—Eidos' *Tomb Raider* (1996)—and be an economic success. English computer artist Toby Gard created Lara in 1996 for Core Design studio (later bought by Eidos). Conceived as a female Indiana Jones, she was initially named Lara Cruise and designed to appeal to male gamers with utopian measurements of 34DD-24-35.[14] However, she also had a distinct personality and a history related in a "bio" to provide the narrative background in the game: Lara is the daughter of English Lord and Lady Henshingly Croft, a loner, and as a child tutored privately at home, with a passion for rock climbing, shooting, and extreme skiing. When on a holiday in the Himalayas she becomes the sole survivor of an airplane crash and has since traveled the world studying ancient civilizations and unearthing archeological treasures. When she was twenty-seven years old the English, aristocratic, tea drinking, and bespectacled adventuress entered her first game, *Tomb Raider*, with huge success in 1996, followed by *Tomb Raider II* (1997), *Tomb Raider III: The Adventures of Lara Croft* (1998), *Tomb Raider: The Last Revelation* (1999), *Tomb Raider Chronicles* (2000), *Tomb Raider: The Angel of Darkness* (2003) and, finally, *Lara Croft Tomb Raider: Legend* (2005). By 1999 Lara had been on the cover of *The Face*, had been featured as major story in *Time* (December 1999) and interviewed in *Newsweek*, *Rolling Stone*, and *Entertainment Weekly*. She had more than a thousand Internet fan sites, and game sales and merchandise generated more than 500 million dollars and inspired the prestigious Elite model agency to develop a division for virtual models.

The fame and popularity of avatar Lara helped make *Lara Croft: Tomb Raider* (Simon West, 2001) and *Lara Croft: The Cradle of Life* (Jan de Bont, 2003) successes, because reviews certainly didn't. Even though the Academy Award nominated Angelina Jolie was chosen to play Lara Croft, both films received scathing reviews. According to *The New York Times* the plot of the first film "seems to have been written on a cocktail napkin during a coffee break" and was a compilation of "holes and clichés that would be inexcusable if written by a high school student."[15] The plot was about a secret society, the Illuminati, trying to find an All-Seeing Eye and a Triangle of Light, items that gave control over "time itself." *Lara Croft: The Cradle of Life* had a similar James-Bond-and-the-end-of-the-world plot with a villainous scientist chasing Pandora's Box so he could unleash a deadly plague in the world. *Variety* concluded that *Lara Croft: Tomb Raider* had "the distinction of being a major motion picture that's far less imaginative, and quite a bit more stupid, than the interactive game it's based on."[16] The review in *The Observer* lamented the film had "no heart" and "as a piece of story-telling [was] absolutely blank, incoherent and insultingly perfunctory" and compared it to a joke about Hitler trying to turn human excrement into butter, however, "'it still smells and tastes just like shit.' That, I'm afraid, is the trouble with *Lara Croft*."[17]

Hitler may have been unable to make human excrement taste and smell like butter, but the high trash heroines films were quite capable of transforming low budget trash into high fashion vintage wear. Even if plots seemed thin there was nothing casual or coincidental about production. The script for *Charlie's Angels* went through sixteen to thirty rewrites, the script for *Lara Croft: Tomb Raider* went through eleven scriptwriters, and with budgets of ninety-two and hundred-and-twenty million dollars for the two *Charlie's Angels* entries, and eighty and ninety million dollars for the two *Lara Croft* films, investments were closer to the continuing *Star Wars* saga than to old television shows.[18] Revenues, luckily, turned out satisfactory in contrast to such femme action extravaganzas as *Cutthroat Island* and *The Long Kiss Goodnight*, the former of which made its production company bankrupt.

Kill Bill Vol. 1 (2003) and *Kill Bill Vol. 2* (2004) fit the "more is more" and the "it's only fun" rule. In the very last image of *Kill Bill Vol. 2* the Bride (Uma Thurman) drives her cabriolet down a road that looks exactly like Mulholland Drive in Hollywood, a black and white scene quoting film noir. Suddenly the Bride winks an eye at us and a brief, conspiratorial smile breaks her serious face. This is her first and only stepping out of character, a metatextual wink letting the audience in on a secret: The bloodshed performed by this female assassin seeking revenge over her former boss and lover Bill and his Deadly Viper Assassination Squad—the DIVAS—for beating up and shooting her; killing her fiancé and eight other people in the little church in El Paso, Texas; subsequently hunting down and killing each and every one of the guilty lot; traveling from Tokyo to Acuna, Mexico; killing Bill and getting back the daughter taken from her womb as she lay in a coma for four years, all of this—it was just for fun.

The characteristic elements of the high trash heroines in *Charlie's Angels* and *Lara Croft*—big budgets, big stars, trash aesthetics, heightened reality, playful mood—all apply to the *Kill Bill* movies. Starting with *Reservoir Dogs* in 1992, auteur Tarantino contributed to postmodern film a cool and aestheticized hyperviolence, an abundance of inter- and extratextual references to high and low film culture, an elevation of "low" elements to "high" drama, and a union of kitsch, camp, exploitation and art, on the way returning fame to John Travolta and Pam Grier and making Uma Thurman a star. Tarantino slowly moved from low budget—*Reservoir Dogs* costing 1.2 million, *Pulp Fiction* eight million and *Jackie Brown* twelve million dollars—to the high budget of the *Kill Bill* films with budgets of fifty-five and thirty million dollars.[19] Originally intended as a single film, the two volume film added up to eighty-five million, thus placing it in the same economic league as the other high trash heroines films. Taratino's casts showcased Hollywood stars on low fees (Harvey Keitel in *Reservoir Dogs*; John Travolta and Samuel L. Jackson in *Pulp Fiction*; Bridget Fonda, Robert De Niro, and Michael Keaton in *Jackie Brown*) and *Kill Bill* was no exception, mixing big stars Uma Thurman, Darryl Hannah, Samuel L. Jackson, and Lucy Liu with cult names like David Carradine and Sonny Chiba.

Quoting and paying homage to obscure films, directors, and genres was a familiar strategy for Tarantino, who this time did it with a vengeance. The revenge-plot came from Japanese *yakuza* (gangster) films; the killer bride from Truffaut's *The Bride Wore Black* (1968); the female samurai assassin from Meiko Kaji in *Lady Snowblood* (1973); Elle Driver's one-eyed assassin from an obscure Swedish rape-revenge movie *They Call Her One Eye* (1974); a seven-and-a-half-minute anime sequence from Production I.G., the producers of classic Japanese anime *Ghost in the Shell* (1995); music from Sergio Leone's spaghetti westerns; scenes and images from Hong Kong films; the Bride's yellow costume with black stripes was inspired by Bruce Lee in *Game of Death* (1978); a femme knife fight from Jack Hill's *Switchblade Sisters* (1976), and the list could go on forever. Like the case of Angel World, we are in the Movie World of Tarantino:

> ... there are two different worlds that my movies take place in. One of them is the "Quentin Universe" of *Pulp Fiction* and *Jackie Brown*—it's heightened but more or less realistic. The other is the Movie World. When characters in the Quentin Universe go to the movies, the stuff they see takes place in the Movie World. They act as a window into that world. *Kill Bill* is the first film I've made that takes place in the Movie World. This is me imagining what would happen if that world really existed, and I could take a film crew in there and make a Quentin Tarantino movie about those characters.[20]

Critics were divided as to whether Tarantino's Movie World was just a fun house for blood spattering samurai mayhem (a twenty-five minute long fight

The white kimono and samurai swords of O-Ren Ishii (Lucy Liu), the snow-covered landscape around her, and the theatrical stance in *Kill Bill Vol. 1* are Quentin Tarantino's homage to the Japanese female samurai vengeance drama *Lady Snowblood* (Miramax Films, A Band Apart, Super Cool ManChu, 1973), whose protagonist fights in similar clothes and setting. (Courtesy of the British Film Institute.)

scene in *Kill Bill Vol. 1* especially stirred a debate) or whether there was a meaning to it all. *The New Yorker* felt, "'Kill Bill' is what's formally known as decadence and commonly known as crap ... coming out of this dazzling, whirling movie, I felt nothing—not anger, not dismay, not amusement. Nothing."[21] Decadence is, indeed, an apt description of the high trash heroines films with their recycling of films and genres. However, if decadent art has no "heart" (like *Lara Croft*), it nonetheless touches us with its visual grandeur, overwrought emotions and heightened sensitivity. Most critics approached *Kill Bill Vol. 1* as "a great-looking Frankenstein monster among motion pictures" with "the confidence, nerve and wild imagination that marked the filmmaker's earlier work, along with increased visual savvy."[22] Some were divided between emptiness and pleasure, like *Hollywood Reporter*: "Instead of rethinking genre movies, here he is a slave to them. Make no mistake. The film is hugely watchable."[23] Others, like the critic in *Time*, bridged the gap between emptiness and pleasure: "Does it have a larger meaning? Do you have to be a moral moron to admire *Kill Bill*? No, no and no. The movie ... is really about the motion, the emotion, the very movieness of movies ... in this sense, *Kill Bill* is the greatest dance film since *West Side Story*."[24]

Energy, unburdened morality and the dead-seriousness of "just fun" replaced the old definition of "content" as something serious. However, playing is for children. "The man is a boy," a commentary in *Screen* claimed about Tarantino, "[w]hich is a way of saying that Tarantino is a sincere artist but a stunted one."[25] High trash heroines cinema marked the stunted phase of decadence and self-conscious playfulness. Psychological "depth" disappeared from characters and narrative along with social consciousness, politics, and morale. Left are style and bodies. Female bodies.

The "Battle of the Bodies"

The body politics of respectively *Charlie's Angels*, *Lara Croft: Tomb Raider* and *Kill Bill* differ in style, setting, and disclosure, or, should we be frank and say, display and eroticization. But their female heroes share an iron grip on the flesh, which can be flexed, folded, displayed, wriggled, and, in the case of Tarantino, exercised, shot, cut, slashed, bound, beaten, and buried and still be victorious. From the great abs of Charlie's angels and the Bride's hard knuckles, to the skin-tight designer clothes and the no-fat and no-wrinkles politics, the body is *the* most important thing in high trash heroines cinema.

In the late eighties and nineties, femme fatale films had placed the female hero in patriarchal and challenging scenarios like all-male prison planets (*Aliens 3*), in antifeminist police stations (*Blue Steel*), and in women-hating military training camps (*G.I. Jane*). They equipped the female hero with gender-critical views (like Sarah's comment in *Terminator 2* that "men" destroy the world, not women), and even, in rare cases, gave her body a feministic edge by toning down traditional feminine signs like long hair, big breasts, and bare flesh, thus allowing female heroes to be skinheads (*Alien 3*, *Tank Girl*), flatchested (*Nikita*), have boyish haircuts (*Blue Steel*), and appear "butch" (*Courage Under Fire*). A woman in a man's world had to work twice as hard and in the eighties and nineties she did so at great pains and costs. Feminism was referred to or inferred in the critique of the patriarchal system and the unfair conditions our female hero was up against. *The Long Kiss Goodnight* played the "nice" version (woman is almost killed but eventually gets family and economic independence), *Courage Under Fire* and *Aliens 3* the "tough" version (woman loses family and becomes martyr).

High Trash Heroines put an end to that. "But really this movie is a tribute to bikini waxing, an excuse to get the Angels (and their nemesis, the shockingly lissome Demi Moore) as near naked as the rating administrators will permit and set them into erotically charged sadomasochistic motion," Richard Schickel noted in *Time* in his review of *Charlie's Angels: Full Throttle*.[26] *Charlie's Angels* self-consciously and spectacularly put the angels' beautiful bodies on display, as in the first scene with Natalie in her bedroom dancing to music, looking down with an ecstatic grin at her butt starting to jiggle—as if driven by its own will—to the rhythm. Natalie is dressed in white cotton panties with an image of Spiderman, and the camera zooms in with a close-up of her swinging butt. "You know, I signed the release waiver, so you can just feel free and stick things in my slot," a smiling and dancing Natalie tells the postman at the door. Thus, sexist jokes are not traded between men but performed by the female heroes doing meta-satirical gags meant to entertain the male viewer while at the same time disarm any accusations of sexism by being tongue-in-cheek, over the top hysterically funny, and hyper sexist. Welcome to Angel World. To underline the "joke" of Natalie as blond bimbo she accidentally bangs her forehead on the doorway—the very same woman who will break into a high security mainframe room in a *Mission Impossible*-esque maneuver without even working up that fatal drop of sweat which nearly gave Tom Cruise's character away. Another joke is Dylan, who is shot at by the villain and falls out the window ... naked! Two little boys arguing whether one of them has seen real "boobies" are interrupted by a naked Dylan outside the veranda glass door begging for clothes! If Natalie and Dylan are sweet bimbo angels, Alex is the dominatrix-bitch angel, established by her cover job as a bikini waxer dressed in a black S-M outfit ("Bummer. I mean, that was sort a turn-on," says boyfriend Jason [Matt LeBlanc], as Alex reveals she is not a bikini waxer) and also established by scenes in both films where she efficiently handles a whip. Both films also have scenes with men trying to make a pass at her: "I was wondering if..." "No." "So there's no chance that..." "NO!"

The strategy of outdoing the (rather innocent) sexism of the original show with postmodern self-consciousness was received by audiences as fun and postfeminist. "America is loving it and millions are flocking to see Cameron Diaz, Drew Barrymore and Lucy Liu flaunt their post-feminist, kitsch machismo," Melinda Wittstock wrote in The Observer.[27] The strategy which I shall return to later in this chapter was to collapse the body politics of the characters with the body politics of the actors, making the Dylan character and producer Drew Barrymore express how she was comfortable with her body, "I like jiggle! I do! ... I'm not a torch-carrying feminist, but I love women ... I think what's great is if you can have intelligence and capability as your foundation and be fun and sexy on top of it." Toby Miller, a professor at New York University, commented on Barrymore's attitude, "She seems to be saying, 'I see no reason to hide my sexuality, my body—I want to celebrate it' ... And all the women I know, even those who thought such a spectacle was tragic in the Seventies, love it. It's a nudge-nudge, wink-wink parody."[28]

The nudge-nudge, wink-wink attitude takes us back to two discourses of postfeminism, namely *choice postfeminism* and *(hetero)sex-positive postfeminism* which Sarah Projansky identifies in *Watching Rape*. High trash heroines and the actors playing them "choose" to exploit their bodies, put them on display as strippers and dancers, work them as masseuses, waitresses and car-licking flirts (the latter is Dylan who distracts a chauffeur by zipping down her leather jacket and licking the steering wheel while Alex places a micro camera in his car). According to Projansky the female action hero in the nineties can choose between "either sculpted muscles or hyperthin bodies" (Lucy Lawless or Jennifer Garner), a "choiceoisie" which opened up for "self-fetishization" by turning the body into a self-created commodity.[29] In feminism, to have a choice is to be empowered. In postfeminism, one's own body becomes a signifier or a commodity—which is one and the same thing here—that can be controlled, groomed, and enhanced like for instance genetically enhanced crops. To feminists like Projansky and Greer, this is not a choice at all since both bodies—thin or muscular—belong to the pleasure-regime of the male gaze. The not-thin and not-muscular body—the ugly, fat, sagging, or "unfeminine" body—is *not* a choice open to the female hero.

This self-conscious commodification of the female body and its status as a "thing" which is an integral part of the actress, yet also separate from her, is reflected in a "battle of the bodies" which took place both in the film *Charlie's Angels: Full Throttle* between the three angels and villainess

Madison and, at the release of the film, between actresses Barrymore, Liu and Diaz and Demi Moore. The retired angel Madison (Moore) is introduced wearing a bikini on the beach in a scene where she talks to Natalie (Diaz). The two women, ten years separating them, were respectively the highest paid Hollywood actresses; Moore in the early nineties, Diaz in 2003. Both flex their muscles, suck in their stomachs and toss their wet hair, the camera tracking Madison in slow motion as she walks to her car then tracking Diaz in slow motion as she throws herself in the waves on her surfboard. The battle is not just between faithful and fallen angel ("Why be an angel when I can be God?" Madison asks Charlie), but also between bodies and star personas. Who is the winner? Displaying Moore's body in such spectacular fashion (and in a later scene she wears high heels, black underwear, a long mink fur, and has five inch-long fake nails) is a reference to the female star's body as weapon: can it "overpower" and "stun" with looks alone?

As I discussed in chapter 10 Moore is famous for changing her star persona through physical transformations and masquerades. Shaving off her long hair on-screen in G.I. Jane is one example, being on the cover of Vanity Fair naked and heavily pregnant or, on another Vanity Fair cover, body painted in male clothes is another. The body is a central part of Moore's star persona; she appeared on The Jay Leno Show in a bikini after Striptease (1996) to prove she had no cellulite, and she did push-ups on the Letterman show to prove that the actor Moore had performed the one-handed push-ups of character Jordan in G.I. Jane (1997). In the article "Body Talk" (1997) Linda Ruth Williams writes about the hair-shaving scene in G.I. Jane, "The 'mondo' pleasure of the scene lies in this—the collision of star and role, with what the scene says about the star as important as how the character develops in the film."[30] The body is the star, and the character's body is the star's body (in opposition to for instance Julia Roberts' use of body doubles in Pretty Woman). The point of Moore's body control is not that this is the "real person" Moore, but that this is the "real body" Moore. In opposition to the stars of classical Hollywood where hard work and fame resulted in villas and designer wardrobes, "in the age of the muscle-clad action heroine, hard work is no longer most visible manifest in consumer rewards ... If it is to be seen anywhere now, 'hard work' must be demonstrated, enshrined, lived out first in the body."[31]

There is, however, a difference between Moore and the high trash heroines. Both display the real body of the actress but in different contextualization. High trash heroines are girlish "fun." Moore, in contrast, has a star persona as a determined bitch obsessed with body control. At the premiere of Full Throttle more attention was given to Moore's new twenty-five-year old boyfriend and her new body—the latter reportedly the result of four hours of exercise a day and 350,000 dollar plastic surgery—than to the three angel actresses, with audiences standing "on seats to get a better look at the revived diva and her maybe boy-toy."[32] Moore was accused of "overshadowing" the film to gain media publicity.[33] Moore's character, her costume, and her private life were united in the media storm. "That body! That bikini! That boyfriend," *Newsweek* commented.[34] Reviewer Cosmo Landesman wondered in *The Sunday Times* if her body was "a miracle of cosmetic surgery" or "a computer-generated image." Yet, in this "battle of the bodies," as Landesman termed it, "40-year-old mother-of-three Demi wins hands down and breasts up." The determination which had made reviewers reject Moore in *G.I. Jane* as cold and "lacking in human component" was now praised as "true" independence. "She has more old-fashioned movie-star presence in her little finger than all the Angels put together. She's the true girl-power role model, not that simpering and sycophantic trio. I wanted to cheer when she says to Diaz, 'I don't take orders from a speaker box—I work for myself.' Right on, sister!"[35]

This battle—not between characters but between actors, as the use of the names Demi and Diaz underlines—is also between generations: "Old-style" movie star Moore and "postfeminist" (as several reviews called them) stars Barrymore, Liu and Diaz. It is between a mother (of three) and three "over-excited little girls," as Landesman called the actresses. In terms of body, the difference is not whether it is surgically enhanced or not, but *the status of* that surgically enhanced body: With high trash heroines, press releases and extra material on later DVDs tell how the training of the stars' bodies was hard yet "fun," and we see the three giggling actresses learning to do wirework and imitate Asian martial arts. The physical bodies of Barrymore, Liu, Diaz, Angelina Jolie, and Uma Thurman are presented to audiences as natural and *not* augmented by silicone implants or any other plastic surgery. Whether this is true or not is irrelevant in this context. The point is that the Demi Moore's "old-fashioned" star body is the result of extreme exercise and "a surgeon to die for," repeated again and again in the media. Hers is a battle against time, against the disappearance of youth and beauty. High trash heroines seem untouched by time, their body terror regime kept invisible. We don't hear about their battle against age, wrinkles, and body fat. They have, according to the press and media coverage, "fun" with their bodies.

If Madison works for herself the angels work for Charlie, work which, like in *Nikita* and *Point of No Return*, is thematized as a relation between pimp and prostitute. Here, however, in the self-conscious humoristic tone characteristic of high trash heroines, Charlie's voice-over—"Once upon a time there were three very different girls who grew up to be very different women

... but they have one thing in common: They're brilliant, they're beautiful, and they work for me"—positions the female heroes as "angels" whose benefactor is hidden, yet almighty and all-seeing like God. The angels do whatever necessary to finish the job, including Dylan sleeping with the client or the angels walking naked on the beach when they take off their diving suits (the camera becomes unfocused at this point), or posing as strippers in *Full Throttle*. Because of the fast editing it is impossible to tell if the wriggle of the three stars convincingly imitates erotic dance, but their facial mimic with each other tells the audience this is a "fun" masquerade, unlike Pamela Anderson in *Barb Wire* where the camera takes a similar stripper scene seriously. The surprised "oops" of Natalie as Alex tears Natalie's bra and panties away with her whip, and the exaggerated "huuh" of the male audience leaning forward in unison to gaze at this sight, signal this is pretend-to-strip, not real strip. A running gag in *Full Throttle* is Alex's father (John Cleese) believing that his daughter and her two colleagues are prostitutes, not detectives, a misunderstanding which is never corrected. "We just took on twelve sailors," Alex proudly tells her father, "you can't even *imagine* the positions we get ourselves into."

Body control works differently in *Lara Croft: Tomb Raider*, the only high trash heroines film to be based on a computer game. Avatar Lara had proved the perfect mix-and-match of Indiana Jones missions, James Bond manners, and Hollywood pinup aesthetics. Kim Walden in her article "Run, Lara, Run: The Impact of Computer Games on Cinema's Action Heroine" describes avatar Lara's body as "closely defined under hot pants and T-shirt which both serve to reveal the contours but conceal the facts. Disproportionately huge breasts but definitely no nipples. Leg displayed but not splayed. The key to this image is revelation of the body by suggestion rather than deed. The figure is adorned with fetishised accoutrements. Lara Croft sports a low-slung belt drawing attention to the hips and the crotch while the gun holsters place visual emphasis on the top of the legs in a manner reminiscent of the clichéd stockings and suspender belts."[36] In a world until now populated with primitive and muscled pixel-heroes, newcomer Lara was very much a *product* of Hollywood cinema, a fact which producers of the movie both wished to acknowledge and overcome. The strategy was to flesh out Lara as faithful to her avatar pixel-physique as possible, yet embed her in an adventure plot and place her in spectacular action scenes which could add kinesthetic excitement to the game. The tone balanced between that of adventure (light fun) and high trash heroines (girlish fun).

Interestingly, the ensuing debate about the lack of a plot and of Angelina Jolie as being disappointing as Lara Croft springs from the game and high trash heroines action cinema being close in nature, and *not*, I will suggest, from the two *Lara Croft* films being "bad" films or Jolie giving a bad performance. Commentaries (with titles like "All the Guys Like to Play With Her" and "Making the Leap From a Game To the Movies") written by people (men) who had played the *Tomb Raider* game were positive and concluded that Jolie's "smart and sexy Lara is so compelling that the Lara of future Tomb Raider games will suffer in comparison" and that Angelina Jolie "gives Lara something she never really had in the game: a genuine personality."[37] Used to pixel–Lara's breasts staying put during somersaults and jumps, game-experienced reviewers were fully satisfied with Jolie's padding up from her original breast size 36C to cinematic Lara's 36D, which was a size below avatar Lara's DD. However, reviewers not familiar with playing *Tomb Raider* compared Jolie to former action heroines, to which they felt she didn't measure up. *The Times* found her a girl instead of a woman: "She is an adolescent boy's fantasy. She wears obligingly preposterous outfits but her sexuality is not remotely threatening or devouring" (a piece entitled "Lara's OK—For a Girl") and *The Observer* felt, "Watching Angelina Jolie performing athletics feats is rather more entertaining than seeing a Jane Fonda aerobics tape..."[38]

Especially Jolie's breasts were a disappointment to reviewers. "[S]he sports what looks like a Wonderbra made of helium. When she runs it looks like a Russ Meyer movie. It is silly. Pure cheesecake."[39] And, in a review aptly entitled "Look Out! It's a Booby Trap," a critic complained, "But it's the expectations raised by her [Jolie's] large breasts that are the problem ... Instead of being shown in a sexy light, they just jut out into space and defy gravity. They are veiled, silent and mute, as if Jolie were wearing not a bra but a muzzle. [Director] West has failed to grasp that the sexiest female action babes—such as Sarah Michelle Gellar, Sigourney Weaver, Lucy Lawless and Carrie-Anne Moss—are not large-breasted. But if you're going to play the big-breast card, then milk 'em for all they are worth; don't go all coy on your audience." The contradictory point here was that actress Jolie was too large-breasted to convince as a female action hero, yet, if playing a large-breasted female action hero, the film should at least exploit her breasts more instead of making them "veiled, silent and mute." This reviewer seemed ignorant about avatar Lara's blend of sexiness, which, as Walden points out, has breasts without nipples and size without movement. We can only speculate what "talking" breasts would look like as opposed to "mute" breasts. Is this the difference between Pamela Anderson's eye-catching erect nipples in the wet stripper scene in *Barb Wire* and Jolie's breasts partially glimpsed (without nipples showing) in a shower scene in *Lara Croft: Tomb Raider*?

Like the famous Barbie—full breast but no nipples—Lara has a sexuality defined by motion and action rather than adult sex. Like the boys

Simon West's *Lara Croft: Tomb Raider* (Paramount Pictures, 2001) finally proved that a computer game could become a blockbuster success. One reason might have been the "breast-question": in the game, Lara Croft was a size 36DD, and actress Angelina Jolie wore breast padding to become a 36D. Critics complained it looked like a "Wonderbra of helium," but audiences were more than satisfied.

gazing at a naked Dylan in *Charlie's Angels*, this is a body to be admired not penetrated. This paradox is characteristic of most high trash heroines' bodies which taunt and flirt yet are not ready for commitment. Lara coolly rejects an invitation (physical and erect) from a former boyfriend in *Lara Croft: Tomb Raider* and, although still in love with him, handcuffs, shoots and kills another former boyfriend in *Cradle of Life*. Like dolls, high trash heroines are dressed and undressed in endless shifts of costume, bent and moved into all kinds of positions, defy gravity, have no need for plots, and don't engage in sex. Albeit able to masquerade as prostitutes and having boyfriends, they are ignorant of sexual threats like rape and torture and a future with family and children. Angel-sex happens off-screen with silly boyfriends, and Jason does propose to Natalie, however, not to marry him but to have a puppy. The future is continued innocence. Indeed, rape can only be alluded to in the form of a joke, as when villain Eric leaves Dylan, tied to a chair, to his men with the words, "You guys like angel cake?" Dylan stops five men from gang raping her by putting her feet in the air and telling them that in a minute she will kick their butts and moonwalk out of the room, "and since my trusty lighter isn't working I'm gonna do all of this with my hands tied behind my back." Indeed, she does, smiling and moonwalking to the music of Michael Jackson with hands tied behind the back as she leaves a room full of unconscious men.

Blessed by the Father

In this last section I want to focus on what *kind* of feminine identity high trash heroines represent, how this identity relates to postfeminism, and how critics and audiences connected these films to postfeminism and empowerment. As we shall see, the three—identity, postfeminism, and the issue of empowerment—are woven together in a confusing and ambivalent pattern.

Most ambivalent of the high trash heroines is the Bride (Uma Thurman). Viewed from afar, she shares the characteristics of Lara and the angels: it's just fun (her wink at the audience), her body is the perfect killing machine, and the *Kill Bill* movies, especially the first, were debated in the press as being about "strong women." At the premiere in Denmark I was interviewed on national television for the evening news (TV2) in a longer feature about *Kill Bill Vol. 1* and asked if the Bride was a new positive role model for women. My answer at that time was that she was not new but rather a fusion of existing archetypes and although I considered *Kill Bill* a superior film I would be cautious about defining the Bride as a positive role model. On the one hand, she represents strength, stubbornness, and persistence, which I find excellent qualities, but on the other hand her killer looks makes her a utopian figure and her method—killing—is hardly one to copy.

I now have the opportunity to deepen my response. The Bride's femininity is different from the self-absorbed sulky teen narcissism of Lara Croft and from the girlish teen narcissism of the angels. Her many names indicate that she is not one character: she is nicknamed the Bride, her operation name is Black Mamba, her false name Arlene Machiavelli, her real name Beatrix Kiddo, and she is finally called Mommy (we learn her names in this order). Lara and the angels all have roots in one and the same archetype, the daughter. The Bride is not one archetype but, like Charly in *The Long Kiss Goodnight*, a fusion of every one of them.

In the first scene before shooting her, Bill calls her Kiddo, which the audience at this time doesn't know is her name. "Kiddo" thus positions her as child and daughter—her first archetype—and Bill as perverse father figure (further so by her remark "it's your baby"). In the beginning of the second film, which goes back to what happened before the massacre in the little town of El Paso, the future husband mistakes Bill for Beatrix' father and asks him to give her away in church. Bill is lover, master, father, and creator of the Bride. He has found and trained her. He sees her off to China to learn martial arts in chapter eight, "The Cruel Tutelage of Pai Mei," where she is turned into an invincible warrior and afterwards joins his Deadly Viper Assassination Squad (the DIVAs) as an assassin. Clearly, Bill has no intention of giving anything away and he shoots her when she tries to leave him for good. However, he also respects her right to vengeance and therefore forgives her when she kills him with the rare five point palm exploding heart technique. "You're not a bad person. You're a terrific person. You're my favorite person. But every once in a while you can be a real cunt." Beatrix is a rebellious daughter intent on breaking the incestuous ties to her father-mentor, just like the daughter-assassins Nikita and Maggie in chapter eight. Like them she will succeed and even advance to the archetype of the mother.

The Bride's second archetype is the Amazon. "Cunt" along with "bitch" are simultaneously derogatory swear words and positive adjectives signaling Amazon strength, independence, and willpower.[40] Like the other female members of the DIVAs—Vernita Green/Copperhead (Vivica A. Fox), O-Ren Ishii/Cottonmouth (Lucy Liu), and Elle Driver/California Mountain Snake (Daryl Hannah)—Beatrix is an Amazon who loves to fight and kill. She introduces herself in *Vol. 1* with her code name, Black Mamba. Her pleasure in killing sets her apart from other high trash heroines and her full dedication to martial arts makes Pai Mei (Chia Hui Liu) teach her the five point palm exploding heart technique which he has taught nobody else.

The fighting is visceral, brutal, physical, and bloody, in every way different from the otherwise rather anemic aesthetics of high trash heroines. "Silly rabbit," says O-Ren when Beatrix kills her teenage bodyguard, the man hating and crazy Gogo (Chiaki Kuriyama). "Tricks are for kids," Beatrix responds, words repeated by O-Ren. Tricks *are* indeed for kids, which is why *Kill Bill Vol. 1* was rated "R" and not PG-13. Here, killing is both stylish and serious, an art calling for respect and the iconography of an action auteur.

All the fights are iconographically planned in minute detail to impress us. Some, like the first knife fight with Vernita Green in *Vol. 1* and the last fistfight in *Vol. 2* with Elle, are rough, realistic, and very visceral. When Elle and B (another nickname for Beatrix) fight in Budd's trailer there is not enough room to swing the Hattori Hanzo swords and the women smash the trailer completely using dirty tricks like kicks to the groin, throwing things in each other's faces ("gross" says Elle), drowning the opponent in the toilet, and, just when Elle thinks they are fighting with swords, Beatrix plucks out Elle's remaining eye and steps on it with her bare feet. Other fights are highly stylized in the Hong Kong tradition with wirework, exaggerated sound effects, balancing on tables and banisters as in the OHM (One Hits Many) where the Bride fights O-Ren's team of killers, the crazy "88"s. When she has had enough, she starts cutting off the opponents' feet with her sword to have it over and done with so she can move on to her main target, O-Ren. Jumping, flying, dancing, she finishes them all and yells, "Those of you lucky enough to still be alive, go and take your life with you. But leave the limbs you have lost behind. They belong to me now!" Spoken by a true Amazon. The sword duel with O-Ren in the snow is Tarantino's homage to Asian action cinema, to Bruce Lee, and of course to *Lady Snowblood*, the connotations of this scene so numerous that Internet sites sprung up with lists of the intertextual references. The triple O's (One On One fights) are all between women (the scenes where the Bride fights Budd and Bill are too short to count as fights as one strike does it in both cases) who in Asian action fashion politely complement each others' skills. "Bill always said you were one of the best ladies he ever saw with an edge weapon," the Bride tells Vernita before killing her. "I taunted you before, and I apologize for that," O'Ren apologizes to the Bride before she dies in the snow. Respect among equals is both an Asian and an Amazon characteristic.

As daughter and Amazon the Bride combines innocence and erotic fantasy, underlined by her symbolic figures "the Bride"—in chapter two's headline called "The Blood-Spattered Bride"—and "Black Mamba." Norwegian film researcher Anne Gjelsvik comments, "The tension is between the innocent woman in a bridal dress versus the black snake, which is a killing machine. Between these extremes is Beatrix Kiddo whose name associates

Call her the Bride, Black Mamba, Arlene Machiavelli, Beatrix Kiddo, or Mommy, one thing is absolutely certain: with the two-volume revenge epic *Kill Bill* (Miramax Films, A Band Apart, Super Cool ManChu, 2003 and 2004), Quentin Tarantino created the ultimate female hero who summed up the five female archetypes. Actress Uma Thurman was rape-avenger, daughter, mother, dominatrix, and Amazon. Who could ask for more?

to both dominatrix ... and a little child..."[41] The white dress and black snake respectively stand for virginity and innocence.

The black snake points to Beatrix as *dominatrix*, her third archetype. Tarantino deliberately avoids making an explicit reference to the dominatrix figure in the Bride's costumes, which are atypical for a female hero: bridal dress; yellow sports outfit copied from Bruce Lee's costume in *Game of Death* (1978); humble training clothes; tight low cut jeans, fitted leather jacket and tricolor cowboy boots when she comes to kill Budd; and pastel-colored summer skirt and loose top when she confronts Bill. No whips, high heels, or black leather. Instead, the typical dominatrix archetype is explicitly embodied by O-Ren, queen of the Japanese yakuza who beheads a man for criticizing her American-Chinese descent, and by Elle who kills the only male member of the DIVAs, Bill's brother Budd (Michael Madsen) and gloatingly reads to him about the venom of the Black Mamba as he lies dying from a bite from this snake.

However, costume is merely a matter of playing with style and distrib-
uting archetypical traits across all the strong women in *Kill Bill*. As this chapter's opening quote from Tarantino indicates, woman-on-woman violence is
"hot" and "naughty" and relates to a pleasure which is essentially masochistic: The pleasure of watching a strong and dominant women punishing and
correcting her victims, literally so when the Bride at one point spanks a
young yakuza boy in the butt with her sword yelling, "This is what you get
from fucking around with yakuzas. Go home to your mother!" The question of whether the film's violence is sadistic or masochistic is raised in the
opening dialogue where Bill shoots Beatrix: "Do you find me sadistic? [He
gently wipes off the blood from Beatrix' face with a white handkerchief] ...
No, Kiddo, I'd like to believe you're aware enough, even now, to know that
there is nothing sadistic in my actions ... this moment, this is me at my most
masochistic." By first training Beatrix to be an expert assassin and then having her come after him, Bill is, psychologically speaking, setting up a
masochistic *contract*. There are rules and ritualistic elements in masochism,
as Gilles Deleuze explained in his classic study of masochism, *Coldness and
Cruelty* (1967), and among these are *spectacular suffering, prolonged suspension*
and *anticipation, ritualization*, and an *aestheticization of violence*. Also, above all,
that *punishment must be enacted according to the rules*. Thus Bill stops Elle from
killing Beatrix when she is in a coma. And when Beatrix asks the pimp Esteban for information on where Bill is, she asks why he gives her this information. Bill would want me to, Esteban replies. Esteban, by the way, is of
the sadistic kind who cuts up his prostitutes and enjoys the sight.

Not just the setting and iconography, the prolonged fights, the dwelling
on aesthetics and theatrical dialogue, the costuming, and the constrained
fight spaces indicate a masochistic universe; so, too, do interviews with Tarantino. He repeatedly compared the intimate relation between himself and
Thurman to that of Josef von Sternberg and Marlene Dietrich and commented on the violence, "Having what you think is the wrong response to
what you're seeing is very sexy and exciting ... Hands down. You know, there's
a special charge."[42] It is characteristic of high trash heroines action cinema
that such reference to a pleasure that Freud found the most dangerous of
all sexual perversions is not designed to provoke. Unlike the WIP films and
rape-revenge films with their castration scenes and male torture, this is a
humorous and intellectual version of masochism. The explicitness of the
quotation, the tongue-in-cheek mode, and the experience of being in Tarantino's Movie World and not Real World leave the audience without a sense
of danger. We recognize the archetype of the dominatrix just like we recognize Bruce Lee's costume: the dominatrix is replayed in mainstream conventions and contained as well as constrained by these.

Next to the daughter, the Amazon, and the dominatrix is the arche-type of the mother, as the Bride was pregnant when she was shot. We recall from the discussions of the maternal rape-avenger in chapter three and the maternal action hero in chapter seven that the mother archetype is about the transformation from "bad" to "new" mother. The new mother is not a traditional "good" mother, but a mother negotiating old-fashioned notions of maternal responsibility with postfeminist values of female strength, inde-pendence, and individualism. Beatrix's decision to retire as assassin after she discovers she is pregnant is an attempt to become the traditional "good" mother with an "ordinary" husband in a small American town. As we get to know her, we realize that this idea—as Bill also tells her before shooting her—is an illusion. Beatrix is not fit for ordinary life (like Vernita Green). Her past will haunt her (as it does Vernita) and to create a future she must accept her past and integrate it into a new personality. The new mother is a woman who can kill the man she loves when he refuses to let her go and cut both arms off a beautiful woman to get the information she needs. Being a mother does *not* soften this female hero. "It's mercy, compassion and for-giveness I lack, not rationality," she tells Vernita who shows her a photo of Vernita's daughter Nikki. "Bitch, you can stop it right there. Just because I have no wish to murder you before the eyes of your daughter does not mean that parading her around in front of me is gonna inspire sympathy. You and I have unfinished business and not a goddamn fucking thing you have done in the subsequent four years, including getting knocked up, is gonna change that."

Ripley, Sarah, and Charly felt obliged to extend their sense of mater-nal responsibility to the rest of society. Beatrix feels no such thing. Her maternity does not turn her into a "better" person and after killing Vernita in front of little Nikki, she calmly says, "Your mother had it coming. When you grow up, if you still feel raw about it, I'll be waiting." *Variety* remarked, "It is doubtful that anyone who had ever had kids could write a scene quite like this." The point, however, is not maternal sensations but loss and revenge. Tarantino does not use the mother archetype as a psychological figure, but as a dramatic device, and Beatrix' cynical words to four-year-old Nikki is Tarantino invoking the child-avenging-a-parent's-death scenario, a cliché of revenge movies. "That woman deserves her revenge. And we deserve to die," as Budd puts it.

A Mother—not even the mother archetype in popular cinema—is not out for revenge. She is motivated by personal loss and the need to defend her child and herself. When Karen gets away with killing the rapist in *Eye for an Eye* it is because he continues raping and killing women and must be stopped to protect other mothers and daughters. Of the female hero archetypes in popular cinema, only the rape-avenger is out for vengeance proper, which is why this archetype is conjured up when the Bride spends four comatose years at the hospital and the nurse Buck sells her body for seventy-five dollar per twenty minutes. Buck, who "came here to fuck," is killed as soon as she wakes up. The rape motive, however, is treated lightly. After smashing Buck's head in the doorway, Beatrix steals the car keys to his "Pussy Wagon" and, in a reference to *Terminator 2*, puts on his sunglasses, a huge pair of goldcoated plastic frames. In this brief moment Thurman's makeup transforms from neutral to—as Beatrix remembers Buck and the rapes—perfectly applied red lipstick in a reference to the eroticized rape-avenger. The light tone stands in sharp contrast to the initial gruesome beating that was visualized with blood and pain. In the revenge film, revenge is motivated by the attack on one's life or the loss of a loved one. The Bride has both motives—the loss of her daughter and her miraculous survival after Bill's execution. Her vengeance is not a maternal issue, but a personal affair. It isn't until *after* torturing Julie that she discovers her daughter is alive and her revenge also becomes a rescue mission of her daughter B.B.

Taken separately, none of the Bride's archetypes form a complete or realistic character; neither so if we add them together. Reviewers were so busy tracking down the many sources of *Kill Bill* that most overlooked Thurman's role in the films. But those who noticed did not criticize the actress for being superficial or "without heart" as the former high trash heroines actresses were described.[43] Quite the contrary, when reviewers noticed Thurman they praised her performance as "a superhero" who was "utterly human" (*The Sunday Times*), a "warrior goddess ... not without honor or humanity" (*Rolling Stone*), an actress who "cuts, so to speak, a terrific figure" (*Variety*).[44] That is, the paradox of a supernatural and humane creature.

Thurman's Bride was compared to Weaver's Ripley, whose passionate and superhuman character she resembles in mentality as well as physique. Like Ripley, the Bride is a female hero cut for adult taste, and the fetishism of *Kill Bill* is far from *Charlie's Angels'* fascination with masseuses, prostitutes, erotic dancers, and girl fun. Tarantino's erotic violence comes in the form of killer girls in school uniforms (Gogo), six-foot blondes beating each other to pulp (Elle and B), beheadings at the table (O-Ren), and pedophile sex and murder (the underage O-Ren in the anime sequence in *Vol. 1*). In terms of identification, the Bride is an adult. However, even if her feminine identity is more fetishized and perversely anesthetized than the female heroes in *Lara Croft: Tomb Raider* and *Charlie's Angels*, the elements uniting the three film series are still more central than what separates them.

First, the three series share irony and distance as narrative strategy and use a "light" and fun mode to address the audience. Where exploitation characterized femme fatale cinema in the seventies, and issues of gender restriction were raised and a realist mode engaged by films like *Aliens* and *G.I. Jane* in the eighties and nineties, an *ironic playfulness* characterizes the present phase of femme fatale cinema. We are in Lara's world, in Angel World, and in Tarantino's Movie World. Not in the Real World. Whether the actress remains clean or covered in dirt, is untouched or raped and beaten, it boils down to fantasy either way. Stepping on an eye is gross, not scary. Like a reviewer commented, criticizing this violence is like criticizing fairy tales.[45]

The second element uniting these films is exactly the recognition, shared by film producers and film audiences, that the female heroes are not "real" persons or "real" women. One could argue that popular cinema always deals in fantasy and pleasure. However, popular cinema also strives at creating characters the audience can identify with, and identification is the corner stone of a feminist film theory criticizing the stereotypical roles offered women and demanding nuanced female characters. In high trash heroines cinema, however, we never enter the Real World. Just like no one contests the fact that Superman flies, nobody complains that Uma Thurman changes into a costume which is an exact copy of a Bruce Lee costume, or that cinematic Lara uses movements that defy gravity but imitate pixel Lara. Lara isn't a "real" person and neither are the angels or Beatrix. Production notes, press releases, gossip and interviews tell us that the actresses, like their characters, were having a great time. Especially the press coverage of *Charlie's Angels* showed that it was all "fun." Like this interview with the three actresses:

BARRYMORE: It is gold.

DIAZ AND LIU: [loudly, imitating Mike Myers from "Austin Powers in Goldmember"] It's gold!!

LIU: We imitate Mike Myers *all* the time. [To Barrymore] Do you think he knows?

BARRYMORE: Oh, he knows!

BARRYMORE AND DIAZ: Because we told him! [Laughter]

BARRYMORE, DIAZ AND LIU: It's gold![46]

This interview makes no sense. A star interview was never meant to be "deep"; however, compared to interviews with stars like Pam Grier, Sigourney Weaver, and Geena Davis, this interview constructs the stereotypical "bimbo." Indeed, the function of the interview is to show three bimbos with nothing to say but nonsense.

Natalie, Dylan, and Alex are not intended as fixed points of identification but as empty signs open for play. Like dolls they are "dead" until played with. We are not meant to regard them as persons but to try them on like new clothes. "It's very simple," as Liu has put it, "to be an Angel, you just have to be yourself. The great thing about our characters is their different personalities. It kind of allows for anyone to be an Angel."[47] To "be an Angel" is not to invest yourself in the character in the sense of matching your own psychological profile to that of a character, but the much more simple operation of putting yourself in the character's place, like "being" an avatar in a computer game. In a similar line of thought Walden argues that the technical helper Bryce (Noah Taylor), who often controls Lara's movements via communication technology (CCTV monitor, satellite phones, walkie-talkies), functions as a stand-in for the male audience in an imitation of the male game player.[48] "Be my eyes," Lara asks Troy in her walkie-talkie headset as from surveillance cameras he monitors the car park where Lara is hiding in *Lara Croft: Tomb Raider* and is able to direct her to the positions of the villains.

To Be an Angel

Analyzing female fans' identification with their favorite stars, Jackie Stacey in *Star Gazing* (1994) argues for a de-psychoanalyzation of the process of identification, "The assumption behind much of the psychoanalytic work discussed earlier is that identification fixes identities," she writes and points out that her cases "contradict this assumption and demonstrate not only the diversity of existing forms, but also that identification involves the production of desired identities, rather than simply the confirmation of existing ones ... Thus, the cultural consumption of Hollywood stars does not necessarily fix identities, destroy differences and confirm sameness."[49] Stacey points to different ways in which her fans relate to stars through "processes of transformation and production of new identities."[50] Some of these processes are *pretending* (to be like the star), *imitating* (the star's behavior) and *copying* (the star's appearance). In her empirical research of fandom, Stacey interviewed (now old) female fans of the classical Hollywood stars in the fifties. If we turn to the present, news media have recently reported an increase in women taking martial arts classes inspired by the female hero in action cinema. "There's a cool factor to it now [says a student inspired to do martial arts after watching *Crouching Tiger, Hidden Dragon*] ... to be a woman and be strong and be able to be a crimefighter, even though I'm a quantitative analyst by day."[51] To be an angel or any other of the high trash heroines need not mean to *be* like the characters but can involve *behaving* or *looking* like them. Today's stars are models of fashion, attitude, and action rather than role models of emotional identity construction.

Stacey's de-psychoanalyzed concept of identification raises the question of where behavior stops and identity begins. Does dressing up or having one's hair cut like the stars change the female viewer's feminine identity? What, then, about martial arts classes? Sociologists speculate that the new female hero is a (bad) role model inspiring young women to violent behavior. In Denmark the recent phenomena of girl gangs and a four times increase in violence committed by female teenagers from 1990 to 2000 were linked to the popular film "Girl Fight. The Backlash of Girl Power. Wild Girls Use Aggravated Violence to Gain Fifteen Minutes of Fame" was the headline of one such article blaming *Kill Bill* and contemporary action movies for providing role models of violent behavior.[52] With names like "Ninja Girls" and "Ghetto Bitches," girl gangs became a new phenomenon in Denmark in the late nineties. As it is beyond the scope of this book to examine the relation between cinema and social behavior, I will leave these questions to be answered by others; however, it is thought provoking that while teenage girls account for still more violence in statistics, the total number of reported violent assaults committed by teenagers remains the same. As teenage girls turn more violent, teenage boys become *less* violent.

If such change in gender behavior is "bad" from one point of view (because women turn violent) it is also significant that as women enter male territory they adopt male behavior, while men reversely renounce violence. Gendered behavior does change. Sociologists and media researchers disagree whether this is "caused" by popular cinema. Xena fans are convinced that female hero Xena changed their lives, as we saw in chapter nine. However, although teenage girls involved in assaults reported that "it was like a film. The only difference was that you were in it," a direct causal relationship between film and social behavior is difficult and problematic to establish.[53] If our social behavior can change from our imitation of the film stars in popular cinema, then these stars are also simultaneously reflections of our social reality. And in the Real World, the female hero in popular cinema is constructed *within* patriarchal society to serve male pleasure. A male framing of female strength is always in place. From Wonder Woman invented by the psychologist William Moulton Marston who was fascinated by masochism, to Lara Croft created by Toby Gard to be "played" by a male game player. From "super bitch" Pam Grier invented by AIP and terminated when she demanded less stereotypical roles, to today's female stars reassuring us that they "like jiggle" (Drew Barrymore) and would like "to dress up sexy every day and have great makeup and hair every minute" (Sienna Guillory playing Jill Valentine in *Resident Evil: Apocalypse*).[54] Tarantino called Thurman his Dietrich, but never used the concept of "feminism." Neither did anyone else. "If there is any kind of feminism in *Charlie's Angels* it's the kind that would come as a free gift in one of those little plastic bags they stick on the front of magazines, next to the hairclips and glitter gel," a female reviewer said and concluded that "I would hoot at anybody who would herald the *Charlie's Angels* franchise as any kind of genuine homage to Girl Power."[55]

The glossy surface of the high trash heroines can be compared to another "battle of the bodies" fought today between "old-fashioned" doll Barbie and "newcomer" doll Bratz, the latter designed by Iranian immigrant Isaaz Larian to be multicultural. Unlike Caucasian Barbie, who has children and boyfriend Ken and fits traditional adult roles like nurse, dentist and bride, Bratz dolls have multiple ethnic identities as white, black, Asian, and Hispanic teenagers going to slumber parties and on vacations with clothes as trendy as the latest adult fashion, fully accessorized down to mobile phones, sushi sticks, tarmaguchis and laptops. In three years, Bratz dolls had beat Barbie in Europe. Why? Children respond that a Bratz doll has "cooler clothes and accessories" and that "she can stand on her own feet" (this because her feet are much bigger than Barbie's, so the doll can actually stand by itself).[56] Like Bratz, high trash heroines aim at a wider audience than the traditional male action audience. Toning down sex and violence (designing sex as unsexy and violence as non-violent) has opened a new market for high trash heroines targeting the eight to twelve-year-old in what Hollywood calls an interesting "ratings creep."[57] With their light humor, cool irony, and (with the Bride as an exception) teenage-like characters, they appeal to tweens as well as teenagers, adults and cult connoisseurs.

This is the paradox of the female hero: She is described positively as a "splashy femme empowerment fantasy," yet compared to and found inferior to Pam Grier.[58] However, as I discussed in chapter one, the star persona of Pam Grier was never feminist and her success not empowering to women in Hollywood. Nonetheless, the actress who fell victim to confusing Hollywood stardom with personal female strength is today hailed as an image of female strength. In postfeminist culture, women walk this tightrope balancing between the illusion and the real, between imitation and identification, between being an angel or being no one at all. In 1975, Laura Mulvey remarked in "Visual Pleasure and Narrative Cinema" that it is said that to analyze beauty is to destroy it. This, she said, was her intention. Thirty years later, beauty has proven indestructible and if we want to conquer a new territory of opposition and opportunity, we must, as Stacey suggested twenty years later, de-psychoanalyze identification itself. Only then can we acknowledge the persistence of female archetypes, and use such archetypes to tap into existing transformations in gender behavior and gender roles. Today, women *can* be beautiful and strong. They *can* be mothers and have a career. But they cannot be feminists and enjoy the female heroes of popular cinema. That takes a postfeminist willing to enter a world of ambivalence. However unreal, today, this world is the Real World.

High Trash Heroines Filmography (Selective)

Charlie's Angels (2000) Dir. McG, filmed in the U.S. and Germany. Angels and private investigators Dylan, Alex, and Natalie, action

Lara Craft: Tomb Raider (2001) Dir. Simon West, filmed in the UK, Germany, U.S. and Japan. Lady and adventuress Lara Croft, action

Charlie's Angels: Full Throttle (2003) Dir. McG

Kill Bill Vol. 1 (2003) Dir. Quentin Tarantino. Female avenger Beatrix Kiddo, also called The Bride, Mommy, Black Mamba, and Arlene Machiavelli, action

Lara Croft Tomb Raider: The Cradle of Life (2003) Dir. Jan de Bont, filmed in the U.S., Germany, UK, Japan and the Netherlands, action

Kill Bill Vol. 2 (2004) Dir. Quentin Tarantino, action

Filmography

I have listed title, year of release, director, and country. A film is a US release if no country is indicated. Television films and television series are included, with year, television network, and (if a finished series) number of episodes.

Above the Law (Zhi fa xian feng), 1986, Corey Yuen, (HK)

Above the Law, 1988, Andrew Davis

Accused, The, 1988, Jonathan Kaplan

Alias, 2001–, ABC, television series

Alien, 1979, Ridley Scott

Alien: Resurrection, 1997, Jean-Pierre Jeunet

Aliens, 1986, James Cameron

Alien3, 1992, David Fincher

All Quiet on the Western Front, 1930, Lewis Milestone

Amazons, 1984, Paul Michael Glaser, television movie

Amazons, 1986, Alejandro Sessa, (Argentina)

Amazons and Gladiators, 2001, Zachary Weintraub, (U.S., Germany)

Anne of the Indies, 1951, Jacques Tourneur

Apocalypse Now, 1979, Francis Ford Coppola

Arena, The, 1974, Steve Carver, (U.S., Italy)

Arena, The, 2001, Timur Bekmambetov, (Russia, U.S.)

Ausgestoßen, 1981, Axel Corti, (Austria)

Azumi, 2003, Ryuhei Kitamura, (Japan)

Azumi 2: Death or Love, 2005, Shusuke Kaneko, (Japan)

Barb Wire, 1996, David Hogan

Barbarian Queen, 1985, Héctor Olivera, (U.S., Argentina)

Barbarian Queen II: The Empress Strikes Back, 1989, Joe Finley, (U.S., Mexico)

Basic, 2003, John McTiernan

Batman Returns, 1992, Tim Burton, (U.S., UK)

Beauty and the Beast, 1987–1990, CBS, 56 episodes

Better Tomorrow, A (Ying hung boon sik), 1986, Tsui Hark, (HK)

Beyond the Valley of the Dolls, 1970, Russ Meyer

Big Bird Cage, The, 1972, Jack Hill, (U.S., Philippines)

Big Doll House, The, 1971, Jack Hill, (U.S., Philippines)

Big House, The, 1930, George W. Hill

Birth of a Nation, The, 1915, D.W. Griffith

Black Angel, The (Kuro no tenshi vol. 1), 1997, Takashi Ishii, (Japan)

Black Angel 2, The (Kuro no tenshi vol. 2), 1999, Takashi Ishii, (Japan)

Black Belt Jones, 1974, Robert Clouse

Black Cat (Hei Mao), 1991, Stephen Shin, (HK)

Black Cat II (Hei Mao II), 1992, Stephen Shin, (HK)

Black Hawk Down, 2001, Ridley Scott

Black Mama, White Mama, 1972, Eddie Romero, (US, Philippines)

Blade Trinity, 2004, David S. Goyer

Blonde Fury (Shi jie da shai), 1989, Hoi Mang, Corey Yuen, (HK, US)

Blood Feast, 1963, Herschell Gordon Lewis

Blood Sabbath, 1972, Brianne Murphy

Blue Lagoon, The, 1980, Randal Kleiser

Blue Steel, 1990, Kathryn Bigelow

Born on the Fourth of July, 1989, Oliver Stone

Bride Wore Black, The (*La Mariée était en noir*), 1968, François Truffaut, (France, Italy)

Bridge on the River Kwai, A, 1957, David Lean, (UK)

Brood, The, 1979, David Cronenberg, (Canada)

Butch Cassidy and the Sundance Kid, 1969, George Roy Hill

Butterfly and Sword (*Xiu liu xig hu die jian*), 1993, Michael Mak Dong-kit, Michael Mak, (Taiwan, HK)

Carrie, 1976, Brian De Palma

Casualties of War, 1989, Brian De Palma

Catwoman, 2004, Pitof

Chained Heat, 1983, Paul Nicholas

Chaplin, 1992, Richard Attenborough, (UK, US, France, Italy)

Charlie's Angels, 1976–81, ABC, television series

Charlie's Angels, 2000, Joseph McGinty Nichol, (US, Germany)

Charlie's Angels: Full Throttle, 2003, Joseph McGinty Nichol

China O'Brien, 1990, Robert Clouse

China O'Brien II, 1991, Robert Clouse

Class of 1999, 1990, Mark L. Lester

Cleopatra Jones, 1973, Jack Starrett

Cleopatra Jones and the Casino of Gold, 1975, Charles Bail, (US, HK)

Coffy, 1973, Jack Hill

Color Me Blood Red, 1965, Herschell Gordon Lewis

Conan the Barbarian, 1982, John Milius

Conan the Destroyer, 1984, Richard Fleischer

Courage Under Fire, 1996, Edward Zwick

Crimson Bat–Blind Swordswoman, The (*Mekura No Oichi monogatari: Makkana nagaradori*), 1969, Sadaji Matsuda, (Japan)

Crimson Bat: Wanted Dead or Alive (*Mekurano Oichi inochi moraimasu*), 1970, Hirokazu , Ichimura, (Japan)

Crouching Tiger, Hidden Dragon (*Wo hu cang long*), 2000, Ang Lee, (Taiwan, HK, US, China)

Cutthroat Island, 1995, Renny Harlin

Cyborg, 1989, Albert Pyun

Damned, The (*La Caduta degli dei*), 1969, Luchino Visconti, (Italy, Switzerland, West Germany)

Dawn of the Dead, 1979, George A. Romero

Day of the Dead, 1986, George A. Romero

Dazed and Confused, 1993, Richard Linklater

Death Wish, 1974, Michael Winner

Deer Hunter, The, 1978, Michael Cimino

Defiant Ones, The, 1958, Stanley Kramer

Deliverance, 1972, John Boorman

Die Hard, 1988, John McTiernan

Dirty Weekend, 1993, Michael Winner

Drum, 1976, Steve Carver

Elektra, 2005, Rob Bowman

Enough, 2002, Michael Apted

Enter the Dragon, 1973, Robert Clouse, (HK, US)

Escape from L.A., 1996, John Carpenter

Extremities, 1986, Robert M. Young

Eye for an Eye, 1996, John Schlesinger

Faster Pussycat! Kill! Kill!, 1965, Russ Meyer

Fatal Attraction, 1987, Adrian Lyne

Female Convict Scorpion Jailhouse 41 (*Joshuu sasori: Dai-41 zakkyo-bô*), 1972, Shunya Ito

Female Prisoner # 701: Scorpion (*Joshuu 701-gô: Sasori*), 1972, Shunya Ito

Female Prisoner Scorpion: Beast Stable (*Joshuu sasori: Kemono-beya*), 1973, Shunya Ito

Female Prisoner Scorpion: # 701's Grudge Song (*Joshuu sasori: 701-gô urami-bushi*), 1973, Yasuharu Hasebe

Fifth Element, The (French title: *Le Cinquieème élément*), 1997, Luc Besson, (France, US)

Firefox, 1982, Clint Eastwood

First Blood, 1982, Ted Kotcheff

Fistful of Dollars, A (*Per un pugno di dollari*), 1964, Sergio Leone, (Italy, Spain, West, Germany)

Fort Apache: The Bronx, 1981, Daniel Petrie

Foxy Brown, 1974, Jack Hill

Friday Foster, 1975, Arthur Marks

Friday the 13th, 1980, Sean S. Cunningham

From Here to Eternity, 1953, Fred Zinnemann

Fugitive, The, 1993, Andrew Davis

Full Metal Jacket, 1987, Stanley Kubrick

Game of Death, 1978, Robert Clouse, (HK, US)

Ghost in the Shell (Kôkaku kidôtai), 1995, Mamoru Oshii, animated film, (Japan, UK)

G.I. Jane, 1997, Ridley Scott

Glorifying the American Girl, 1929, John W. Harkrider and Millard Webb

Guardian Angel, 1994, Richard W. Munchkin

Halloween, 1978, John Carpenter

Hamburger Hill, 1987, John Irvin,

Hannie Caulder, 1972, Burt Kennedy, (UK)

Hart's War, 2002, Gregory Hoblit

He Got Game, 1998, Spike Lee

Heartbreak Ridge, 1986, Clint Eastwood

Hercules: The Legendary Journeys, 1994–1999, synd, 116 episodes

Hercules: The Legendary Journeys, "The Warrior Princess" 1:9, March 13, 1995

Hercules: The Legendary Journeys, "The Gauntlet" 1:12, May 1, 1995

Hercules: The Legendary Journeys, "Unchained Heart" 1:13, May 8, 1995

Heroic Trio, The (Dung fong saam hap), 1993, Johnny To, (HK)

Heroic Trio 2: Executioners, The (Xian dai hao xia zhuan), 1993, Siu-Tung Ching, Johnny To, (HK)

House on Turk Street, The, 2002, Bob Rafelson, (U.S., Germany)

Hunter's Blood, 1986, Robert C. Hughes

I Spit on Your Grave (also called *Day of the Woman*), 1978, Meir Zarchi

Inferno (also called *Coyote Moon*), 1999, John G. Avildsen

Ilsa, She-Wolf of the SS, 1974, Don Edmonds

Ilsa, Harem-Keeper of the Oil Sheiks, 1976, Don Edmonds

Ilsa, The Tigress of Siberia, 1977, Jean LaFleur

Ilsa, The Wicked Warden (also called *Greta–Haus ohne Männer; Greta the Torturer; Greta, the Mad Butcher; Greta, the Sadist; Ilsa: Absolute Power; Wanda, the Wicked Warden*), 1977, Jess Franco, (U.S., Schweizerland, Germany)

In My Daughter's Name, 1992, Jud Taylor, television movie

Inspector Wears Skirts, The (Ba wong fa), 1988, Jackie Chan, (HK)

Irma Vep, 1996, Olivier Assayas, (France)

Irréversible, 2003, Gaspar Noé, (France)

Jackie Brown, 1997, Quentin Tarantino

Justice League, 2001–, Cartoon Network, animated series

Kill Bill: Vol. 1, 2003, Quentin Tarantino

Kill Bill: Vol. 2, 2004, Quentin Tarantino

Killer, The (Die xue shuang xiong), 1989, John Woo, (HK)

King Arthur, 2004, Antoine Fuqua, (U.S., Ireland)

Kiss of the Dragon, 2001, Chris Nahon, (France, U.S.)

L Word, The, 2004–, Showtime, television series

La Femme Nikita, 1997–2001 U.S.A (96 episodes)

Ladies' Club, The, 1986, Janet Greek

Ladies of the Big House, 1931, Marion Gering

Lady Avenger, 1989, David DeCoteau

Lady Dragon, 1992, David Worth, (Indonesia)

Lady Snowblood: Blizzard from the Netherworld (Shurayukihime), 1973, Toshiya Fujita, (Japan)

Lady Snowblood 2: Love Song of Vengeance (Shura-yuki-hime: Urami Renga), 1974, Toshiya Fujita, (Japan)

Lara Craft: Tomb Raider, 2001, Simon West, (UK, Germany, U.S., Japan)

Lara Croft Tomb Raider: The Cradle of Life, 2003, Jan de Bont, (U.S., Germany, UK, , Japan, Netherlands)

Last House on the Left, 1972, Wes Craven

Léon, 1994, Luc Besson (France, U.S.)

Lethal Weapon 4, 1998, Richard Donner

Lipstick, 1976, Lamont Johnson

Long Kiss Goodnight, The, 1996, Renny Harlin

Love Camp 7, 1969, Lee Frost

Mädchen in Uniform, 1931, Leontine Sagan, (Germany)

Madigan, 1968, Don Siegel

Magnificent Warriors (Zhong hua zhan shi), 1987, David Chung, (HK)

Magic Crystal, The (Mo fei cui), 1986, Jing Wong, (HK)

Matrix, The, 1999, Andy and Larry Wachowski

Memoirs of a Geisha, 2005, Rob Marshall

Messenger: The Story of Joan of Arc, The (also called *Joan of Arc; Jeanne d'Arc*), 1999, Luc , Besson, (France)

Million Dollar Hotel, The, 2000, Wim Wenders, (Germany, UK, U.S.)

Millionaire's Express, The (Foo gwai lit che), 1986, Sammo Hung Kam-Bo, (HK)

Moonlight Express (Sing yuet tung wa), 1999, Daniel Lee, (HK)

Mr. and Mrs. Smith, 2005, Dough Liman

Ms. 45, 1981, Abel Ferrara

Mulan, 1998, Tony Bancroft, Barry Cook

Night of the Living Dead, 1990, Tom Savini

Nikita, 1990, Luc Besson, (France, Italy)

No Retreat, No Surrender 2: Raging Thunder, 1989, Corey Yuen, (HK, U.S.)

Officer and a Gentleman, An, 1982, Taylor Hackford

Once Upon a Time in China (Wong Fei Hung), 1991, Hark Tsui, (HK)

One, The, 2001, James Wong

Original Gangstas, 1996, Larry Cohen

Owl and Dumbo (Mao tou ying yu xiao fei xiang), 1984, Sammo Hung and Kam-Bo, (HK)

Passion de Jeanne d'Arc, La (also called *The Passion of Joan of Arc*), 1928, Carl T. Dreyer, (France)

Patton, 1970, Franklin J. Schaffner

Performance, 1970, Donald Cammell and Nicolas Roeg, (UK)

Platoon, 1986, Oliver Stone

Point Blank, 1967, John Boorman

Point of No Return, 1993, John Badham

Police Story 3 (Jing cha gu shi III: Chao ji jing cha), 1992, Stanley Tong, (HK)

Positive I.D., 1987, Andy Anderson

Pretty Woman, 1990, Garry Marshall

Princess Blade, The (Shura yukihime), 2001, Shinsuke Sato, (Japan)

Private Benjamin, 1980, Howard Zieff

Project S (Chao ji ji hua; also called *Police Story 3 Part 2; Once a Cop; Supercop 2)*, 1993, Stanley Tong, (HK)

Pulp Fiction, 1994, Quentin Tarantino

Pumping Iron, 1977, George Butler and Robert Fiore, documentary

Pumping Iron II: The Women, 1985, George Butler, documentary

Quick and the Dead, The, 1995, Sam Raimi, (U.S., Japan)

Rage and Honor, 1992, Terence H. Winkless

Rage and Honor II: Hostile Takeover, 1992, Guy Norris, (Indonesia, U.S.)

Raging Bull, 1980, Martin Scorsese

Rambo: First Blood Part Two, 1985, George P. Cosmatos

Rape Squad (also called *Act of Vengeance; The Violator*), 1974, Bob Kelljan

Red Sonja, 1985, Richard Fleischer

Replicant, 2001, Ringo Lam

Reservoir Dogs, 1992, Quentin Tarantino

Resident Evil, 2002, Paul W.S. Anderson, (UK, Germany, France)

Resident Evil: Apocalypse, 2004, Alexander Witt, (Germany, France, UK, Canada)

Return to the Blue Lagoon, 1991, William A. Graham

RoboCop, 1987, Paul Verhoeven

Royal Warriors (Wong ga jin si, also known as *In the Line of Duty* and *Ultra Force)*, 1986, David Chung, (HK)

Samouraï, Le, 1967, Jean-Pierre Melville, (France, Italy)

Saturday Night Fever, 1977, John Badham

Savage Streets, 1984, Danny Steinmann

Saving Private Ryan, 1998, Steven Spielberg

Seven Maidens (Wu xia qi gong zhu; Holy Weapon; Seven Maidens), 1993, Jing Wong, (HK)

Shane, 1953, George Stevens

Sheba Baby, 1975 , William Girdler

Silver Hawk (Fei ying), 2004, Jingle Ma, (HK)

Sin City, 2005, Frank Miller and Robert Rodriguez

Sister Street Fighter, (*Onna hissatsu ken)*, 1974, Kazuhiko Yamaguchi, (Japan)

Sister Street Fighter 2 (Onna hissatsu kenikki ippatsu), 1974, Kazuhiko Yamaguchi, (Japan)

Sister Street Fighter 3, (*Kaette kita onna hissatsu ken)*, 1975, Kazuhiko Yamaguchi, (Japan)

Sisters, 1973, Brian De Palma

Sleeping with the Enemy, 1991, Joseph Ruben

Soldier's Sweetheart, A, 1998, Thomas Michael Donnelly, television movie

Something Wicked This Way Comes, 1983, Jack Clayton

Soong Sisters, The (Song jia huang chao), 1997, Mabel Cheung, (HK, Japan, China)

Stalingrad, 1993, Joseph Vilsmaier, (Germany)

Starship Troopers, 1997, Paul Verhoeven

Strange Days, 1995, Kathryn Bigelow

Stray Cat Rock: Sex Hunter (*Nora-neko rokku: Sekkusu hanta*), 1970, Yasuharu Hasebe

Stray Cat Rock: Wild Measures '71 (*Nora-neko rokku: Bôsô shudan '71*), 1971, Toshiya Fujita

Straw Dogs, 1971, Sam Peckinpah

Striptease, 1996, Andrew Bergman

Stunt Woman, The (*Ah Kam*), 1996, Ann Hui, (HK)

Sudden Impact, 1983, Clint Eastwood

Switchblade Sisters, 1975, Jack Hill

Sweet Sugar, 1973, Michel Levesque

Sworn to Justice (also called *Blonde Justice*), 1996, Paul Maslak

Tai-Chi Master, The (*Tai ji zhang san feng*), 1993, Woo-ping Yuen, (HK)

Tank Girl, 1995, Rachel Talalay

Terminal Island, 1973, Stephanie Rothman

Terminator, The, 1984, James Cameron

Terminator 2: Judgment Day, 1992, James Cameron

Texas Chain Saw Massacre, The, 1974, Tobe Hooper

Thelma and Louise, 1991, Ridley Scott

They Call Her One Eye (Thriller—en grym film), 1974, Bo Arne Vibenius, (Sweden)

Thin Red Line, The, 1998, Terrence Malick

37(2 le matin (U.S. title: *Betty Blue*), 1986, Jean-Jacques Beineix, (France)

Three Kings, 1999, David O. Russell

Tiger Claws, 1992, Kelly Makin, (Canada, U.S.)

Time to Kill, A, 1996, Joel Schumacher

Tomorrow Never Dies, 1997, Roger Spottiswoode, (UK, U.S.)

Touch, The (Tian mai chuan qi), 2002, Peter Pau, (HK, China, Taiwan)

Trapped! The Crimson Bat (*Mekurano Oichi jigokuhada*), 1969, Sadaji Matsuda, (Japan)

28 Days Later..., 2002, Danny Boyle, (Netherlands, UK, U.S.)

Two Moon Junction, 1988, Zalman King

Two Thousand Maniacs!, 1964, Herschell Gordon Lewis

Ultraviolet, 2006, Kurt Wimmer

Universal Soldier, 1992, Roland Emmerich

Vampires, Les, 1915, Louis Feuillade, 10 episodes silent film serials (France)

Watch Out, Crimson Bat (*Mekurano Oichi midaregasa*), 1969, Hirokazu Ichimura, (Japan)

We Were Soldiers, 2002, Randall Wallace

Week End, 1967, Jean-Luc Godard, (France, Italy)

Westward the Women, 1951, William A. Wellman

Wham Bam Thank You Spaceman, 1975, William A. Levey

Wing Chun (*Yong Chun*), 1994, Woo-ping Yuen, (HK)

Women in Cages, 1971, Gerardo de Leon (U.S., Philippines)

Wonder Seven, The (*7 jin gong*), 1994, Siu Tung-Ching, (HK)

Xena: Warrior Princess, 1995–2001, synd, 134 episodes

Xena: Warrior Princess, "Sins of the Past" 1:1, September 15, 1995

Xena: Warrior Princess, "Chariots of War" 1:2, September 22, 1995

Xena: Warrior Princess, "A Day in the Life" 2:15, March 2, 1997

Xena: Warrior Princess, "The Bitter Suite" 3:12, February 14, 1998

Xena: Warrior Princess, "The Rheingold" 6:7, November 18, 2000

Xena: Warrior Princess, "The Ring" 6:8, November 25, 2000

Xena: Warrior Princess, "Return of the Valkyrie" 6:9, December 2, 2000

Yes, Madam (*Huang gu shi jie*, also known as *In the Line of Duty 2* and *Ultra Force 2*), 1985, Corey Yuen, (HK)

You Stupid Man, 2002, Brian Burns, (U.S., Germany)

Zatoichi, (*Zatôichi monogatari*), 1962, Kenji Misumi, (Japan)

Zoolander, 2001, Ben Stiller, (U.S., Australia, Germany)

Chapter Notes

Preface

1. I borrow this term from Judith Halberstam who calls a person whose gender is not clearly identifiable as male or female "in-between" and use in-betweenness to describe the experience of not fitting one gender. Judith Halberstam, *Female Masculinity* (Durham, N.C.: Duke University Press, 1998), 192.

2. Thaïs E. Morgan, "A Whip of One's Own: Dominatrix Pornography and the Construction of a Post-Modern (Female) Subjectivity," *The American Journal of Semiotics* 6, no. 4 (1989): 126.

3. Sarah Projansky, *Watching Rape: Film and Television in Postfeminist Culture* (New York: New York University Press, 2001), 67.

4. As I write this preface yet another book on female heroes is coming out, Dominique Mainon and James Ursini's non-academic *The Modern Amazons: Warrior Women On-Screen* (Pompton Plains, N.J.: Limelight Editions, 2006).

5. Judith Butler, *Gender Trouble: Feminism and the Subversion of Identity* (New York: Routledge, 1999), xiv.

Introduction

1. Richard Dyer, "Action!" *Sight and Sound*, October 1994, 9.

2. Yvonne Tasker, "Soldier's Stories: Women and Military Masculinities in *Courage Under Fire*," in Rikke Schubart and Anne Gjelsvik (eds.), *Femme Fatalities: Representations of Strong Women in the Media* (Göteborg: Nordicom, 2004), 92.

3. Greer quoted in Maja Mikula, "Lara Croft, Between a Feminist Icon and Male Fantasy," in Schubart and Gjelsvik (eds.), *Femme Fatalities*, 57.

4. John M. Wilson, "A Swarm of Superheroes Due Back in Strength," *Los Angeles Times*, May 7, 1978.

5. "Stinkende premiere" ["Stinking Premiere"], Danish review of *Ilsa, She-Wolf of the SS, Aarhus Stiftstidende*, April 26, 1976.

6. Halberstam, *Female Masculinity*, 192.

7. Sharon Willis, *High Contrast: Race and Gender in Contemporary Hollywood Film* (Durham, N.C.: Duke University Press, 1997), 1.

8. Willis, *High Contrast*, 2.

9. Horror and porno are also male genres; however, neither has traditional heroes. See Carol Clover, *Men, Women and Chain Saws: Gender in the Modern Horror Film* (London: BFI, 1992) for a discussion of male audiences and the horror movie, and Linda Williams, "Film Bodies: Gender, Genre and Excess," *Film Quarterly* 44, no. 4 (Summer 1991): 2–13, for a discussion of male audiences and the porno movie.

10. Jeanine Basinger, *A Woman's View: How Hollywood Spoke to Women 1930–1960* (New York: Alfred A. Knopf, 1993), 9.

11. Basinger, *Woman's View*, 13.

12. *Ibid.*, 36, 505.

13. *Ibid.*, 17.

14. Thomas Schatz, *Hollywood Genres: Formulas, Film-Making and the Studio System* (New York: McGraw Hill, 1981), 34–36.

15. Will Wright, *Sixguns and Society: A Structural Study of the Western* (Berkeley: University of California Press, 1975), 40.

16. David D. Gilmore, *Manhood in the Making: Cultural Concepts of Masculinity* (New Haven: Yale University Press, 1990), 223.

17. Basinger, *Woman's View*, 448.

18. *Ibid.*

19. *Ibid.*, 477.

20. *Ibid.*, 467.

21. Laura Mulvey, "Visual Pleasure and Narrative Cinema," in Gerald Mast, Marshall Cohen, and Leo Braudy (eds.), *Film, Theory and Criticism* (New York: Oxford University Press, 1992), 750–51.

22. Studies in masculinity point to pain and masochism as essential to the construction of

masculine identity. See, for instance, Klaus
Theweleit, *Male Fantasies* (Minneapolis: Univer-
sity of Minnesota Press, 1996) on the German
Freikorps soldiers; Gilmore, *Manhood in the
Making* on anthropological studies of initiation
rituals; Anthony Easthope, *What A Man's Gotta
Do: The Masculine Myth in Popular Culture* (New
York: Routledge, 1992) on cultural notions of
masculinity; psychoanalyst Roger Horrocks,
Masculinity in Crisis (New York: Palgrave Macmillan, 1994); and in film studies, Peter Lehman,
*Running Scared: Masculinity and the Representa-
tion of the Male Body* (Philadelphia: Temple University Press, 1993) is one example of an analysis of masculinity as heterogeneous.

23. As a joke, the journal *Citizen News*
awarded Clint Eastwood "the decade's open
wound award" for his beatings in Sergio Leone's
spaghetti westerns. "Clint Eastwood Bidding
for Black-and-Blue Honors," *Citizen News*, December 16, 1968. Sylvester Stallone was, among
several reviews, called "Jesus" in a review of
Rocky II (1979) by Frank Rich, "Plastic Jesus,"
Time, June 25, 1979. See also Rikke Schubart,
"Birth of a Hero: *Rocky*, Stallone and Mythical
Creation," in Angela Ndalianis and Charlotte
Henry (eds.), *Stars in Our Eyes: The Star Phenomenon in the Contemporary Era* (Westport, Conn:
Praeger, 2002), 140–164. The Jean-Claude Van
Damme quote is from Stephen Rebelle, "The 8
million Dollar Man," *Movieline*, August 1994,
82.

24. Rebelle, "8 Million Dollar Man," 82.

25. Publicity stills from *Rambo IV* (1985)
played with the expectations of Dolph Lund-
gren's homosexual fans. One still had him pose
in front of a huge poster with Marlene Dietrich; in another he wore a military peaked cap.

26. Willis, *High Contrast*, 102.

27. Clover, *Men, Women and Chain Saws*, 53.

28. Barbara Creed, *The Monstrous-Feminine:
Film, Feminism, Psychoanalysis* (London: Routledge, 1993), 151.

29. Creed, *Monstrous-Feminine*, 7.

30. Sarah Projansky, *Watching Rape: Film and
Television in Postfeminist Culture* (New York: New
York University Press, 2001), 66.

31. Germaine Greer, *The Whole Woman*
(London: Anchor, 2000), 3.

32. Quoted in Pamela Aronson, "Feminists
or 'Postfeminist'? Young Women's Attitudes toward Feminism and Gender Relations," *Gender
and Society* 17, no. 6 (December 2003): 903–922,
911. For further discussion of postfeminism see
chapter 2, "The Postfeminist Context: Popular
Redefinitions of Feminism, 1980–Present," in
Projansky; and Elaine J. Hall and Marnie
Salupo Rodriguez, "The Myth of Postfeminism," *Gender and Society* 17, no. 6 (December
2003): 878–902.

33. This section is based on Projansky,
Watching Rape, 66–89.

34. Elizabeth Wurtzel, *Bitch: In Praise of
Difficult Women* (New York: Doubleday, 1999),
291.

35. Projansky, *Watching Rape*, 80.

36. *Ibid.*, 68.

37. Tasker, "Soldier's Stories," 100.

38. *Ibid*, 19.

39. Jeffrey Brown, "Gender and the Action
Heroine: Hardbodies and the *Point of No Return*," *Cinema Journal* 35, no. 3 (1996): 52, 54,
56.

40. *Ibid.*, 52, 54.

41. *Ibid.*, 56.

42. F.X. Feeney, "Conan: Primordial Postcards," *L.A. Weekly*, May 14–20, 1982.

43. Projansky, *Watching Rape*, 150.

44. Joan Riviere, "Womanliness as a Masquerade" (1929) in Victor Burgin, James Donald, and Cora Kaplan (eds.), *Formations of Fantasy* (London: Methuen, 1986), 35–44.

45. Bev Zalcock, *Renegade Sisters: Girl Gangs
on Film* (London: Creation Books, 1998), 8.

46. Martha McCaughey and Neal King, eds.,
Reel Knockouts: Violent Women in the Movies
(Austin: University of Texas Press, 2001), 6.

47. The last quote is Read quoting Andrea
Stuart. Jacinda Read, *The New Avengers: Feminism, Femininity and the Rape-Revenge Cycle* (Manchester: Manchester University Press, 2000),
254.

48. Willis, *High Contrast*, 110.

49. Projansky, *Watching Rape*, 232.

50. *Ibid.*

51. Greer, *Whole Woman*, 413.

52. *Ibid.*, 377.

53. *Ibid.*

54. See Susan E. Linville, "'The *Mother* of
All Battles': *Courage Under Fire* and the Gender-
Integrated Military," *Cinema Journal* 39, no. 2
(Winter 2000): 100–120, for a discussion of
rape trials in the U.S. army and *Courage Under
Fire.*

55. Two women—Lynndie England and Sabrina Harman—posed in the infamous torture
photographs from the Abu Ghraib prison in
Iraq. They were later put on trial. The image of
female American soldiers torturing male prisoners were distributed by news media across
the world, and recently the scenes from the
photographs were incorporated as scenes in the
blockbuster Turkish action drama *Valley of the
Wolves–Iraq* (*Kurtlar vadisi–Irak*, 2006).

56. See Chapter 5, "Male Rape," in Sue
Lees, *Ruling Passions: Sexual Violence, Reputation,
and the Law* (Buckingham: Open University
Press, 1997).

57. Frances Early and Kathleen Kennedy,
eds., *Athena's Daughters: Television's New Women*

Warriors (Syracuse, N.Y.: Syracuse University Press, 2003), 6. Recent studies in the field of the new female hero also include Sherrie A. Inness, *Tough Girls: Women Warriors and Wonder Women in Popular Culture* (Philadelphia: University of Pennsylvania Press, 1998); Sherrie A. Inness, ed., *Action Chicks: New Images of Tough Women in Popular Culture* (New York: Palgrave Macmillan, 2004); Schubart and Gjelsvik (eds.), *Femme Fatalities*; Elyce Rae Helford, ed., *Fantasy Girls: Gender in the New Universe of Science Fiction and Fantasy Television* (Lanham, Md.: Rowman and Littlefield, 2000).

58. Inness, *Action Chicks*, 14.

59. Projansky, *Watching Rape*, 32.

60. Read, *New Avengers*, 94.

61. *Ibid.*, 41.

62. Lees, *Ruling Passions*, 103.

63. *Ibid.*

64. Creed, *Monstrous-Feminine*, 130.

65. Read, *New Avengers*, 49.

66. Creed, *Monstrous-Feminine*, 17, 27.

67. Ben Singer notices the lack of mothers in his analysis of sixty serial-queen melodramas produced between 1912 and 1920. "While a benevolent father figure is generally established, the heroine is always without a mother and none is ever referred to. These films depict a world in which there simply is no such social and biological entity as a mother." Ben Singer, "Female Power in the Serial-Queen Melodrama: The Etiology of an Anomaly," *Camera Obscura*, no. 22 (1990): 99.

68. Yvonne Tasker, *Working Girls: Gender and Sexuality in Popular Cinema* (London: Routledge, 1998), 27.

69. Brown, "Gender and Action Heroine," 67.

70. Blake Tyrrell, *Amazons: A Study in Athenian Mythmaking* (Baltimore, Md.: Johns Hopkins University Press, 1984), 77.

71. *Ibid.*, 63.

72. Elyce Rae Helford, "Feminism, Queer Studies, and the Sexual Politics of *Xena: Warrior Princess*," in Helford (ed.), *Fantasy Girls*, 135–162, 143.

Chapter 1

1. Mark Jacobson, "Sex Goddess of the Seventies," *New York*, May 19, 1975, 43–45, 44.

2. From interview with Pam Grier in Bob Ellison, "Pam Grier: A Matter of Survival," *Los Angeles Times*, August 19, 1979, Calendar.

3. Jacobson, "Sex Goddess," 44.

4. Jamaica Kincaid, "Pam Grier: The Mocha Mogul of Hollywood," *Ms.*, 50, 49–53. (Date and issue number missing from my copy from The Margaret Herrick Library. The year is probably 1975.)

5. Mary Murphy, "Pam's Stranglehold on Violent Roles," *L.A. Times*, January 4, 1976.

6. American WIP movies flourished in the seventies with *The Big Doll House* (1971); *The Big Bird Cage* (1972); *Black Mama, White Mama* (1973); *Terminal Island* (1973); *Caged Heat* (1974); and the notorious *Ilsa* movies: *Ilsa, She-Wolf of the SS* (1975), *Ilsa, Harem-Keeper of the Oil Sheiks* (1976), and *Ilsa, Tigress of Siberia* (1977). The eighties saw more sadistic epics like *Chained Heat* (1983), *Red Heat* and *Hellhole* (1985). Modern WIP films have roots in films like *Women in Bondage* (1943), *Caged* (1950), *Women's Prison* (1955), and *Blonde Bait* (1956). The genre is discussed in Nicolas Barbano, "Mondo Bleeder," article included on the DVD of the film *Bleeder*, and in David Henry Jacob, "Women in Chains," *Toxic Horror*, no. 4 (June 1990). See also James Robert Parish, *Prison Pictures From Hollywood: Plots, Critiques, Casts and Credits for 293 Theatrical and Made-for-Television Releases* (Jefferson, N.C.: McFarland, 1991).

7. See Anne Morey, "'The Judge Called Me an Accessory': Women's Prison Films, 1950–1962," *Journal of Popular Film and Television* 23, no. 2 (1995): 80–87.

8. Ed Morales, "Mama Said Knock You Out," *Voice*, August 15, 1995.

9. Parish, *Prison Pictures*, 28.

10. See chapter 1, "Women in Prison," in Bev Zalcock, *Renegade Sisters: Girl Gangs on Film* (London: Creation Books, 1998); Morey, "Women's Prison Films"; Pam Cook, "'Exploitation' Films and Feminism," *Screen* 17, no. 2 (Summer 1976): 122–27; Birgit Hein, "Frauengefängnisfilme," *Frauen & Film* 43 (December 1987): 22–26.

11. Peter Lehman, "'I'll see you in small claims court': Penis-Size Jokes and Their Relation To Hollywood's Unconscious," in Peter Lehman (ed.), *Running Scared: Masculinity and the Representation of the Male Body* (Philadelphia: Temple University Press, 1993), 105–129, 129.

12. Murphy, "Pam's Stranglehold."

13. For a discussion of masculinity as cultural performance see anthropologist David Gilmore, *Manhood in the Making: Cultural Concepts of Masculinity* (New Haven: Yale University Press, 1990) and Danish ethnologist Anne Knudsen, "Masculinity as Challenge—The Fantasmatics of Honour" in Hand Bonde (ed.), *Mandekultur* (Copenhagen: Center for Kvindeforskning, 1991). For the construction of masculinity and its relation to cinematic pleasure and popular film genres see, e.g., Antony Easthope, *What a Man's Gotta Do: The Masculine Myth in Popular Culture* (New York: Routledge, 1992); Lehman, *Running Scared*; Dennis Bingham, *Acting Male: Masculinities in the Films of James Stewart, Jack Nicholson and*

Clint Eastwood (New Brunswick, N.J.: Rutgers University Press, 1994); Steven Cohan and Ina Rae Hark, *Screening the Male: Exploring Masculinities in Hollywood Cinema* (London: Routledge, 1993); Susan Jeffords, *Hard Bodies: Hollywood Masculinity in the Reagan Era* (New Brunswick, N.J.: Rutgers University Press, 1994).

14. *Filmfacts*, vol. xvi, no. 5 (1973): 136.

15. Jack Hill on the commentary track of the 2001 DVD *Coffy*.

16. "Coffy," *Variety*, May 14, 1973.

17. "Coffy," *Boxoffice*, May 28, 1973.

18. "Foxy Brown," *Variety*, April 17, 1974.

19. Linda Gross, "Pam Grier in 'Sheba, Baby,'" *Los Angeles Times*, March 28, 1975, Part IV.

20. Alan Ebert, "Pam Grier," *Essence*, January 1979, 107.

21. Murphy, "Pam's Stranglehold."

22. Jacobson, "Sex Goddess," 43.

23. Kincaid, "Mocha Mogul," 52–53.

24. See Sumiko Higashi, "Hold it! Women in Television Adventure Series," *Journal of Popular Film and Television* vol. 8, no. 3 (Fall 1980), for an analysis of the seventies' television series *Police Woman, Bionic Woman* and *Wonder Woman*.

25. Kincaid, "Mocha Mogul," 52.

26. Ibid, 53.

27. Ebert, "Pam Grier," 107.

28. Jacobson, "Sex Goddess," 44.

29. Ebert, "Pam Grier," 104.

30. Kincaid, "Mocha Mogul," 53.

31. Ebert, "Pam Grier," 107.

32. For an introduction to Pam Grier's career till 1990 see Lars Krogh, "Pam Grier," *Moshable* no. 11. (The year is missing from my copy but is probably 1992.)

Chapter 2

1. Darrin Venticinque and Tristan Thompson, *The Ilsa Chronicles* (Northants, U.K.: Midnight Media, 2000), 57.

2. Venticinque and Thompson, *Ilsa Chronicles*.

3. "Stinkende premiere" ("Stinking Premiere"), *Aarhus Stiftstidende*, April 26, 1976.

4. "Nazifilm om SS-tortur tages af plakaten fordi publikum bliver dårlige" ("Nazi movie about SS torture is pulled because the audience gets sick"), *Ny Dag*, December 16, 1976. Even if people were "sickened," there was an audience. The American *Ilsa* films all premiered in Danish cinemas, as did other American WIP films such as *The Big Doll House* (1971), *Black Mama, White Mama* (1972), *Chained Heat* (1982), and *The Concrete Jungle* (1983).

5. Wade Major, "Ilsa, She Wolf of the SS," *Boxoffice Magazine Online*, accessed from http://www.rottentomatoes.com on May 12, 2002.

6. Anonymous review of "Ilsa, She Wolf of the SS," accessed from www.prisonflicks.com/ilsa-shewolf.htm on May 12, 2002.

7. The only article I know of about the *Ilsa* films is by Frank Furseth, "Ilsa, Nazisternes Hunndjevel" (Ilsa, the Nazi She-Devil), *Z filmtidsskrift* 67, no. 1 (1999): 30–34.

8. I have come across four articles and one paper: Pam Cook, "'Exploitation' Films and Feminism," *Screen* 17, no. 2 (Summer 1976): 122–127; Birgit Hein, "Frauengefängnisfilme," *Frauen & Film* 43 (December 1987): 22–26; Anne Morey, "The Judge Called Me an Accessory," *Journal of Popular Film & Television* 23 (Summer 1995): 80–87; Suzanna Danuta Walters, "Caged Heat: the (R)evolution of Woman-in-Prison Films," in Martha McCaughey and Neal King (eds.), *Reel Knockouts: Violent Women in the Movies* (Austin: University of Texas Press, 2001), 106–124; Omayra Cruz, "Between Cinematic Imperialism and the Idea of Radical Politics: Philippines Based Women's Prison Films of the 1970s," Paper presented at the SCS Conference in Denver, Colorado, 2002.

9. Exploitation cinema is the "bastard child" of cinema, an uncivilized lower stratum of cinema history. However, since New Hollywood and feminist film theory, exploitation films have been a source of inspiration to researchers. Directors such as Herschell Gordon Lewis, John Waters, and Russ Meyer have been reevaluated as innovative in their portrayal of strong women, perverse sexuality, and a provocative aesthetics of camp, kitsch, and trash. Films like *The Texas Chain Saw Massacre* (1974) and *I Spit on your Grave* (1978) were embraced by feminist film scholars as almost avant-garde cinema. But not Ilsa.

10. "This brutal and shameless exercise in depravity and relentless sadism..." Venticinque and Thompson, *Ilsa Chronicles*, 4.

11. Characters' names vary in spelling and most of the credits appear to be pseudonyms. The prisoner Rosetta—the only woman to escape Camp 9—is not in the end credits and is not mentioned in *The Ilsa Chronicles* or on IMDB.

12. Kaja Silverman, *Male Subjectivity at the Margins* (London: Routledge, 1992), 33, 32.

13. After *She-Wolf* in 1974 followed *SS Girls, Women's Camp 119, SS Experiment Camp, SS Camp 5 Women's Hell, Achtung! The Desert Tigers, Horrifying Experiments of the SS Last Days, Gestapo's Last Orgy, Nazi Love Camp 27*—all produced in 1976.

14. Quoted in Silverman, *Male Subjectivity*, 34.

15. Sigmund Freud, "The Economic Problem of Masochism" (1924), in James Strachey (trans.), *The Standard Edition of the Complete Psychological Works of Sigmund Freud vol. XIX* (London: Hogarth Press, 1980), 159.

16. Freud, "Economic Problem," 162.

17. *Ibid.*

18. For a thorough discussion of Freud's writings on masochism see Silverman, *Male Subjectivity*, chapter 5, which is a longer version of the article "Masochism and Male Subjectivity." About homosexuality in male masochism, Reik comments, "There cannot be any doubt as to the existence and efficaciousness of the passive-homosexual idea in masochism—but much doubt as to its prevalent importance. It does not show up regularly nor is its importance always the same." Theodor Reik, *Masochism in Modern Man* (New York: Farrar, Straus, 1941), 206.

19. Reik, *Masochism in Modern Man*, 216.

20. Freud, "Economic Problem," 162.

21. Reik, *Masochism in Modern Man*, 41.

22. *Ibid.*, 42.

23. On the commentary track to *Wicked Warden* Dyanne Thorne says she receives letters from women thanking her that the *Ilsa* films saved their marriage. I may be conservative, but my guess is that if women watch these films they do so on male initiative. When asking, I did not find one woman who had seen an *Ilsa* film, whereas many male friends, colleagues and acquaintances surprised me by having watched one or several. My private asking is not a survey poll, but the result is supported by the fact that during research I have not met any women commenting on the films.

24. *Ilsa, She-Wolf of the SS.*

25. Richard Scheib, "Ilsa, She Wolf of the SS," accessed from http.//members.fortunecity.com/roogulator/horror/ilsa1.htm on May 12, 2002.

26. Chris Steltz, "She Wolf of the SS," accessed from www.dvdangle.com/reviews/ on May 12, 2002.

27. Silverman, *Male Subjectivity*, 50.

28. Quoted in Barbara Creed, *The Monstrous-Feminine: Film, Feminism, Psychoanalysis* (London: Routledge, 1993), 125.

29. The Spanish sequel is an exception to this rule. It follows the traditional sadistic path of WIP films with female victims, evil lesbian wardens who are killed in the end, and sadistic voyeurism.

30. Brian Matherly, "She Wolf of the SS," *Daily-Reviews.com*, accessed from www.daily-reviews.com/i/bmilsa1.htm on May 12, 2002.

31. Gaylyn Studlar, "Masochism, Masquerade, and the Erotic Metamorphoses of Marlene Dietrich," in Jane Gaines and Charlotte Herzog (eds.), *Fabrications: Costume and the Female Body*, (London: Routledge, 1990), 236–7.

32. Cook, "'Exploitation' Films," 127.

33. "Ich war gleich beim ersten Film von den Frauen begeistert (. .) Sie prügeln sich nach allen Regeln der Kunst. Sie gehen ganz selbstverständlich mit Schusswaffen und Messern um. Sie sind hinterhältig und skrupellos. Sie sind sehr geil aufeinander und, wenn es darauf ankommt, sehr solidarisch und mutig." Hein, "Frauengefängnisfilme," 22.

34. Walters, "Caged Heat," 121.

35. Georges Bataille, *Eroticism* (London: Penguin Books, 2001), 63, 65.

Chapter 3

1. Jacinda Read, *The New Avengers: Feminism, Femininity and the Rape-Revenge Cycle* (Manchester: Manchester University Press, 2000), 242.

2. Carol Clover, *Men, Women and Chain Saws: Gender in the Modern Horror Film* (London: BFI, 1992), 137.

3. For an analysis of *Deliverance* see Carol Clover, *Men, Women and Chain Saws*, chapter 3, and Linda Ruth Williams, "Blood Brothers," *Sight and Sound*, no. 9 (1994): 16–19.

4. It is unclear if Drew voluntarily throws himself from the canoe because he is unable to live with his complicity in the murder of the rapist, or if he is shot by the second mountain man. Both possibilities are kept open, since Ed and Bobby do not search Drew's body for bullet wounds. To stick with their story (that Drew drowned in the river and they never met the two mountain men) they hide Drew's body in the river.

5. Stephen Farber, "'Deliverance'—How It Delivers" *The New York Times*, August 20, 1972.

6. Review of *Deliverance, The New Yorker*, December 8, 1972.

7. For a comparison between James Dickey's novel and John Boorman's film see James J. Griffith, "Damned If You Do, and Damned If You Don't: James Dickey's 'Deliverance,'" *Post Script* v, no. 3 (Spring(Summer 1986): 47–59; R.A. Armour, "'Deliverance': Four Variations of the American Adam," *Literature/Film Quarterly* 1, no. 3 (Summer 1973): 280–285; Robert F. Willson, Jr., "'Deliverance' From Novel to Film: Where Is Our Hero?" *Literature/Film Quarterly* 2, no. 1 (Winter 1974): 52–58.

8. Barbara Creed, *The Monstrous-Feminine: Film, Feminism, Psychoanalysis* (London: Routledge, 1993), 131.

9. Sue Lees, *Ruling Passions: Sexual Violence, Reputation, and the Law* (Buckingham: Open University Press, 1997), 95.

10. *Ibid.*, 99.

11. *Ibid.*, 103.

12. *Ibid.*, 105.

13. Ironically, the real Chattooga River separating Georgia and the Carolinas, which was

Deliverance's fictitious Cahulawassee River, became a popular excursion goal after the movie. In 1975, three years after *Deliverance*, nineteen men died trying to go down the river without a guide. Newspapers coined this "The Deliverance Syndrome." The stunt man doubling for Jon Voigt opened a company specializing in taking groups down the Chattooga River and was interviewed by *The New York Times*, "The river is a lady ... You respect her. Some say she's haunted. Every time you get careless, lose your respect for her, she'll kill you. The river is totally implacable, she won't turn you loose." Wayne King, "Wild 'Deliverance River' Lures Adventurers South," *The New York Times*, June 8, 1975, Section K, National Topics.

14. Clover, *Men, Women and Chain Saws*, 122.

15. For a discussion of 60,000 daily unreported male rapes in jail see Lees, *Ruling Passions*, 96.

16. James Wolcott, "Meat Grinders," *Village Voice*, February 18–24, 1981.

17. "Day of the Woman," *Variety*, March 16, 1983.

18. Joan Mellen, *Big Bad Wolves: Masculinity in the American Film* (New York: Pantheon Books, 1977), 296.

19. Gilles Deleuze, *Coldness and Cruelty* (1967) in Jean McNeil (trans.), *Masochism: Coldness and Cruelty by Gilles Deleuze, Venus in Furs by Leopold von Sacher-Masoch* (New York: Zone Books, 1994), 68.

20. Clover, *Men, Women and Chain Saws*, 157.

21. On initiation rites see David D. Gilmore, *Manhood in the Making: Cultural Concepts of Masculinity* (New Haven: Yale University Press, 1990), 14.

22. Read, *New Avengers*, 39.

23. Germaine Greer, *The Whole Woman* (London: Anchor, 2000), 384.

24. Read, *New Avengers*, 35.

25. Mary Ann Doane, *Femmes Fatales: Feminism, Film Theory, and Psychoanalysis* (New York: Routledge, 1991), 2–3.

26. Creed, *Monstrous-Feminine*, 130.

27. In 1996, the same year as *Eye For an Eye*, Joel Schumacher presented audiences with a paternal avenger in *A Time to Kill*.

28. Production information for *Enough*, 1.

29. Lael Lowenstein, "Vigilantism's New Face," *Los Angeles Times*, May 30, 2002.

30. Richard Corliss, "Girls Just Wanna Have Guns," *Time*, April 22, 2002. Corliss is referring to Ashley Judd in *High Crimes*, to *Murder by Numbers* with Sandra Bullock, Jennifer Lopez in *Enough*, and Jodie Foster in *Panic Room* (yet another mother whose daughter's life is threatened), all from 2002.

31. Charlotte Brunsdon, "Feminism, Post-feminism, Martha, Martha, and Nigella," *Cinema Journal* 44, no. 2 (Winter 2005): 114.

32. Slim is positioned as a WASP, although she is played by the light-skinned Latino Jennifer Lopez. Her racial heritage is disavowed by surrounding her with white people: Ginny is played by actress Juliette Lewis, the husband Mitch and his family are white, the French mistress is positioned as foreign (in one exchange Mitch answers his phone with "is this my little croissant?" to which Slim replies, "no, this is your loaf of bread," thus positioning a *white* loaf of bread against the beige croissant), and Slim devaluatively comments on the Indian food cooked by a dark-skinned Indian woman. White is clearly the color of this female hero.

33. Read, *New Avengers*, 245.

Chapter 4

1. My information on Meiko Kaji has been cross-checked with several sources, and my résumés of her films are from my viewing of them. Information on the Internet varies in quality. A review of *Female Convict Scorpion: Jailhouse 41* describes Kaji's role in the *Stray Cat Rock* series as "the leader of a vicious gang of female bikers." However, the girls are not "vicious" (no random violence) and they are not bikers but walk on foot in the city (http://www.midnighteye.com/reviews/femaconv.shtml). Still, the reviews of Meiko's films on www.midnighteye.com are the most reliable. Also "Urami-bushi" performed by Kaji is on www.imdb presented as the title song of the third *Scorpion* film, while it is the title song of the first film in the series, reappearing in slightly different versions in each sequel (http://www.imdb.com/). Some sites claim Meiko starred in all five *Stray Cat Rock* films, while others credit her with only the third and fourth film in the series. From my research carried out in 2004 at the National Film Center in Kyobashi, Tokyo, the latter seems true. English, German, and French websites list her under the third and fourth *Stray Cat Rock* film.

2. Kazuo Koike, *Kozure Ōkami*, manga published from 1970 to 1976 in 28 volumes of 300 pages, in all 7,000 pages. See http://www.mangamaniacs.org/reviews/lonewolf.shtml for a review of the original and the English translation. The manga was turned into a series of six films, a television series, and records. An American film, *Lone Wolf and Cub* by director Darren Aronofsky, is listed on imdb as being in production.

3. The *Zatoichi* figure was extremely popular just as chanbara cinema was a huge hit at the end of the sixties and beginning of the seven-

ties; a staggering number of 25 *Zatoichi* films were produced between 1962 and 1973.

4. The all-female pop-group singing in the nightclub where The Alleycats and The Eagles hang out is the real Japanese pop group "The Golden Half" whose five members are half-breeds with Japanese mothers and fathers of American, Thai, German, Italian and Spanish descent. Ichiro is half Japanese, half Afro-American (thus half black), and Kazuma appears to be half Japanese, half Spanish-American.

5. Carol Clover, *Men, Women and Chain Saws: Gender in the Modern Horror Film* (London: BFI, 1992), 207.

6. Barbara Creed, *The Monstrous-Feminine: Film, Feminism, Psychoanalysis* (London: Routledge, 1993), 76.

7. Creed, *Monstrous-Feminine*, 75.

8. After *The Witches of Eastwick* (1987) the witch became a popular figure with films like *Teen Witch* (1989), *The Craft* (1996), *Practical Magic* (1998), and the television series *Sabrina, The Teenage Witch* (1996–2003) and *Charmed* (1998–2006) where witchcraft is a positive feminine force and the witches are young and beautiful instead of old and hideous. Similarly, the vampire became a heroic and sometimes tragic figure since *Innocent Blood* (1992) followed by *Blade* (1998), *Blade II* (2002), *Blade: Trinity* (2004), and the television series *Buffy the Vampire Slayer* (1997–2003).

Chapter 5

1. Hong Kong born Maggie Cheung went on to serious roles in the dramas *Chinese Box* (Wayne Wang, 1997) with Jeremy Irons and *Clean* (Olivier Assayas, 2004) with Nick Nolte. She married Olivier Assayas in 1998 and divorced him in 2001.

2. Helle Hellmann, "007 er ingen dinosaurus" ("007 Is No Dinosaur"), *Politiken*, November 18, 1997.

3. Craig Reid, "Fighting Without Fighting: Film Action Fight Choreography," *Film Quarterly* 47 (Winter 1994/95): 31.

4. Rick Baker and Toby Russell, *The Essential Guide to Hong Kong Movies* (London: Eastern Heroes Publications, 1994), 181.

5. Susanne Johansen, "Hun gi'r Bond tørt på" ("She hangs Bond out to dry"), *B.T.*, December 18, 1997.

6. These are typical comments by fans on Internet Movie Data Base: "Jackie really plays second fiddle to co-star Michelle Yeoh in this film, the only time he let this happen with a female co-star" (anonymous fan, "Jackie Chan is Outshone by His Female Co-Star," October 13, 2003, accessed from http://www.imdb.com/

title/tt0104558/usercomments on August 15, 2005) and "The duo of Michelle Kahn (Yeoh) and Chan is amazing, and Yeoh almost steals the show in her own right—her persona and her insistence to do her own stunts (like Chan) makes her a marvel to watch—this is why she is so damn good in Tomorrow Never Dies, but it's a shame the director of TND never captured her in the same way Stanley Tong does!" (anonymous fan, "The Best Jackie Chan Action Film Yet," November 28, 2000, accessed from http://www.imdb.com/title/tt0104558/usercomments?start=10 on August 15, 2005).

7. Anonymous fan, "One of the Best Hong Kong Martial Arts Buddy Films Ever—Yeoh Is Terrific!" August 12, 2000, accessed from http://www.imdb.com/title/tt0104558/usercomments?start=10 on August 15, 2005.

8. Tony Rayns, "The Heroic Trio," *Sight and Sound*, vol. 3 (March 1995): 56.

9. "The Heroic Trio," *Video Watchdog*, nb. 35, 1995, 64–66, 65.

10. Baker and Russell, *Essential Guide*, 267.

11. Anita Mui died from cervical cancer on December 30, 2003.

12. Henrik List, "Sexet stuntkvinde" ("Sexy Stuntwoman"), *Berlingske Tidende*, December 13, 1997, Section 2.

13. Shelly Kraicer, "Ah Kam," accessed from http://www.chinesecinemas.org/ahkam.html on August 18, 2005.

14. Bey Logan, *Hong Kong Action Cinema* (London: Titan Books, 1995), 159.

15. Nicolas Barbano, "Kampmaskinen fra Hongkong" ("The Fight Machine from Hong Kong"), *Ekstrabladet*, November 18, 1997.

16. Hellmann, "Ingen dinosaurus."

17. Cathy Greenhalgh, "High-Flying Romance," *Vertigo* 2, no. 1 (Spring 2001): 6.

18. David Bordwell, *Planet Hong Kong: Popular Cinema and the Art of Entertainment* (Cambridge, Mass.: Harvard University Press, 2000), 245, 232.

19. Ibid., 231–2.

20. Peter Culshaw, "Fusion Cinema," *Vertigo* 2, no. 1 (Spring 2001): 7.

21. Ibid.

22. Baker and Russell, *Essential Guide*, 96.

Chapter 6

1. Andy Meisler, "The Biggest Star You Never Heard Of," *The New York Times*, July 3, 1994, H 21.

2. "Cynthia Rothrock Biography," accessed from http://www.cynthiarothrock.org/biography.htm on August 25, 2005.

3. "Cynthia Rothrock Biography."

4. Danny Shamon, "Interview: Cynthia

Rothrock, the Lady Dragon," *Kung Fu Cinema*, year unknown, accessed from http://www.kungfucinema.com/ on August 25, 2005.

5. Bey Logan, *Hong Kong Action Cinema* (London: Titan Books, 1995), 157.

6. For a discussion of Hong Kong film production, see Logan, *Hong Kong Action Cinema*, 170, and David Bordwell, *Planet Hong Kong*, 152.

7. "The construction is all the more admirable for the fact that it was developed on the set in a single day, with the director quickly deciding on each shot as each bit of action was conceived. This twenty-four seconds of cinema puts to shame the storyboarded fights in big-budget Schwarzenegger films, where firepower substitutes for briskness and finesse," Bordwell, *Planet Hong Kong*, 243.

8. Paradoxically, this technique actually prolongs the duration of the fight while at the same time giving an impression of speed. For a discussion of Hong Kong action choreography see Bordwell, *Planet Hong Kong*, 238–42 and Reid, "Fighting Without Fighting.

9. Shamon, "Interview: Cynthia Rothrock."

10. It seems Cynthia Rothrock also made the films *Fight to Win* (1987, Leo Fong, U.S.), *Rapid Fire* (1988, no director, Canada), and *Jungle Heat* (1988, George Chung, U.S.), about which there are little information. Only the first is available today and appears to be a completed movie.

11. Quoted from Richard Norton's biography on the Internet Movie Data Base, accessed from http://www.imdb.com/name/nm0636280/bio on September 5, 2005.

12. Yvonne Tasker, *Spectacular Bodies: Gender, Genre and the Action Cinema* (London: Routledge, 1993), 25.

13. My spelling of the martial arts terms is phonetic as my DVD film had no subtitles. I am not familiar with these Asian terms.

14. The press material for *Invasion U.S.A.* (1985) quoted Norris: "Call me a flag-waver. That's what I am. I love this country and I believe in it, and I hope my movies make people proud of the U.S.A." In his autobiography, Norris sums up his "Code of Ethics" as, among other things, "I will continually work at developing love, happiness, and loyalty in my family and acknowledge that no other success can compensate for failure in the home. I will maintain respect for those in authority and demonstrate this respect at all times. I will always remain loyal to my country and obey the laws of the land." Chuck Norris with Joe Hyams, *The Secret of Inner Strength: My Story* (Boston: Little Brown, 1988), 194–5.

15. Pat H. Broeske, "Sly's Match?" *Los Angeles Times*, January 29, 1989, Outtakes.

16. Judith Halberstam, *Female Masculinity*

(Durham, N.C.: Duke University Press, 1998), 180.

17. *Ibid*.

18. See also Gilles Deleuze's study of masochism *Coldness and Cruelty* (1967) in Jean McNeil (trans.), *Masochism: Coldness and Cruelty by Gilles Deleuze, Venus in Furs by Leopold von Sacher-Masoch* (New York: Zone Books, 1994).

19. Anonymous fan, "He's So Good, They Call Him Martial Law! Awesome," February 26, 2005, accessed from http://www.imdb.com/title/tt0104822/#comment on September 20, 2005.

20. Anonymous fan, "Ok Action," February 16, 2000, accessed from http://www.imdb.com/title/tt0105592/#comment on September 20, 2005.

21. Linda Williams, "Film Bodies: Gender, Genre, and Excess," *Film Quarterly* 44, nb 4 (Summer 1991): 2–13, 10. The full quote runs, "These enigmas are located in three areas: the enigma of the origin of sexual desire, an enigma that is 'solved,' so to speak, by the fantasy of seduction [porno]; the enigma of sexual difference, 'solved' by the fantasy of castration [horror]; and finally the enigma of the origin of self, 'solved' by the fantasy of family romance or return to origins [melodrama]," my brackets.

22. Richard Dyer, "Action!" *Sight and Sound*, October 1994, 7–10, 10.

23. In *Passion og acceleration: Maskulinitet og myte i actionfilmen, 1968–2000 (Passion and Acceleration: Masculinity and Myth in the Action Movie, 1968–2000)*, unpublished Ph.D. dissertation from Department of Film and Media Studies, University of Copenhagen, 2001. The dissertation was published as *Med vold og magt: Actionfilmen fra Dirty Harry til The Matrix (Mission Complete: The Action Movie from Dirty Harry to The Matrix*, Copenhagen: Rosinante, 2002).

24. Robert Warshow, "Movie Chronicle: The Westerner," in Gerald Mast, Marshall Cohen, and Leo Braudy (eds.), *Film Theory and Criticism*, (New York: Oxford University Press, 1992), 453–66, 455.

James Cameron's *True Lies* (1994) and Brad Bird's Pixar animation movie *The Incredibles* (2004) are two examples of action comedies that engage the problem of how a secret superhero can sustain an ordinary family life. Both "overcome" the conflict through further (comical) denial, drawing the family into the narcissist fantasy of almightiness.

25. Jeffrey A. Brown, "Gender, Sexuality, and Toughness: The Bad Girls of Action Film and Comic Books," in Sherrie A. Inness (ed.), *Action Chicks: New Images of Tough Women in Popular Culture*, (New York: Palgrave, 2004), 49.

26. *Ibid*., 50.

27. Quoted from the press material for *Above the Law*.

28. As far as I know, the first time Rothrock undresses for the camera is in *Sworn to Justice* (1996).

29. Tasker, *Spectacular Bodies*, 149.

30. Kurt Andersen, "And Now, a Wham-Bam Superstar," *Time*, May 20, 1985.

31. "Poorly Plotted, Poorly Acted, Poorly Paced—Stay Away!" accessed from http://www.imdb.com/title/tt0117803/usercomments on September 25, 2005.

32. "Rothrock Makes the Movie ... And Kurt McKinney Breaks It," accessed from http://www.imdb.com/title/tt0117803/usercomments on September 25, 2005.

33. "The Unofficial Cynthia Rothrock Home Page," accessed from http://www.interlog.com/~tigger/crprint.html on September 25, 2005. The quote is a comment on photos taken for an interview in *Femme Fatales Magazine* 4, no. 1 (Summer 1995).

34. Meisler, "The Biggest Star."

35. Charles Fleming, "That's Why the Lady Is a Champ," *Newsweek*, June 14, 1993.

36. Anonymous fan, "Just For Fans," September 25, 2003, accessed from http://www.imdb.com/title/tt0117803/usercomments on September 25, 2005.

Chapter 7

1. Anonymous fan, "Aliens is the Sci-Fi Genre," December 6, 1998, accessed from http://www.imdb.com/title/tt0090605/usercomments on October 25, 2005. All further comments from the Internet Movie Data Base were accessed from this address on October 25, 2005.

2. Anonymous fan, "Gets Better Every Time I See It," December 8, 2004. Second quote, anonymous fan, "I Knew You'd Come..." February 6, 2003.

3. John Brosnan, *The Primal Scene—a History of Science Fiction Film* (London: Orbit, 1991), 190. Dan O'Bannon who conceived the story of *Alien* was inspired by science fiction films such as *The Thing From Another World* (1951) where an arctic expedition finds a spaceship with a frozen pilot and a flesh-devouring alien, and *It! The Terror From Beyond Space* (1958) about a spaceship that returns to Earth with a monster as blind passenger.

4. Ivor Powell quoted from the 68 minute documentary *The Alien Legacy* (Michael Matessino, 1999) which is in the DVD box-set *Alien Legacy* (1999).

5. *The Alien Legacy* (1999, Michael Matessino).

6. Rhona Berenstein, "Mommie Dearest: *Aliens*, *Rosemary's Baby* and Mothering," *The Journal of Popular Culture* 24, no. 2 (1990): 55.

7. *Ibid.*, 57.

8. *Ibid.*

9. *Ibid.*, 60.

10. Barbara Creed, *The Monstrous-Feminine: Film, Feminism, Psychoanalysis* (London: Routledge, 1993), 18.

11. H.R. Giger quoted from *The Alien Legacy*.

12. Creed, *The Monstrous-Feminine*, 25.

13. See Creed, *The Monstrous-Feminine*, chapter 2 "Horror and the Archaic Mother: *Alien*" and chapter 10 "The Castrating Mother: *Psycho*" for a further discussion of the mother figure in horror.

14. *Ibid.*, 26.

15. *Ibid.*, 27.

16. *Ibid.*, 28.

17. Carol Clover, *Men, Women and Chain Saws: Gender in the Modern Horror Film* (London: BFI, 1992), 39–40.

18. One could argue that the attempt to save the cat Jonesey feminizes Ripley. Even if the cat adds feminine qualities to Ripley—such as being protective and emotional—still, it does not make her fearful or soft.

19. *Ibid.*, 53.

20. *Variety*, January 8, 1986, 22. Number one was *Back to the Future*, number three *Rocky IV*.

21. Richard Schickel, "Help! They're Back!" *Time*, July 28, 1986. Accessed from Time Magazine Archive on November 11, 2005.

22. *Ibid.*

23. Tim Blackmore, "'Is this Going to be Another Bug-Hunt?': S-F Tradition Versus Biology-as-destiny in James Cameron's *Aliens*," *Journal of Popular Culture* 29, no. 4 (1996): 219. Blackmore provides an excellent analysis of images of the Vietnam war in *Aliens*, "Cameron's grunts talk about 'getting short,' (a reference to the end of the 365 day tour), demand 'immediate dust off' (helicopter evacuation to safety)" and the flight vessel was designed to resemble and move like "an Apache AH-64 helicopter." (219).

24. *Ibid.*, 217.

25. Berenstein, "Mommie Dearest," 63.

26. Susan Jeffords, "'The Battle of the Big Mamas': Feminism and the Alienation of Women," *Journal of American Culture* 10, no. 3 (1987): 80.

27. Harvey R. Greenberg, "Fembo: *Aliens*' Intentions," *Journal of Film & Television* 15, no. 4 (Winter 1988): 171.

28. The daughter is also in the novelization of *Aliens* from 1986.

29. Adrienne Rich, *Of Woman Born* (New York: W.W. Norton, 1976), 34, quoted from Berenstein, "Mommie Dearest," 55.

30. Lynda K. Bundtzen, "Monstrous Mothers: Medusa, Grendel, and Now Alien" *Film Quarterly* 40, no. 3 (1987): 16.

31. Jeffords, "Big Mamas," 73.

32. Greenberg, "Fembo," 171.

33. Only a small number of reviewers and critics acknowledged Ripley as a new kind of hero. David Ansen in *Newsweek* (1986) found Ripley "human macho" and "a strong, unsentimental heroine," and Richard Schickel in *Time* (1986) thought the film "gives her something, someone wonderful to fight for" and saw Ripley as "a sign of grace." David Ansen, "Terminating the Aliens," *Newsweek*, July 21, 1986, 64–5, quoted from Jeffords, "Big Mamas," 73. Schickel, "Help! They're Back!"

The only positive critic I have found is Rebecca Bell-Metereau (writing in 1985 and thus referring to Ripley in *Alien*, not *Aliens*) who pointed out Ripley is a different role than what science fiction usually offers women and "a prototype for a new female lead ... because she is not stunning, stunned, or simpering" and welcomed Ripley as "true role reversal" and "a subtle hurrah for the human race, and for womankind at that..." Rebecca Bell-Metereau, *Hollywood Androgyny* (New York: Columbia UIP, 1993), 209, 222.

34. Bundtzen, "Monstrous Mothers," 16.

35. Bell-Metereau, *Hollywood Androgyny*, 212, 210.

36. Berenstein, "Mommie Dearest," 68. Blackmore makes the same point about the heterogeneous pleasures of popular culture.

37. Blackmore, "Bug-Hunt," 222.

38. Germaine Greer, *The Whole Woman* (London: Anchor, 2000), 398.

39. See Fredric Jameson, "Reification and Utopia in Mass Culture," *Social Text* 1 (Winter 1979): 130–148. I have read Wilhelm Dilthey and Hans-Georg Gadamer in Danish translations in Jesper Gulddal and Martin Møller, eds., *Hermeneutik: En antologi om forståelse* (København: Gyldendal, 1999).

40. Judith Halberstam, *Female Masculinity* (Durham, N.C.: Duke University Press, 1998), 205.

41. Halberstam repeats this analysis of Vasquez twice, twice mis-remembering her death. *Ibid.*, 181, 205.

42. Greenberg, "Fembo," 170.

43. *Ibid.*, 171.

44. The same year *Alien* launched Ripley, David Cronenberg's Canadian horror movie *The Brood* portrayed a mother giving birth to mutant killer children through an external uterus she had grown from the energy of her rage.

45. Clover, *Men, Women and Chain Saws*, 54.

46. Anonymous fan, "Outstanding blend of sci-fi, action, and humor," February 23, 2000.

47. Anonymous fan, "'I Knew You'd Come...'" February 6, 2003.

48. Anonymous fan, "Quite possibly, the greatest film ever..." September 12, 2002.

49. Anonymous fan, "Excellent Film! Unmissable!" September 24, 2005.

50. "'I Knew You'd Come..." February 6, 2003.

51. Greenberg, "Fembo," 170, 171.

52. Such discussions belong to science fiction proper and are marginal in femme fatale cinema whose female bodies do not question the *biological nature* of that body, but what it means to *live* and *behave* as a woman in patriarchal society. That is, where science fiction questions the essence of human nature and within this area the essence of respectively male and female *bodies* and *identities*, femme fatale cinema deals with the socially constructed *gender roles*.

53. With 667 comments *Aliens* has the most comments, second is *Alien* with 605, third *Alien: Resurrection* with 457, and last is *Alien3* with 450 comments, which is still a very high number. Of the approximately forty films I checked for comments on the Internet Movie Data Base, 450 comments place *Alien3* as number twelve on the list of the most commented on femme fatale movies.

54. A longer "Special 'Assembly Cut' Version" was issued in 2003, 145 minutes long. This is not a director's cut as Fincher wanted nothing to do with the film in neither the old nor the new cut, but most of the inserted material came from his originally rejected cut.

55. For an analysis of *Alien3* and AIDS see Amy Taubin, "The 'Alien' Trilogy: From Feminism to Aids," in Pam Cook and Philip Dodd (eds.) *Women and Film: A Sight and Sound Reader* (London: Scarlet Press, 1993): 93–100. The threat of anal rape is also a threat in the rape assault on Ripley and a subtext in the film's dialogue—"nobody ever gave me nothing. So I say fuck it," and "what makes you think they're gonna care about you here at the ass-end of the universe?"

56. Taubin, "The 'Alien' Trilogy," 100.

57. The eight million dollar budget for *Alien* is director Ridley Scott's number in the documentary *The Alien Legacy*. The figures for the other three films is from the Internet Movie Data Base. Figures differ significantly in various sources; *Alien* is estimated to cost between eight and eleven million dollars, *Aliens* between fifteen and eighteen-and-a-half, *Alien3* between thirty-five and fifty, and *Alien: Resurrection* between seventy and eighty million dollars.

58. Anne Balsamo, *Technologies of the Gendered Body: Reading Cyborg Women* (Durham, N.C.: Duke University Press, 1997), 5.

59. *Ibid.*, 9.

60. *Ibid.*, 23.

61. Anonymous fan, "You have got to be kid-

ding me," September 11, 1998. Accessed from http://www.imdb.com/title/tt0118583/user comments?filter=chrono;start=450 on October 25, 2005.

62. Dion Farquhar, "(M)other Discourses," in Gill Kirkup, Linda Janes, Kath Woodward, and Fiona Hovenden (eds.), *The Gendered Cyborg: A Reader* (London: Routledge, 2000), 216.

63. The film *The Handmaid's Tale* (1990), based on the novel of the same name by Margaret Atwood from 1986, is one example of involuntary surrogate mothers. Another example is *The Island* (2005) where clones are "grown" to supply their owners with genetic material (limbs, organs, children).

64. Farquhar, "(M)other Discourses," 211.

65. It could be argued that the pirates, male as well as the one female, are "good." However, they make a living from crime and do not ask questions, which is "bad." The only pirates to survive are the crippled Vriess and the stupid Johner which, symbolically speaking, are two castrated examples of masculinity.

66. *Ibid.*, 213, 216.

Chapter 8

1. Ovid, *Metamorphosis* book 10, section Pygmalion, in Karl K. Hulley and Stanley T. Vandersall (eds.), *Ovid's Metamorphosis: Englished, Mythologized, and Represented in Figures by George Sandys* (Lincoln: University of Nebraska Press, 1970), 460.

2. Eva Jørholt, "The Big Red," *Information*, January 13, 1995.

3. Hulley and Vandersall, *Ovid's Metamorphosis*, 461.

4. Jeffrey A. Brown, "Gender and the Action Heroine: Hardbodies and the *Point of No Return*," *Cinema Journal* 35, no. 3 (Spring 1996): 57, 52.

5. *Ibid.*, 54.

6. *Ibid.*, 56.

7. *Ibid.*, 60, 61.

8. *Ibid.*

9. *Ibid.*, 63. Brown uses *Nikita* (1990) and *Point of No Return* (1993) interchangeably, "[a]s a remake *Point of No Return* was unusually faithful to the original, so in effect any reference to one film is a reference to both," 63. The remake is loyal but different in several aspects: Maggie never cross-dresses as a man, she kills her last victim, she fights with the "Cleaner" who attempts to kill instead of rescue her as in *Nikita*, and the age difference between her fiancé and agent Bob is accentuated.

10. *Ibid.*, 54.

11. Maggie escapes through a laundry chute in the kitchen.

12. Joan Riviere, "Womanliness as a Mas-

querade," in Victor Burgin, James Donald, and Cora Kaplan (eds.), *Formations of Fantasy* (London: Methuen, 1986), 37.

13. *Ibid.*, 38.

14. *Ibid.*, 42.

15. Brown, "Action Heroine," 56, 69.

16. Judith Butler, *Gender Trouble: Feminism and the Subversion of Identity* (New York: Routledge, 1999), 179.

17. *Ibid.*, 173.

18. *Ibid.*, 180.

19. Brown, "Action Heroine," 55, 56.

20. Laura Ng, "'The Most Powerful Weapon You Have': Warriors and Gender in *La Femme Nikita*," in Frances Early and Kathleen Kennedy (eds.), *Athena's Daughters: Television's New Women Warriors*, (Syracuse, N.Y.: Syracuse University Press, 2003), 106.

21. *Ibid.*, 114.

22. Brown, "Action Heroine," 56.

23. *Ibid.*, 64.

24. *Ibid.*

25. Quoted in Brown, 64.

26. Jacinda Read, *The New Avengers: Feminism, Femininity and the Rape-Revenge Cycle* (Manchester: Manchester University Press, 2000), 187.

27. *Ibid.*, 192.

28. Brown, "Action Heroine," 54, 67.

29. *Ibid.*

30. Butler, *Gender Trouble*, 144.

31. Yvonne Tasker, *Working Girls: Gender and Sexuality in Popular Cinema* (London: Routledge, 2000), 59.

32. Butler, *Gender Trouble*, xiv.

33. Tasker, *Working Girls*, 27.

34. *Ibid.*

35. Riviere, "Womanliness as Masquerade," 43.

36. Nikita and Maggie are both twenty-three when they leave the agency. In *Nikita* the actress Anne Parillaud (Nikita) is thirty, actor Tchéky Karyo (Bob) is thirty-seven, and Jean-Hugues Anglade (Marco) is thirty-five. In *Point of No Return* the age difference was underlined by having twenty-nine-year-old actress Bridget Fonda (Maggie) play opposite the forty-three-year-old Gabriel Byrne (Bob), which made the actual age difference between the two fourteen years. Dermot Mulroney (J.P.) was thirty.

37. Tasker, *Working Girls*, 28.

38. The switch between selves is complex in *The Long Kiss Goodbye*. The change of the "ordinary" Samantha into "extraordinary" Charly is visually rendered as an initial transformation (her change in personality is followed by a change in appearance). However, "Samantha" is not a real self, but the cover identity Charly was using at the time she got amnesia. Throughout the plot the "Samantha" and "Charly" characters alternate until in the end a third self is de-

veloped: A woman with feminine clothes who adeptly throws her knife into a trunk. This woman is independent (she has taken the money) but remains with the family and in the home.

Chapter 9

1. Anonymous fan comment on *Amazons and Gladiators* (2001), "Conflicted," July 20, 2003, accessed from http://www.imdb.com/title/tt0275913/usercomments?start=0 on January 30, 2006. From the content and the fan's name—ada.p—I guess it is a woman. An anonymous fan commenting on *Barbarian Queen II: The Empress Strikes Back* thus calls himself (I guess it is a he) Hugh G. Rection, "Half-nekkid amazon warriors follow their busty queen," August 13, 2005, accessed from http://www.imdb.com/title/tt0103768/#comment on January 28, 2006.

2. Anonymous fan comment on *Barbarian Queen* (1985), "Memorable," August 26, 2002, accessed from http://www.imdb.com/title/tt0088771/usercomments. Later comments on this film are from the same webpage.

3. There may of course be pure Amazons in popular cinema that I do not know of. The closest is Sabrina in *Amazons and Gladiators* who discovers that her mother was an Amazon before marrying her father. The pure Amazon may be too intimidating and too predictable to be of interest. Instead, her psychological and sexual content is transferred to the postmodern female hero, the negotiated Amazon, who is part of patriarchy.

4. William Blake Tyrrell, *Amazons: A Study in Athenian Mythmaking* (Baltimore, Md.: The Johns Hopkins University Press, 1984), 17.

5. Pierre Grimal, *The Dictionary of Classical Mythology* (Oxford: Blackwell Reference, 1986), 36. However, Marina Warner suggests a possible different interpretation of the word Amazon as meaning instead "many-breasted": "...no Amazon in a Greek vase painting or sculpture of classical times is mutilated in this way ... the word may mean 'many-breasted,' as indeed was the Amazon's special goddess Diana of the Ephesians." Marina Warner, *Joan of Arc: The Image of Female Heroism* (New York: Alfred A. Knopf, 1981), 215.

6. The raped Amazon is first nameless but in later versions becomes Hippolyte (the Amazon queen), Antiope (the queen's sister), Melanippe, or Glauce. Tyrrell, *Amazons*, 5. To be precise, the Amazons attack twice. The first attack is in response to the rape and abduction. Then a treaty is agreed on which has Theseus marry the abducted Amazon. When he deserts her for a Greek wife, she returns to his wedding feast

and attacks with the Amazons. The avenging Amazon is killed by Theseus and the Amazon race is annihilated.

7. Tyrrell, *Amazons*, 45.
8. *Ibid.*, 65.
9. *Ibid.*, 31.
10. *Ibid.*, xv, xvi.
11. *Ibid.*
12. By some accounts the Amazons met at night in the hills with men from a neighbor nation, so that they would not be able to recognize the father if they met him in daylight. The point was to have children without fathers.
13. The Amazon Dawn thus raped Tithonus, Cephalus, and Orion. *Ibid.*, 80.
14. *Ibid.*, 52–53.
15. *Ibid.*, 78.
16. *Ibid.*, 81.
17. *Ibid.*, 18.
18. *Ibid.*, 63.
19. Jane Gaines, "Costume and Narrative: How Dress Tells the Woman's Story" in Jane Gaines and Charlotte Herzog (eds.), *Fabrications: Costume and the Female Body*, (London: Routledge, 1990), 188. I must thank Jeffrey A. Brown's article "Gender and the Action Heroine: Hardbodies and the *Point of No Return*" for bringing Gaines work to my attention.
20. See, for instance, the fantastic swimsuit costume on the poster of *Love Slaves of the Amazons* (1957).
21. In this respect the Amazon costume may not be different from costumes in other film genres. Jane Gaines points to the illusion of the costume as something to be worn, "One of the most successful fictions woven by Hollywood publicity is that costumes created by the studio departments were worn. Screen costumes, on the contrary, were not made to be worn, they were made to be photographed. These improbable clothes were often too heavy for actresses to wear without becoming exhausted or were too tight for them to sit in; hence they leaned against reclining stands called 'costume boards' between takes and sometimes were even carried to their places on the set." Gaines, "Costume and Narrative," 20.
22. Scott Bukatman, "X-bodies (the torment of the mutant superhero)," in Rodney Sappington and Tyler Stallings (eds.), *Uncontrollable Bodies: Testimonies of Identity and Culture*, (Seattle: BayPress, 1994), 112. Bukatman places superheroes' aesthetics and costumes in the psychological context of adolescence torn between narcissistic "aggrandizement and anxiety, mastery and trauma." Bukatman, 94.
23. Thaïs E. Morgan, "A Whip of One's Own: Dominatrix Pornography and the Construction of a Post-Modern (Female) Subjectivity," *The American Journal of Semiotics* 6, no. 4 (1989): 114.

24. *Ibid.* Morgan is drawing on Eco's semiotic theory of code and hypercode and Goffman's cognitive theory of frames.

25. *Ibid.*, 116.

26. *Ibid.*, 119, 131.

27. Anonymous fan comment on *Barbarian Queen*, "For Your Eyes Only," October 28, 2001.

28. Anonymous fan comment from Italy on *Barbarian Queen*, "Better than the First."

29. Anonymous fan comment on *Red Sonja*, "Conditions," April 25, 2002, accessed from http://www.imdb.com/title/tt0089893/user comments?count=54&filter=best;start=0 on January 30, 2006.

30. Sherrie A. Inness (ed.), *Tough Girls: Women Warriors and Wonder Women in Popular Culture* (Philadelphia: University of Philadelphia Press, 1999), 62–63.

31. See discussion of Lola's costume in Kim Walden, "*Run, Lara, Run!* The Impact of Computer Games on Cinema's Action Heroine," in Rikke Schubart and Anne Gjelsvik (eds.), *Femme Fatalities: Representations of Strong Women in the Media* (Göteborg: Nordicom, 2004), 84.

32. Anonymous fan comment on *Barbarian Queen*, "Best Reason to See This Movie: Lana Clarkson on the Rack," October 30, 1998.

33. "William Moulton Marston," in *Wikipedia, the Free Encyclopedia*, accessed from http://wikipedia.org/wiki/William_Moulton_Marston on February 16, 2006. Later Marston quotes are from the same source.

34. *Catwoman* was the first female superhero, invented in 1940 as Batman's opponent. Then came *Wonder Woman*, also in 1940, *Batwoman* followed in 1956, *Supergirl* in 1958, *Invisible Girl* from the team of The Fantastic Four in 1961, *Marvel Girl* from The X-Men in 1963, *Red Sonja* crossed from Ron E. Howard's Conan universe (where she was born in 1934) into the comics in the early seventies, *She-Hulk* was born in 1980, and during the eighties the X-Men had *Rogue*, *Psylocke* and *Shadowcat*, while *Spider-Girl*, *Hawkgirl*, and *Witchblade* saw daylight in the nineties—along with *Mantra*, *Lady Rawhide*, *Shi*, *Vampirella*, and *Lady Death* to name but a few. For a study of Wonder Woman see Lillian S. Robinson, *Wonder Women: Feminisms and Superheroes* (New York: Routledge, 2004).

35. Helen Damico, *Beowulf's Wealhtheow and the Valkyrie Tradition* (Madison: The University of Wisconsin Press, 1984), 41.

36. *Ibid.*, 42.

37. Quoted from Joanne Morreale, "*Xena: Warrior Princess* as Feminist Camp," *Journal of Popular Culture* 32, no. 2 (September 1998): 79.

38. Sharon Delaney, "The Genesis of *Xena*," *Xena: Warrior Princess The Official Magazine*, no. 1, 8–11, 9.

39. Damico, *The Valkyrie Tradition*, 49.

40. Helen Caudill points out in "Tall, Dark, and Dangerous: Xena, the Quest, and the Wielding of Sexual Violence in *Xena* On-Line Fan Fiction" that the quest was always female as well as male and gives the myths of Isis/Osiris and Ishtar/Tammuz as examples. Frances Early and Kathleen Kennedy (eds.), *Athena's Daughters: Television's New Women Warriors* (Syracuse, N.Y.: Syracuse University Press, 2003), 27–40.

41. Elyce Rae Helford, "Feminism, Queer Studies, and the Sexual Politics of *Xena: Warrior Princess*," in Elyce Rae Helford (ed.), *Fantasy Girls: Gender in the New Universe of Science Fiction and Fantasy Television* (Lanham: Rowman and Littlefield, 2000), 135.

42. Gabrielle and Xena are both Caucasian: Xena has blue eyes and white skin and, in fact, actress Lucy Lawless was so white that she had to sunbathe regularly to keep her skin tanned.

43. Helford, "Sexual Politics," 149.

44. *Ibid.*, 151.

45. *Ibid.*, 139.

46. *Ibid.*, 144.

47. At the end of "The Reckoning" Xena says she "owes" Gabrielle. "I owe you too," Gabrielle replies and hits Xena. "What was that?" "Payback for hitting me!" This is done in a comic tone while Gabrielle's earlier comment on Xena's violence was serious and indicated Gabrielle's reluctant acceptance of an Evil Xena.

48. Helford, "Sexual Politics," 146.

49. Actually, in the saga Sigurd first awakes a sleeping Brynhilde who swears to marry him. Later, in a ring of fire, Sigurd, magically transformed into the shape of Gunnar, leaps through the fire on Gunnar's horse. Brynhilde does not recognize the transformed Sigurd and marries Gunnar in the belief he was the man without fear. The tragic confusion of Gunnar/Sigurd eventually results in the murder of Sigurd and Brynhilde's suicide.

50. Helford, "Sexual Politics," 138.

51. *Ibid.*, 136.

52. *Ibid.*, 137.

53. Quoted from Helford, 144.

54. Quoted from Morreale, "Feminist Camp," 85.

55. Walter Alesci, "*Xena: Warrior Princess* Out of the Closet? A Melodramatic Reading of the Show by Latin American and Spanish Lesbian and Gay Fans," in Schubart and Gjelsvik (eds.), *Femme Fatalities*, 206.

56. Morreale, "Feminist Camp," 80.

57. Caudill, "Dark and Dangerous," 39.

58. Morgan, "Whip," 113.

59. Quoted in Alesci, "Out of the Closet?" 212.

60. Anonymous fan quoted in Helford, "Sexual Politics," 143.

61. Rogers Cadenhead, "Bad Girls: Who says female characters don't sell? Don't tell that to these women—or their creators," *Wizard*, no. 38, 46.

Chapter 10

1. Richard Rayner, "The Warrior Besieged," *New York Times*, June 22, 1997, Magazine Desk. Accessed from http://www.nytimes.com/ on March 1, 2004.

2. With the exception of Goldie Hawn in the comedy *Private Benjamin* (1980), the only professional (i.e., trained) female combat soldiers I have found in American war films were pilots. The distance between the aviatrix and the enemy keeps her "out of harms way" whereas a female combat soldier on the battlefield is a different thing. An early title such as *They Flew Alone* (1942) has a female pilot and *She Goes to War* (1929) has a woman cross-dressing as a soldier. The more well-known *So Proudly We Hail* (1943) and *Cry Havoc* (1943) are about army nurses, not soldiers. For literature on women and war movies see, for instance, Thomas Doherty, *Projections of War: Hollywood, American Culture, and World War II*, chapter 7 "Women Without Men," (New York: Columbia University Press, 1993), 149–179; and Michael T. Isenberg, *War On Film: The American Cinema and World War I, 1914–1941*, chapter 13 "War and Women" (East Brunswick, N.J.: Farleigh Dickinson University Press, 1981), 189–203.

3. See Kathryn Kane, "The World War II Combat Film," in Wes D. Gehring (ed.), *Handbook of American Film Genres* (Westport, Conn.: Greenwood Press, 1988), 85–102, for a discussion of war movies as a genre. For the purpose of analyzing women in war movies, I use an essentialist and semiotic description of the war movie. There exist other definitions, some of which include historical films; others include science fiction films. The war movie has several subgenres: combat movies (*Hamburger Hill*), prison camp movies (*The Bridge on the River Kwai*), boot camp movies (*Heartbreak Ridge*), special mission war movies (*Black Hawk Down*). Also, each war seems to generate its own subgenre: Vietnam war films, World War II combat films, et cetera. The anti-war film is a subgenre cutting across the war movie.

4. The two themes of the war narrative are from Kane's seminal "The World War II Combat Film," which treats only World War II combat movies.

5. *Ibid.*, 93.

6. Amy Turbin, "Dicks and Jane," *Village Voice*, August 26, 1997.

7. Klaus Theweleit, *Male Fantasies*, 2 vols.

(Minneapolis: University of Minnesota Press, 1996), vol. 2, 162.

8. *Ibid.*

9. Tasker, *Working Girls*, 47 (see Introduction, n. 68).

10. And the "real" person is, ironically, in director Ridley Scott's take on Jordan, a "bitch" whose determination relates her to the famous "bitch" Ripley in *Alien 3*, a film taglined "The bitch is back." Ripley/actress Sigourney Weaver also shaved her head to look like the men on the planet.

11. In *Virtuous War* James Der Derian writes, "The sanitization of violence that began with the Gulf War has come to overpower the mortification of the body that marks communal wars in Nagorno-Karabakh, Somalia, Bosnia, Rwanda, and elsewhere." James Der Derian, *Virtuous War: Mapping the Military-Industrial-Media-Entertainment Network* (Boulder, Colo.: Westview Press, 2001), xvi. A *Soldier's Sweetheart*, however, does present us with mutilated male bodies. This made-for-cable movie merits a much closer analysis than I provide here, as it inverts many Hollywood conventions in its complex critique of gender and war.

12. Kane, "World War II," 89.

13. Barbara Ehrenreich, foreword to *Male Fantasies*, Theweleit, ix–xix, xiii.

14. The exact same words actress Geena Davis says as Charly in *The Long Kiss Goodnight* in 1996.

15. See Susan E. Linville, "'The *Mother* of All Battles': *Courage Under Fire* and the Gender-Integrated Military," *Cinema Journal* 39, no. 2 (Winter 2000) for a highly interesting discussion of real-life rapes in the U.S. military and representations of rape in *G.I. Jane* and, symbolically, in *Courage Under Fire*. Linville quotes Lynda Boose on rapes during the first Gulf War, "...probably more American women recruits were concurrently being raped on military bases by their fellow soldiers than Kuwaiti women had been by the Iraqi military. In fact, the instance of reported rape and sexual assault at U.S. military installations escalated so dramatically in the months leading up to the war that the Pentagon and the chairman of the Senate Armed Services Committee were embarrassed into ordering investigations," 117. Rape was also an issue in the Jessica Lynch incident, where Pentagon spokesmen accused Iraqi soldiers of raping Lynch, allegations which were refuted by the Iraqi doctors treating her in the hospital. Her clothes, the doctors said, were found bloodied and in ruins as claimed by U.S. military, since the doctors removed them from her unconscious body before operating. See J. Kampfner, "The Truth About Jessica," *The Guardian*, May 15, 2003; D. Priest, B. William and S. Schmidt,

"A Broken Body, a Broken Story, Pieced Together," *Washington Post*, June 17, 2003; and R. Russell, "Iraqi Doctors Deny Jessica Lynch Raped," November 11, 2003; Rikke Schubart, "Gennemhullede myter: Jessica Lynch og den amerikanske 'tilfangetagelses-fortælling,'" *MedieKultur* no. 38 (April 2005): 15–23.

16. Peter Rainer, "Naval Gazing," *New Times L.A.*, August 21, 1997.

17. Terry Diggs, "*G.I. Jane* Is Such a Drag," *The Recorder*, Wednesday October 1, 1997.

18. Taubin, "Dicks and Jane."

19. Halberstam, *Female Masculinity*, 21 (see Introduction, n. 6).

20. The percentage numbers are from Linville, "All Battles," 117.

21. George L. Mosse, *Nationalism and Sexuality: Respectability and Abnormal Sexuality in Modern Europe* (New York: Howard Fertig, 1985), 18.

22. *Ibid.*, 97.

23. *Ibid.*, 98. Mosse notes that the aggressive Marianne in Eugène Delacroix' painting *Liberty Leading the People at the Barricades* (1830) was an exception and as "Marianne became established as a national symbol, the nation clipped her revolutionary wings" (91). However, it is worth noting that she is not a soldier and does not bear weapons. In Delacroix' painting she is half-naked and carries a tattered flag, looking like a cross between a prostitute and a rape victim.

24. See for instance J. Holsøe, "U.S.A. ind i Saddams paladser" [U.S.A. Goes Into Saddam's Palaces], *Politiken*, April 8, 2003.

25. Creveld quoted in Richard Raynar, "The Warrior Besieged," *New York Times*, June 22, 1997, Magazine Desk, accessed from http://www.nytimes.com/ on March 18, 2004

26. See note 15.

27. In Denmark all television stations and every major newspaper covered the Jessica Lynch story. See P. Høi, "Savnet" [Missing], Magasinet, *Berlingske Tidende*, March 30, 2003.

28. "Captivity narratives (both historical and fictional) were among the most popular and prevalent form of American adventure story for most of the eighteenth century. The hero of the captivity narrative is a White woman (or minister) captured by Indians during a 'savage war.' The captive symbolizes the values of Christianity and civilization that are imperiled in the wilderness war. Her captivity is figuratively a descent into Hell and a spiritual darkness which is akin to 'madness.' By resisting the physical threats and spiritual temptations of the Indians, the captive vindicates both her own moral character and the power of the values she symbolizes. But the scenario of historical action developed by the captivity narrative is a passive one that emphasizes the weakness of colonial power and ends not with a victorious conquest but with a grateful and somewhat chastened return home." Richard Slotkin, *Gunfighter Nation: The Myth of the Frontier in Twentieth-Century America* (New York: University of Oklahoma Press, 2002): 14–15.

29. See note 15. See also Rick Bragg, *I Am a Soldier, Too: The Jessica Lynch Story* (New York: Alfred A. Knopf, 2003) and N. Gibbs, "The Private Jessica Lynch," *Time Magazine*, November 17, 2003.

30. The Black Diamond story by Rory Carroll was printed in *Politiken*, "Oberst med lange negle" [Colonel With Long Nails] August 31, 2003. It was translated from English where it had appeared in *The Guardian*. The stories of Lynch and Black Diamond both include rapes, Lynch as allegedly raped, Black Diamond as a rape victim and former child-slave, now a soldier with a daughter left in a refugee camp.

31. An article in *Glamour* about a female reporter, a policewoman, and a female doctor in Iraq is an example of how women in war are featured in a non-threatening way as helping, nursing, keeping up order and holding off chaos. Cordelia Kretzschmar, "Women in the Line of Fire," *Glamour*, July 2003, 66–74. The infamous incident of female soldiers Lynndie England and Sabrina Harman, who participated in the torture at the Abu Ghraib prison in Iraq and were on the torture photographs taken by the soldiers as trophies, illustrates how women become unheimlich when they are too close to aggressive behavior. The media saw the participation of women in the torture as incomprehensible, as if it was comprehensible (and, of course, wrong) that men would behave in such a way.

32. Tasker, "Soldier's Stories," 209, 215 (see Introduction, n. 2).

33. Linville, "All Battles," 108.

34. When the combative female soldier is not a protagonist or is paired with a male lead—as in John McTiernan's *Basic* (2003)—ambivalence disappears. *Basic* has room for a combative female elite soldier in a smaller role as well as the female military police investigator Osborne (played by Connie Nielsen) as protagonist opposite Hardy (played by John Travolta).

Chapter 11

1. Eric Layton, "The Messenger: The Story of Joan of Arc," *Entertainment Today*, November 12, 1999; Walter Addiego, "Blame The Messenger," *San Francisco Examiner*, November 12, 1999.

2. Annlee Ellingson, "The Messenger: The Story of Joan of Arc," *Boxoffice*, accessed from http://www.boxoffice.com/scripts/fiw.dll?GetReview&where.... on May 20, 2003.

3. Ginette Vincendeau, "Joan of Arc/ Jeanne d'Arc," *Sight and Sound*, April 2000, accessed from http://www.bfi.org.uk/sightand sound/reviews on May 20, 2003.

4. However, what some consider "just" entertainment may by others be considered sick and dangerous films that should be banned, as was the case with the *Ilsa* films discussed in chapter two.

5. "But trust me, if my mom had been a figure skater, I'd be the best figure skater in the world now," Milla Jovovich told *Playboy* in 2002 (answer to question eighteen). Robert Crane, "Milla Jovovich—20Q," *Playboy*, May 2002, accessed from http://www.millaj.com/art/play boy0502.shtml on September 16, 2002.

6. Giselle Benator, "Another Fairy Tale, a New Star," *L.A. Herald Examiner*, June 20, 1988.

7. Crane, "Milla Jovovich—20Q." Next quote is also from Crane.

8. Steve Beale, "Wonder Woman," *Arena*, July 2002, accessed from http://www.millaj. com/art/arena0702.shtml on September 16, 2002. Alienness is also underlined in Christopher Hemblade, "Alien Apparent," *Empire*, issue 97 (July 1997): 56–57.

9. Beale, "Wonder Woman."

10. Christopher Bagley, "Major Milla," *W*, May 1998, 230–32, 232.

11. Kirk Honeycutt, "Directors in Fight Over Joan of Arc," *Hollywood Reporter*, June 9, 1998.

12. Christian Monggaard Christensen, "The Million Dollar Hotel," *Information*, August 18, 2000, Section 1, page 8. A review of the film's soundtrack pointed out one of her two songs, "The actress Milla Jovovich, who plays the young Eloise in the movie, uses her drawling, sensual voice to do a beautiful and melancholic interpretation of Lou Reed's 'Satellite of Love.' It can hardly be done more beautiful or intense" (this and all other quotations from Danish reviews are my translation). Lars Rix, Review of soundtrack "The Million Dollar Hotel," *Aktuelt*, August 18, 2000, Section 1, page 17.

13. Johs. H. Christensen, "Visdom og visuel kraft" [Wisdom and Visual Power], *Morgenavisen Jyllands-Posten*, August 1, 1997.

14. Kim Williamson, "The Fifth Element," *Boxoffice Magazine*, accessed from http://www. boxoffice.com on May 20, 2003.

15. Chris Chang, "Escape From New York," *Film Comment* 33, no. 4 (July/August 1997): 58.

16. Barbara Shulgasser, "Chaos Theory," *San Francisco Examiner*, accessed from www.sf.gate. com/cgi-bin/article.cgi?f=/e/a/1997/05/09/ WEEKEND8772.dtl on May 20, 2003.

17. Roger Ebert, "The Fifth Element," *The Sunday Times*, accessed from www.suntimes. com/ebert/ebert_reviews/1997/05/050903. html on May 20, 2003.

18. Reviews in, for instance, *Los Angeles Times*, May 9, 1997, and the big and national Danish newspapers *Ekstra Bladet* August 1, 1997; *Politiken*, August 1, 1997; and *Morgenavisen Jyllands-Posten*, August 1, 1997, do not comment on Milla Jovovich's performance.

19. This and the former "neurosis" quotation are from the film's press material, 14.

20. Addiego, "Blame The Messenger."

21. "It all started with a picture of me that Luc and I were looking at," says Jovovich. "It's one of my favorite pictures. It's sepia-toned and very crazy. The hair is really wild, and the make-up is very smoky, very strange. And I was looking at it, and I said to Luc, 'This is Joan. This is her.' That picture really made us want to make the movie." Page 7 in the 25 page long press material for *The Messenger: The Story of Joan of Arc*.

22. Ellingson, "The Messenger."

23. Vincendeau, "Joan of Arc."

24. Jonna Gade, "En fotomodel som martyr" [A Martyr Model], *Ekstra Bladet*, January 28, 2000.

25. Eva Jørholt, "Ny film: På herrens slagmark" [New Film: Abandoned on the Battlefield], *Information*, January 28, 1997.

26. Niels Frid-Nielsen, "Rustningen holder" [The armor is still strong], *Aktuelt*, January 28, 2000.

27. The character in the *Resident Evil* computer game is called Claire, not Alice. The name Alice is director Paul W.S. Anderson's homage to *Alice in Wonderland* as is also the name The Red Queen for the Hive's computer.

28. A script written by director George A. Romero was rejected as too visceral by Constantin Films, even if his *Living Dead* trilogy was the inspiration for the *Resident Evil* games. It would be interesting, however, to see how Romero would have imagined the female hero. Thus, Barbara in the remake *Night of the Living Dead* (Tom Savini, 1990) is a female hero of the nineties who survives, in contrast to the passive and panicked Barbara in the original *Night of the Living Dead* (George A. Romero, 1968).

29. The first quotation is Stephen Holden, "They May Be High-Tech, But They're Still the Undead," *New York Times*, March 15, 2002, the second quotation is Jan Stuart, "Resident Evil's Gore Is Guilty Fun," *Newsday*, March 15, 2002. Other examples of reviews that ignore Milla Jovovich are the *San Francisco Chronicle*, March 15, 2002, which only mentions Rodriguez; review in *The Examiner*, March 15, 2002, which mentions Milla in six words; and Roger Ebert's mere mention of her name in *The Sunday Times*, March 15, 2002.

30. Marina Warner describes the test of Joan's virginity in her excellent study *Joan of*

Arc: The Image of Female Heroism (New York: Alfred A. Knopf, 1981), 16. All historical information about Joan is either from Arthur James Evesham (ed.), Joan of Arc: The Image of Female Heroism or The Trial of Joan of Arc (Guernsey: Arthur James, 1996). This latter publication is a transcript of the trial of Jeanne with an introduction by Marina Warner.

31. The three quotes are from Warner, Joan of Arc, 148.

32. Ibid., 156, 157.

33. In the transcript from the trial Joan said that the first time she heard her voice, she vowed her virginity as long as it should be pleasing to God. She was then thirteen years of age or thereabouts. Evesham, Trial of Joan, 96.

34. Freud must have been aware that this was pure speculation since he continues, "I do not think there is any harm in employing such speculations, so long as one avoids setting too much value on them." Sigmund Freud, "The Taboo of Virginity" (1918) in James Strachey (trans.), The Standard Edition of The Complete Psychological Works of Sigmund Freud vol. 11, (London: The Hogarth Press, 1980), 205.

35. Ibid, 208.

36. Evesham, Trial of Joan, 28.

37. Ibid., 143.

38. Ibid., 27.

39. In his Transgender Warriors: Making History from Joan of Arc to Dennis Rodman (Boston: Beacon Press, 1996) Leslie Feinberg mentions several historical cross-dressers and androgynous virgins. In Albania in the early twentieth century, a virgin was recognized as a man and could carry weapons and work with the men if she swore in front of twelve witnesses that she would never marry. Another example is Catalina de Erauso who in the early seventeenth century cross-dressed as a conquistador, slaughtered many natives and received the Pope's blessing to continue cross-dressing. Yet another example is Liberté (Angélique Brulon), a decorated officer who served in Napoleon's army from 1792 to 1799 and during the French Republique Liberté replaced Joan of Arc as a female national hero.

40. Sigmund Freud, "Hysterical Phantasies and their Relation to Bisexuality" (1908), Standard Edition, vol. 9, 163.

41. Rob Nelson, "Ultraviolet," The Village Voice, March 7, 2006, accessed from http://www.villagevoice.com/film/0610,nelson,72461,20.html on May 18, 2006.

Chapter 12

1. Brent Simon, "Raider of the Lost Hearts," Entertainment Today, June 15–21, 2001.

2. Sean M. Smith, "Threesome," Newsweek, June 23, 2003, 62.

3. Rolling Stone, "Quentin's Kung-Fu Grip," October 30, 2003, 43.

4. Sean Macaulay, "Firsts Amon Equines" (review of Lara Croft Tomb Raider: The Cradle of Life), The Times, July 28, 2003.

5. See also Marc O'Day's article "Beauty in Motion: Gender, Spectacle and Action Babe Cinema" for a discussion of the same films in Yvonne Tasker (ed.), Action and Adventure Cinema (London: Routledge, 2004), 201–218.

6. Cosmo Landesman, "Out on a Limb" (review of Charlie's Angels: Full Throttle), The Sunday Times, July 6, 2003.

7. Kenneth Turan, "The Real Powerpuff Girls," Los Angeles Times, November 3, 2000.

8. Todd McCarthy, "Sassy, Snappy 'Angels': A Devil of a Good Time," Variety (W), October 30, November 5, 2000.

9. Joe Morgenstern, "Who Needs a Plot? 'Angels' Has Eye Candy to Spare—And Infectious Self-Delight," Wall Street Journal, June 27, 2003.

10. "Welcome to Angel World," documentary on the DVD with the director McG, the art director, production designer, and property master on Charlie's Angels.

11. See Umberto Eco, "Casablanca, or The Cliches Are Having a Ball" in Travels in Hyperreality: Essays (London: Pan Books, 1987). T.J. Hooker (1982–86) is a television series that has not yet been turned into a movie.

12. Quoted from Hsiung-Ping Chiao, "His Influence on the Evolution of the Kung Fu Genre," Journal of Popular Film and Television 1, no. ix (Spring 1981): 30.

13. The strategy may have been lethal; Lee died at only thirty-two years old, some say of exhaustion and over-exercising, the coroner's report concluded he died from an allergic reaction to headache medicine.

14. For an analysis of Lara Croft see, for instance, Maja Mikula, "Lara Croft: Between a Feminist Icon and Male Fantasy," and Kim Walden, "Run, Lara, Run: The Impact of Computer Games on Cinema's Action Heroine," both in Rikke Schubart and Anne Gjelsvik (eds.), Femme Fatalities: Representations of Strong Women in the Media (Göteborg: Nordicom, 2004), 57–70 and 71–88, or Claudia Herbst, "Lara's Lethal and Loaded Mission: Transposing Reproduction and Destruction," in Sherrie A. Inness (ed.), Action Chicks: New Images of Tough Women in Popular Culture (New York: Palgrave MacMillan, 2004). See also "All the Guys Like to Play With Her," The Sunday Times, June 24, 2001.

15. Charles Herold, "Making the Leap From a Game To the Movies," The New York Times,

June 21, 2001. See also Jan Holmberg, "Film/Dataspel" [Film/Computer Games], *Filmhäftet* 30, no. 3 (2002): 10–17 for a discussion of plot and filmatizations of computer games.

16. Todd McCarthy, "Lara Croft: Tomb Raider," *Variety* (D), June 15, 2001.

17. Philip French, "She Does Have Some Good Points," *The Observer*, July 8, 2001.

18. The script for *Charlie's Angels* is in Manohla Dargis, "*Charlie's Angels* and *The World Greatest Sinner*," *L.A. Weekly*, November 3, 2000. Screenwriters for *Lara Croft: Tomb Raider* appear in Sean Macaulay, "Lara's OK—For a Girl," *The Times*, June 18, 2001. In comparison, budgets for *Star Wars: Episode I—The Phantom Menace* (1999) and *Star Wars: Episode II—Attack of the Clones* (2002) were respectively 115 and 120 million dollars.

19. Economic figures are taken from "Martial Law: Will Kill Bill Kick Butt in Asia?" *Screen International*, October 10, 2005, and from box office information on http://www.imdb.com/.

20. The quote is from the film's production notes, "Kill Bill Vol. 1—production notes."

21. David Denby, "Cries and Whispers," *New Yorker*, October 13, 2003.

22. Todd McCarthy, "Asian-Style Fever Dream" (review of *Kill Bill Vol. 1*), *Variety* (W), September 29, 2003.

23. Kirk Honeycutt, "Kill Bill—Vol. 1," *Hollywood Reporter*, September 29, 2003.

24. Richard Corliss, "And Now ... Pulp Friction," *Time*, October 20, 2003.

25. Richard Alleva, "About a Boy," *Screen*, December 5, 2003, 13.

26. Richard Schickel, "Ladies Who Lunge," *Time*, July 7, 2003.

27. Melinda Wittstock, "It's Bond Meets Barbie," *The Observer*, November 12, 2000.

28. *Ibid.*

29. Sarah Projansky, *Watching Rape: Film and Television in Postfeminist Culture* (New York: New York University Press, 2001).

30. Linda Ruth Williams, "Body Talk," *Sight and Sound* 7, no. 11 (1997): 18–21, 20.

31. *Ibid.*, 21.

32. Liz Smith, "Demi and Ashton: Is It True Romance," *Los Angeles Times*, June 27, 2003.

33. Jason Solomons, "Angels with Dirty Faces," *The Observer*, October 19, 2003.

34. B.J. Sigesmund and Sean M. Smith, "Ashton Wants Her. But Will Hollywood?" *Newsweek*, June 23, 2003.

35. Landesmark, "Out On a Limb." The *G.I. Jane* quote is from Kenneth Turan, "Shipping Out with Demi," *Los Angeles Times*, August 22, 1997.

36. Kim Walden, "Run, Lara, Run: The Impact of Computer Games on Cinema's Action Heroine," in Schubart and Gjelsvik (eds.), *Femme Fatalities*.

37. Herold, "Making the Leap."

38. Macaulay, "Lara's OK."

39. *Ibid.*

40. Both the nurse Buck and the lover Bill call the Bride "cunt" and the sheriff in El Paso calls her "cock sucker." Anne Gjelsvik points out the ambivalence of such oral abuses going unpunished when made by "positive" male figures like Bill and the sheriff but being punished when made by negative figures like Buck. Anne Gjelsvik, "Fiksjonsvoldens etiske betydninger i Quentin Tarantinos *Kill Bill*, med særlig henblikk på kjønn" [The Ethical Significance of Fictitious Violence in Quentin Tarantino's *Kill Bill* With Special Focus on Gender], unpublished paper delivered as part of defense of the Ph.D., December 10, 2004.

41. Gjelsvik, "Fictitious Violence," 9.

42. In the context of Uma Thurman's unexpected pregnancy Tarantino said, "I've said that this is my grindhouse movie ... but it's also my Josef von Sternberg movie. If you're Josef Von Sternberg, and you're about to start shooting *Morocco* in 1930, and Marlene Dietrich gets pregnant, what do you do? Do you go ahead and make the move with someone else? Of course not. You wait for Dietrich. And film history will thank you." Quentin Tarantino quoted from production notes to *Kill Bill Vol. 1*, 14, 2003; the "hands down" quote is from Wright, "Quentin's Kung-Fu Grip," 44.

43. To this we can add the harsh critique of Halle Berry in *Catwoman*, 2004, another film that fits the high trash heroines action film category.

44. Cosmo Landesman, "Blade Simple" (review of *Kill Bill Vol. 1* directed by Quentin Tarantino), *The Sunday Times*, October 12, 2003; Peter Travers, "A Paradise of Pulp," *Rolling Stone*, October 30, 2003, 99; McCarthy, "Fever Dream."

45. Gjelsvik, "Fictitious Violence," 1.

46. Smith, "Threesome," 61.

47. Production notes for *Charlie's Angels*, 12, 2000.

48. Walden, "Run, Lara, Run," 74.

49. Jackie Stacey, *Star Gazing* (London: Routledge, 1994), 172.

50. *Ibid.*

51. Lorraine Ali, "Coming to a Gym Near You," *Newsweek*, December 11, 2000, 76.

52. Camilla Mehlsen, "Pigekamp. *Girl power* giver bagslag. De vilde piger tyr til grov vold for femten minutters berømmelse" [Girl Fight. The Backlash of Girl Power. Wild Girls Use Aggravated Violence to Gain Fifteen Minutes of Fame], *Politiken*, December 16, 2003.

53. Per Straarup Søndergaard, "Attacked by a group of Ninja girls," in Per Straarup Søndergaard (ed.), *Seje tøser, stakkels piger* [Cool Chicks, Poor Girls] (Vejle: Kroghs forlag, 2003), 57.

54. Quoted from interviews with the actors in *Game Babes*, a ten-minute documentary on the DVD *Resident Evil: Apocalypse* (2004).

55. Barbara Ellen, "Bold as Bras," *The Times*, July 3, 2003, T2.

56. Line Aarsland, "Bratz Banker Barbie" [Bratz Beats Barbie], *Politiken*, October 14, 2004, Section 1, 4. Comment about feet is from my own daughter who now has seventeen Bratz dolls—"much less than my friends," she tells me.

57. Tony Allen-Mills, "Tomb-Raider Lara Is Hero of Tweeny America," *The Sunday Times*, June 17, 2001.

58. The "femme empowerment" quote is from McCarthy, "Snappy Angels"; the comparison to Pam Grier is in J. Hoberman, "Enter the Dragon Lady," *Village Voice*, October 8–14, 2003.

Bibliography

Aarsland, Line. "Bratz Banker Barbie" [Bratz Beats Barbie]. *Politiken*, October 14, 2004, Section 1, p. 4.

Addiego, Walter. "Blame The Messenger." Review of *The Messenger: The Story of Joan of Arc*, directed by Luc Besson. *San Francisco Examiner*, November 12, 1999.

Alesci, Walter. "*Xena: Warrior Princess* Out of the Closet? A Melodramatic Reading of the Show by Latin American and Spanish Lesbian and Gay Fans." In *Femme Fatalities: Representations of Strong Women in the Media*, edited by Rikke Schubart and Anne Gjelsvik, pp. 203–19. Göteborg: Nordicom, 2004.

Ali, Lorraine. "Coming to a Gym Near You." *Newsweek*, December 11, 2000, p. 76.

Allen-Mills, Tony. "Tomb-Raider Lara Is Hero of Tweeny America." *The Sunday Times*, June 17, 2001.

Alleva, Richard. "About a Boy." Review of *Kill Bill Vol. 1*, directed by Quentin Tarantino. *Screen*, December 5, 2003, p. 13.

Andersen, Kurt. "And Now, a Wham-Bam Superstar." *Time*, May 20, 1985.

Aronson, Pamela. "Feminists or 'Postfeminist'? Young Women's Attitudes toward Feminism and Gender Relations." *Gender and Society* 17, no. 6 (December 2003): 903–22.

Bagley, Christopher. "Major Milla." *W* (May 1998) 230–32.

Baker, Rick, and Russell, Toby. *The Essential Guide to Hong Kong Movies*. London: Eastern Heroes Publications, 1994.

_____. *The Essential Guide to Deadly China Dolls*. London: Eastern Heroes Publications, 1996.

Balsamo, Anne. *Technologies of the Gendered Body: Reading Cyborg Women*. Durham, N.C.: Duke University Press, 1997.

Barbano, Nicolas. "Kampmaskinen fra Hongkong" [The Combat Machine from Hong Kong]. *Ekstrabladet*, November 18, 1997.

Basinger, Jeanine. *A Woman's View: How Hollywood Spoke to Women, 1930-1960*. New York: Alfred A. Knopf, 1993.

Bataille, Georges. *Eroticism*. London: Penguin Books, 2001.

Beale, Steve. "Wonder Woman." *Arena*, July 2002, http://www.millaj.com/art/arena 0702.shtml. Accessed September 16, 2002.

Bell-Metereau, Rebecca. *Hollywood Androgyny*. New York: Columbia UIP, 1993.

Benator, Giselle. "Another Fairy Tale, a New Star." *L.A. Herald Examiner*, June 20, 1988.

Berenstein, Rhona. "Mommie Dearest: *Aliens, Rosemary's Baby* and Mothering." *The Journal of Popular Culture* 24, no. 2 (1990): 55–73.

Blackmore, Tim. "'Is this Going to be Another Bug-Hunt?': S-F Tradition Versus Biology-as-destiny in James Cameron's *Aliens*." *Journal of Popular Culture* 29, no. 4 (1996): 211–26.

Bordwell, David. *Planet Hong Kong: Popular Cinema and the Art of Entertainment*. Cambridge, Mass.: Harvard University Press, 2000.

Broeske, Pat H. "Sly's Match?" *Los Angeles Times*, January 29, 1989, Outtakes.

Brosnan, John. *The Primal Scene: A History of Science Fiction Film*. London: Orbit, 1991.

Brown, Jeffrey A. "Gender and the Action Heroine: Hardbodies and the Point of No Return." *Cinema Journal* 35, no. 3 (Spring 1996): 52–71.

_____. "Gender, Sexuality, and Toughness: The Bad Girls of Action Film and Comic Books." In *Action Chicks: New Images of Tough Women in Popular Culture*, edited by

Sherrie A. Inness, pp. 47–74. New York: Palgrave Macmillan, 2004.

Brunsdon, Charlotte. "Feminism, Postfeminism, Martha, Martha, and Nigella." *Cinema Journal* 44, no. 2 (Winter 2005): 110–16.

Bukatman, Scott. "X-bodies (the torment of the mutant superhero)." In *Uncontrollable Bodies: Testimonies of Identity and Culture*, edited by Rodney Sappington and Tyler Stallings, pp. 92–129. Seattle: BayPress, 1994.

Bundtzen, Lynda K. "Monstrous Mothers: Medusa, Grendel, and Now Alien." *Film Quarterly* 40, no. 3 (1987): 11–17.

Butler, Judith. *Gender Trouble: Feminism and the Subversion of Identity.* New York: Routledge, 1999.

Cadenhead, Rogers. "Bad Girls: Who says female characters don't sell? Don't tell that to these women—or their creators." *Wizard*, nb, pp. 38, 42–47.

Cassell, Justine, and Jenkins, Henry. *From Barbie to Mortal Combat: Gender and Computer Games.* Cambridge, Mass.: MIT Press, 1998.

Caudill, Helen. "Tall, Dark, and Dangerous: Xena, the Quest, and the Wielding of Sexual Violence in *Xena* On-Line Fan Fiction." In *Athena's Daughters: Television's New Women Warriors*, edited by Frances Early and Kathleen Kennedy, pp. 27–40. Syracuse, N.Y.: Syracuse University Press, 2003.

Chang, Chris. "Escape From New York." *Film Comment* 33, no. 4 (July-August 1997): 56–61.

Chiao, Hsiung-Ping. "His Influence on the Evolution of the Kung Fu Genre." *Journal of Popular Film and Television* 1, no. ix (Spring 1981): 30–42.

Christensen, Christian Monggaard. "The Million Dollar Hotel." Review of *The Million Dollar Hotel*, directed by Wim Wenders. *Information*, August 18, 2000, Section 1, page 8.

Christensen, Johs. H. "Visdom og visuel kraft" [Wisdom and Visual Power]. Review of *The Fifth Element*, directed by Luc Besson. *Morgenavisen Jyllands-Posten*, August 1, 1997.

"Clint Eastwood Bidding for Black-and-Blue Honors." *Citizen News*, December 16, 1968.

Clover, Carol. *Men, Women and Chain Saws: Gender in the Modern Horror Film.* London: BFI, 1992.

"Coffy." *Boxoffice*, May 28, 1973.

"Coffy." Review of *Coffy*, directed by Jack Hill. *Variety*, May 14, 1973.

Cook, Pam. "'Exploitation' Films and Feminism." *Screen* 17, no. 2 (Summer 1976): 122–27.

Corliss, Richard. "And Now ... Pulp Friction." *Time*, October 20, 2003.

_____. "Can a Woman Be a Man?" *Time*, August 5, 1991.

_____. "Girls Just Wanna Have Guns." *Time*, April 22, 2002.

Crane, Robert. "Milla Jovovich—20Q." *Playboy*, May 2002, http://www.millaj.com/art/playboy0502.shtml. Accessed September 16, 2002.

Creed, Barbara. *The Monstrous-Feminine: Film, Feminism, Psychoanalysis.* London: Routledge, 1993.

Cruz, Omayra. "Between Cinematic Imperialism and the Idea of Radical Politics: Philippines Based Women's Prison Films of the 1970s." Paper presented at the Society for Cinema Studies Conference in Denver, Colorado, May 23–26, 2002.

Culshaw, Peter. "Fusion Cinema." *Vertigo* 2, no. 1 (Spring 2001): 7.

Damico, Helen. *Beowulf's Wealhtheow and the Valkyrie Tradition.* Madison: University of Wisconsin Press, 1984.

Dargis, Manohla. "*Charlie's Angels* and *The World Greatest Sinner*." *L.A. Weekly*, November 3, 2000.

"Day of the Woman." Review of *I Spit On Your Grave*, directed by Meir Zarchi. *Variety*, March 16, 1983.

Delaney, Sharon. "The Genesis of *Xena*." *Xena: Warrior Princess The Official Magazine*, no. 1, pp. 8–11.

Deleuze, Gilles. *Coldness and Cruelty.* Original title "Le Froid et le Cruel" in Présentation de Sacher-Masoch, published in 1967 by Editions de Minuit, France. Reprinted in *Masochism: Coldness and Cruelty by Gilles Deleuze, Venus in Furs by Leopold von Sacher-Masoch*, translated by Jean McNeil, pp. 9–143. New York: Zone Books, 1994.

Denby, David. "Cries and Whispers." Review of *Kill Bill Vol. 1*, directed by Quentin Tarantino. *New Yorker*, October 13, 2003.

Der Derian, James. *Virtuous War: Mapping the Military-Industrial-Media-Entertainment Network.* Boulder, Colo.: Westview Press, 2001.

Diggs, Terry. "*G.I. Jane* Is Such a Drag." *The Recorder*, October 1, 1997, Comment.

Doane, Mary Ann. *Femmes Fatales: Feminism, Film Theory, and Psychoanalysis.* New York: Routledge, 1991.

Dyer, Richard. "Action!" *Sight and Sound* 4, no. 10 (October 1994): 7–10.

Dyer, Richard. *White.* London: Routledge, 1997.

Early, Frances, and Kennedy, Kathleen, eds. *Athena's Daughters: Television's New Women Warriors.* Syracuse, N.Y.: Syracuse University Press, 2003.

Ebert, Alan. "Pam Grier." *Essence*, January 1979.

Ebert, Roger. "The Fifth Element." Review of *The Fifth Element*, directed by Luc Besson. *The Sunday Times*, www.suntimes.com/ebert/ebert_reviews/1997/05/050903.html. Accessed May 20, 2003.

Ellen, Barbara. "Bold as Bras." *The Times*, July 3, 2003, T2.

Ellingson, Annlee. n.d. "The Messenger: The Story of Joan of Arc." Review of *The Messenger: The Story of Joan of Arc*, directed by Luc Besson. *Boxoffice*, http://www.boxoffice.com/scripts/fiw.dll?GetReview& where.... Accessed May 20, 2003.

Ellison, Bob. "Pam Grier: A Matter of Survival." *Los Angeles Times*, August 19, 1979, Calendar.

Evesham, Arthur James, ed. *The Trial of Joan of Arc.* Guernsey: Arthur James, 1996.

Farber, Stephen. "'Deliverance'—How it Delivers." *The New York Times*, August 20, 1972.

Farquhar, Dion. "(M)other Discourses." In *The Gendered Cyborg: A Reader*, edited by Gill Kirkup, Linda Janes, Kath Woodward, and Fiona Hovenden, pp. 209–20. London: Routledge, 2000.

Feeney, F.X. "Conan: Primordial Postcards." *L. A. Weekly*, May 14–20, 1982.

Fleming, Charles. "That's Why the Lady Is a Champ." *Newsweek*, June 14, 1993.

"Foxy Brown." Review of *Foxy Brown*, directed by Jack Hill. *Variety*, April 17, 1974.

French, Philip. "She Does Have Some Good Points." Review of *Lara Croft: Tomb Raider*, directed by Simon West. *The Observer*, July 8, 2001.

Freud, Sigmund. "Hysterical Phantasies and their Relation to Bisexuality" (1908). In *The Standard Edition of The Complete Psychological Works of Sigmund Freud*, translated by James Strachey, 9:157–66. London: Hogarth Press, 1980.

____. "The Taboo of Virginity" (1918). In *The Standard Edition of The Complete Psychological Works of Sigmund Freud*, translated by James Strachey, 11:191–208. London: Hogarth Press, 1980.

____. "The Economic Problem of Masochism" (1924). In *The Standard Edition of The Complete Psychological Works of Sigmund Freud*, translated by James Strachey, 19:157–70. London: Hogarth Press, 1980.

Frid-Nielsen, Niels. "Rustningen holder" [The armor is still strong]. Review of *The Messenger: The Story of Joan of Arc*, directed by Luc Besson. *Aktuelt*, January 28, 2000.

Furseth, Frank. "Ilsa, Nazisternes Hunndjevel" [Ilsa, the Nazi She-Devil]. *Z filmtidsskrift* 67, no. 1 (1999): 30–34.

Gade, Jonna. "En fotomodel som martyr" [A Martyr Model]. Review of *The Messenger: The Story of Joan of Arc*, directed by Luc Besson. *Ekstra Bladet*, January 28, 2000.

Gaines, Jane. "Costume and Narrative: How Dress Tells the Woman's Story." In *Fabrications: Costume and the Female Body*, edited by Jane Gaines and Charlotte Herzog, pp. 180–273. London, Routledge, 1990.

____. "Introduction: Fabricating the Female Body." In *Fabrications: Costume and the Female Body*, edited by Jane Gaines and Charlotte Herzog, pp. 1–27. London, Routledge, 1990.

Gaines, Jane, and Herzog, Charlotte, eds. *Fabrications: Costume and the Female Body.* London: Routledge, 1990.

Gilmore, David D. *Manhood in the Making: Cultural Concepts of Masculinity.* New Haven: Yale University Press, 1990.

Gjelsvik, Anne. "Fiksjonsvoldens etiske betydninger i Quentin Tarantinos *Kill Bill*, med særlig henblikk på kjønn" [The Ethical Significance of Fictitious Violence in Quentin Tarantino's *Kill Bill* With Special Focus on Gender]. Unpublished paper delivered as part of Ph.D. defense, December 10, 2004.

Glaessner, Verina. *Kung Fu: Cinema of Vengeance.* London: Lorrimer, 1974.

Greenberg, Harvey R. "Fembo: *Aliens'* Intentions." *Journal of Film and Television* 15, no. 4 (Winter 1988): 165–71.

Greenhalgh, Cathy. "High-Flying Romance." *Vertigo* 2, no. 1 (Spring 2001): 6.

Greer, Germaine. *The Whole Woman.* London: Anchor, 2000.

Gross, Linda. "Pam Grier in 'Sheba, Baby.'" *Los Angeles Times*, March 28, 1975, Part IV.

Halberstam, Judith. *Female Masculinity.* Durham, N.C.: Duke University Press, 1998.

Hall, Elaine J., and Rodriguez, Marnie Salupo. "The Myth of Postfeminism." *Gender and Society* 17, no. 6 (December 2003): 878–902.

Hein, Birgit. "Frauengefängnisfilme" [Women-in-Prison Films]. *Frauen & Film* 43 (December 1987): 22–26.

Helford, Elyce Rae, ed. *Fantasy Girls: Gender in the New Universe of Science Fiction and Fantasy Television.* Lanham, Md.: Rowman and Littlefield, 2000.

_____. "Feminism, Queer Studies, and the Sexual Politics of *Xena: Warrior Princess.*" In *Fantasy Girls: Gender in the New Universe of Science Fiction and Fantasy Television*, edited by Elyce Rae Helford, pp. 135–62. Lanham, Md.: Rowman and Littlefield, 2000.

Hellmann, Helle. "007 er ingen dinosaurus" [007 Is No Dinosaur]. *Politiken*, November 18, 1997.

"Heroic Trio, The." Review of *The Heroic Trio*, directed by Johnny To. *Video Watchdog*, no. 35 (1995): 64–66.

Herold, Charles. "Making the Leap From a Game To the Movies." *The New York Times*, Thursday, June 21, 2001.

Higashi, Sumiko. "Hold It! Women in Television Adventure Series." *Journal of Popular Film and Television* 8, no. 3 (Fall 1980): 26–37.

Hoberman, J. "Enter the Dragon Lady." Review of *Kill Bill Vol. 1*, directed by Quentin Tarantino. *Village Voice*, October 8–14, 2003.

Holden, Stephen. "They May Be High-Tech, But They're Still the Undead." Review of *Resident Evil*, directed by Paul W.S. Anderson. *New York Times*, March 15, 2002.

Honeycutt, Kirk. "Kill Bill—Vol. 1." *Hollywood Reporter*, September 29, 2003.

Hulley, Karl K., and Vandersall, Stanley T., eds. *Ovid's Metamorphosis: Englished, Mythologized, and Represented in Figures by George Sandys.* Lincoln: University of Nebraska Press, 1970.

"Ilsa, She-Wolf of the SS." Review of *Ilsa, She-Wolf of the SS*, directed by Don Edmonds. www.prisonflicks.com/ilsashewolf.htm. Accessed May 12, 2002.

Inness, Sherrie A., ed. *Tough Girls: Women Warriors and Wonder Women in Popular Culture.* Philadelphia: University of Pennsylvania Press, 1998.

_____, ed. *Action Chicks: New Images of Tough Women in Popular Culture.* New York: Palgrave Macmillan, 2004.

Jacobs, David Henry. "Women in Chains." *Toxic Horror* no. 4 (June 1990): 35–38.

Jacobson, Mark. "Sex Goddess of the Seventies." *New York*, May 19, 1975, pp. 43–45.

Jeffords, Susan. "'The Battle of the Big Mamas': Feminism and the Alienation of Women." *Journal of American Culture* 10, no. 3 (1987): 73–84.

Johansen, Susanne. "Hun gi'r Bond tørt på" [She hangs Bond out to dry]. *B.T.*, December 18, 1997.

Jørholt, Eva. "The Big Red." Review of *Nikita*, directed by Luc Besson. *Information*, January 13, 1995.

_____. "Ny film: På herrens slagmark" [New Film: Abandoned on the Battlefield]. Review of *The Messenger: The Story of Joan of Arc*, directed by Luc Besson. *Information*, January 28, 1997.

"Kill Bill Vol. 1—Production Notes." Production notes to *Kill Bill Vol. 1*, directed by Quentin Tarantino, 2003.

Kincaid, Jamaica. "Pam Grier: The Mocha Mogul of Hollywood." *Ms.*, 49–53. (Year missing from original in The Margarat Herrick Library, probably 1975.)

King, Wayne. "Wild 'Deliverance River' Lures Adventurers South." *The New York Times*, June 8, 1975, Section K, National Topics.

Kraicer, Shelly. n.d. "Ah Kam." Review of *The Stunt Woman* (original title *Ah Kam*), directed by Ann Hui. http://www.chinesecinemas.org/ahkam.html. Accessed August 18, 2005.

Landesman, Cosmo. "Blade Simple." Review of *Kill Bill Vol. 1*, directed by Quentin Tarantino. *The Sunday Times*, October 12, 2003.

_____. "Out on a Limb." Review of *Charlie's Angels: Full Throttle*, directed by McG. *The Sunday Times*, July 6, 2003.

Layton, Eric. "The Messenger: The Story of Joan of Arc." *Entertainment Today*, November 12, 1999.

Lees, Sue. *Ruling Passions: Sexual Violence, Reputation, and the Law.* Buckingham: Open University Press, 1997.

Lehman, Peter. "'I'll see you in small claims court': Penis-Size Jokes and Their Relation to Hollywood's Unconscious." In *Running Scared: Masculinity and the Representation of the Male Body*, edited by Peter Lehman, pp.

105–129. Philadelphia: Temple University Press, 1993.

Linville, Susan E. "'The *Mother* of All Battles': *Courage Under Fire* and the Gender-Integrated Military." *Cinema Journal* 39, no. 2 (Winter 2000): 100–20.

List, Henrik. "Sexet stuntkvinde" [Sexy Stuntwoman]. *Berlingske Tidende*, December 13, 1997, Section 2.

Logan, Bey. *Hong Kong Action Cinema*. London: Titan Books, 1995.

Lowenstein, Lael. "Vigilantism's New Face." *Los Angeles Times*, May 30, 2002.

Lyons, Deborah. *Gender and Immortality: Heroines in Ancient Greek Myth and Cult*. Princeton, N.J.: Princeton University Press, 1997.

Macaulay, Sean. "Lara's OK—For a Girl." *The Times*, June 18, 2001.

_____. "First Amon Equines." Review of *Lara Croft Tomb Raider: The Cradle of Life*, directed by Jan de Bont. *The Times*, July 28, 2003.

Mainon, Dominique, and Ursini, James. *The Modern Amazons: Warrior Women On-Screen*. Pompton Plains, N.J.: Limelight Editions, 2006.

Major, Wade. n.d. "Ilsa, She Wolf of the SS." Review of *Ilsa, She-Wolf of the SS*, directed by Don Edmonds. *Boxoffice Magazine Online*, http://www.rottentomatoes.com. Accessed May 12, 2002.

"Martial Law: Will Kill Bill Kick Butt in Asia?" *Screen International*. October 10, 2005.

Mast, Gerald, Cohen, Marshall, and Braudy, Leo, eds. *Film Theory and Criticism*. New York: Oxford University Press, 1992.

Matherly, Brian. n.d. "She Wolf of the SS." Review of *Ilsa, She-Wolf of the SS*, directed by Don Edmonds. *Daily-Reviews.com*, www.daily-reviews.com/i/bmilsa1.htm. Accessed May 12, 2002.

McCarthy, Todd. "Lara Croft: Tomb Raider." *Variety* (D), June 15, 2001.

_____. "Sassy, Snappy 'Angels': A Devil of a Good Time." Review of *Charlie's Angels*, directed by McG. *Variety* (W), October 30(November 5, 2000.

_____. "Asian-Style Fever Dream." Review of *Kill Bill Vol. 1*, directed by Quentin Tarantino. *Variety* (W), September 29, 2003.

McCaughey, Martha, and King, Neal, eds. *Reel Knockouts: Violent Women in the Movies*. Austin: University of Texas Press, 2001.

Mehlsen, Camilla. "Pigekamp. *Girl power* giver bagslag. De vilde piger tyr til grov vold for femten minutters berømmelse" [Girl Fight. The Backlash of Girl Power. Wild Girls Use Aggravated Violence to Gain Fifteen Minutes of Fame]. *Politiken*, December 16, 2003.

Meisler, Andy. "The Biggest Star You Never Heard Of." *The New York Times*, July 3, 1994, H 21.

Mellen, Joan. *Big Bad Wolves: Masculinity in the American Film*. New York: Pantheon Books, 1977.

Mikula, Maja. "Lara Croft, Between a Feminist Icon and Male Fantasy." In *Femme Fatalities: Representations of Strong Women in the Media*, edited by Rikke Schubart and Anne Gjelsvik, pp. 57–70. Göteborg: Nordicom, 2004.

Morales, Ed, "Mama Said Knock You Out." *Voice*, August 15, 1995.

Morey, Anne. "'The Judge Called Me an Accessory': Women's Prison Films, 1950–1962." *Journal of Popular Film and Television* 23, no. 2 (1995): 80–87.

Morgan, Thaïs E. "A Whip of One's Own: Dominatrix Pornography and the Construction of a Post-Modern (Female) Subjectivity." *The American Journal of Semiotics* 6, no. 4 (1989): 109–37.

Morgenstern, Joe. "Who Needs a Plot? 'Angels' Has Eye Candy to Spare—And Infectious Self-Delight." Review of *Charlie's Angels: Full Throttle*, directed by McG. *Wall Street Journal*, June 27, 2003.

Morreale, Joanne. "*Xena: Warrior Princess* as Feminist Camp." *Journal of Popular Culture* 32, no. 2 (September 1998): 79–86.

Mosse, George L. *Nationalism and Sexuality: Respectability and Abnormal Sexuality in Modern Europe*. New York: Howard Fertig, 1985.

Mulvey, Laura. "Visual Pleasure and Narrative Cinema." In *Film Theory and Criticism*, edited by Gerald Mast, Marshall Cohen, and Leo Braudy, pp. 746–757. New York: Oxford University Press, 1992.

Murphy, Mary. "Pam's Stranglehold on Violent Roles." *Los Angeles Times*, January 4, 1976.

"Nazifilm om SS-tortur tages af plakaten fordi publikum bliver dårlige" [Nazi Movie About SS Torture Is Pulled Because the Audience Gets Sick]. *Ny Dag*, December 16, 1976, film.

Neiiendam, Jacob. "Navnet er Croft—Lara

Croft" [The Name is Croft—Lara Croft]. *Politiken*, May 31, 2001.

Nelson, Rob. "Ultraviolet." Review of *Ultraviolet*, directed by Kurt Wimmer. *The Village Voice*, March 7, 2006, http://www.villagevoice.com/film/0610,nelson,72461,20.html. Accessed May 18, 2006.

Ng, Laura. "'The Most Powerful Weapon You Have': Warriors and Gender in *La Femme Nikita*." In *Athena's Daughters: Television's New Women Warriors*, edited by Frances Early and Kathleen Kennedy, pp. 103–15. Syracuse, N.Y.: Syracuse University Press, 2003.

Norris, Chuck, with Hyams, Joe. *The Secret of Inner Strength: My Story*. Boston: Little Brown, 1988.

O'Day, Marc. "Beauty in Motion: Gender, Spectacle and Action Babe Cinema." In *Action and Adventure Cinema*, edited by Yvonne Tasker, pp. 201–218. London: Routledge, 2004.

Parish, James Robert. *Prison Pictures From Hollywood: Plots, Critiques, Casts and Credits for 293 Theatrical and Made-for-Television Releases*. Jefferson, N.C.: McFarland, 1991.

Projansky, Sarah. *Watching Rape: Film and Television in Postfeminist Culture*. New York: New York University Press, 2001.

"Quentin's Kung-Fu Grip." *Rolling Stone*, October 30, 2003, pp. 43–46.

Rainer, Peter. "Naval Gazing." *New Times L.A.*, August 21, 1997.

Rayner, Richard. "The Warrior Besieged." *New York Times*, June 22, 1997, Magazine Desk. http://www.nytimes.com/. Accessed March 1, 2004.

Rayns, Tony. "The Heroic Trio." Review of *The Heroic Trio*, directed by Johnny To. *Sight and Sound* 3, March 1995, p. 56.

Read, Jacinda. *The New Avengers: Feminism, Femininity and the Rape-Revenge Cycle*. Manchester: Manchester University Press, 2000.

Rebelle, Stephen. "The 8 million Dollar Man." *Movieline*, August 1994.

Reid, Craig. "Fighting Without Fighting: Film Action Fight Choreography." *Film Quarterly* 47 (Winter 1994–1995): 30–35.

Reik, Theodor. *Masochism in Modern Man*. New York: Farrar, Straus, 1941.

Review of *Deliverance*, directed by John Boorman. *New Yorker*, December 8, 1972.

Rich, Frank. "Plastic Jesus." Review of *Rocky II*, directed by Sylvester Stallone. *Time*, June 25, 1979.

Riviere, Joan. "Womanliness as a Masquerade" (1929). In *Formations of Fantasy*, edited by Victor Burgin, James Donald, and Cora Kaplan, pp. 35–44. London: Methuen, 1986.

Schatz, Thomas. *Hollywood Genres: Formulas, Film-Making and the Studio System*. New York: McGraw Hill, 1981.

Scheib, Richard. "Ilsa, She Wolf of the SS." Review of *Ilsa, She-Wolf of the SS*, directed by Don Edmonds. http.//members.fortunecity.com/roogulator/horror/ilsa1.htm. Accessed May 12, 2002.

Schickel, Richard. "Help! They're Back!" *Time*, July 28, 1986.

_____. "Ladies Who Lunge." Review of *Charlie's Angels: Full Throttle*, directed by McG. *Time*, July 7, 2003.

Schiff, Stephen. "Gun-totin' Women." *Film Comment*, January–February, 1982.

Schubart, Rikke. "Woman With a Gun Does Not Signify Man With a Phallus: Gender and Narrative Change in the Action Movie." *Nordicom Review: Special Issue 19*, no. 1 (June 1998): 205–15.

_____. "Birth of a Hero: *Rocky*, Stallone and Mythical Creation." In *Stars in Our Eyes: The Star Phenomenon in the Contemporary Era*, edited by Angela Ndalianis and Charlotte Henry, pp. 149–64. Westport, Conn.: Praeger, 2002.

Schubart, Rikke, and Gjelsvik, Anne, eds. *Femme Fatalities: Representations of Strong Women in the Media*. Göteborg: Nordicom, 2004.

Shamon, Danny. n.d. "Interview: Cynthia Rothrock, the Lady Dragon." *Kung Fu Cinema*, http://www.kungfucinema.com/. Accessed August 25, 2005.

Shulgasser, Barbara. "Chaos Theory." Review of *The Fifth Element*, directed by Luc Besson. *San Francisco Examiner*, www.sf.gate.com/cgi-bin/article.cgi?f=/e/a/1997/05/09/WEEKEND8772.dtl. Accessed May 20, 2003.

Sigesmund, B.J., and Smith, Sean M. "Ashton Wants Her. But Will Hollywood?" *Newsweek*, June 23, 2003.

Silverman, Kaja. *Male Subjectivity at the Margins*. London: Routledge, 1992.

Simon, Brent. "Raider of the Lost Hearts." *Entertainment Today*, June 15–21, 2001.

Singer, Ben. "Female Power in the Serial-Queen Melodrama: The Etiology of an Anomaly." *Camera Obscura*, no. 22 (1990): 91–129.

Slotkin, Richard. *Gunfighter Nation: The Myth of the Frontier in Twentieth-Century America.* New York: Atheneum, 2002.

Smith, Liz. "Demi and Ashton: Is It True Romance." *Los Angeles Times,* June 27, 2003.

Smith, Sean M. "Threesome." *Newsweek,* June 23, 2003, pp. 60–62.

Solomons, Jason. "Angels With Dirty Faces." *The Observer,* October 19, 2003.

Søndergaard, Per Straarup, ed. *Seje tøser, stakkels piger* [Cool Chicks, Poor Girls]. Vejle: Kroghs forlag, 2003.

Stacey, Jackie. *Star Gazing.* London: Routledge, 1994.

Steltz, Chris. n.d. "She Wolf of the SS." Review of *Ilsa, She-Wolf of the SS,* directed by Don Edmonds. www.dvdangle.com/reviews/. Accessed May 12, 2002.

"Stinkende premiere" [Stinking Premiere]. Danish review of *Ilsa, She-Wolf of the SS,* directed by Don Edmonds. *Aarhus Stiftstidende,* April 26, 1976.

Stuart, Jan. "'Resident Evil's Gore Is Guilty Fun." Review of *Resident Evil,* directed by Paul W.S. Anderson. *Newsday,* March 15, 2002.

Studlar, Gaylyn. "Masochism, Masquerade, and the Erotic Metamorphoses of Marlene Dietrich." In *Fabrications: Costume and the Female Body,* edited by Jane Gaines and Charlotte Herzog, pp. 236–7. London: Routledge, 1990.

Tasker, Yvonne. *Spectacular Bodies: Gender, Genre and the Action Cinema.* London: Routledge, 1993.

_____. *Working Girls: Gender and Sexuality in Popular Cinema.* London: Routledge, 1998.

_____. "Soldier's Stories: Women and Military Masculinities in *Courage Under Fire.*" In *Femme Fatalities: Representations of Strong Women in the Media,* edited by Rikke Schubart and Anne Gjelsvik, pp. 91–110. Göteborg: Nordicom, 2004.

_____, ed. *Action and Adventure Cinema.* London: Routledge, 2004.

Taubin, Amy. "The 'Alien' Trilogy: From Feminism to Aids." In *Women and Film: A Sight and Sound Reader,* edited by Pam Cook and Philip Dodd, pp. 93–100. London: Scarlet Press, 1993.

Theweleit, Klaus. *Male Fantasies.* 2 vols. Minneapolis: University of Minnesota Press, 1996.

Travers, Peter. "A Paradise of Pulp." Review of *Kill Bill Vol. 1,* directed by Quentin Tarantino. *Rolling Stone,* October 30, 2003, p. 99.

Turan, Kenneth. "Shipping Out with Demi." *Los Angeles Times,* August 22, 1997.

_____. "The Real Powerpuff Girls." *Los Angeles Times,* November 3, 2000.

Turbin, Amy. "Dicks and Jane." *Village Voice,* August 26, 1997.

Tyrrell, Blake. *Amazons: A Study in Athenian Mythmaking.* Baltimore, Md.: Johns Hopkins University Press, 1984.

Venticinque, Darrin, and Thompson, Tristan. *The Ilsa Chronicles.* Northants, U.K.: Midnight Media, 2000.

Vincendeau, Ginette. "Joan of Arc/Jeanne d'Arc." Review of *The Messenger: The Story of Joan of Arc,* directed by Luc Besson. *Sight and Sound,* April 2000, http://www.bfi.org.uk/sightandsound/reviews. Accessed May 20, 2003.

Walden, Kim. "*Run, Lara, Run!* The Impact of Computer Games on Cinema's Action Heroine." In *Femme Fatalities: Representations of Strong Women in the Media,* edited by Rikke Schubart and Anne Gjelsvik, pp. 71–90. Göteborg: Nordicom, 2004.

Walters, Suzanna Danuta. "Caged Heat: The (R)evolution of Woman-in-Prison Films." In *Reel Knockouts: Violent Women in the Movies,* edited by Martha McCaughey and Neal King, pp. 106–124. Austin: University of Texas Press, 2001.

Warner, Marina. *Joan of Arc: The Image of Female Heroism.* New York: Alfred A. Knopf, 1981.

Warring, Anette. *Tysker Piger: Under besættelse og retsopgør.* København: Gyldendal, 1993.

Warshow, Robert. "Movie Chronicle: The Westerner." In *Film Theory and Criticism,* edited by Gerald Mast, Marshall Cohen, and Leo Braudy, pp. 453–66. New York: Oxford University Press, 1992.

Williams, Linda. "Film Bodies: Gender, Genre and Excess." *Film Quarterly* 44, no. 4 (Summer 1991): 2–13.

Williams, Linda Ruth. "Body Talk." *Sight and Sound* 7, no. 11 (1997): 18–21.

Williamson, Kim. "The Fifth Element." Review of *The Fifth Element,* directed by Luc Besson. *Boxoffice Magazine,* http://www.boxoffice.com. Accessed May 20, 2003.

Willis, Sharon. *High Contrast: Race and Gender in Contemporary Hollywood Film.* Durham, N.C.: Duke University Press, 1997.

Wilson, John M. "A Swarm of Superheroes Due Back in Strength." *Los Angeles Times,* May 7, 1978.

Wittstock, Melinda. "Its Bond Meets Barbie." *The Observer*, November 12, 2000.

Wolcott, James. "Meat Grinders." *Village Voice*, February 18–24, 1981.

Wright, Will. *Sixguns and Society: A Structural Study of the Western*. Berkeley: University of California Press, 1975.

Wurtzel, Elizabeth. *Bitch: In Praise of Difficult Women*. New York: Doubleday, 1999.

Zalcock, Bev. *Renegade Sisters: Girl Gangs on Film*. Creation Books: London, 1998.

Index

353